PRINCIPLES

OF

GOVERNMENT

A

TREATISE

ON

FREE INSTITUTIONS

INCLUDING

THE CONSTITUTION OF THE UNITED STATES.

BY NATHANIEL CHIPMAN, LL. D.

THE LAWBOOK EXCHANGE, LTD.
Clark, New Jersey

ISBN 9781584770466 (hardcover)
ISBN 9781616191740 (paperback)

Lawbook Exchange edition 2011

The quality of this reprint is equivalent to the quality of the original work.

THE LAWBOOK EXCHANGE, LTD.
33 Terminal Avenue
Clark, New Jersey 07066-1321

*Please see our website for a selection of our other publications
and fine facsimile reprints of classic works of legal history:*
www.lawbookexchange.com

Library of Congress Cataloging-in-Publication Data

Chipman, Nathaniel, 1752-1843.
    Principles of government : a treatise on free institutions, including the
Constitution of the United States / by Nathaniel Chipman.
        p.   cm.
        Originally published : Burlington, Vt. : E. Smith, 1833.
        Includes bibliographical references.
        ISBN 1-58477-046-5 (cloth : alk. paper)
        1. Political science. 2. United States. Constitution. I. Title.
JC211 .C56 2000
    320.473—dc21   99-048863
                                                            CIP

Printed in the United States of America on acid-free paper

PRINCIPLES

OF

GOVERNMENT

A

TREATISE

ON

FREE INSTITUTIONS

INCLUDING

THE CONSTITUTION OF THE UNITED STATES.

BY NATHANIEL CHIPMAN, LL. D.

BURLINGTON:

EDWARD SMITH,

(Successor to Chauncey Goodrich.)

. . . .

1833.

PREFACE.

The subject of government has employed the pens of the first philosophers of every age, from the time of Plato and Aristotle to the present day. To them the world are much indebted, especially to some of the moderns. None of them, however, as far as recollection serves, have attempted, or at least, have succeeded in an investigation of first principles; in analyzing the social nature of man, and deducing from the relations thence resulting, the principles that ought to be pursued in the formation of civil institutions; and yet it is believed, this is the only certain ground of investigation, the only mode in which any general, consistent, and practical principles in the science of government can be established. The greater number of those who have written on this subject have employed themselves in illustrating and recommending the principles and form of some government, for which they had conceived a predilection; while others in their theories have consulted the imagination rather than the understanding. It will, therefore, be readily perceived that the theories and principles of neither class of these writers can be of general, much less of universal application; that they cannot be applied, at least, indiscriminately, to governments of a different construction, and embracing different, and in many respects opposite principles. Such are the civil and political institutions of these United States; they differ in principles and construction very essentially from all that have preceded them. The Author convinced of that difference of principles and the excellence of our institutions owing chiefly to that difference, published as early as the year 1793, a small work entitled, "Sketches of the Principles of Government," with a view of briefly illustrating the principles on which they are founded. That little work which was well received at the time, has long been out of print.

The Author had entertained a design, as no treatise had appeared fully embracing the subject, of publishing a revised edition of that work; but on a review, he found it too limited in its plan, as well as deficient in arrangement. He, therefore, resolved to new-cast the whole, to enlarge the plan, to give it a more regular and scientific arrangement, and as far as he was capable, to make it an elementary treatise on that kind of government which has been adopted in these United States. In the execution of this task, although the work consists principally of new and additional matter, the Author has in several instances, admitted portions of his former work with such corrections as were suggested by a long course of observations and experience.

He has enjoyed many advantages favorable to the accomplishment of his design,—he has been an attentive observer of passing events, and not unfrequently an actor in the political scenes that have occurred in a period of more than half a century commencing with the controversy between the states (then colonies) and the mother country,—which eventuated in their independence, and, finally, in the establishment of the present government on the true principles of freedom—a period agitated and occupied with revolutions and revolutionary movements, which have extended with various effects to all the civilized nations of Europe and the whole of the American continent, and which have produced a more thorough investigation, and discussion of the social and individual rights of man and the nature and principles of free governments than is to be found in any other age, indeed, than all preceding ages within the reach of history. With what success the work has been executed must be left to the decision of the public. Such a work adapted to the civil and political institutions of the country has been hitherto, a *desideratum*, which it was the Author's ambition to supply. If, however, he has failed in this, it will be a sufficient consolation, should what he has attempted, excite some writer of more leisure and of a higher order of talents to accomplish the task, although, now at the advanced age of fourscore he can hardly expect personally to enjoy that consolation.

The Author has throughout the whole endeavored at the investigation of natural principles, and to follow truth wherever it led ;—he has several times been induced to differ from the opinions of some writers of the first talents and reputation. Although he has examined these opinions with the freedom of philosophical discussion, it has been his constant aim to treat the writers with that decent respect which they merit from every lover of science.

As to the manner and style of the work, if it should be thought that they savor of former times, the apology is, that the author himself, more properly belongs to an age that is now past.

Tinmouth, Vermont, July 10, 1833.

CONTENTS.

BOOK IV.

Of Rights and Liberty.

BOOK V.

Of the formation of government—the distribution and limitation of the civil and political power.

BOOK VI.

Of Laws.

BOOK VIII.

Of the Government of the United States.

APPENDIX.

ERRATA.

The Publisher regrets that the errors of the press have been so numerous as they appear to be by the following list. He trusts, however, that it will be a sufficient excuse to the candid reader, that the greater part of the work was printed from manuscript at such a distance from the author, as to prevent an inspection of the proof-sheets by him. To the same cause, as well as to imperfections in the manuscript, some slight errors are owing, all of which may not be noted below. The work having been sent to the publisher at different times, and in separate portions, one parcel was accidentally mislaid, and was not observed to be wanting, until it had been passed by in the order of printing. It was afterwards inserted in its place, *after the 144th page*, the letter *(a)* being annexed to the number of the pages. No inconvenience can result from this slight irregularity; but it has the effect of making the contents of the work appear less than they are in fact, by 44 pages.

Page	Line from	for	read	Page.	Line from	for	read
2	12 bottom,	resulting,	result,	103	13 bottom before speech dele 'the,'		
18 & 19	19	mean,	means,	114	14 top,	nation,	nations,
22	3 do after progress, insert in the knowledge			114	8 bottom,	sacred.	second,
41	19 top, after furnish insert 'us,'			133	1 do	second	remaining,
53	17 do	nature,	motive,	143	6 top,	indeed,	induced,
59	18 do	getting,	keeping,	176a	5 do	served,	succeed,
65	7 do after given insert 'up,'			182a	12 bottom, after and, insert 'if,'		
do	8 do	good,	goods,	174	5 top,	see,	seek,
66	3 do	relating,	relate,	184	16 top,	to,	by,
74	16 do	alternately,	ultimately,	189	11 bottom,	agreements,	arguments,
81	9 do before custom insert 'a,'			193	2 top,	decreeing,	directing,
82	18 bottom,	Menort,	Mentor,	198	17 top,	representation,	perception,
83	12 top	part,	poet,	207	11 bottom,	sentence,	sanction,
88	18 bottom,	divisions,	decisions,	217	15 on, read an, institutions, institution,		
100	8 top, after rated dele 'to,'			250	16 bottom,	on,	or.
do	19 bottom,	learners,	learning,	243	top l. before representatives insert 'Every		
102	12 top,	priest,	priests,		law passed by the senate and house of'		

BOOK I.

INTRODUCTORY.

CHAPTER I.

THE SUBJECT PROPOSED.

A theory has been adopted by some European philosophers,* and strenuously advocated by their followers, that the first rude state of society, which, among civilized nations, is usually denominated the savage state, is the only natural state of man; that in this state alone he is capable of attaining the acme of perfection in virtue and happiness. They have supposed, that, what are generally called social improvements, serve only to deprave, and either inevitably generate a wicked disposition in man, or at least, invigorate an original propensity to vice, which might otherwise forever lie dormant, in what they so emphatically style the state of nature.—They have even gone farther, and maintained, that civil government, so far from proving a remedy for these evils, necessarily becomes the corrupt cause and fruitful source of all the miseries to be found in society.

Others have maintained, that true virtue and pure benevolence in man, would, in every stage of society, supersede the necessity of municipal laws and civil subordination. With a shade of difference from the former, they hold, that wickedness alone has imposed the necessity of civil government. They appear to imagine, that civil polity is not to be derived from principles founded in the social nature of man; but that it is a

---

*Rousseau and others.—The Abbé Raynal inclines to the same opinion.—This chapter was written in the year 1792.

system of rules contrived to meet his wicked disposition, and to restrain the violence of individuals by the violence of laws. According to them, civil government was not so much designed, by the Author of our nature, to lead men to happiness in society, as to prevent the miseries, which they are ever ready to inflict on each other.——In short, that there is to man, a necessity for civil government, but not an adaptation of his nature to that state.

Some political writers of great eminence* have admitted, that man was originally designed for civil government, and is under a certain necessity of nature to adopt it. At the same time, they have maintained that, on entering into civil society, he, of necessity, gives up a portion of his natural liberty, of his natural rights. By these expressions "natural liberty" and "natural rights" is to be understood, that liberty, and those rights, to which man is entitled as constituted by the Author of his being. This clearly implies that man is but partially fitted for civil society. Compelled, however, to adopt that state, from a necessity which is admitted to arise from a law of his nature, he is supposed to sacrifice a part of his natural rights to secure the remainder, and even to acquire others, to which he was not by the laws of his nature originally entitled.

It is proposed in the following work to inquire, whether man is, by the constitution and laws of his nature, fitted for society; whether his happiness does not require social improvements, and laws, which resulting from his whole nature, lead to the adoption of civil institutions; or whether he is compelled to adopt that state by a single, and that a vicious principle in his nature, in opposition to others. Whether, considered as a moral being, the laws of his nature have indulged to him any liberty which he may not enjoy under civil institutions; and whether government and laws be not, to any secure enjoyment, both of natural and civil rights, in fact, necessary to all subordinate social beings, with whatever virtues they may be endued.

The great end in these inquiries will be, to find the leading principles of government in the laws of social nature, and to trace them into exercise in the establishment of civil

---

*Locke, Beccaria, Blackstone, and many others.

institutions. In the United States of America, political opinions, though considered as merely theoretical, cannot be wholly inconsequential. In these states, government is professedly founded in the rights of man.—It derives all its efficacy in the prevention of evil, all its energy in the production of happiness, from the sentiments of the people. The opinions, generally entertained, of government, of the necessity of laws, of the end to be attained by them, and the proper mode of attaining that end, will have an influence on the sentiments of the people and the reasonings of the legislator. They will, in a good measure, form the features of the government, and give a tone to all its acts in every department of the administration.

CHAPTER II.

Of the sense in which the term, "principles of government," is used in the following work.

From Montesquieu the term "principle" or "principles," when applied to government, has been used in a more appropriate sense, than in other sciences. In other sciences it is always used to signify something fundamental, some leading rule, law, or maxim. Thus we speak of the principles, on which any thing is constructed, as, a watch. The term principles, here, comprehends not only, the laws of mechanics, but those rules by which the relative proportions of the several parts are determined, to direct the motions to a certain end. These are properly called the principles of construction. There are also rules by which the moving force is applied and made to

operate on the machine, with a view to the end proposed.
These are called the principles of operation. The term is
frequently used to signify some passive quality, capacity or
susceptibility ; that condition of a subject, by which it is fitted
to exhibit, in consequence of the operations of certain agents
upon it, certain effects agreeable to certain laws. Thus we
speak of the principle of fluidity, the inflammable principle,
the principle of malleability ; and thus we say of man, that the
principles of society and government are implanted in his nature,
by which we mean that he is fitted for such state, or at least that
his nature requires it.

In the science of government, there are the principles of
construction, by which the government is constituted and
organized ; the principles of operation, by which its activity
and efficiency are produced. There are also the passive
principles arising out of the susceptibilities of man, through
which he becomes subject to all the variety of passions and
emotions, that are excited by means of impressions made
on his mind, by a multiplicity of agents and objects both
corporeal and mental. To these the operative principles
are adapted to produce the end intended—obedience to the
laws. These principles, however, are, or ought to be,
directed by ulterior principles, to be sought in the social nature
of man, and by those laws established by the Author of nature,
in his formation, designed to promote the general happiness.
The operative and passive principles in any government are
determined by the constructive principles employed, or the
nature of the constitution. They will therefore be different
according to the different constitution or nature of the
government. Those which are here denominated the operative
and passive principles, Montesquieu, has, by way of eminence
called the principles of government ; and this is altogether
proper to his design, which was to treat of the spirit of the
laws peculiar to the different constitutions of governments in
being ; not of the principles on which governments ought to
be formed. But in the view we have proposed to take of the
subject, the principles of government are not capable of being
thus simplified, or reduced to any single principle. Far from
it, they are often very complex and subject to a great variety

of modifications, from the admission of different principles in the construction. Each government, however, has its predominant and characteristic principles. The same may be said of other principles beside those of Montesquieu. He has in one place defined the principle of a government to be the human passions, which set it in motion.* This, taken in the author's sense, does not militate against what has just been observed of the passive principles arising out of a susceptibility of passions and emotions. The passions, it may be said, when excited, alone, give activity and vigor to the operative principles.

He has introduced three different principles, which he tells us, are peculiar to the three principal forms of government, the despotic, monarchical, and republican. Fear, he tells us, is the principle of a despotic government. This, in his sense of the term principle, is undoubtedly just. The instruments of despotism are a military force at the beck of the sovereign, which, by the terror of punishment, or rather of vengeance, secures obedience to his mandates. Inveterate habits of superstition often come in aid of the military force, and clothe the messenger of the prince, with the power of armies. Fear is that passion of human nature, to which the measures of this government are principally addressed, and without which the despot could procure obedience only by the constant and present application of force in each particular case.

Honor he assigns as the principle of a monarchy. This I will venture to say, is, taken in his sense, very deficient. That passion of emulation, that desire of excellence, which is natural to man, and which, by cultivation, is capable of an infinity of directions, good and evil, is with the higher orders in a monarchy, modified into what is called the principle of honor; but its direct effect in securing obedience to the sovereign, is confined principally to those orders. The multitude, the great majority of the nation are under a complicated despotism. The nobles, in conjunction with the military order, are the instruments employed to awe the people to obedience. Religion, transformed into a gloomy superstition, has been often employed to the same end.

---

* Book III, Chapter 1.

In the same sense he makes virtue the principle of a republic.
We are liable to be misled by the use of this term, in a sense
different from that, in which it is commonly received. As the
principle of republican government he has therefore defined it
to be "a love of the laws and of our country."* It is necessary
here to observe, that the term " republic" in its usual acceptation
comprehends several kinds of government very different in
their nature and principles ; they may, however, be reduced to
two principal kinds,—an aristocracy, of which oligarchy is a
degenerate species ; and a democracy, of which a government
by representatives, periodically elected by the people, is an
improved form. A form of government unknown to the ancients,
and which has not been distinguished by an appropriate name.†
An aristocracy differs from a monarchy as an aggregate from a
sole corporation. The people are under the same slavery, both
civil and political, as under a monarchy ; and are indeed farther
removed from all prospect of honors. A sole monarch is under
a necessity, in administering the government, to communicate
honors and authority to some of his subjects ; but an aristocracy
always confines the distribution of honors and authority to its
own members and their families. The principle of virtue, the
love of the laws and of the country is, in strictness, no more
applicable to this kind of government than to a monarchy.
Both the monarch and the members of the aristocracy love their
country ; they love their people, in a certain sense ; because
they are the source of their political consequence, and the
machines of their power ; but as for a love of the laws, they are,
in both governments, made for the people, not for the rulers.
In a democracy, where the powers of government are retained
in the body of the people, and in the representative form, where
the powers are vested in delegates periodically elected by the
people, and accountable to them, the laws are made for all, as
well for the rulers as the people, and are or ought to be, an
expression of the will of the society, being an aggregate of the
individual wills. Now if the will of the aggregate, in all cases,
coincide with each individual will, the observance of the law

---

* Book IV. Chapter 5.　　† Note.

must be as necessary as the power of willing; but this can, perhaps in no instance be the case. The will of the whole, that is the law, is the result of mutual concessions or a compromise of the individual wills, as determined by the majority. Hence the necessity of our author's principle of virtue, which he has appropriated to republican government, and which I have ventured to call a predominant sentiment of attachment to the community, its institutions and laws, which alone can secure for the laws a general acquiescence, and the ready obedience of the individual members. Under this kind of government, no force can be applied in the execution of the laws but what depends on this principle. It is certainly no more entitled to the appropriate appellation of virtue, than other social passions and sentiments common to man; but it has this pre-eminence over the other principles, mentioned above, that it is, when rightly informed, perfectly in harmony with all the other moral and social virtues, and is best promoted by them.

In the following work the term " principle" and " principles of government," will sometimes, according to the nature of the subject, be used in the appropriate sense of Montesquieu, but more generally, in the same sense, in which it is used in other sciences, as explained above.

BOOK II.

OF MAN AS FORMED FOR THE SOCIAL STATE.

CHAPTER I.

Of the first rude state. Whether this is a state of virtue and happiness in preference to a state of improvement.

That the savage state is a state of nature to man cannot with truth, be denied. There is not, at this day, a people on earth, who may not trace their origin to a race of savages; some indeed more and some less remote. The Jews, as the writings of Moses and their subsequent historians abundantly prove, are far from being an exception. The question is not, whether a rude unpolished state be ever a natural state to man; but whether, in the original constitution of his nature, he is so formed for happiness in this state, as to exclude any benefit to be derived from progressive improvement. We are at a loss, at what period of the progress of society, to fix the precise state of nature intended. Shall we go back to the rude state of the inhabitants of New Holland, who have learned to draw no part of their subsistence from the earth by cultivation, or the inhabitants of Terra-del-Fuego, whose sole dependence, for food, is said to be in the shell fish found in the sand at the ebb of the tide, neither of whom have any notions of honesty or the rights of property, beyond the circles of their little tribes? Shall we make a little farther advance and place it among the savages of North America, when first discovered by Europeans, some of whom continue in the same rude state to this day? They are simple, they are honest, as far as the circle of their several tribes. They obtain their food from the river, or the forest, furnished by the bounty of nature, and the little deficiencies are supplied by a scanty cultivation of the earth. The skins of the chase furnish them with coarse, but comfortable clothes, or are exchanged for the products of European looms. They are contented with their present situation, or rather resigned to it as their inevitable lot. All this was true, and still is true of all the American natives, whose manners have not been affected by intercourse with European settlers, who have occupied a large portion of their country ; and yet it gives us hardly a glimpse of their character. The savages of America, like other men, have their predominant passions. They esteem war and hunting almost the only pursuits worthy of a man. Address in these constitutes their highest point of honor, while every other labor of life is imposed on the women, who are no better than slaves. Hence they derive an excessive ferocity of manners : their resentment is keen, and revenge their most darling gratification. This arises from their state of society, in which every one is left to judge in his own cause, and to avenge his own wrongs. As they never forget a favor, so they never forgive an injury. Among the different tribes, the injuries of an individual are resented as national ; the possession of a hunting ground is to them the possession of an empire, and these are the sources of frequent wars waged with the most savage ferocity. The butchering and scalping of old men, women, and children, the torturing and burning of prisoners in cold blood with the most shocking circumstances of cruelty are among their pastimes. These are not secret acts of violence— are by none considered as wrong ; they are public transactions, performed under what is to them, the law of nations. Nor have they been free from ambition of conquest,—from that lust of power, which when acquired, has generally proved the scourge of the human race. The Mexicans, when first visited by the Spaniards, were in possession of an extensive empire acquired by the conquest of neighboring nations and tribes. In later times, the Iroquois, or five nations, formed a powerful confederacy of conquerors, and became the terror even of distant tribes.—Nor were these singular incidents. We find every where among them, traditions and even monuments of powerful nations, who made extensive conquests, and were again conquered or exterminated by some more powerful nation, or by a coalition of neighboring tribes. Notwithstanding this trait of character, which has been exhibited by some of the North American tribes, at different and distant periods, it is generally true of all, that as they are not anxious about the future, for the same reason they are almost wholly improvident. When not engaged in their favorite pursuits of war or hunting, they are too indolent to think of making an adequate provision against the inclemency of the seasons, or of any future want. As they have fewer vices, so they have fewer virtues than more civilized nations, and both are more prominent, more distinctly marked. This arises from the paucity of the objects with which they are conversant. With them numerous passions, correcting and restraining each other, are not, as in a state of civilization, equally excited, by a multiplicity of objects. When any object rouses their attention, the whole force of the mind, the whole vigor of the soul is collected and exerted on one point. Hospitality is always a virtue, and is peculiarly so to a savage people, and the finest trait in their character. When we contemplate this virtue, among such a people, it strikes the mind with all the advantage of vivid sentiment, singularity of impression and contrast of manners. Every recollection is accompanied with an enthusiastic admiration, that makes us regret the loss of those manners, which are, alone, capable of giving lustre to this sublime virtue. Will it be thought strange to assert, that this virtue derives its origin and takes its principal lustre, from the barbarous manners of the age? and yet such is the fact. It does not, however, consist with the rudest state of society and of manners. Some advance in civilization, some progress in the arts of life, is necessary to give a relish for hospitality, and to supply the means of indulging it. Among a people in the hunter state it makes but little figure: depending on the fortune of the chase, or the gleanings of the forest, they find but a scanty and precarious subsistence. With neither the foresight, nor the means of making a secure provision for the future, they are frequently in want of necessary sustenance. Among such a people, the pressing demands of nature, leave little of their scanty stores for the uses of hospitality. They have little curiosity, and no conception of any knowledge, which can be of use beyond that of forming the bow or some instrument of the chase. With such a people always exposed, and not unfrequently reduced to a famishing condition, what can compensate for an additional tax on their precarious and scanty means of subsistence? The North American natives have never been equally noted, for the practice of this virtue, with the ancient Germans, or the more ancient inhabitants of Greece. They draw but a small share of their subsistence from the earth; all the care of their tillage, consisting in the cultivation of maize, beans, and a few edible roots, is left to the women. The labor of these, spared from their attendance on the men in hunting, and other drudgeries of a domestic nature, without the assistance of useful animals, and with such rude implements as they can either form or procure, can yield but a scanty supply for one part of the year ; the other is, for the most part, as scantily supplied by the fortune of the chase. They appear to have little relish for any new arts of life, unless they have some relation to their principal occupations of war and hunting; and very little curiosity for any information to be derived from an intercourse with strangers. Instances are not however, wanting, in which they have discovered all that fidelity to their guests, all that warmth of attachment, which gives such a charm to the patriarchal times of the old world. Although the instances are less frequent, they bear the same genuine character of heroic integrity.

The shepherd state supplies a more ready and abundant supply of food and domestic conveniences. Then, more at ease, conversation begins to acquire a charm; more arts become necessary. The useful and the convenient engage the attention. New objects afford gratification to an awakened curiosity; still they are divided into small tribes ; their domestic manners are sincere, but rough ; to strangers, they are fierce, cruel and faithless. So universal has always been the state of war, among such a people, that, in almost every language, the same word originally signified both foreigner and enemy. Disputed boundaries are often the occasion of wars : they are often waged to avenge a private quarrel ; and to surprise and plunder the neighboring tribes of their herds is the principal object of their hostile enterprises. Their whole history is a continued scene of war, pillage and reprisal. So frequent were these predatory expeditions, among the petty tribes of ancient Greece, that they were early honored with a particular name.* In such a state of society and nations the use of coin is unknown. Their whole commerce, whatever they may have, consists in exchange of commodities in kind. These are usually bulky and unfit to attend the person of the owner, to answer his occasions in travelling ; nor could they attend him with safety, among a people, who reckon the plundering of strangers a lawful means of acquisition. Inns for the accommodation of travellers are unknown. Were it not for the hospitality of individuals, there could be no passing from one country to another. There is something in the practice very congenial to the frank, rough and generous manners of a rude people. Their generosity, however, in this favorite instance rises, as it were, through a cloud. We find from Homer that strangers often applied to their intended hosts, in the posture of suppliants, and entreated the rights of hospitality as for their lives. His instances may, indeed, be considered as poetic fiction ; but they were, undoubtedly, relative to the spirit and manners of the age. To grant the rights of hospitality was to grant protection. The host or patron was considered as the protector of his guest; an office which suited with a martial spirit. It gave the host consequence, in his own estimation and in the estimation of others. The practice of this virtue, among rude nations, affords not only a gratification to curiosity, but the opportunity of indulging in the exercise of humanity to strangers, without incurring the imputation of a want of attachment to the tribe. The advantages are national and reciprocal ; in no other way can they acquire a knowledge of foreign nations, their arts and manners. Like the safety of heralds it passes into their law of nations. In ancient writers, we often read of the right of hospitality, and of wars to protect those rights or to avenge their violation. Indeed, it is to be considered no less a national, than a private virtue. In the present state of improvement, among civilized

---

* *Βοηλασια, abactio bovum, præda* taking cattle, prey.

nations, almost every reason, which, among savages, concurred to the establishment of hospitality, has ceased, and the practice, in the ancient sense, has ceased of course. The arts of writing and printing have furnished innumerable vehicles of intelligence always at command. Knowledge of all the arts of life is diffused with facility, safety, and accuracy, as far as the use of letters is known. The cultivation of the gentle passions, an improved sense of the duties of humanity, a knowledge of its rights, and the protection afforded to those rights, by the law of nations and the civil laws of most countries, have superseded the necessity of individual protection ; and public accommodations have been much more convenient for travellers, than private hospitality. The universal introduction and currency of money, and the facilities of commerce, have given men the command of a kind of property, which may with ease and safety attend their persons, and provide for them in their peregrinations. Most men, who travel at this day, are engaged in pursuits of interests or gratifications of a private nature. In this state of things, hospitality, in the *ancient practice,* would be unnecessary, unjust, and intolerably burdensome. It has therefore been well exchanged for those courtesies, that better accord with the manners as well as the interests of civil society : and why should we regret the exchange ? Let those who entertain such an enthusiastic veneration for hospitality and other ancient virtues of the same origin, reflect, that they cannot have the effect without the cause ; and that those precious gems of savage virtues would lose their lustre and estimation without the foil of savage vices. This short sketch is sufficient to prove, that the first rude state of man, or if we choose the expression, the first simple state of society does not most abound in virtue and happiness. I have given, indeed, a short, but in a general view I believe, a true sketch of every uncivilized tribe on earth.

This opinion of a preference of the savage to a civilized state of society has been inculcated by some, who, irritated and disgusted with the numerous abuses of a corrupt government, have unjustly attributed to civilization those evils, which we always find aggravated, the nearer we approach to the savage state, their favorite state of nature ; and by the glowing minds of some whose zeal in the cause of virtue exceeded their information. Had they attended to the science of human nature, the development of the human mind, the powers, faculties, passions and appetites of man ; had they studied attentively the history—not of battles and sieges only, the intrigues of statesmen, and the revolution of empires—but the history of man in society, the history of the human mind, they would have found reason for correcting their opinion. This science, so important to man, has been too much neglected. In the first stages, none are capable of making or recording proper observations, and one half of the progress has generally passed unnoticed. In the following ages, historians, hurried away by the more splendid events of history, have too much neglected to mark the progressive improvement of the mind ; and readers have been equally inattentive to the few facts that have been recorded, throwing any light upon the subject. In America, the best opportunity that ever presented for supplying these deficiencies in the early history of man, by actual observation on real life and manners, has been too much neglected, and suffered to escape hitherto with but little improvement.

CHAPTER II.

Of the appetite or propensity for society—the appetite which leads to the propagation of the species—ambition—sympathy.

We will now, briefly, inquire how far man, without a consideration of mutual wants, or a necessity for mutual defence, arising merely from a sense of weakness or wickedness, is by nature fitted for society. That, surely, is to him a natural state, to which the laws of his nature, general and particular, all tend. Here let me premise, that, with man, a state of improvement is not opposed to a state of nature. Perhaps as good a definition as any which has been given of man is, that he is a being capable of improvement, in a progression, of which he knows not the limits. Deity has. implanted in his nature the seeds of improvement, furnished him with powers and faculties for the cultivation, and to these superadded a sense that the cultivation is a duty. The first thing which strikes the mind, in the course of our inquiry is an appetite for society. Man desires to associate with man, and feels a pleasure at the approach of his kind.

The appetite is so universally prevalent, it cannot be denied, that it originates in his nature. The same appetite, under the name of instinct, produces all those associations which are found to prevail among all gregarious animals of the brute creation and with them, it is allowed to be natural. Why not allow it to be so with man, to whom it isso much more extensively useful? This appetite, which may with equal, or perhaps, more propriety be denominated a propensity to society, is common to all men;—and although I have compared it to

instinct, in the lower order of animals it is I conceive, in its origin
a susceptibility merely of certain mental impressions, that is,
such as excite feelings in the mind, either agreeable or
disagreeable, according to the constitution of nature. The infant
receives its first impressions from its mother or nurse ; these are
effected by soothing attentions to the wants of the infant, in
its helpless state ; exciting pleasurable sensations : until the
presence of the soothing object constantly suggests, or is
accompanied with those pleasurable sensations agreeable to
the laws of association, by which the pleasure excited in
the mind, by any object, is transferred to that object and
considered as an inherent quality. These feelings are soon
extended from the mother or nurse to all whose presence
has become familiar ; until it embraces every acquaintance.
The pleasurable sensation is frequently counteracted by another,
that of fear excited by some new and unusual object ; which,
however, is removed by familiarity, and gives place to the
former agreeable impressions. This appears to be the origin of
the social affections. The susceptibility, only, is innate and is
common to all ; and as the very life of every infant, that comes
into the world, necessarily depends on the kind attention of
others, every one, that lives, must necessarily experience the
impressions, and the social affections become as common as the
susceptibility. They vary, indeed, in degree and extent, from
circumstances ; from constitution, which renders one less
susceptible than another ; but more frequently from education
and habit, which are, principally, effected through a propensity
to imitation. If there be any thing instinctive in man, it is
this propensity to imitation. It was long ago observed by
Aristotle, that man is an imitative being. In the early stages
of life, this propensity to imitation opens the only avenue to
improvement. Infants, children, and youth take, by imitation,
not only their actions, but their feelings, sentiments, and
opinions, from others, particularly from those to whom they
are most attached, and for whom they have the greatest respect.

It has been made a question whether the propensity to society
be limited in the number of its objects ? This question, I think,
will admit, though not a precise, yet a satisfactory answer. It
is adapted to the occasions, the powers and faculties of men,

and admits of equal extension by improvement; accordingly, in the early stages of society, while the powers and faculties of men were in their infancy, men have every where been found associated in families and small independent tribes. If at any time, larger associations were formed, like some of the great empires of antiquity, they were not the effect of choice, but of superior force. Agreeable to this opinion, we find the parts were but loosely connected, and every where crumbled in pieces, as soon as that force was removed. As mankind increase in knowledge, as their powers and faculties extend, and the comprehension of the mind is enlarged, they voluntarily extend their associations; to determine therefore the limits of the social propensity, or the social affections, we must determine the limits of social improvements. This appetite is accompanied with other appetites, propensities, and passions, that nature has made essential parts of the constitution of man, which have no use, no gratification but in society. Hardly can we find one which terminates wholly in self, not one that stands opposed to society. Of compassion, sympathy, and the train of benevolent passions and emotions, society is clearly the ultimate object. The principal end of some is the preservation of the individual; of others, the continuation of the species—such is the hoarding appetite, and the passion for riches to which it gives rise; the appetite which leads to the propagation of the species and its consequent passions;—even these are not solitary;—they do not terminate wholly in self—no, not the hoarding appetite, which, if any, might be thought an exception. Here, self often predominates; but in general the passion for riches, stript of every view to society, becomes very faint, if not totally extinct. The man, who is intent upon gain, has some connexion, some friend, whom he wishes to benefit, by his acquisition. He views the acquisition of riches as a mean, not an end; a mean of future support and personal indulgence, it is true; but at the same time, as a mean of benefiting some, and of acquiring esteem, confidence, and influence among all. Some instances have, indeed, been known of solitary misers, who have made the amassing of riches the sole end of their pursuits: some individuals have, likewise, conceived an aversion for man, and secluded themselves from society. These are considered as deviating from the common sense of their species, the common standard of man ; they are instances of the abuse of natural passions, or are the anomalies of the race. There are other anomalies ; but from such we do not take the common nature of man. The appetite which leads to the propagation of the species is, perhaps, in its origin, a vague indeterminate impulse to gratification. The principal end of this appetite, doubtless, is the continuation of the species by a perpetual re-production, in which view it is the constant revivifying principle of society ; but the Author of our being, whose all comprehensive plan is adjusted, in the most perfect harmony, has made it farther subservient to social happiness. Nature, by making it the source of a specific passion, corrects the vagueness of the appetite ; and thus it becomes the fountain of domestic felicity and one of the strongest bonds of society.

Ambition, when in balance with the other passions and appetites, is not opposed to the general good of society.—Far from being detrimental, it is highly useful to man. By this passion, many actions, the noblest and most beneficial in society, are produced. It is only in the extreme, that the passion becomes hurtful ; when the acquisition of power or influence is no longer considered as a mean of doing good ; when the passion aims solely or principally at its own gratification: But this is doing violence to the laws of nature, which result from the whole nature of man. The passions of hatred, revenge, and some other passions and emotions, not unfrequently very pernicious in society, are reserved for the next chapter. In the remainder of this, we will attend to some emotions purely of a social tendency. Sympathy is an ingredient in the social nature of man, deserving of very particular attention. The modus agendi, or how the emotion of sympathy is produced ; whether it be wholly mental, the reflection of a sentiment, or whether it be partly organical, partly mental, is perhaps, one of the secrets of nature ; but the effect is evident and the final cause illustrious. It is one of those nice adjustments in the nature of man, which give us the most exalted idea of the wisdom and benevolence of its Author. In the smaller circles of life, its influence is more immediate, more direct, but its influence extends to whole nations and empires. Sympathy

is generally produced through the medium of an organic
impression. We see something in the countenance, the
movement, the whole figure of the person, which we take for
the expression of a sentiment, or a particular state of mind in
that person. We instantaneously, seemingly by a direct
impression, without time for reflection, find excited in ourselves
a corresponding tone of mind, corresponding sentiments,
producing similar expressions. The emotion, though we may
have a sense of pain and distress in the object, is not repulsive.
On the contrary we feel a powerful attraction to objects of
distress. Thus man is sweetly prepared to mourn with those
who mourn and to rejoice with those who rejoice. The emotion
of sympathy not only prevents a thousand discords, but produces
in society a kind of instinctive harmony. There is one
impression of sympathy, which seems to be mostly organic, or
an effect on the nerves only. A yawn from one person in
company, will produce a spontaneous yawn in all present, at
least all who see the act. When we see a person suddenly
hurt, or hear of one being wounded in a particular part, we
feel a particular affection of the nerves in that part, which
thence thrills through the whole frame, conveying at once
to the heart a sense of the pain supposed to be felt by the
patient. This may be one reason why, when we hear of a
person being wounded, we are anxious to learn the manner and
particular place of the wound. Where our information is general
the effect on us is general ; we endure something like a state of
suspense. This is a situation apparently of greater uneasiness,
than when the sensation is reduced to a corresponding part.
Lord Kaims has beautifully unfolded what he calls the
sympathetic emotion of virtue* and which ought not to be
omitted here. When we are witnesses, or hear of the
performance of any great, noble, and benevolent action, we
find excited in ourselves a strong desire to perform the same
kind of action. The mind swells with an ardent desire to find
a proper opportunity, or a proper object. Notwithstanding some
opinions to the contrary, I am persuaded these emotions of

---

*Elements of Criticism. Vol. I. Chapter II. p. 1. Sec. 4.

sympathy are not the effect of reasoning from the object to our own situation ; they rather resemble instinctive impulses. Sympathy, without the intervention of words, blends the thoughts, sentiments, and the virtuous disposition of individuals ; it diffuses joys of the heart from countenance to countenance, commands relief in distress, and consolation in affliction. Montesquieu alludes to this principle in human nature when he says,—"Parents are generally able to communicate their ideas to their children ; but are still better able to transmit their passions." This disposition to sympathy helps to account for all that similarity of sentiments, character, and even of features, which is observable in families, societies and nations ; less perfect, indeed, the more extensive the connexion.

CHAPTER III.

Of hatred and revenge—Envy and some other dissocial passions.

Hatred and revenge are not, in their nature, opposed to society, although, from their abuse they become at times very pernicious. On a candid inquiry it will be found, that those passions do not arise from any malignity in the nature of man ; but are given for good and wise purposes. They are necessary to a being capable of injuring as well as benefiting others, and liable to be himself the subject of injuries from those of his own species. Men are conscious of a freedom of action, of a choice in what they do—we know at the same time, that man is not a perfect being, that he has many weaknesses, that there fall in his way motives to action infinitely various. Sometimes his choice is influenced by ignorance, by error, by the prevalence of particular passions or appetites, a present desire of gratification.

Sometimes he is confounded by a combination of circumstances, the result of which, he wants the power, or the patience, to evolve. He is frequently tempted to a deviation from right, by an opposition of interests, originating, not in a direct intention of the parties, but the want of an early foresight in each, of the other's intended pursuits. To a being thus circumstanced, powerful moral restraints are necessary. Such restraints are provided for man, and come in aid of his moral perceptions of right, and are made to arise from the consequence of his actions. It is evidently a general constitution of providence, that the general tendency of *vice* is to produce misery to the agent, of *virtue*, to produce happiness, connected in both by the relation of cause and effect. The passions of hatred and revenge will be found to accord with this constitution.

The more fully to investigate this subject, it will be necessary to take a nearer view of human nature. Man, in an unimproved state, is very little acquainted with the operatiuns of his own mind, the extent of his powers and faculties and the result of their various combinations. For their development, he is furnished with internal perceptions and external senses, accompanied with the powers of reason and investigation. As in physics, no reliance can be had on reasonings a priori; experience alone can decide. Man, therefore, fully to discover the extent of his powers and faculties, and the right tendency of his whole nature, must with sufficient attention and presence of mind to mark the result, pass through such a variety of situations as will bring all into exercise, and put all to the test, in every variety of combination. It is a matter of great difficulty for a man to make just and accurate observations on a subject so evanescent, as are the operation of his own mind, and always in transitu. They are past ere there is time for reflection : on the most important occasions, the whole mind is wrapped in attention to some external objects. Add to this, subjected as man is, though for wise purposes, to the influence of habit, his observations will be frequently partial, and his conclusions warped by some present prevailing bias.—It is evident, therefore, that the progress of moral and social combinations beyond those that are the most simple and obvious, will be slow ; how slow a slight attention to the history of the human mind will evince,

We are taught by reason and experience, that the less a man is able to discern agreements and tendencies, the moral relations of things, the more liable he is to do wrong; the more liable from partial views, instead of seeking a compromise, to sacrifice to his own the interest of others; at the same time he is the less able to devise and enforce those social rules, which might remedy the evil. In the first rude stages of society, men have no notion of general laws or of public punishments, for the prevention of private injuries; they are unable to connect private injuries with the public concerns of the nation or tribe. The redress or prevention of these, are left to each individual. In such a situation hatred and revenge are the only practical checks. Hatred is a fixed aversion of one man to another, on account of a real or supposed intentional opposition to his interest or happiness.—Revenge is a desire in one person to inflict an evil on another for a real or supposed injury received. —Hatred alone dictates the avoidance of its object as disagreeable or noxious: revenge pursues its object, and is gratified only with retaliating the injury; such conduct is dictated by the law of self preservation, and is necessary, in that state, as there is no other external restraint, no other means of escaping, or preventing future injuries. Thus limited and directed, they are necessary for the prevention of a licentiousness in injuries unrestrained by any fear of the consequences.

In the progress of improvement an extension of social intercourse, useful discoveries, the invention of arts, the separation of property, a gradual change of manners, the multiplication of desires and objects of gratification, form a scene too intricate, a combination of interests too complicated, for the former simple mode of society; liability to injuries is increased in proportion. The passion of revenge, almost constantly called into exercise would, in this state of society, if laid under no restraint, become the most cruel scourge and render society a curse instead of a blessing. Nature is always equal to her occasions. Active enterprise and more extensive pursuits invigorate and enlarge the powers of the mind, and render men equal to the task of a more extensive legislation. They are led by degrees, in some measure, to comprehend their situation; to evolve the combinations of their various interests ; to form those laws, which may have a tendency to prevent a direct opposition ; to provide for a reparation of injuries, and punishments for the restraint of wanton violence. Still the progress is slow ; it is long before men can be persuaded to accept merely a reparation for injuries, and submit to society the sole right of punishing for prevention which comes in the place of revenge. The right to revenge private injuries, in the most improved state of society, in the highest refinement of manners, never wholly ceases ; nor is it demanded. There will exist many little oppositions, many little injuries, to which the law cannot descend, and which if neglected, become the source of greater violence. The exercise of hatred and revenge, by the party injured, is still the only restraint in these cases. In a state of improvement, however, in a well regulated civil society, these passions stripped of their violence, and under the restraint of laws and moral discipline, are hardly known for the same passions. Still they are the same, only chastised and accommodated to a more improved state of society. Before, justified by the law of self preservation, they acted a primary part as sovereign in the distribution of punishments.—Now they act a subordinate part in coming in aid of the law, in matters of smaller moment. They are however, under every guard of law and of morals, liable at times to great abuses ; and what, when left to the direction of a fallible being, is not liable to abuse ? We should be ill fitted for society, without them. In an improved and well regulated society, the abuse can never be very extensive in its consequences. Let us not rashly attempt to correct the wisdom of Deity, much better is it for us that we should suffer the abuse of them than the total extinction.

Envy, malice, and avarice have been accounted instances of natural passions which are dissocial, and tend to prove, that man is little fitted for happiness in society. I will not here contend about the term natural. It is true that man is capable of these passions, and of many other vicious passions and habits ; a little reflection, however, will discover that these are not original in his nature ; but have their origin in the abuse of those natural passions, which are necessary to his happiness, both as a social being and as an individual. Envy is generally said to be emulation carried to excess. This is undoubtedly correct; but in the exercise it certainly partakes of the passion of revenge. Emulation is a desire to excel others, in the public estimation. While a person strives by the acquisition of superior excellence, to deserve a preference in the public opinion, it may emphatically be called the strife of virtue.— The happiness of society is interested in the contest. When a person deserts the prime object, the acquisition of real excellence, and strives, by the depression of a competitor, to enjoy the public estimation unrivalled, it has degenerated into envy, and is now the contest of vice. A person under the dominion of this passion is prone to exaggerate every little fault in a competitor, and to convert even his virtuous actions into vices by attributing them to corrupt motives. Every excellence in a rival is viewed as hostile, every advance as a personal injury. To complete the turpitude of the passion, and fill up the measure of vice, the passion of revenge is called into its aid.

Malice is a disposition to inflict evil on others without just cause. This disposition, by indulgence, is inflamed into a permanent passion, the most detestable, as well as pernicious in its effects. It may be called a perpetual anger, and is equally irrational with that passion in the extreme. Some persons appear to derive from their organization, an irritability of mind, which easily admits this disposition. In general, malice prevails most among a people of fierce and rough manners, where the common tone of the mind borders upon anger. It is more rare in an improved state of society and manners, and where it is discovered, may generally be traced to its source, in disappointments, insults, and hard usage, which have habituated the mind to a state of irritation. In all these cases it is easily perceived, that a malicious disposition is, originally, no part of the common nature of man, but is wholly adventitious. It is a vicious habit of mind admitted and confirmed by a too ready indulgence of the irritable feelings. Avarice is the excess of that passion which accompanies the hoarding appetite; the passion which prompts man to provide for his future necessities or convenience. It is the foundation of all his providence. Like other passions it is liable to abuse, to be

4

converted into avarice, and become indirectly an incentive to the most horrid vices. There are passions which originate in habit ; every habit gives rise to an attendant passion, which impels to the indulgence of the habit. Vicious habits are attended with vicious passions, many of which have the most pernicious consequences in society. Such passions have no pretence of being natural or original, in the mind of man. The habits from which they are derived, are formed in the mind, through the neglect or abuse of some natural power, faculty, or propensity. They may like every vice be admitted or excluded at the election of the mind ;—they may, therefore, withthe greatest propriety, be denominated, adventitious. That any of the passions, faculties, or propensities of man may be abused, proves only that he is a moral agent capable, in his actions, of choosing between good and evil, or that he is imperfect and liable to deception, and sometimes to aberrations from virtue, without designing the consequences. Were it an objection to any passion, propensity, power, or faculty, that it might be abused to the injury of mankind, not one would escape condemnation. The faculty of reason would not be exempt. Generosity must be accounted an evil, because it sometimes misjudges and sometimes turns to prodigality.

Upon a candid view of the whole subject, the conclusion is undeniable, that man is, by the laws of his common nature as constituted by the Author of his being, fitted for a state of society and social improvements ; that his happiness depends on the right use of his passions, appetites, powers, and faculties agreeable to the laws of social nature ; that as a moral being, capable of vicious as well as virtuous actions, he may deviate from his destination, and disturb his own happiness, as well as the happiness of others.

BOOK III.

OF MAN AS FITTED FOR CIVIL GOVERNMENT AND LAWS.

CHAPTER I.

Of the moral faculty, or moral constitution of man.

In the preceding book, we have seen that man, as far as depends on his natural appetites, powers, and propensities, is fitted, and intended, for the social state. We shall now inquire, how far he is fitted for government,—to be the subject of civil institutions and laws.

The first thing, that presents itself in this inquiry, is the moral faculty, or the moral constitution of man; moral perception or the power of discerning what is morally right or wrong in human actions, both as it relates to himself and others; and a sense of obligation to do what is right accordingly, and to forbear what is wrong. Without such power of perception and sense of obligation, he could not be a subject of government, could be subject to no laws, human or divine, except to the laws of instinct and to those physical laws, which are appointed for the lower orders of the animal creation, and which are to them, laws of necessity, not of obligation. I shall endeavor to investigate fully, but with as much brevity as is consistent with perspicuity, the nature of that constitution, the origin of the moral faculty, and the nature of moral obligation, and in what way it renders him a proper subject of government and laws.

Before entering upon this inquiry I shall briefly notice some opinions of Mr. Paley, who sustains a very eminent character as a moral writer. In his treatise of moral philosophy, he very justly discards the notions of innate maxims, of an instinctive perception of moral right and wrong, or what may be called a moral instinct. He admits that man has, from nature, a capability of attaining the perception of moral right and wrong, and accounts for his approbation of the one and disapprobation of the other, in the following manner. "Having experienced in some instances, a particular conduct to be beneficial to ourselves, or observed that it would be so, a sentiment of approbation arises in the mind, and which sentiment afterwards accompanies the idea or mention of the same conduct, although the private advantage, which first excited it, no longer exists," and e converso of a conduct injurious. He farther attributes the continuation of such sentiments, or as I understand him, their propagation, and what renders them common in society, to imitation, of which he says—"The efficacy of this principle is most observable in children; indeed, if there is anything in them, which deserves the name of instinct, it is the propensity to imitation." However just these observations may be, and however applicable to the manner in which moral sentiments become habitual, and the manner in which they are frequently propagated, they do not at all serve to explain the original principle of the moral faculty, in the common nature of man. That there is such a common principle, is evident from the common and universal effect.—Every man endued with human faculties is found capable of moral sentiments, and of attaining the perception of the moral quality of actions. This common principle, I shall endeavor, presently, to demonstrate. The same author when treating of moral obligation, says,— "When I first turned my thoughts to moral speculations, an air of mystery appeared to hang over the whole subject, which arose, I believe, from hence, that I supposed, with many authors, whom I had read, that to be obliged to do a thing was very different from being induced to do it, and that the obligation to practice virtue, do what is right, just &c., was quite another thing and another kind, than the obligation, which the soldier is under to obey his officer, a servant his master, or any of the other civil and ordinary obligations of human life ; whereas it appears from what has been said, that it is like all other obligations, and that obligation is nothing more than an inducement of sufficient strength, and resulting from the command of another." He had before given what he calls a definition of virtue, that it is " the doing good to mankind, in obedience to the will of God, for the sake of everlasting happiness,"—and a definition of obligation,—" A man is said to be obliged, when he is urged by a violent motive resulting from the command of another." I do not know that any one, who has at all considered the subject, has supposed that obligations differ in kind, but in species. A general definition, if correct, is true of all the species comprehended in the general term, but cannot mark their specific distinction ; and when it becomes necessary or proper to mark their specific distinctions, something must be added to the general definition. It is true that moral obligation is superinduced upon every legitimate obligation or blended with it ; but I believe that Mr. Paley would not have hazarded the assertion, that all civil obligations, and moral obligations, are specifically the same, and that the world have hitherto been amused with distinctions merely nominal. I will here only point out a marked distinction between civil and moral obligation, which will be more fully explained in another place. Civil obligation is considered as fulfilled by the mere performance or forbearance of the act enjoined or prohibited, without regard to the intention of the agent ; but moral obligation cannot be fulfilled as such, without the good intentions of the agent ; and besides, moral obligation is much more comprehensive than civil obligation. In these definitions, and indeed in his whole account of the moral constitution of man, although he makes his duty to consist in doing good to mankind, yet Mr. Paley seems not sufficiently to have considered him as a social being by the constitution and laws of his nature ; that the social affections are necessary to that moral constitution, and that without them he could not be the subject of moral obligation. Accordingly, when he introduces the principle of utility, which is indeed the end of all moral laws, he leaves it a mere selfish principle, with the agent. Besides, his plan of treating actions in the abstract and that only, according to his own confession, excludes the intention of the agent, without which actions are neither virtuous nor vicious; in fine, have no moral quality, but are to be considered, as merely useful or detrimental, as chance directs.

Let us inquire, what, according to his definition of virtue and obligation, is the inducement.--Is it the will or command of God? the consequence alone? or both united? The consequence alone replies the author. "We can be obliged to nothing but what we ourselves are to gain or lose something by it; for nothing else can be a violent motive to us. As we should not be obliged to obey the laws or the magistrate, unless reward or punishments, pleasure or pain, somehow or other, depended on our obedience; so neither should we, without the same reason, be obliged to do what is right, practice virtue, or obey the commands of God." But this motive must result from the command of another; in the case of moral obligation, from God. On this same plan, that the motive must result from the command of another, can only be explained to mean a firm belief that the author of the command has the power and the will to reward the obedient and punish the disobedient. Do the sentiments of the mind, under a sense of moral obligation respond to this? I think not. The sense of desert, of praise or blame, due to our conduct, seems not to be consistent with it; or at least to intimate that something more is wanting. Why do we feel ourselves accountable to God, or to our fellow men? Is that sense of accountability to be resolved into a mere dread of power? or is it a mere sentiment of regret for what we may lose? or of pleasure for what we may gain? and shall we for merit and demerit, substitute useful and injurious to ourselves, and consider our accountability as a mere account of profit and loss?

What then is wanting in this system? Clearly the affections, which involve the disposition and intention of the agent, and which, as he tells us in a note, his plan excluded, and at the same time acknowledges that the agent is virtuous or vicious according to his design, or, which is the same thing, actions as they relate to the agent are virtuous or vicious according to that design; from hence they derive their moral quality.—But he tells us at the same time, that actions are right or wrong according to their tendency to produce good or evil. In this plan, then, that actions are right, means only that they are useful, and wrong, that they are injurious, but they are not therefore virtuous or vicious. If, as he tells us in the same note, his concern was with actions in the abstract, and that only, he should have adhered to that plan, and in all instances, have substituted utility for virtue, useful for virtuous, and injurious for vicious. His definition of virtue would then have been consistent as a definition of utility, and with this his definition of obligation would correspond. Had he, through the whole of his treatise so deservedly esteemed, adhered strictly to his plan of considering action, in the abstract only, excluding the intention of the agent, it would have been found very little in harmony with that practical moral system, which the Author of nature has ordained for man. He that would write a practical system of morality, to be useful, must study the moral constitution and situation of man ; the end and design of that constitution, and the means provided for attaining that end, for carrying the design into effect. This will keep him in a constant communication with human action, with moral action, which can never be found to exist without intention. In such a system, utility will be the important end, but it will be a social not a selfish utility, and virtue will be the means of attainment. Such, notwithstanding the plan which he had announced, of treating actions in the abstract only, was clearly, the author's practical opinion ; for we find him almost constantly bringing down his theory to practical morality, which gives to his work its principal value. Thus we find him almost in the outset, in the sixth chapter of his preliminary book, making human happiness first of all, to consist in the exercise of the social affections. By the social affections he must mean a kind disposition in one toward his fellow men, at least, those within the sphere of his connection, which is, in fact, an habitual intention to do them good, as occasion presents. The social affections make the man an integral part of society, and in degree, identify his happiness with that of others ; they add what was wanting in the author's definition, the doing good to mankind with affection, that is with good intentions, and unite benevolence with prudence ; but the definition includes prudence only in the motive, —"for the sake of everlasting happiness." And it would have been the same had the avoidance of everlasting misery, been made the motive. There is certainly in the motive nothing of benevolence.—If I am correct in this, it proves that the social affections must, in any moral view, constitute an essential part of that violent motive, which he makes the inducement to moral obligation; it proves also the deficiency of the explanation above given, "that we can be obliged to nothing, but what we ourselves are to gain or lose something by, for nothing else can be a violent motive to us." If the social affections be necessary, which must be the case, to render the obligation moral, what we are ourselves to gain or lose makes but a part, both must unite to complete the motive; one or the other may prevail according to the situation. Where our own life is in immediate danger, self preservation will be the prevailing motive; where the life of another, the social affections. Nor is it any answer to say that blending the social affections in the motive serves to promote our own happiness. It proves that our own happiness is not a mere isolated, selfish, consideration.

We will now proceed to inquire into the moral constitution of man the origin and progress of the moral faculty, and the nature and end of moral obligation, as it relates to the individual, and to society. We have before noticed, in the human mind, a susceptibility of impressions,—impressions exciting in the mind feelings agreeable or disagreeable, of pleasure or pain which I shall denominate moral impressions. These are the germ of moral sentiments, and differ from sensation, or those impressions, whether agreeable or disagreeable, pleasurable, or painful, which are received through the organs of sense, and which are for the most part felt at the organ and terminate in the pleasure or pain excited; and though they are perceived and distinguished by the mind, yet they are perceived as impressions immediately on the respective external organs. The feelings excited by moral impressions are perceived to be in the mind itself, and to be independent of the organs of sense. There is, indeed, often a sensible and a moral impression from the same object. The sensible impression is direct; but the moral impression appears to be made by way of suggestion; both excite feelings of pleasure or pain ; but from habit, if they excite pleasure in a common degree only, they pass for indifferent. We are more sensible to any thing in a small degree painful. The feelings excited by moral impression are of the social kind ; they have always some relation to society, to others ;—not so the mere sensible impression. Where they do not, by way of suggestion, cause some moral impression, the feelings excited terminate in self. Nor is it an objection, that we wish others to enjoy with us a fine picture or a fine present. That wish is a moral sentiment, introduced by suggestion.— Indeed, there is not perhaps a sensible impression or sensation, which may not, on occasion, impress some moral sentiment, suggest some moral reflection. Moral sentiments may be just or unjust. It is not their rectitude that constitutes them moral in the sense of the term here used, but their social nature.

But some entertain unsocial sentiments ; are these of a moral nature ? Certainly they are, and it is still in relation to society, that they have their moral quality. Of the susceptibility of moral impressions we have the same proof, as we have of a susceptibility of sensations, a universal consciousness of the impressions. We may therefore consider it to be clearly established as a first principle. Such is the constitution of the human mind, that the feelings excited by those impressions, whether agreeable or disagreeable, are always reflected back upon the object, and are considered as belonging to the object as the cause. In proportion as the feelings excited are pleasant or agreeable, they are accompanied with complacency toward the object; if disagreeable or painful, with disgust or resentment. These feelings appear to rise spontaneously, or rather without any intention in the mind to excite them ; nay, to be often uncontrollable ; although they may, by a course of discipline, be brought under restraint. That these things are so, we know from observation and experience ; but why they are so, until we are able to discover further principles, we must resolve into the constitution of the human mind, or rather into the great first cause where all our researches must finally terminate. In infancy the range of moral impressions is very limited, because the comprehension of moral objects is also limited, and it is extended only as the comprehension of those objects is

extended. It is not easy to determine, how early the human
mind is capable of these impressions, how early the susceptibility
exists ; but we have reason to believe it to be co-existent with
mind. For the first mental acts which we observe in children
are complacency in acts of kindness and resentment of injuries.
In that state, however, from the absence or weakness of
intellect, these acts are not considered as moral, in the sense of
being imputable ; it seems like the embryo state of the moral
powers. Nor do infants distinguish, as moral, the objects from
which they receive the impressions, and often resent with the
same violence an injury received from an inanimate as an
animate, from an irrational as a rational, object ; nor do they
begin to distinguish between intentional and unintentional
injuries, until some development of the rational powers has
taken place. The susceptibility of moral impressions, having
its origin in nature, is entitled to be considered as a first
principle, and as much an essential part of the mental, as the
organs of sense are of the animal constitution. The moral
faculty is, however, yet in its germ—something farther is
necessary towards its cultivation and improvement; we find it
here wrapt in self. It cannot be said fully to act a moral
part ; and the means of improvement are found intimately
connected with its first principle. I have before said, that
moral sentiments are of a social nature, and have shown that
the social affections, by which man is connected with, and
becomes an integral part of society, have their origin in
a mental susceptibility of impressions. This is the same
susceptibility which we have now found to be the first simple
principle of the moral faculty ; and the process by which the
social affections, springing from that natural source, were shown
to be cultivated, is in every step a moral process. Thus by
this simple natural principle, the social and moral relations are
found to be indissolubly connected, or with more strict propriety
may be said to be identified. The sentiments of complacency
and resentment excited in the infant mind, by the impressions
made by different objects, are but the germ of moral sentiments,
not being yet accompanied with a conception of moral right
and wrong, which is necessary to their becoming practically
moral, in the sense to be imputable. The cultivation of the

social affections contributes to this end, but which can be fully attained, only by a development of the intellectual powers. A degree of intellect is, we have before said, necessary, not only to the development of the moral faculty, but to the moral quality of human actions, as imputable to the agent. Without this a human action is no more imputable than the actions of a brute animal, or the movements of a machine. It is the province of the intellectual powers to combine and distinguish the moral relations, to discern and appreciate their results in duty, and to direct the performance of those duties, as they are found to conduce not only to the interest of the individual, but to the general interest of society, and the promotion of human happiness. Still, the moral powers must always be imperfect. They are the moral powers of man, liable to be led astray by his vicious habits, by his passions and appetites, by his weakness and sometimes by his reason.

In this same constitution, and originating in the same principle, nature has founded her moral law, the law of human conduct; and the next inquiry is, what provision is made for enforcing on the human mind a sense of obligation to observe and obey that law? This will be found originating in the same principle and an essential part of the same moral constitution. When actions come to be considered as right or wrong, according to their beneficial or injurious effects and tendency, from this circumstance, the sentiment of complacency in regard to a beneficent act, becomes as referred to the agent, a rational sentiment of approbation, and that of resentment for an injurious act, of disapprobation. Nature has also given an early and ready discernment of analogy by which not only man, but animals in general, distinguish their species, and each discerns that the species to which it belongs, has a common nature, on which they all rely with confidence in their mutual intercourse. Hence every man relies that all other men have, under the same circumstances, the same feelings and the same sentiments with himself, and finds it confirmed by observation and experience. In viewing the conduct of others, he is conscious of a sentiment of approbation of the right, and disapprobation of the wrong, accompanied with a sense of desert, of praise for the one, and of censure for the other. In viewing his own conduct he is conscious of the same sentiment of approbation and disapprobation accordingly, and the same sense of desert ; but in the latter case, the sentiment is more vivid, more pointed as being brought home to the mind by its own consciousness. Thus a provision is made by nature for the reward and punishment of moral actions. On the same principle every man is led to seek the approbation and to dread the censure of his fellow men, which he considers in the one case, the reward due to his good conduct, and in the other, the punishment due to his crimes. On the same principle, but by a stronger motive, he is led to seek the approbation and to dread the censure of that Omniscient Being, who is the Author of nature, and nature's laws ; from whom he received his own existence, and to whose goodness he is indebted for all his enjoyments, for all his prospects of happiness. Under these inducements, to seek the approbation of his own conscience, of his fellow men, and of his God, he finds himself bound by a three-fold cord of accountability—in other words under a moral obligation to do what is good and right,—to practice virtue.

Thus we find that moral obligation, of which I have here given an account, without attempting to force it into a definition, is an important part, or rather is the result, of the moral constitution, and is indissolubly connected with the same universal principle in the nature of man, which is the source of all our moral sentiments, of all the social affections. It will perhaps be remarked, that in explaining the origin and progress of this moral faculty, I have scarcely more than alluded to what is, or ought to be, the great end of all moral actions,—general utility, or the general interest of society ; but the subject, so far as it was here found necessary to pursue it, did not require its discussion. It was sufficient to consider it so far as the individual is affected ; and besides, the laws of nature, rightly understood, are found to aim, as well at the promotion of the individual as the general interests—or rather the promotion of the general interest of the community, through the private interests of the individual members ;—for the general interest consists of an aggregate of the individual interests, properly estimated. If ever they clash or run in opposite directions, it is owing so some error in the estimate; and indeed, with man there can never be a perfect estimate; it will at best, be but a near approximation.

Let us now see how far man, provided with such moral constitution, is, notwithstanding some seeming incongruities, fitted to become the subject of civil government and laws. The moral sense, (for I will now venture to use that term to express the perception of moral right and wrong, including a sense of moral obligation,) is to man the final arbiter of justice, veracity, and of all the moral virtues, of all his moral actions. When he perceives his actions to be right, or productive of good, agreeable to the laws of his nature, he is conscious of a pleasurable emotion of approbation ; when wrong, of a painful emotion of disapprobation. Hence his love of justice, veracity, and all the moral virtues. What he is conscious of in himself, he expects to find in others. This is the foundation of his confidence in the justice of others, and his reliance on human testimony. That he sometimes violates these virtues, is not sufficient proof that he does not admire and even love them. Justice, for instance, is the result of certain reciprocal relations, subsisting between the agent and the object; it is often therefore not a little complex. A little more or less comprehension of the relations may wholly vary the result, as to the moral quality of the action.

Viewing things through the medium of prejudice, or some present passion, man is liable to err in his estimate of those relations, and while he loves virtue in general, to admit vice in particulars. Considered as to his mind, man has not only active powers, but susceptibilities, in regard to which, the mind appears to be merely passive. He is capable of deliberation and choice. He is likewise susceptible of various impressions, from objects both external and internal; for the affections and operations of the mind, by reflection become objects, and have their impressions. The impressions made, produce a change in the mind, which is the subject ; a difference in the subject causes a difference in the effect. Hence it is, that, not only different men, but the same man at different times, may be differently affected by the same object, and the same apparent motive have a different influence. And hence comes a fluctuation of choice. This fluctuation is corrected by the moral sense, and by the force of reason and of habit, which places the choice of objects, or the admission of the causes of such impressions, in the power of the mind.

Were man unassailable by external impulses, were the influence of motives excluded, he would be wholly unaccommodating, wholly unaccountable. Law might as well be promulgated to a machine—rewards and punishments could add no inducement to obedience. However such a state may be suitable or necessary to any other order of beings, it is very ill suited to man, intended as he is for a state of government and laws. The sense of accountability, arising more immediately from the deep interest which we feel in the approbation of others, as above explained, is a principal ingredient in the moral constitution of man. When he has done well, he is conscious that he is deserving of the approbation of others; when ill, of their censure. Judging in the same manner of others, he is made to perceive the necessity of government, and the necessity and propriety of submitting his conduct in society to the regulation of laws, as well civil as moral.

CHAPTER II.

Idea of a community—Of Patriotism.

Man, by the force and habit of association and abstraction, acquires the conception of an aggregate of individuals, as forming a distinct entity,—a moral person, capable of rights and duties. Such is the idea of a community, of a society.

When a man considers himself as connected with any society, he is, if I may use the expression, conscious of a kind of individuality of himself with the aggregate. The conception of this individuality is more or less distinct and forcible, as the connexion is more or less intimate,—and if it be not the germ of every attachment to the community, certainly gives strength to the attachment and vigor to patriotism itself. It is essential to the social nature of man, and of great importance to government. It is not only the soul of individuality to the whole government; but as there will always be numerous subordinate connexions forming smaller societies in the same government, it makes all the members of the same connexion, in some degree, responsible for the actions of each. They enjoy the virtues and the advantages both of the individuals and of the community, and each in the same degree, the reproach of the other's crimes, and the justice of their punishment.

This sentiment has, however, given rise to a principle, which has been grossly abused to the oppression of mankind. In many governments, the practice has prevailed of involving in the same punishment of offenders, all of the same family and connexion,—the innocent with the guilty. It has prevailed most generally in despotic states, where it coincides with the principles of the government, which makes it a crime for a man to be placed even by nature herself, in a situation in which he might dare to think himself injured by the act of the prince. Although this conception of the unity of a connection is no justification of the practice, yet it fully accounts for its origin. In this also has originated the practice of retaliation, reprisals, and many things of a similar nature, permitted by the laws of nations ;—and here humanity may vindicate her rights, and assert that the practice is too often carried farther than the principle will in justice warrant.

Patriotism or love of country, is a noble passion, and illustrates the character of every people, who enjoy any just portion of liberty under civil institutions. It is indispensably necessary to any good degree of security or prosperity, in a nation. The whole community is the object of this passion ;— in its effects, it unites the individual members in the pursuit of public measures, and on necessary occasions, gives a preference of the public to private good. To the common interest in the defence and prosperity of the nation, it adds an affection great as the object, on which it is exerted.

It has been made a question whether the passion may be reckoned among the natural passions of man. The Abbé Raynal has asserted that it cannot. Speaking of the aboriginal inhabitants of Brazil—he says, " They show no particular attachment to their native place. The love of country, which is a ruling passion in the civil state, which in a good government rises to enthusiasm, and in bad ones becomes habitual—this love of country is but a factitious sentiment arising from society, but unknown in a state of nature."

Let us examine this opinion.—At this day, facts and not names give to opinions their just weight and currency. Although in speaking of the aborigines of Brazil, he mentions only their want of attachment to their native soil ; yet in his general position, he comprehends all the distinctive properties of that love of country which is generally denominated patriotism. In this sense love of country is a love of the community. An attachment to the soil collects, limits, and confines the passion, and gives a locality to its objects ; but does not of itself constitute the passion. Take from the country the community, take from it the inhabitants, and the object ceases.

Were this passion not discovered in the first rude state of man, no conclusive argument could be drawn from that circumstance. All the passions of man are, originally, capacities only, and capacities may and do often exist antecedent to the objects to which they are adapted. They can be discovered in exercise only; and they cannot be exhibited in exercise, until a proper object be presented. Many, if not all, of them are like plants in the germ; they discover not their species, until expanded by cultivation. Shall we say, the oak is not a tree of nature, because in its first state it is but a germ in the acorn? Or shall we say, the appetite in man, which leads to the propagation of the species, and its consequent passions, are not natural, because not discovered in the infant of a day?

If we rely upon facts, history has not recorded, nor modern researches discovered, a single people in this supposed state of nature, a state in which a love of country, an attachment to the community, does not make a conspicuous figure. The ancient Barbarians of the north of Europe, from whom most of the modern inhabitants of that country are descended, furnish with proofs of the existence of this passion among them, of vigorous national attachments. It is true, their attachment to any portion of the soil was not so strong. This attachment to the soil is fixed by the cultivation of the earth for subsistence, which collects the interest and attention to one spot and gives a locality to conveniences. It is not, however, generally true, that savages have but a feeble attachment to the soil of their country. In this respect, they are, in a great measure, capable of the same habits, passions, and sentiments as the man of civilization. They occupy, with their habitations, but a small part of what they call their country. The rest is reserved for pasture or hunting grounds; it is the great farm of the tribe. They readily remove their temporary habitations from one part of this to another; but war, famine, or some very powerful cause is necessary to compel them to a total abandonment. The ancient Scythians, from whom the modern Tartars are descended, were nations of herdsmen. Their riches consisted principally in their horses, which supplied them both with food and carriage. Their habitations were booths or tents of easy construction. In a country of great extent, they preferred those places, in which the greatest plenty of fresh pasture were found; for the sake of these, they made frequent and distant removals. We learn that among this people, as early as the reign of Darius the son of Hystaspes, the love of country was a vigorous passion. Their national attachments were strong, and they were attached to the soil, not so much because it afforded them subsistence by cultivation, as because it contained the tombs of their fathers. According to Herodotus, Indasarthus, a prince or head warrior in that country, sent the following message to Darius then attempting the conquest of Scythia—" If I flee before thee, Prince of the Persians, it is not because I fear thee. What I do now, I am used to do in times of peace. We Scythians have neither houses nor lands to defend. If thou hast a mind to force us to come to an engagement, attack the tombs of our fathers, and then thou shalt know what manner of men we are." Such a people could be no strangers to patriotism.

The savages of America are a living instance, of the strength of this passion, among a rude and uncultivated people. The European writers have been very much abused in their information of the American natives. Buffon has asserted, " that among them, paternal love and filial affection are very faint ; the most intimate connexion, that of family, has but feeble ties ; there is no intercourse between one family and another ; of course there is no national union, no republic, no social state." The Abbé Raynal has copied many things from Buffon, and probably here he found that state of nature, of which he speaks in the passage recited above. In the same account of the native inhabitants of Brazil, the Abbé gives an account of their ancient mode of life, in that country. What but a local attachment, an attachment to the soil, could have been the cause of this people continuing in the same country through a succession of ages ? To what but a national attachment shall we attribute their national manners, and national resentment, of which he tells us ? In another place, he furnishes an instance, which contradicts almost every part of the character given of the American natives by Buffon, and ought to have corrected his own opinion, that in what he calls a state of nature, the love of country is unknown. He tells us, the French proposed to a native tribe in Canada to remove to a distance from their ancient habitation; on which occasion, one of their chiefs made the following speech. "We were born, said he, on this ground—our fathers lie buried in it,—shall we say to the bones of our fathers, arise and go with us into a foreign land?" Is this the language of a people, who are almost void of parental and filial affection,—who have no national attachments, no republic, no social state?

Logan a Mingo chief, in his speech sent to the governor of Virginia, at the close of an Indian war, in the year 1774, discovers the same sentiments of patriotism. The reader will not be displeased to see the whole speech. It is more than equal to volumes, collected in the closet, on the character of that people. "I appeal, says he, to any white man to say, if ever he came to Logan's camp hungry, and he gave him not meat, if he ever came cold and naked, and he clothed him not.—During the last long and bloody war, Logan remained idle in his cabin, an advocate for peace. Such was my love of the whites, that my countrymen pointed as they went and said, *Logan is the friend of white men**. I had even thought to have lived with you, but for the injuries of one man. Colonel Cresap, last spring, in cold blood and unprovoked, murdered all the relations of Logan, not sparing even my women and children; there runs not a drop of my blood in the veins of any living creature.—This called on me for revenge—I have fought—I have killed many. I have fully glutted my vengeance. For my country, I rejoice at the beams of peace. But do not harbor a thought that mine is the joy of fear. Logan never felt fear. He would not turn on his heel to save his life. Who is there to mourn for Logan? Not one."

Where shall we find the love of country and family attachment more emphatically, more beautifully expressed? The people of these United States, who have known the aboriginal inhabitants of North America, both in peace and in war, and have often treated with them in their national councils, know full well the strength of their national attachments. Indeed the farther we go back toward that state so fondly and partially

* Jefferson's notes on Virginia.—67.

deemed by some the only true state of nature, the more vigorous we find that passion which attaches them to their little communities. What then is the result? Why clearly, that the Author of existence, to fit man for society and civil government, has implanted the principles of this passion in his nature.

CHAPTER III.

Of a disposition in man to abuse the powers of government with which he is intrusted.

The question whether man be originally depraved ; whether a disposition to evil, a relish for vice as such, be a part of his nature in the present state, I leave to be discussed by the moralist and the divine. I am here to consider his natural powers, his disposition and actions, as they relate solely to his political state.

Moralists have embraced different systems respecting the origin of moral evil, and the natural disposition of man, as affected to virtue and vice. Political writers have uniformly agreed. From Machiavel to Dr. Price, all have asserted or admitted, that, in a political character, when intrusted with power, man is totally depraved, wicked, and corrupt; that in power, the utmost perverseness is inherent in his very nature ; that he is never good, but through necessity. Hence mutual checks, restraints, and opposition of powers are found necessary to guard against the oppression of rulers. This, if true, refutes the opinion which I have attempted to establish; that man, by the original constitution of his nature, is fitted for civil government; or, as I have elsewhere expressed it, Deity has implanted in him the germ of every necessary qualification for that state. Little, however, is man fitted for civil government, if no one can be found fit to be intrusted with the execution of its powers. Before we admit an opinion which so much vilifies the nature of man, and must, if fully believed, almost tempt one to call in question the goodness of the Author of that nature, let us candidly consider the reasons on which the opinion is founded.

It is said, and truly, that every page of history furnishes us with instances of the abuse of power. The long line of Roman Emperors, with very few exceptions were scourges of the earth. All the kings and princes of ancient and modern times, not excepting the philosophic Frederick of Prussia,* have given full and convincing proofs of the danger of intrusting the powers of government to be exercised without control. An effect so universal, it is said, must have a universal cause in the nature of man. All this is true ; and yet I will venture, at the hazard of being thought to be singular, to dissent from the common opinion, respecting the real cause. I apprehend the effect so general is not produced by any malignity, any culpable disposition in the nature of man ; but that it is mostly the effect of situation. I do not doubt of the universality of the effect, or if you please, of the event, of a constant abuse of power in certain situations. I doubt of the cause only. I think the cause to be very different from that which has been usually assigned ; that it is more complex, and is the effect of other causes, some existing in the nature of man, others arising from the nature of the power, and from the mode in which it has been intrusted or assumed.

· It may perhaps be urged, that if experience has evinced a general propensity in rulers, to abuse the powers which they possess, it is of little consequence to the science of government, what may be the particular cause of that propensity. The same checks, the same opposition of powers, will be necessary to guard against the abuse. But let it be remembered, that in applying a remedy to any evil, little success can be expected, if the cause of the evil be unknown or mistaken. It is much more eligible, where there is a possibility, to remove or prevent the cause, than to be obliged to maintain a constant struggle

---

* Note.

against the effect, or be perpetually employed, in palliating or diverting its malignity. According to our different apprehension of the cause, the remedy applied will be different, and the event more or less successful.

It must be remembered that man is a complex being, and by nature constituted with a variety of passions, appetites, powers, propensities, and susceptibilites; with external senses, and an internal discernment adapted to the perception of objects physical and moral. Some of these have a more immediate relation to his individual being and happiness, yet so as not to be opposed to society; while others relate more immediately to society, yet not to the exclusion of self. He was not made for independence, but for mutual connexion, mutual dependence; and to this every thing in his nature is more or less relative.

On the right discernment of moral relations, either singly, or in their various combinations, arising from various objects, situations, and circumstances, depends the justness of his moral perceptions; on a full and right comprehension of the result, depends the knowledge of his duty. He is from the constitution of his nature, capable of impressions from an infinite variety of objects external and internal; for the operations and affections of the mind by reflection become objects, and again have their impressions. These impressions give an equal variety to the modifications of his passions, appetites, powers, and faculties. The result of all these constitutes the temper, disposition, and character of the man; and from the various modification arises, in a principal degree, the various influence of motives. Were man left in this situation he would be the sport of blind impulses;—there is evidently a necessity for a balance, as well as some arbiter of moral action. Reason, by which he combines, compares, distinguishes, and marks the result, has been considered by many, if not most of our ethical writers, as being to man the balance of his moral powers and the arbiter of his actions. I think this is not the office of reason. Reason is the hand that adjusts the balance, extends and limits it, rather than the balance itself. Let it be observed, that reason is here used, not for simple intellect or intelligence, but for ratiocination or the power of reasoning. However nice and metaphyisical these distinctions may appear, they lead to some important consequences in the moral economy of man.

What then, it will be asked, is to man the arbiter of his actions? what the balance of his moral powers? I answer, the moral sense or conscience, as explained in the preceding chapter, is, in all cases, the arbiter of moral action. Reason is an advocate to argue, compare, and inform ; but to conscience or the moral sense, is left the ultimate decision. I believe every one will be capable of perceiving this distinction. The remaining part of the subject is, indeed, a little more intricate ; but I hope to make it intelligible to all, who will attend to what passes in their own minds.

We have seen that man is a being constituted with a great variety of powers, faculties, passions, and appetites ; that these, from the various impressions to which the mind is subjected, are capable of an almost endless variety of modifications and combinations, which furnish to motives different directions, and different degrees of force. To a being thus constituted, some balance, to prevent the utmost capriciousness of conduct, and give him a command of choice in his actions, some constant regulator is necessary. A little attention to those faculties, that constitute the reasoning powers, to their operation, to the manner in which they are affected, influenced, and biassed by impulses internal and external, will discover that reason, instead of being qualified to serve as a regulator, has itself need of a balance, some steady principle for its regulation. Nature, always equal to her wants, has provided such a principle. This, in addition to the moral sense, is found in that sense of accountability, which is common to man. The sense of accountability has already been investigated and explained ; but it will be here necessary to examine it with a little more attention, and that we may have at once, an entire view of the subject, to repeat some things that have been said before.

The principle of accountability having its immediate origin in the sentiment of approbation and disapprobation, of which a man is conscious in regard to his own actions, it will be necessary to keep in view, as well the faculty, by which we discern moral relations, and the moral quality of actions, as the sense of desert which accompanies that consciousness. Man, as before observed, has a passion, a desire, an appetite call it by what name you please, for the approbation of others ;

and he extends it to all intelligent beings, whom he conceives to be, in any way conusant of his actions, (and its force is increased or diminished according to the relation in which he considers himself placed, in respect to those beings.) When he perceives that his actions are morally right, he is conscious that he deserves their approbation ; on the contrary, if he has done wrong, he is conscious that he is deserving of their censure. He is conscious to himself of a feeling of approbation and disapprobation of the conduct of others, as he views it to be right or wrong. Judging from his own feelings, and the expressions he observes in others, he justly expects to find the same sentiments in all ; and thus, as before expressed, he finds himself bound to his duty by a three-fold cord of accountability—to God, to his own conscience,* and to his fellow men. The sense of accountability constantly operating with the moral sense, though not exempt from the imperfections incident to the nature of man, constitutes the balance of his moral powers, and a steady principle for the regulation of his actions. Reason, by comparing circumstances, marking the result, and detecting the impositions, to which, not only the external sense, but the internal faculties, are more or less liable, is qualified to adjust the balance. Here we may again observe, that neither the moral sense, nor the sense of accountability is given in perfection to man ; they are but plants in the germ, the growth and improvement of which can be expected, only from a proper cultivation. I cannot but flatter myself, that the distinctions I have endeavored to make, are intelligible, and the principles clearly established. By the assistance of these principles, we shall be able to throw some light on the question, respecting so universal an abuse of power.

The correctness of a man's conduct will depend, principally, on a just discernment of moral relations, a clear perception of what, in his situation, is right or wrong, in moral action ; on the means of information, the strength and impartiality of his reason, and a just sense of accountability, to God, to his conscience, and to his fellow men. In proportion as there is a

---

* Note.

deficiency in one or all of these, he will be liable to a deviation from right, and every deviation, by changing the force of habit to the weaker side, will strengthen and confirm the bias. He, therefore, who in life and action would persevere in a course of virtue, must beware, how he indulges any deception on his moral discernment, any bias upon his reason or any relaxation of his sense of accountability. Free a man from his sense of accountability only, he is left to the dominion of his passions and appetites, and driven precipitately into vice; it is like detaching the balance of a watch in motion.

That branch of the sense of accountability by which a man perceives that his actions are of right, subjected to the praise or censure of his fellow men, is not least efficacious in preserving the balance of his moral powers; yet his sense of accountability to them may become extinct, from the situation merely, in which he may be placed. Place him, in a situation to consider himself either above or below the regard of his fellow men, he will no longer feel himself accountable to them for his conduct. He, who in such a situation, can maintain the guard of his virtue, and successfully resist the solicitations of his passions and appetites, the covert approaches, and the open attacks of vice, must be something more than human. Such is the original adjustment of the moral constitution of man, its parts, connexions, and dependencies, mutually supporting and supported, that not a pin can be loosened, without endangering a derangement of the whole structure.

That political situation which places a man in any degree of independence on those, over whom he exercises a power, in the same degree cherishes the emotions of pride, and transforms that which before was only a contempt of what is low, mean and unworthy of the man, into haughtiness, under the name of grandeur. It engenders a contempt for men, and extinguishes those sentiments which ought to subject his conduct to their approbation or censure, according to his desert. Such has been more or less the situation of all hereditary monarchs on the globe; of all aristocrats and aristocratical bodies; of all men in authority; who have had, or have conceived themselves to have the ability to continue their authority independent of those, over whom it was exercised; in a word such is the situation of all who hold their power in contempt of the people, they govern. A situation not indulged to man by the laws of his nature, and which providence has often, though hitherto with little effect, warned him, by the pernicious consequences, not to intrust to any one of the race. The wonder is not that men, in such a situation, should have been guilty of so many vices, but that they should have exhibited even a few virtues; how few have been those virtues, could we strip the actions of princes and nobles of the false glare of character, we should learn from every page of their history.

Instances of constant and flagrant abuse of power, by men thus situated, demonstrably prove that it is dangerous to exceed the limits of our nature, to step beyond the limits of its laws, but they prove no original malignity in man. In a different situation within the limits assigned, by the laws of human nature, men have administered the powers of government, with the greatest abilities and the most exalted virtues, for the sole good of the community. May we not instance more than one, may we not instance many examples in these United States? In situations in which rulers have held themselves fully accountable to the general sentiments of the people for the exercise of the powers, with which they were intrusted, they have conducted with as much integrity and virtue as have been exhibited in the more private scenes of life. It must be allowed that few such situations have been devised by political wisdom.

When any people are capable of forming a constitution of government, on natural principles, and establishing a power of administration within the limits of those principles, they will be able to secure themselves from the danger of all exorbitant abuses. Care must always be taken, that the ruler shall feel in a proper degree, his responsibility to the people, for his public conduct, and to provide, that he shall administer, not his own powers, but the powers of government intrusted to him as a sacred deposit.

If, then, the observations here made, upon this subject are just, and the reasoning correct, we may say, whatever human institutions have done, nature has not disqualified man for any of the functions of civil government.

CHAPTER IV.

Of the necessity of civil laws and government.

Having in the preceding chapters shown, that men, by the constitution of their common nature, are fitted and designed for civil government, we shall conclude this part of the subject, by an inquiry into the nature and origin of the necessity by which they are compelled to enter into that state.

As was formerly observed, some have thought, the necessity arises, solely, from the perverseness of human nature. They assert, that men have, inherent in their nature, a relish for vice, an original propensity to evil, to restrain the malignity of which, they were laid under the necessity of civil government and laws; that true virtue, genuine benevolence, would have carried them happily through the most complicated scenes, that could have fallen to their lot in society. How the account stands between them and their Maker, it is not my present purpose to inquire. I shall observe only, that their civil and political conduct does not avow a consciousness of such depravity of nature. They appear, in all cases, where no particular bias of passion or interest is discoverable, to have full reliance on the justice, integrity, and veracity of each other.

Some, who have entertained less gloomy views of human nature, have holden, that the necessity arises from the weakness only of individuals, requiring mutual aid for the supplying of their mutual wants, and protection against physical evils. This, however, would lead no farther than the social state. It would not, alone, induce the necessity of civil government. We have seen that man was, by nature, intended for the latter state; and we shall now find, arising from his nature, a necessity for adopting it; but, a necessity different from what has been

suggested. Although men have a relish for society ; although
it is the scene of their improvements, and the great source of
their happiness ; yet no goodness of heart can enable them to
enjoy its benefits, without an establishment of laws. Perception,
consciousness, and volition, or those powers which originate
and direct external action in men, belong to them individually.
A society consisting of a number of individuals, can have no
common, united perception, consciousness, or volition. Could
this be the case, a society might will, and, by the single act
of volition, direct and control the actions of all and every
member, with the same ease and regularity, with which an
individual directs and controls the motions of his body and
its members. But this is denied to man in the aggregate, and
in every combination of society. The will of a society is
made up of the wills of the individual members, collected.
Had man been formed with faculties enabling him, with an
intuitive glance, to penetrate and comprehend the individual
wills of all the members of the society, and of all whose conduct
might, in any way, affect it ; to penetrate and comprehend the
passions, appetites, and pursuits of every individual ; in a word
to comprehend all the causes, by which God governs the
actions of moral agents ; were he endued with reason sufficient
to arrange the whole, so as to prevent every interference in
human pursuit ; goodness of heart and firmness of mind, to
enable him to pursue the arrangement ; in such a state both
of knowledge and disposition, he would stand in no need of
civil laws, or rules prescribed by common consent, for the
regulation of social conduct. But such a state falls not to the
lot of any finite being.

Our positive knowledge, both of the present and past, is
partial and depends on actual and accurate observation. There
is, however, given us some clue to the future. We are able
to perceive certain relations of cause and effect ; and as far as
experience leads, we find a uniformity in the course of nature.
We discover some of the causes and some of the laws, by
which physical effects are produced in a chain ; while of
others we are wholly ignorant, or can at best, obtain but an
imperfect glimpse. Much more imperfect is our knowledge
of the causes that produce and vary human actions, subject to

the influence of motives, to the choice of the agent and to those causes that govern and connect the chain of human events. In an extensive society, individuals can have but a limited knowledge of the present actions of the whole. Their knowledge of the intentions and causes, upon which future actions depend, is much more limited ; or rather is reduced to conjecture. We are able to gain some knowledge of the leading principles of action, of the motives, which generally prevail, and of the species of action, which they will produce, in certain characters and in certain situations. To descend to every situation, to every character, and thence to learn, fully, the particular influence of motives, and the individual actions that will follow in each, is far beyond the reach of human sagacity.

In a society composed of any considerable number of individuals, and of any considerable activity, there will be many and very different situations. The influence of nature with different persons will be very different. They will have a variety of distinct interests and pursuits, and those not at all, or very imperfectly, known to each other, .in their origin. However innocent and right those interests and pursuits may be, when considered separately, they will by frequent, though unintentional, interferences and oppositions, form a scene too intricate for the powers of the human mind to evolve. Could we suppose every person in the society to be actuated by principles of the most disinterested benevolence, and the most accommodating spirit, the whole time must be consumed in compromise ; none would be left for action. Without a social perception, consciousness, and volition, with any goodness, and with any wisdom, short of infinite, the state of society would, at best, be a scene of inextricable confusion. To remedy this confusion, nature has pointed out to man the necessity of civil establishments, and the promulgation of laws. Here is a provision analogous to his nature. By the establishment of laws, which all the individuals of the community have become bound to observe, as the rules of their future conduct, each is enabled to foresee, with a sufficient degree of certainty, the future interests and pursuits of others. By following the line prescribed, all may avoid any considerable inconvenience, or by applying the general rule, may remedy the evil. In no other way, is it possible to connect a community either in sentiments, or interests, to unite the public force to direct it to the attainment of any common good, or to the avoiding or repelling of any common evil; in no other way is it possible to obtain any security of public or private rights.

Still men are imperfect. They will be guilty of deviations from the rule, transgressions of the law, and infringements of each other's rights. This will happen, sometimes, through ignorance of the law or the right; sometimes through weakness in judging, or inattention in examining; sometimes it will happen through the prevalence of interest, the violence of passion, or from a disposition habitually profligate and vicious. Therefore to provide to the laws a compulsory force, they must be so calculated, that every member of the community shall find a convenience in the observance, and a certain inconvenience in the neglect or violation. Hence, arises the necessity of penalties. These penalties are, from the weakness of men, in discerning tendencies, and their consequent liability to vice, necessarily enhanced. Hence also arises the necessity of subordination, and of civil rulers, to give activity and efficiency to the laws. In a state of greater perfection, than is to be found in the present state of society, a greater perfection in knowledge and virtue, penalties may make a less formidable appearance; but in every state, the necessity of penalties will equally exist.

In a community, composed of a few individuals, in a simple state of manners and of property, the motives to action are few; consequently, there is but little activity of the members, little eagerness of pursuit. A few simple rules, mostly adopted and supported by custom, supply the place of a more regular polity. They are the first rude essays in civil institutions. Still in every state of morals and of manners, the necessity of civil government, the necessity of laws, of known and established rules, equally exists. On the whole, we may safely conclude, that no order of beings, short of infinite perfection, in wisdom as well as goodness, can subsist in society without an establishment of government and laws.

BOOK IV.

OF RIGHTS AND LIBERTY.

CHAPTER I.

Of natural, political, and civil rights and liberty.

The first great object of all civil institutions is, or ought to be, the security of those personal rights, in the full and free enjoyment of which true liberty consists.

The word right, when applied to action, signifies what is fit and proper to be done, as opposed to wrong.—As a substantive, it is used to express the just title or claim which a person has to any thing ; and signifies that the thing belongs to him, who is said to have the right. There are several classes of rights distinguished by some law, custom, or institution, in which they are supposed to originate, or by which they are sanctioned, and are accordingly denominated, First, natural rights—Secondly, political rights, and Thirdly, civil rights.

Natural rights are generally said to consist in the right of personal liberty, personal security, and of private property. These rights originate in the laws of our nature and are as universal as the social nature of man ; they cannot be justly forfeited unless by the commission of some crime against the good and wholesome laws of the community. They may be violated, and their exercise by the subjects suspended, by the will of a tyrant, aided by superior force ; but are never extinguished. The subjects always retain the right to reassume their full exercise, whenever they find themselves able to resist the force of the oppressor.

Political rights have been very generally confounded with civil rights; although they clearly are, and from their importance ought to be considered, a distinct class. They consist of the rights and powers retained by the people in the fundamental law, the constitution of the state—as in a democracy, the power of making all laws as well of the constitution as of the municipal code, and the appointment and control of all the officers and ministers of the government,—in a mixed monarchy the right of electing a co-ordinate branch of the government,— and in a representative government, the right and power of electing directly or indirectly the public functionaries, through which they are all, in a good degree, held accountable to the people for their conduct in the administration, and also the power of changing, altering, and amending the constitution itself, agreeably to the regulations prescribed in the original compact.

Civil rights are those that are guarantied to the citizens by civil institutions and are contained in the class of natural rights above mentioned; the right of personal liberty, of personal security, and of private property, and the rights derived from, .and subordinate to these, which are very numerous. They are called natural rights as they have their foundation in the laws of social nature; but as practical rights they may well be denominated conventional, because for their secure enjoyment, they depend on the social or civil compact; whether established by usage or by express stipulation.

Judge Blackstone tells us, that "the rights of persons considered in their natural capacities, are of two sorts, absolute and relative,—Absolute, which are such as appertain and belong to particular men merely as individuals or single persons.— Relative, which are incident to them as members of society and standing in various relations to each other." He farther says, "by the absolute rights of individuals we mean those which are so in their strictest sense; such as would belong to their persons merely in a state of nature, and which every man is entitled to enjoy whether out of society or in it." This distinction is, I think, in some degree, incorrect.—There cannot, strictly speaking, be any such thing as absolute rights, as the author has here explained them.—What are the rights of man, if we suppose one excluded from all society, from all relation to any other human being? In such a situation, a man may have and exercise his natural powers.—He may take and use for his support any of the productions of nature, for food, for covering, or for any other purpose; but this power to use is very different from the notion of right in the appropriate sense intended. With a man in the situation we have supposed, the right of personal liberty, so important in a state of society, must sink into the mere power of locomotion, limited only by the laws of his nature. The notion of right, in the sense of the author, vanishes with the notion of relation.

There is, certainly, a distinction between the rights here denominated absolute, and relative. The former, such as the rights of personal liberty, personal security, and of private property, universally result from the social relations, are recognized by the primary laws of our nature, and continue through every stage of society, although subject to certain modifications. The latter are not permanent nor universal. They result from those relations in which a man is placed in a state of society;—such as the right to obtain a legal redress for the violation or neglect, by others, of those rights which are recognized by the laws and constitution of the state; or from those relations, which he has the liberty and capacity of forming; such is the married state and the relations thence resulting. Beside, the former are not absolute in any sense: for although they cannot be alienated by a voluntary transfer, yet they may, agreeably to just and necessary laws of the community, be forfeited and lost, by the criminal act of the individual. On the whole, therefore, these two classes of rights are not properly distinguished, by calling one absolute and the other relative. The one arising from the primary, universal, and permanent relations of social nature; the other from those relations that are subsequent, limited, and fluctuating, they will, with much greater propriety, be denominated primary and secondary rights, by which the nature of the several classes will be more clearly distinguished. Of the origin of rights on natural principles, we shall have occasion to treat more particularly in the next chapter on the inception and progress of the right of property.

Liberty, applicable to man, in the general sense of the term, consists in the free exercise and enjoyment of his rights, and is natural, civil, or political liberty, according as reference is had to one or the other of those rights. Of natural liberty Judge Blackstone says. " The absolute rights of man considered as a free agent, endowed with discernment to know good from evil and with the power of choosing those measures, which appear to him most desirable, are usually summed up in one general appellation, and denominated the natural liberty of mankind. This natural liberty consists, properly, in a power of acting as one thinks fit, without any constraint or control, unless by the laws of nature, being a right inherent in us by birth, and one of the gifts of God to man at his creation, when he endued him with the faculty of free will." Notwithstanding the little inaccuracy to be found in this passage, in making liberty to consist in the rights themselves, instead of the exercise and enjoyment of those rights, it might have been admitted as a just exposition of natural liberty had he said, " without any restraint or control, unless by the laws of social nature." It would then have been liable to no misconception ; but instead of including, the author has, perhaps inadvertantly, excluded the notion of social from his law of nature ; for he immediately adds. " But every man, on entering into society, gives up a part of his natural liberty, as the price of so valuable a purchase, and in consideration of receiving the advantages of mutual commerce, obliges himself to conform to those laws which the community have thought proper to establish." The author, here, has evidently confounded the natural liberty of man, with that range of action permitted to all animals of the brute creation, even the most ferocious ; a range of action, for it cannot claim the appellation of liberty, not permitted to man by the laws of his nature. On this subject, Mr. Christian has very justly observed that "the libertas quidlibet faciendi, or the liberty of doing every thing which a man's passions urge him to attempt, or his strength enables him to effect, is savage liberty, the liberty of a tiger and not of a man."

Burlamaqui has given us a definition of natural liberty, which is free from this objection. " Moral or natural liberty is the right which nature gives to all mankind of disposing of their persons, and property, after the manner they shall judge most consonant to their happiness; on condition of their acting within the limits of the laws of nature, and that they do not any way abuse it to the prejudice of other men." The author of this definition has, with the utmost propriety, considered natural liberty as of the moral, that is, of the social kind. Such are the rights of man, and such to him are the laws of nature. These laws not only prohibit the doing of what is prejudicial, but enjoin many things to be done, that are beneficial to individuals, as well as to society; they enjoin positive acts as well as restraints. The definition, therefore, leaving out all the active moral duties, appears to me to be materially deficient. To correct this, and a small inaccuracy in the forepart, I would express it thus. Moral or natural liberty consists in the free exercise and enjoyment of that right which nature gives all mankind, of disposing of their persons and property in the manner they judge most consonant to their happiness, on condition of their getting within the limits of the laws of nature, and that they observe towards others, all the moral duties enjoined by that law. Such limitation is necessary, unless we admit that the natural liberty of a moral and social being may dispense with moral obligation.

Civil liberty consists in the secure exercise and enjoyment of all civil rights, which comprehend the natural rights, and the subordinate rights which in the civil state flow from these, and in a strict sense, limited only by the necessary, equal, and expedient laws of the community; but in a more general sense, limited also, by moral obligation. This definition agrees very nearly with the concise definition of Judge Blackstone. "Civil liberty, which is that of a member of society, is no other than natural liberty so far restrained—and no farther—as is necessary and expedient for the general advantage of the public," and with that of Mr. Paley which is, "civil liberty is the not being restrained by any law, but what contributes in a greater degree to the public advantage,"—and we may here add, that civil liberty can be enjoyed only under an upright and impartial administration of just, equal, and expedient laws.

Political liberty consists in the exercise and enjoyment of those rights which we have distinguished by the denomination of political rights, rights reserved to the people, by the fundamental laws, the constitution of the state, in such manner and under such regulations only, as are provided and authorized by those laws. Mr. Christian, who has observed, that, "no ideas or definitions are more distinguishable than those of civil and political liberty, yet they are generally confounded," tells us, that "political liberty may be defined to be the security, with which, from the constitution and form of the established government, the subject enjoys civil liberty." But this is a definition of the end and intended effect of political liberty, not of the liberty itself.

The important end of political liberty, and for which alone it is valuable, is to secure the permanent enjoyment of civil liberty. It is the only security the wisdom of man has been able to devise against civil and political slavery. It may be laid down as an unfailing maxim that the extinction of political liberty is the establishment of slavery. From its importance in this view, it is not to be wondered, that where any idea of a free government has existed, this species of liberty has been always the idol of mankind. The writer last mentioned, indeed, asserts, that civil liberty may exist in perfection under an absolute monarch, and to this purpose cites a passage from Claudian, who wrote under a Roman Emperor.—

> Fallitur egregie, quisquis sub principe credit
> Servitium ;—nunquam libertas gratior exit,
> Quam sub rege pio—

and then in favor of political liberty asks the question—" But what security can the subjects, have for the virtues of his successor ? With the same propriety, and the same emphasis, it might be asked—What security can the subjects have for the virtues of the present possessor, placed as he is supposed to be, beyond the reach of accountability ? It is true, they may enjoy the semblance of liberty, such as the veriest slave may enjoy under an indulgent master ; both may, from ignorance of a better state, and a comparison with others, be contented, and even feel a happiness in their condition ; but both are nevertheless slaves ; this, under a private—those, under a public absolute master.

It appears from what has been said in this chapter, that there
is a closer coincidence between those rights which have been
denominated natural, civil, and political, than writers on law
and government have generally been disposed to allow ; and
as it is one great end of this work, to refer all necessary civil
institutions to such natural and moral principles as may give
satisfaction to every serious inquirer, we shall treat the subject
a little more at large.

That man, on entering into civil society sacrifices a part of
his natural liberty, has been very generally asserted, or taken
for granted, by all political writers. They speak of it as a
necessity arising from the very nature of all civil institutions,
even the best as well as the worst, differing in degree only.
This notion of a sacrifice must have been adopted from a very
indefinite and, indeed, very absurd notion of natural liberty ;
what this notion was has been already noticed ; but we will
take it from the Marquis Beccaria in his admirable work on
crimes and punishments. He there tells us, that man, on
entering into society, makes a sacrifice of that liberty of action
common to all sensible beings, and limited only by our natural
powers. What sort of liberty is that which is common to man,
to the lion, and the tiger ? Man is allowed by all to be a
moral being. The laws of nature applicable to him, as such,
are of the moral kind—when we speak of the liberty common
to man, liberty, and a right to act are convertible terms. Man
indeed, has a natural, that is, a physical power to injure both
himself and others. But is a right to do this conceded to
him by the laws of his nature ? That is, a right to transgress
those laws : power and liberty are not synonymous. Power is
here, that by which we exercise our liberty, not the liberty itself,
when considered as a right. In a larger sense liberty
comprehends both the power and the right. Civil liberty is
generally taken in this sense. It will not, I presume, be
suggested that the natural liberty of man, a moral being, is at
variance with moral obligations ; it therefore follows, that the
liberty common to man is limited by his natural powers, by the
obligations of morality, in a word, by the laws of his nature.
For a moral being to forbear the performance of any action,
that is forbidden by the laws of moral and social nature, can

never be deemed a sacrifice, and is no more a duty in civil society than out of it.

But it is said, that every man has a right to pursue his own interest and happiness, and that in the commerce of civil society, there will arise oppositions, which will oblige one man to sacrifice his interest and happiness, to that of others. I answer—First, The nearer we approach to a state of individual independence, the supposed state of nature, and the less men direct their conduct by mutual laws, the more frequently will such oppositions arise, and sacrifices be necessarily made, and that under circumstances of violence.—Secondly, That a man, sociable by the laws of his nature, has no right to pursue his own interest or happiness, to the exclusion of that of his fellow men.— Thirdly, The reciprocal relations of social beings dictate, that when, for want of foresight, or from the nature of the objects of pursuit, an opposition arises, and there is no preference of right, there should be an amicable compromise. Beyond this, nature may have given power; but she has accorded no liberty, no right, to man. This is the true principle of all commerce amongst men; of the accommodation of all claims, natural and civil, and the mutual submission of private opinion to public sentiment. It is true, men in their private intercourse, often lose sight of this principle, and in public bodies, it is too much neglected. The interests of the minority, which, on the principle of mutual compromise, where, in the nature of the case admissible, are entitled to a proportionable regard, are too often neglected, or wholly sacrificed to the more powerful interests of the majority. Still the principle, however neglected, is founded in the immutable relations of nature.

It is further said, there are some rights which are conceded to be natural rights, and which are necessary to be exercised in a state of nature; but are not allowed in any well constituted civil society; one of which is, that every individual shall, in case of injury, be his own judge, and may take satisfaction, or rather, revenge, at his own pleasure. Such right has been, and still is admitted by some savage nations, among whom the law of retaliation, instead of a reparation of injuries, obtains, as mentioned in a former chapter, such as the right of the next of kin to avenge the blood of the slain; and in that state it is allowed to be natural right. On this we may observe that the right of judging is relative to the rights of justice, and is permitted for the sake of those rights. Men have a reciprocal right to demand justice of each other, and are reciprocally bound to make an adequate satisfaction for injuries. A right of judging amounts to a right of deciding what is right and just between one individual and another—a right of determining what satisfaction ought to be made for injuries, and in what manner. It is the duty of the judge to decide justly; if he decide otherwise, a second injury is committed. But such is the nature of man, we know, as a general rule, that he is incapable of judging justly and impartially in his own cause; and to this we may add, that he must frequently want the power to give effect to his decisions. In matters that depend on a mutual compromise, every man is, under the best regulated government, of right allowed to be the judge of his own interest, and an actor in his own cause. So in a present invasion of his rights by violence, he is his own judge, both of the means and the measure of defence, and this from the necessity of the case; but he must judge rightly, agreeably to the occasion, at the peril of becoming an aggressor; for the right is not independent and without appeal. There is, therefore, a deficiency as well in point of capacity to judge, as of power to execute.

From a little consideration it will be evident, that this right of judging in his own cause is a temporary right, permitted to man from necessity only, until he shall arrive at a maturity to be capable of comprehending and carrying into effect that law of his nature which makes him accountable to the judgment of others, and which dictates in all controversies a submission to an impartial judge. Each one, as well the party injuring as the party injured, has a right to an impartial decision; and the laws of nature have pointed out the means of obtaining it. The right of justice is perpetual; the right of judging is incidental, and comes in, lest there should be a failure of the former. When men become capable of providing for a regular administration of justice in government, that right, which nature designed to be temporary only, ceases of course, so far as such provision is made. It cannot be said to be sacrificed or given up by any act of the individual. Such rights may, as it respects society, be well denominated, juvenile rights. In the progress of society toward maturity, the same thing happens to them, that happens to the juvenile passions and appetites of an individual. Many little passions and appetites exist in infancy and early youth, which, though necessary and proper for that state, are, nevertheless, unbecoming the state of manhood. These are never given up by any specific act of the mind; but, agreeable to the constitution of nature, give place in the progress of the individual, to passions and appetites proper to an advanced state, and one after another become extinct.

I am apprehensive that the legal notion of the necessity of a consideration to the validity of a contract introduced or has, at least, long supported the opinion that men, on entering into civil society, give up a part of their natural rights, their natural liberty, as a consideration for the security of the ramainder. Writers on government have been anxious to discover, on the part of the people, some consideration given for the right of protection and the right of justice. While government is supposed to be finally established, not by a compact between the individuals of the people, but between the people and the rulers, this appeared to be a matter of great importance; but it can be of no moment, when it is understood that all legitimate government is produced by the people entering into a compact among themselves for that purpose. There is no occasion to look for any consideration for the duty of obedience to the laws on the one part, or a just and equal consideration on the other, but the mutual and inviolable obligations of such compact as enjoined by the laws of social nature.

I am happy to find one authority in favor of the opinion here advocated—the authority of Montesquieu himself, equal to a host. In treating of a subject, which led him to make a comparison between a state of individual independence, the supposed state of nature, and a state of civil government, he says.* "Liberty principally consists, in not being forced to do a thing, which the laws do not oblige; people are in this state only as they are governed by civil laws; and because they are governed

---

* Spirit of the Laws. Book xxvi. Ch. 20.

by civil laws, they are free. Hence it follows, that princes who live not among themselves, under civil laws, are not free; they are governed by force, they may continually force or be forced." Sovereign princes are, in respect to each other, in a state of natural independence. In another place he observes.*
"As men have given up their natural independence, to live under political laws; they have given the natural community of good, to live under civil laws; by the first they acquired liberty, by the second property." From these passages it appears that Montesquieu differed from other writers, in his opinion of the liberty to be enjoyed in the two states. He clearly supposes, that man, on entering into civil society, makes an acquisition of liberty, without any sacrifice; that he thereby secures himself, from the danger of deprivation by force, of the common rights of his nature.

Still it may be urged, that if no rights are necessarily sacrificed by men, on entering into the civil state, yet it must be acknowledged that in most of the governments that now exist, or ever have existed, many rights are established which do not originate in any natural principles, the exercise and enjoyment of which, by the few who possess them, is a restraint, and often a violation of the common and natural rights of all others.— This is true of all governments, that have established ranks and privileges, whether hereditary or for life, whether annexed to persons and families, or estates. These factitious rights have been assimilated to the natural rights, particularly to the right of property, and have followed the same laws; but they all have their origin, not in the principles of nature, but in the inventions of men. They have no place in a government founded in true natural principles; and we are treating of natural rights as it respects such governments only.

In every government formed and administered on just and natural principles, all the secondary and subordinate rights, both civil and political, are but species of one or other of the great primary rights;—the right of personal liberty, personal security, or of private property, modified and adapted to the state of

---

* Sp. L. B. xxvi Ch. 15.

society. It needs no arguments, to prove that all the civil rights, which a man in the civil state has to a remedy for every case of injury, whether direct or consequential, relating to his freedom from restraint, his life, his reputation, or his property—whether the injury proceed from violence, from fraud, neglect or breach of trust, or from the non-fulfilment of any lawful agreement, either express or implied, they relate either to his person or his property, and fall under one or the other of those primary rights.

Those rights which we have denominated political rights, are but the modified rights of self government, which belongs to natural liberty,—"That right which nature gives to all mankind, of disposing of their persons and property, after the manner they shall judge most consonant to their own happiness." Now all the laws of civil society affect either the person or property.—In every government where the people have no voice in framing the laws, whether the law of the constitution or of the municipal code, they are, so far as those laws extend, deprived of the right of self government. Where the people have a voice in framing and administering the laws, either by themselves, or by their representatives, accountable to them for their conduct, they enjoy all that right of self government, which the laws of nature permit in civil society. On a careful review of the whole, we arrive at this fair and undeniable conclusion, that the rights of man are all relative to his social nature, and that the rights of the individual exist, in a coincidence only with the rights of the whole, in a well ordered state of society and civil government.

CHAPTER II.

Of the right of property.

The right of property makes so great a figure in the institutions and laws of every country, that in a work like the present, the origin of that right, and the foundation upon which it is so universally established are deserving of a very particular investigation.

Judge Blackstone observes, "there is nothing which so universally strikes the imagination, and engages the attention of mankind, as the right of property, that sole and despotic dominion which one man claims and exercises over the external things of this world, in exclusion of every other individual in the universe," and he might have added, nothing has so much employed the labor, attention, and researches of jurists, statesmen, and legislators. The right, although under different modifications, is recognized in every state of society, from that of the rudest savage, up to the highest state of civilization and refinement. It seems then, a just conclusion, that a right, so universally acknowledged, has its foundation in the laws of nature, in the social nature of man. Indeed it is conceded by all to be a natural right; but I think, most writers on the subject have in their researches, stopt short of the true origin.

A brief notice of the opinions of some of the principal of those writers will not be wanting in entertainment or instruction. They have generally agreed to consider occupancy, as one thing necessary to the commencement of the right of property in the thing to be appropriated; but that occupancy alone, is not sufficient for its completion. Mr. Locke maintains, that as every man's time and labor is something that is his own, he, by the very act of occupancy, mixes with the thing that something of his own, which cannot afterwards be taken from him without injustice. But it is difficult to conceive how, or by what mysterious operation a substance not mine before should become my exclusive property, on my mixing with it something that is mine. Others, as Grotius and Puffendorf, have held that the right of property by occupancy is founded on a tacit consent of mankind, that the first occupant, should become the owner. That a custom introduced and established by the tacit consent of any society is a law of that society; which may secure the property, is true,—and when it has become a confirmed custom, that the first occupant shall be considered the owner, occupancy will become a proof of the right; but this does not account for the right among men, which must accompany or precede the custom which attaches upon it.

Judge Blackstone* derives the right of private property from occupancy; but first derives to man a general and common right of property in every thing on which that right can attach, from an original grant of the Creator to man, that he should have dominion over all the earth, and over the fish of the sea, and over the fowls of the air, and over every living thing that moveth upon the earth.† This does not, however, assist us in the least, in solving the question, how, if all have a common property in a thing, the occupation of a part by one should sever that part from the common stock, and without the consent of the others, vest an exclusive right in the occupant. It rather enhances the difficulty; what the author considers in a technical sense, as the grant of a common property, is to be taken as an expression of man's superiority and a declaration of the intention of the laws of nature, established at the creation, that man was to have the use of all these things in such way and manner, with such use of rights and enjoyment as shall be suited to his nature and situation, and with such regulations and modifications, as he should devise, leaving to him the discovery and application of those laws under the guidance of reason and experience.

It is not necessary to suppose, nor is it true, that all things were the common property of man; but all were intended for

---

* 2 Comm. p. 2.   † Gen. i. 28.

his use, and capable of being appropriated, as he should find the capacity, the necessity, and the occasion. Mr. Paley has expressed himself on this subject a little differently, but from his concluding observations, it is evident that his opinion does not essentially differ from that of Judge Blackstone just recited. After stating the various opinions on this subject, he says—" A better account of this right of ownership is the following ; that God has provided these things, for the use of all ; he has of consequence, given each leave to take what he wants ; by virtue therefore of this leave, a man may appropriate what he stands in need of, without waiting for the consent of others." But he says,—"This reason justifies property as far as our necessaries alone ; or at most, as far as a competent provision for our natural exigencies." Here he is speaking of moveable property ; but with regard to property in land he says, "The real foundation of our right is in the law of the land," and his reason is that " the land cannot be divided into separate property, without leaving it to the law of the country to regulate that division."

All this does not go to the origin of the right of property ; and the notion of a formal and equal division, we shall find has no foundation in the law of nature upon this subject. Judge Blackstone observes that " the dispute concerning the origin of the right of property savors too much of nicety and scholastic refinement."—But, replies his annotator, Mr. Christian, " It is of great importance, that moral obligations and the rudiments of laws should be referred to true and intelligible principles, such as the minds of serious and well disposed men may rely upon with confidence and satisfaction"—and after having remarked on the insufficiency of former theories, he says,—"But how then does property commence ? I conceive no better answer can be given, than by occupancy ; or when a thing is separated for private use from the stores of nature, this is agreeable to reason and the sentiments of mankind, prior to all civil establishments. When an untutored Indian has set before him the fruit, which he has plucked from the tree that protects him from the heat of the sun, and the shell of water raised from the fountain that springs at his feet, if he is driven by any daring intruder from this repast, so easy to be replaced, he instantly feels and resents the violation of the law of property, which nature herself has written on the hearts of all mankind."

From an observation of this early and universal sentiment of the right of property, some have supposed that man is by nature furnished with an internal sense, by which he has a direct perception of this right, and which has been denominated a sense of property.—This seems to be nearer the truth than any of the former theories—and indeed it is the truth, but it is drawn from the stream in its course, not from the fountain head. It is a complex notion and capable of being resolved into its simple principles.

It has been already shown, that man is by nature, or rather the God of nature, furnished with a susceptibility of impressions, by which moral sentiments are excited in his mind. (By moral sentiments is meant such as in some way relate to society, to social rights and duties.) This susceptibility is, as we have seen, the point at which the social nature of man commences, and in which commence all his notions of rights and duties as a social being. The right of property is one of those social rights : it can exist in society only. An isolated being, who never had any knowledge of society, or of any person but himself, could have no conception of a right of property. For it is essential to any conception of this right, that the subject belongs to one in exclusion of all others. The isolated individual could be conscious of his power only to use the fruits, or whatever he had collected for his sustenance; but there is nothing in this situation that can suggest to his mind in the remotest degree any notion of right.—Place him in society with others, let one attempt to deprive him of the fruit he has gathered, or any thing he has collected for his sustenance, it makes an impression on his mind that at once suggests his right to the fruit or other thing, and excites a feeling of resentment against the intruder for a violation of that right in himself.

This is not, however, sufficient to establish a general notion of a right of property. It is yet an individual right, confined to himself, or rather it is but the inceptive notion of the right; and to this extent many of the brute creation appear to have a feeling of the right. The wild beast defends its cavern or any place of shelter for rest, or the protection of its young, and the bird its nest, with the same resentment and the same apparent consciousness of their right; but they evidently have no notion of a general right. To the conception of a general right, something further is necessary; and this nature has furnished to man, in the perception of analogy, mentioned in a former chapter, in which brutes partake to a certain degree, and through which they discern, that the species to which they respectively belong has a common nature, on which they rely with confidence in their intercourse with each other. Hence, every man in society relies, that all others have the same conceptions of right, and the same feelings of resentment, for a violation, which he experiences in himself; and hence, all for their own ease and quiet, in time, become disposed to respect that right and those feelings generally; and such general respect is the first complete establishment of the right of property in society. To respect the right of property thus becomes a custom which is the origin of law in the primeval state. As this law, originating in natural principles, is found by experience to be beneficial to all, so a violation of the law is equally resented by all. Thus we find, that the right of property originates in natural principles, is confirmed by them, and finally sanctioned by the principle of utility, the general interest, which is the great end of all the laws of nature.

The natural principle of the acquisition of property was adopted in the civil law, so far as respected those natural subjects, which that law had left unappropriated,—as we learn from the following passage in Justinian's Institutes. "There are various modes, by which things may become the property of individuals; of some we obtain the dominion by the law of nature; which we have said, is likewise called the law of nations, of others by the civil law; but it will be most proper to begin with the most ancient law, that law which nature established at the birth of mankind.—Wild beasts then, birds, fishes, and all animals, which are bred in the sea, the air, or upon the earth, as soon as they are taken, become, by the law of nations, the property of the captors; for natural reason gives to the first occupant, that which before had no owner."* The

* B. II. T. 1. Sec. 11. 12.

same law, in relation to the same subjects, still prevails in every country, where game laws have not been interposed in favor of certain classes of the community.

It is obvious to remark, that the right of property belongs to the same moral system, which we have been advocating—originates in the same first principle. It is also matured in its progress by the same moral principles, and involves the same moral obligation. In the early state of society, these principles first secured to each the quiet enjoyment of the fruits and productions of the common earth, which he had collected for the use of himself, and those who were dependent on him for support, the quiet possession of the hut he had built for shelter, and the spot of ground which it occupied. In the progress of society, the same principles appropriated to any one the animals he had taken and domesticated; and as barter and exchange always accompany the introduction of private property, the right of the first occupant was soon extended to any successor by his consent. When agriculture was introduced, the right was extended to the field which any one cultivated. Nor could it be long before the utility of a permanent occupation was perceived, and the occupant came to be considered as the exclusive owner; and the right of disposal followed of course.

As to the objection, that property in moveables, that is, in the natural fruits and productions of the earth, could not, in the state supposed, be justified beyond a competent provision for necessaries; and that land could not be divided into separate property without leaving it to the law of the country to make a division; the whole is founded in a mistake. It supposes the whole human race, few or many, previous to the introduction of private property, to have had a joint and equal right of property in the common earth and its productions; that each was an owner in common of some undivided aliquot part, so that all that was necessary to be done to make any portion of it the private property of an individual was, to make a fair division of his part to be set off to him, by the consent of all others, and until that should be done he was permitted to occupy so much as might be necessary for his immediate use and no more, lest he should exceed his right and violate the right of others.

73

But it is impossible to suppose, that men, before they could
have any clear conceptions of the right of private property,
had yet attained to the abstract and complex notion of an
aggregate community consisting of the whole human race,
vested with a common property in the earth and its productions;
and to suppose men to be bound, or assume to act upon a right
or a principle of which they had yet the means of obtaining no
possible conception, is wholly absurd. The conception of a
public right of property must, from necessity and the nature of
things, be derived from a knowledge of the private right in an
individual. Nothing, while it remains common to all men, can
partake of the nature of property, nor can it become property,
until it is appropriated by some individual or company of
individuals occupying it to the exclusion of others. If then, we
suppose a time, when all things remained common to all, neither
public or private property would exist while all continued
common.

Probably an idea of the necessity of a division of the land,
to be made by law, was suggested by the situation of the
common, or as generally called, public lands, in all modern
governments, in which the right of property to such lands is
vested in the state by their institutions. The state, indeed,
parcels out these lands; not however, by a division, but by a
sale and transfer to individuals, in such portions, and on such
terms, as is deemed most for the public good. But such was
not the original state of things. The earth was not given in
property to man; but was, with all it contains, provided and
designed to become the subject of property, by the separate
occupation of individuals, as we have already shown, to be
possessed and enjoyed under such regulations, and in such
way and manner as men, in the progress of society, should find
most conducive to the general interest.

The laws of nature do not, in making a division for the
purpose of vesting a right of private property, descend, as
seems to be supposed, to such minute calculations, or such
useless, and I may add, in the primitive state, impracticable
formalities; but have submitted, nay I may say, enjoined as the
most useful, and in the state supposed, the only practicable
mode, that the division, or rather separation be made, by each

taking into his private occupation, such portion as he should judge convenient for his own use. Nor have the laws of nature in this case any regard to equal quantities in the division, but to a sufficiency for each. Whether any choose to make a more or less ample provision, no one is injured, no right infringed. The declaration of nature in the primitive state is, " There is ample provision for all—come and select what portion you choose, with these only restrictions, that you interfere not with prior selections, and that you make no unnecessary waste."

From what has been said of the origin and progress of the right of property in society, it will be evident to every reflecting mind, that all just conceptions of the legitimate rights of man, natural, civil, and political, are the genuine offspring of the same natural principle, a susceptibility of moral impression. All social rights are founded alternately in the same principles, and, consequently, all the duties corresponding to those rights are enforced by the same moral obligations.

As the end and design of all the laws of nature is general utility or the promotion of the general interest and happiness of social man, the sure test of any rule set up as a law of nature is its general tendency to promote that end. If the test fail, the rule must at once be pronounced spurious. The execution of those laws, and the means of enjoying their benefit, and the means that may be employed to that end, are submitted to the same test, their tendency to promote the general interest. Among enlightened nations, the end sought is first proposed, and, with the means of attaining it, made a matter of deliberation. In the early and inexperienced state of mankind, they generally act with no remote views; but, by following the suggestions of present interest and convenience, they not unfrequently arrive at the same important end without having seen the final result. So intimately have the laws of nature, if simply pursued, united individual with the general interest, present interest with the future.

We have traced the right of property, in its progress from its commencement, in natural principles by occupancy, through the modes of acquisition by barter, and exchange or bargain, until it has become a permanent right. We may still trace those principles in the modifications which the right has received in the progress of society, and show more particularly their connection with hereditary right and a right of testamentary disposition ; but these are reserved for another chapter. The modes of acquisition, although all proceed from the same principles, are found to be very various according to the state and varying interest of society. In the earliest stages of society, the objects of property are few, and the modes of acquisition as few and simple. The objects of property are those things only that are necessary to support existence. The modes of acquisition are mostly confined to occupancy ; The simple mode of gift and exchange are soon added. In the progress of society men learn to apply to their use, either for their necessities, or their pleasure, most of the productions of nature. By the assistance of art, as the powers of the human mind are expanded, new productions, considered either necessary, convenient, or agreeable, are multiplied without end. In proportion as men extend their views of what is useful or agreeable, the hoarding appetite gains strength ; they become eager of the present, and provident of the future, and the objects of property become equally numerous with the objects of desire. In such a state of society the modes of acquisition are greatly diversified, and made the subject of a great variety of regulations.

The whole business of property now appears to be an artificial system ; but the mode of acquisition and the tenure and use only, are the subjects of artificial regulations. The right of property itself, still remains founded in natural principles; the modes of acquisition serve only to bring the subjects of property within those principles. In this, which appears to be the only correct view of the origin of the right of property, it is not true as asserted by many writers, that it is merely a creature of the civil law ; and the consequences, which they have drawn from that position, on a dissolution of government all property is annihilated, and that every revolution or radical reformation of government is destructive of the right itself, are wholly groundless. In such case, civil protection only is lost, the secure enjoyment is endangered, but the right, founded in a primary law of nature, remains unchanged.

We shall conclude this chapter with a few brief remarks.—If a discovery of the right of property, (if, indeed, such right could have otherwise existed,) was left to reason and experience, instead of being discovered in the natural principle that has been unfolded, and rendered obvious to every one possessed of the common feelings and sentiments of our species, it must, if at all attainable, exact at least a considerable maturity of the reasoning powers.—To children and all of weaker intellects, it must be wholly unattainable. Force alone could prevent a constant violation of property ; prohibitory laws would be considered, as so many arbitrary impositions. How much better is the plan of nature. Who can forbear to admire the wisdom and goodness displayed in adapting the nature of man to that social and civil state, which he has ever found necessary, not only to his happiness, but to any tolerable existence in life. The Deity has implanted in man the germ of every necessary qualification, and left to him the cultivation.—More it is probable, could not be indulged to a moral agent.

CHAPTER III.

Of the right of inheritance and of making a testamentary disposition.

In the preceding chapter, we have found the inception of the right of property in a moral principle of our nature, that susceptibility of moral impressions which is common to all mankind; and have pursued its progress in natural principles, to its general reception, a right of transfer, and its final consummation, in the permanent and exclusive right of the individual; but the right has universally been carried farther, to the right of the owner to make a testamentary disposition, to direct who shall succeed to his property after his death, and to the right of inheritance and succession in next of kin to the deceased. We shall now enquire, how far these rights are founded on natural principles, and how far they are consistent with each other.

Judge Blackstone, who held that the permanent right of property in any one was not a natural, but a mere civil right, consistently with that doctrine tells us, *" All property must therefore cease upon death, considering men as absolute individuals, unconnected with civil society; for then, by the principles before established, the [next immediate occupant would acquire a right in all the deceased possessed; but as under civilized governments, which are calculated for the peace of mankind, such a constitution would be productive of endless disturbances, the universal law of almost every nation,—which

---

*2 Comm. 10.

is a kind of secondary law of nature—has either given the dying person a power of continuing his property, by disposing of his possession by will, or in case he neglects to dispose· of it, or is not permitted to make any disposition at all, the municipal law of the country then steps in and declares who shall be the successor, representative, or heir of the deceased ;" and he further adds,—" The right of inheritance, and descent to the children and relations of the deceased, seems to have been allowed much earlier than the right of devising by testament. We are apt to conceive at first view, that it has nature on its side ; yet we often mistake for nature, what we find established by long and inveterate custom. It is certainly a wise and effectual, but clearly, a political establishment, since the permanent right of property vested in the ancestor himself, was no natural but a mere civil right.*

The author seems to have been not a little confused upon this subject. He has reckoned the right of private propertyamong the absolute rights, which he says belongs to every individual, whether in society or out of it, and says it is probably derived from nature.† Yet he appears to suppose, that in its progress before it could become permanent, it ceased to be a natural, and became a mere civil right. Believing it, therefore, to have become a mere civil right, the creature of civil institutions, he very consistently supposes, that thereafter every legitimate mode of acquisition and disposal, the transfer of the right and mode by which it passes from one to another, must originate solely in the same institutions.

But it has been clearly proved, that the right of property originates in natural principles, independent of civil institutions, and is permanently established in society by the laws of nature, which are the sure foundation of all institutions, civil and political. It is therefore a reasonable conclusion, that the laws of nature reach also future acquisitions and disposals, and embrace the cases under consideration, to the exclusion of that constitution, which, as the author well observes, would be productive of endless disturbances ; and that the almost universal

---

*2 Comm. p. 10, 12.   † 1 Comm. 123, 138.

law of every nation upon this subject is, in fact, a secondary law of nature, in this sense, that it follows and is a species of that primary law, which establishes the right of property itself ;—and I am persuaded, that it will be found on enquiry, that on this foundation rests the right of the possessor to dispose of his property by will, and the right of the children and next of kin to inherit. Civil institutions, have only confirmed and modified these rights. The right to inherit, is indeed a qualified and subordinate right, subject to the right and occasions of the predecessor.

I am happy to be able to oppose to the author of the Commentaries two authorities of the first respectability. Mr. Christian, in a note on the passage last cited says*—"I am obliged to differ from the learned Judge and all writers upon general law, who maintain that children have no better claim by nature to succeed to the property of their deceased parents than strangers, and that the preference given to them, originates solely in political establishments. I know no other criterion, by which we can determine any rule or obligation to be founded in nature, than by its universality, and by inquiring whether it has not in all countries and ages, been agreeable to the feelings, affections, and reason of mankind." And Vattel, in his treatise on the law of nations,† lays it down as a fixed principle, that " Every man may naturally choose the person to whom he would leave his wealth after his death, as long as his right is not limited by an indispensable obligation ; as, for instance, that of providing for the subsistence of his children. The children have also naturally the right of succeeding in an equal proportion to the property of their father."

Our first enquiry will be concerning the early and general acknowledgment of these rights. In every nation, among whom property as a provision for the future has been an object of pursuit, the right of the children to succeed to the property of their deceased parents, is found in their customs, and confirmed by their civil institutions. Neither authentic history nor tradition reaches the origin of those customs and institutions.

---

* 2 Comm. 11. n. 3.   † B. 1. C. 20. s. 256.

In the history of the Jews, the most ancient history extant, the right of inheritance is constantly spoken of as a thing well known, and the right of making a testamentary disposition, or of a man to appoint his heir, is frequently implied, and that long before the law of Moses. Abraham is introduced saying,—"Thou hast given me no seed, and lo, one born in my house shall be my heir;*—alluding to his steward Eliezer;—the meaning is, that for want of children he had appointed Eliezer to be his heir. "And the word of the Lord came unto him, saying, this shall not be thine heir, but he that shall come forth of thine own bowels shall be thine heir." The following passages also imply, or clearly express, the right of making a testamentary disposition. "And Abraham gave all that he had to Isaac; but to the sons of the concubines, which Abraham had, he gave gifts, and sent them away from Isaac his son, while he yet lived, eastward into the eastern country."† If this was a transaction between the living, it was nevertheless an appointment by the parent, how his property should be enjoyed by his children after his death. Of the same nature was the gift made by Jacob, just before his death, to his son Joseph. "Moreover I have given to thee one portion above thy brethren, which I took from the Amorite with my sword and my bow."‡

In the laws of Moses, given some centuries after, inheritance is often mentioned and alluded to as a well known right, which we must suppose had been long established by custom; for the Jews had not before, any written laws or any civil institutions, except their customs. But no general rule or precept is in that law given on the subject.—There are but two instances, of regulating inheritances, and those only partial. One case is, if a man have two wives, one beloved and the other hated, and they have children, both the beloved and the hated, and the first-born be her's who was hated, then it shall be, when he maketh his sons to inherit, he may not make the son of the beloved first-born before the son of the hated, who is indeed the first-born; but he shall acknowledge him the first born by giving him a double portion of all that he hath; for he is the

---

* Genesis, Ch. 15. † Ch. 25. ‡ Ch. 48.

beginning of his strength ; for the right of the first born is his.* This was agreeable to a well known custom among the Jews, and probably a custom of their ancestors in Mesopotamia. For we have an account of Jacob, many ages before, purchasing of his elder brother Esau, his birthright as something valuable in those times. This precept of the law is here given, not for the purpose of establishing the right of the first-born, already known, but to prevent partiality, which might induce the father to violate custom already established. The other instance is that of the daughters of Zelophehad.—The father was dead leaving no sons, but daughters, who applied to Moses to be admitted to the inheritance of their father, whereupon the following law was given. " If- a man die, and have no son, then ye shall cause his inheritance to pass unto his daughter, and if he have no daughters, then ye shall give his inheritance unto his brethren, and if he have no brethren, then ye shall give his inheritance unto his father's brethren, and if his father have no brethren, then ye shall give his inheritance unto his kinsman that is next to him of his family and he shall possess it ; and it shall be to the children of Israel for a statute of judgment as the Lord commanded Moses".†

Before this law, it appears that, among the ancient Jews, daughters were in all cases excluded from the inheritance. The reasons of this exclusion may be found, partly in institutions peculiar to the Jews, and partly in customs common to the age. The nation were divided into tribes and families, a thing very common among the most ancient nations. The lands of their inheritance, were alotted, in distinct portions, to each tribe and family, and were on no account to pass from one tribe to another ; but which, were the daughters generally admitted to the inheritance, might frequently happen, by their marriage into different tribes. To prevent this effect of the law recited above, a subsequent law ‡ was given, by which it was ordained, that every daughter that possesseth an inheritance in any tribe of the children of Israel, shall be wife unto one of a family of the tribe of her father, that the children of

---

* Deuteronomy 21.   † Numbers 27.   ‡ Numbers 36.
11

Israel may enjoy every man the inheritance of his fathers ;—
neither shall the inheritance remove from one tribe to another
tribe, but every one of the tribes of the children of Israel
shall keep himself to his own inheritance.

There was another reason, not only with the Jews, but with
the ancients generally, why daughters were excluded from the
inheritance, especially where there were any sons. The
continuance of the family name was considered as a matter of the
utmost importance, and its extinction the greatest curse—a
demonstration of the divine anger. But in the common course,
the name could be continued in the male line only.*—The
female, by her marriage, sunk her family name in that of her
husband. It was also the custom for men to purchase their
wives. The dowry, frequently mentioned, was not advanced
by the father to the daughter or her husband, but by the
husband to the father. The wife thus purchased was considered
and treated little other, than a favorite slave. Thus Jacob
served seven years for each of his two wives,—and David paid to
Saul the dowry stipulated for his daughter Michel. This custom
is frequently alluded to by Homer, the most ancient profane
writer, and indeed by most ancient authors. I will cite but
one instance from the Odyssey. It is in the advice given by
Minerva under the character of Menort, to Telemachus.—
" And if your mother is determined to marry, let her return
to the house of her illustrious father, and let these—the suitors,
settle the affair of the marriage, and provide the many valuable
presents, which it is meet to give for a beloved daughter."†
Yet, notwithstanding the general custom, the father had the
power of appointing that the daughters should inherit with
the sons,—among many instances of this, one is found in
Job, where, in speaking of the daughters of Job, it is said that
their father gave them an inheritance among their brethren ;
which is mentioned as a thing, not in the common course.—
Where there were no sons but daughters, the father often gave
the inheritance to them on their marriage, to some of his

* The word for male in Hebrew, is Zacar—remembrance, one who supports
the memory of the family.   † Od. 1 v. 276—277.

kindred ; or if a daughter in that case was married to a stranger, the father, to continue his name, adopted the husband into the family.

We further learn from Homer, that the right of the children to the inheritance was admitted among the Greeks before his time, and was supposed to be a common custom among other nations ; it had even gone farther than the inheritance of property ; for we find his kings, generally deriving their authority as well as possessions by hereditary right. Allusions to this custom are without number. It will be sufficient to mention two or three.—In the second book of the Iliad, the part speaking of the sceptre of Agamemnon says—" It was made by Vulcan, and by him presented to Saturnian Jove, by Jove it was given to the god Mercury, by Mercury to Pelops, Pelops gave it to Atreus Thastor,—that is, king of the people ; Atreus, at his death, left it to Thyestes, who left it to Agamemnon."* Here its being given by Pelops to Atreus, for he had other sons, seems to mark an appointment in the nature of a devise, and in the other instances being left on the death of the father to the son to mark a course of descent. In the fifth book, on Xanthus and Thoon, sons of Dolops, who were Trojans, being slain by Diomede, we are told, " The father had no other son to whom he might leave his possessions, but his remote kindred shared it amongst them." In the first book of the Odyssey Antinous, expresses himself thus ;—" Telemachus son of Ulysses, may the gods never make thee a king in Seagirt Ithaca, which is your paternal right by birth."

The right of making a testamentary disposition, and the right of inheritance were regulated by the laws of Athens ; but these laws only adopted, or probably modified, customs more ancient than their oldest lawgivers, Draco and Solon. Sophocles who lived not far from two centuries after Solon, in his tragedy of Trachinia,† relates that Hercules, when he departed on his last expedition, left a written will directing how, if he should not return, his property should be divided among his family.—As to the facts, they are undoubtedly

---

*v. 101—109.   †v. 160—166.

poetic fictions ; but their relations are evidence of what the laws and customs were at the times they wrote, and the general opinion of their high antiquity.

These rights must have been long established in ancient Italy ; for we find them both regulated in the laws of the twelve tables. The first law of the fifth table is,—" After the death of the father of a family, let the disposition be made of his estate, and his appointment concerning the guardianship of his children be observed."—The second—"If he dies intestate, and has no children, let his nearest relation be his heir ; if he have no near relation, let a man of his name be his heir,"—that is, of his family name, the family being supposed to be descended from one common stock. Here the right of making a disposition, by will, is necessarily supposed to be already known and long established,—and the right of the next of kin to the succession seems to have been extended, rather than introduced by this law.

Among the ancient Germans, according to Tacitus, children were heirs and successors to their parents. If there were no children, then the next of kin succeeded, first the brothers of the deceased ; if no brothers, then the uncles of the father's side, and next the uncles of the mother's side. Honors were also hereditary in families, as they were in Gaul and Britain, in the time of Julius Cæsar ;—but Tacitus says that wills were not in use among the Germans. I think, however, there is reason to question the accuracy of his information on this point. For with the Anglo Saxons, in addition to the law of inheritance found among their German ancestors, the custom of making a testamentary disposition, although under certain restrictions, prevailed, and there is every reason to believe that they brought this custom with them from the forests of Germany, rather than that they adopted it from the miserable remnant of ancient Britons, whom they had reduced to a state of the most abject slavery.

It was, perhaps, unnecessary to be thus particular ; for I believe no nation where property is considered to be absolute

---

* 160 to 166   † De Moribus Germanorum.

in the owner, has been found, however rude, among whom the
right of children to inherit to their deceased parents has not
prevailed, as well as the right of the possessor to make some
sort of testamentary disposition. A custom in any nation, has
its origin in the common feelings and sentiments of the people;
and if we find the same custom prevailing universally among
all nations, it is a proof that the same feelings and sentiments
are universal, and may generally be admitted as a proof that
the custom is a law of nature upon the subject which it
embraces. It is true, that circumstances very general may
produce a perversion of feeling and sentiment, on certain
subjects, equally general. Such were the ancient laws of
war, which gave to the conqueror, a right to take the lives
of the vanquished, and consequently, on sparing their lives
as a favor, to hold or dispose of them in perpetual slavery—
a perversion which might easily be accounted for, if here
necessary.

To a final decision, whether a custom be founded in natural
principles, it is necessary to bring it to the unerring test, its
tendency to general utility. The question is, if it relate to a
particular society only—Is its general tendency to promote
the interest of that society without injury to others? If it relates to the whole human race,—Is its general tendency to
promote the interest, the happiness of mankind? The good
tendency of the laws and customs which we have been
advocating, is seen, felt, and acknowledged by all. Judge
Blackstone, and all the writers upon general law, fairly
acknowledge, that they are necessary to the general good,
the general peace and happiness of mankind, although they
contend that they are mere civil institutions. But we may go
farther and connect both these rights with natural principles.
We will first examine the right to make a testamentary
disposition;—and I think it is fairly and fully included in that
sole and despotic dominion, which, as Judge Blackstone
expresses it, one man claims and exercises over the external
things of this world, to the exclusion of every other individual
in the universe; and which we have clearly shewn to be a
natural right. It cannot be contended that this dominion, so
despotic and absolute, is only a right of use for the present

necessities, convenience, or pleasure of the possessor.—No, it comprehends equally in itself, the right equally natural, of a disposition of the property by sale, gift, or exchange, to take effect immediately or at any future time, or upon contingency either in possession or reversion, in his life time, or at his death, which may lawfully be the contingency. Nor can it be justly subject to any other limitations, than such as the public good requires, a limitation to which every right of man is subject by the laws of social nature. But as we have seen, so far is the public good from opposing this claim of right, that it imperiously requires its allowance.

The natural right of the children and kindred, especially of the children, to succeed to the inheritance of the deceased, is, if possible, still more clear. The union of parents and children forms a society the most intimate and the most purely natural. The reciprocal right and duties, parental and filial, are derived solely from the relations of nature, and are in their origin independent of the modifications of art or of civil institutions. Not only the members of the several families, but others forcibly feel what I have ventured to call the individuality of these little communities of nature. The perception may be resembled to that of the members to form the body. All the members of a family, one of these little communities, feel the tenderest interest in the good or evil, moral or natural, that befalls each other ;—no one hesitates when he observes an instance of a contrary disposition, to pronounce it unnatural. When a child is arrived at maturity ready to branch into a new family, it is perceived, from the natural connexion, to be the duty of the parent, according to his ability, and with a due regard to the subsisting or growing relations of the family, to contribute to the advancement of such child. If a parent, in common cases, neglect to contribute, every one conceives him to be guilty, though not of a civil, yet of a moral crime ;—He is at once believed to be under the dominion of avarice, or some other vicious passion, that has stifled the voice of nature.—On the whole we may with propriety adopt the elegant and forcible language of Mr. Christian upon the subject. " The affection of parents toward their children is the most powerful and universal principle, which nature has implanted in the human breast, and it cannot be conceived, even in the most savage state, that any one is so destitute of that affection and of reason, who would not revolt at the position, that a stranger has as good a right as his children to the property of a deceased parent.

When there are no children, the same natural relations, differing in degree, extend to the next of kin, whether ascending, descending, or collateral, who on the same natural principles have a right to succeed as heirs to the possessions of the deceased. In proportion to the distance the relations are less strongly marked; and although the inconvenience arising from the numerous claimants that may appear in the more remote degrees, has sometimes been thought a good reason for a limitation; yet it has generally been agreed to allow the claim as far as the relations can be traced. The relations, however remote, clearly carry a right preferable to that of a total stranger. If then, the right of property be a natural right; if those are natural rights, that commence in natural principles, then the right of making a testamentary disposition, and the right of the children and next of kin, according to their several degrees, to succeed to their parent and kinsman, are natural rights; they have their inception in natural principles, are admitted and approved by the universal sentiments of mankind, and they abide the sure test of all the laws of nature, their general tendency to promote the peace and happiness of human society.

It may be suggested, however, by some, that if the right of the children be founded in the laws of nature, those laws are immutable, and, consequently, the right; which must necessarily abridge, or wholly supersede the parent's right of disposal in this case. The laws of nature are determined in their application by the existing relations. The relations remaining under the same combinations and modifications, the result will be the same, and, consequently, the same law will invariably apply. The relations are subject to different arrangements.—They may be enlarged, diminished, or wholly cease. In all these cases the result will vary, and, consequently, the law will vary in application precisely as the relations themselves; or we may say, the cases vary, and therefore come under different rules of the same general law.

The parent, during his life, has a full right to direct the use and disposal of his property. That he is under a natural, or moral obligation to provide for his household and to advance his children with his property as his occasions admit, and their circumstances require, no more effects his rights than any moral obligation affects the freedom of moral action. The right of the children, during the life of the parent, constitute claims of a moral nature only, of the admission of which, he is by nature made the sole judge. There are other claims on his property beside those of his children. His property is subject civilly, to all claims of right both of the public and individuals—it is subject to other claims of a moral nature, of which he is also the sole judge. He may think it his duty to give some of his property for the public use, for the relief of distress, for the encouragement of learning and virtue, the reward of humanity or exemplary instances of filial piety. It is subject during his life to all his occasions, natural, civil, and moral, and a disposition to take effect after his death is no more inconsistent with the rights of the children than a disposition for the same purposes, while living. In such cases a parent may misjudge, he may do wrong, but it is generally an affair of too much delicacy to endure the divisions of the civil law.

On the death of the parent, the relation in which he stood while living, being determined, the right of the children, as far as respects the property of which no disposition has been made remains, and that right, which before was only contingent and of a moral nature, is now perfected and realized ; and when the just demands of others are satisfied, all the children have an equal claim and an equal right to the remaining property of their common parent. If nature dictates any preference, it is generally in favor of the younger, and not of the elder, branch. It appears not unreasonable, that when any of the younger children are left in a state of helpless infancy, the common property left by the parent, should assist in some degree in making the provision for their support and education, which, were he living, he would consider not as an advancement, but an indispensable obligation of nature.

Thus, upon a careful examination of the right of descent,

upon natural principles, we find no intimation of the right
of primogeniture, no preference in succession, but what tends
to an equal enjoyment of the goods of fortune. We may
repeat that the equal laws of nature, if rightly understood and
practised in government, tend to prevent every dangerous
excess. The more we examine these laws, the more will
appear their coincidence with the best feelings of the human
heart, and the genuine principles of equal law and government.

CHAPTER IV.

Of the extension of the right of property and its abuse.

It should seem at first view, that the right of property could
attach on no subject, which is not an object of sense; no
subject of a mere incorporeal nature, and that man, the only
being in whom nature has vested a right of property, could not
himself become the subject of that right; and yet the right
has prevailed in both kinds.—There are many instances of the
right of property recognized in the laws of civilized countries,
in which the subjects of that right exist only in the contemplation
of the mind. They are not objects of sense; and such right
is called an incorporeal right. The right may be temporary
or perpetual. If perpetual, it is called an incorporeal
hereditament; which has been defined by Judge Blackstone,
to be "a right issuing out of a thing corporeal, whether real
or personal, or concerning, or annexed to, or exercisable
within the same. It is not the thing corporate itself, which
may consist in lands, houses, jewels or the like; but something
collateral thereto, and issuing out of those lands or houses, or

an office relating to those jewels ;"*—and farther on he says—
An annuity, for instance, is an incorporeal hereditament ; for
though the money, that is, the fruit of that annuity, is doubtless
of a corporeal nature, yet the annuity itself, which produces
that money, is a thing invisible, has only a mental existence,
and cannot be delivered over from hand to hand."

However abstract the notion, yet I think the conception of
it very easy ; and although it cannot be supposed to exist in
the very early stages of society, or until the right of property
has become general and permanent, yet when it comes into
existence, so far as it is connected with, or issues out of a
thing corporeal, a natural subject of property, it will readily
be perceived to be comprehended in the natural right of
property. But no grant of an annuity merely personal and not
issuing out of something corporeal, comes within the natural
right, of which it partakes no more than the right acquired by
one man to a sum of money, which another has by contract
promised to pay him. There is the same distinction, as to the
nature of the right, where it issues not out of the thing
corporeal, but is annexed to some office or trust concerning it.
The right is to a reward for care and pains, whether it be in
the shape of a pension, or salary, or of perquisites, as fees for
services to be performed in the exercise of the office. The
reward issues not out of a thing corporate—for the jewel,
mentioned as an instance, yields nothing,—nothing issues out of
it. The reward, or wages if in the shape of a salary, is paid by
the owner or employer ; it is a personal concern between the
employer and the person employed, and that, whether the
employment be of a public or a private nature. If the reward of
an office be in the shape of perquisites as fees, it is then paid by
those for whom the official services are performed. There is no
differencein the nature of the thing from the right of a laborer in
agriculture, or an artificer hired for certain wages, or as it
sometimes happens, for a certain share of the profits, by the
day, month, or year. If the office be for life, it has an analogy
to a freehold, a life estate. If it be granted to one and his

---

*2 Comm. 20.

heirs, it has, in that respect, an analogy to an estate of
inheritance ; but as in this case the right does not inhere in,
or issue out of, anything corporeal, any natural subject of
property, the analogy is imperfect. It is true, these offices
and employments produce something that is property, the wages
paid or recieved. Such is the case with all offices and
employments, whether of a public or a private nature.

Under the inducements of these analogies, the laws have
generally classed these rights with the rights of property, and
have provided remedies, accordingly, in cases of ouster and
violation. These analogies have been extended much farther.
Monarchs and independent princes are held to have a sacred
right of property in their authority, and that inheritable ; not
only so, but to inherit the states and kingdoms over which
they preside, and the allegiance and services of their subjects,
who are left to inherit the duty of submission. The same
observations will apply to the members of a sovereign
aristocracy.

With respect to a hereditary nobility under a monarchy,
forming a branch of the government, they inherit certain
subordinate powers, which they exercise conjointly with the
monarch, or in a mixed government, with the prince, and the
popular branch, and their rights are supported by the same
principles, and the same analogies. There are also, in most, if
not all monarchies, enjoyed hereditary titles, of mere rank,
connected with no authority, no power, no office, either of
trust or profit. The analogy here consists merely in the
hereditary quality of a factitious rank, which has been aptly
compared to a mouthful of moon-shine ;–yet they are considered
as having a property in this rank.

All these rights of property in offices, in power, ranks, titles,
and dignities, will with one consent, be pronounced, by all
those who have been born and educated under a free and well
regulated popular government, to be flagrant abuses ; while
the subjects of a mild, or a mixed monarchy, although they
may acknowledge them to be factitious, yet from the force of
education and habit, will consider them inventions of wisdom
almost super-human, for the peace and happiness of mankind.
Still they will admit the abuse under a despotic government ;

but will attribute the abuse, not so much to the nature of the institution as to the character of the reigning prince, or the absence of certain preventives of the evil, certain checks and balances, consisting of the like institutions.

We cannot here omit an enquiry concerning the other species of property mentioned at the beginning of this chapter; which claims a right of prescription beyond all authentic history, beyond the most remote tradition; the right of property, which one human being claims in another being of the same species; the right which the master claims in his slave. This is also deemed an hereditary right, but of a corporeal nature. The master has an inheritance in his slave extending through him to his children, and children's children, to the remotest generation.

The practice of slavery is indeed, very ancient, has prevailed generally if not universally, and has been confirmed by the civil institutions of most countries. The antiquity and general reception of the custom of holding slaves, has been, and still is urged as a proof, that it is just, and founded in the laws of nature. It is acknowledged, that the antiquity and generality of a custom is a strong, but by no means, a conclusive proof that it is so founded. It has been observed that circumstances very general may happen, that will produce a general perversion of sentiments,—and the consequence will be, the adoption of customs equally perverse. Such circumstances were found in the early ages of society, which introduced the ferocious custom that subjected to the mercy—mercy did I say?—to the brutal fury of the conqueror, the lives of the vanquished, from the soldier taken in arms, to the child in the womb of the mother,—of which the practice of slavery is the legitimate offspring. But a more particular discussion of this subject will be deferred, until we come to treat of the laws of nature and the laws of nations.

Notwithstanding the antiquity of the practice of slavery, and confirmed as it is, and has been, by the civil institutions of so many countries, we cannot hesitate to say, it is supported by no right, no principle, acknowledged by the laws of nature; that it is inconsistent with all natural right;—the right of personal liberty, of personal security, and of private property,—all are violated or rather annihilated in the person of the slave.—Not only does it violate rights and principles allowed natural, but it fails in that safe and sure test of every law of nature, and of all civil institutions as founded in those laws, its tendency to promote the general interest and happiness of the society where it prevails, as well as of mankind in general.—Its general tendency is, in every just view, directly the reverse,—so generally is this now understood, that to attempt the proof, would be as tedious as it is unnecessary.

Is it necessary then, to support the institution of slavery in any country, to discard the general tendency of a law or action as a moral test? or shall we say that those rights, which have so generally been considered as appertaining to every individual, whether in society or out of it, and which are still claimed even by slave holders themselves, in their own case as founded in the irreversible laws of nature are but a vain illusion, and adopt the opinion of a modern writer, " That all right is founded upon power, and all obligation upon self interest?"* An opinion that explodes the benevolent and divine precept,— " Thou shalt love thy neighbor as thy self," which has so generally, and it seems so weakly been considered as inculcating one of the first principles of morality and religion, and substitutes in its place, as a universal precept—" Thou shalt love thyself alone"—a precept, which the most ferocious tribe of savages would, in their intercourse among themselves, reject with contempt.

What then shall we say of this species of private property? is it wholly condemned by morality? is there no moral obligation to respect it?—certainly there is. In a country where slavery is introduced and permitted by law or general custom, the right of the master to his slave is as complete, while remaining within the limits of the law or custom, as to any, the most common subject of property, considering the right, as before explained, a title, an allowed claim, the jus suum of the civil law. The private right in a moral view, is distinct from the moral of the law or custom, and its tendency to

---

* Cooper's Justinian.—Note 412. vide. Note at the end of this chapter.

promote the interest of the society, where it exists, or the general interest and happiness of the human race. From these sources, arguments may be drawn to persuade the people to reform their general sentiments and to change their laws; but until that be done the private right of property, ought, as far as the law or custom extends, to be considered inviolable. Still there is an important distinction between this and other kinds of property. The right of the master in the slave is truly a mere civil and not a natural right.—The right of the owner in the common, or as we may say, natural subjects of property is a natural right and is every where respected and supported by the laws of nature as well as of society. The right of the master ceases the moment he passes with his slave into a country or state, where there is no law or custom to support it; or unless, as in the United States, there is some provision to protect his property in the slave accompanying him. So a slave escaping into such a state becomes free, unless a provision have been made, enabling the master to reclaim him. But if a slave owner remove with his slave into a state to reside where there is no law to protect his right, it ceases at once, and the slave becomes ipso facto free; because the laws of that state protect all men alike in their natural rights.

NOTE.

The passage, a part of which is quoted in the text, ought to be recited at large, that it may meet that execration which it deserves from every lover of mankind, every friend of morality and religion.

"As to the right of slavery, I look upon it as a point completely settled, that all right is founded upon power, and all obligation upon self interest. What right have we to sieze and castrate a horse or an ox, and condemn the one to perpetual slavery and the other to slaughter? The question about the abstract right of making slaves is a futile discussion.—If one being has the power of subjecting another to his dominion, service and control, and can do it with perfect impunity, why should he not? Let the answer to this question be given, and pursued to its ultimate term, and the dispute is at an end. In fact, throughout all nature, this is the law. I have greatly changed my opinion on this, and many other subjects in consequence of thirty years' observation, and reflection. I do not treat it now as an abstract but a practical question."

And can this be so ? Is all right resolved into power, and all moral obligation, into self interest? Let us examine this question.—If one being has the power of subjecting another to his dominion, service, and control, and can do it with perfect impunity, why should he not? And he might have added, on his own principle,—If self interest requires, he is under an obligation to do it. We will answer the question, why should he not? and pursue it to its ultimate term.

But first let it be premised, that the being having the power, and the being to be subjected, are both human beings.—For I have too much respect for the human race, of which I happen to be one, to place them in the same grade of being and of rights, with oxen and horses. I answer then,—Power merely, gives no right, because every man, as a moral being, is by the laws of social nature, under a moral obligation, not only to abstain from such acts as are immediately or in their general tendency, injurious to others, but to do that which tends to promote the interest and happiness of his fellow men, including himself, according to the relations in which he stands connected with them.

But says the author—All obligation is founded upon self interest—a man is under no obligation to abstain from any act by which his own present interest will, in his view, be promoted, however injurious to others, provided only that he can do it with perfect impunity. If he cannot do it with perfect impunity, it may injure instead of promoting his interest, and so be a violation of his obligation.

To this I answer—If by self interest the author means the isolated interest of the individual, it is not true, when asserted as the foundation of moral obligation. To say that a man is, in any strict sense, under an obligation to himself, is absurd. If one person owes a duty or is under an obligation, on the one hand it must, necessarily, be to some person, on the other, who has a corresponding right—a right to demand the performance of that duty. I am here speaking of duties of perfect obligation, as sufficient for the present purpose.—If the duty and the right, as sometimes happens, unite in the same person the duty merges and becomes extinct.—In a word, to say that all obligation is founded upon self interest, in this isolated sense, is to assert, that one man can be under no obligation to another.—But if by self interest the author means an expanded interest, which is co-extensive and identifies itself with all the social relation of which the individual makes a constituent part, it does indeed put an end to the dispute but by giving a full and decided negative to his conclusion.

" The dispute about the abstract right of making slaves is a futile discussion." But the dispute is not about a mere abstract, but, a practical right—the right of one man to reduce another to slavery. Let it always remain an abstract right never to be carried into practice, and the discussion will be as futile as the right.

" In fact," concludes the author, " throughout the whole system of nature this is the law."—that is,—" that all right is founded upon power"—that the stronger shall subject the weaker,—and is man then like the brutes, subject only to the law of instinct? are the laws of morality and the benevole' precepts of religion a mere imposition? What a triumphant defence of all the villains, public and private, that have ever infested society—of all the tyrants civil and ecclesiastical, who have existed from the days of Nimrod down to the present period of the holy alliance!—I ask the author's pardon—of all who have been able to exercise their villainies and their tyranny with perfect impunity.—Those who have not been able, I suppose the author will allow, to have been guilty of a miscalculation of their power; and that they might justly suffer the penalties due for such criminal miscalculation.

It will, I think, readily be perceived, that Mr. Cooper has fallen into this error from a misconception of the position, that utility is the foundation of all obligation, which is true only, if understood of general, and social utility, the general good, and which includes the good of each individual capable of obligation. But he has confined it to the isolated good of the individual actor; an error, to the very verge of which Mr. Paley has sometimes pushed his principles of moral philosophy.

This passage of the author was intended as a defence of the slave holders in the United States; but surely those slave holders will feel themselves under little obligation to him for placing their defence upon a principle, that will equally justify their slaves, and make it a duty, if they think it can be done with impunity, that is, with success, to attempt their own emancipation by force,—and which will, in the same manner, justify each individual slave in the murder of his master.

They have a better—they have a just defence in their situation; a situation derived to them from their ancestors, and in producing which they had no participation; a situation in which the law of self preservation, a law of necessity, forbids a general emancipation, that must inevitably prove the ruin both of the master and the emancipated slave, and reduce the country to something worse than a mere desert,—nor has it been found an easy—if a possible—thing to introduce any gradual emancipation, which shall prove safe and effectual.

CHAPTER V.

Of the right of Opinion.

A private opinion, while confined to the breast of an individual, does not belong to the cognizance of human laws, or of human tribunals. It is a matter between the individual and his conscience, and is cognizable only by the Great Searcher of the human heart. It has never been claimed by any human tribunal, except that of the Romish Church. The Pope, the head of that Church, who claims to be God's Vicegerent on earth, claims also the right and power to search the human heart. Accordingly the Court of Inquisition, a tribunal erected by the authority of the Pope, have assumed, as a right which they exercise, an authority to compel, by the most excruciating tortures, any person suspected of secretly entertaining any opinion inserted in their catalogue of heresies, to confess that opinion, and recant the same, upon which, they sometimes dismiss him on penance ; sometimes, as a favor, suffer him to perish in their prisons ; or, if he obstinately refuse to recant, they condemn him to perish in the flames. But so gross is the absurdity of the claim, that in the present age, and with those for whom I write, to attempt a refutation, would be like an attempt to heighten the splendor of the meridian sun by the feeble light of a candle.

I shall, therefore, assume it as an incontrovertible position—as a first principle—that the right of private opinion, which is, in fact, no other than the right of private judgment, upon any subject presented to the mind, is a sacred right, with which society can, on no pretence, authoritatively interfere, without a violation of the first principles of the law of nature. But when a man extends this right, and assumes the liberty of acting upon it, his actions become subject to human control, as they may be injurious to others, injurious to the community. The right of private opinion still remains sacred, while the right of acting upon it is, like all other rights, and for the same reasons, subject to be controlled by political and civil regulations. The right of merely propagating an opinion is a matter of great delicacy and can rarely be subject to civil restraint. The right of acting in this case, as here proposed to be discussed, presents a two-fold division agreeable to the subjects, on which it is exercised. First, religious liberty, or the liberty of a man to act agreeable to his religious opinions ; and secondly, the liberty of political opinion. I might have introduced a third division,— The right of moral opinion ; but this is nothing more than that natural liberty, of which sufficient has been said in former chapters.

It may appear to some, that little need be said on the subject of religious liberty ; but a moment's reflection will convince any one that no subject has occasioned more disputes in the world, or produced a greater variety of conflicting opinions, which have brought the most cruel calamities on mankind. Nor is there, it is believed, a nation in the old world, in which religious liberty is allowed in its full and just extent. Religious liberty has been denominated " Liberty of conscience," and " The rights of conscience" always with a reference to the same subject.—It is properly defined to be, " The liberty which a man has of discussing and maintaining his religious opinions and of worshiping God in that way and manner, which he believes in his conscience to be most acceptable to his Maker, without being liable on that account to any degradation, penalties, or disqualifications, civil or political. Strictly just as this definition may appear to us in this land of liberty ; however consistent with the true spirit of religion and the best interests of mankind, civil and moral, there are nations calling themselves christians, who would deem it a blasphemous heresy, and condemn to the stake any one who dare to maintain it. Many of them tolerate dissenters from the national Church, under various restrictions and disqualifications. Even in England, that boasted land of liberty, dissenters from the established Church, have on that account, been deprived of many important rights and privileges, both civil and political, or permitted to enjoy them on conditions and compliances inconsistent with any just measure of religious liberty. One is astonished and disgusted on reading in Judge Blackstone's commentaries, the long catalogue of vexations, penalties, disabilities, and degrading disqualifications imposed by numerous laws on the different sects of dissenters, under which they were tolerated in worshiping God according to their consciences. These penalties, disabilities, and disqualifications in a civil and political point of view have been mitigated and even removed since the commentaries were written. But still, while there remains the establishment of the national Church, so regarded by law, the dissenting sects enjoy their religious liberty under the idea of toleration, which is in itself sufficiently degrading. Indeed a national establishment of religion, however necessary it may have been thought in former times to the support of the established government, had its commencement in error, in bigotry, and superstition, which are always exclusive, always intolerant.—It is at best, inconsistent with a full and just measure of rational religious liberty.

However demonstrable the existence of the Supreme Being, his extensive attributes, and the duty of all to obey his will, and to serve and worship him, may be to common reason, the mode and manner of that worship which will be most acceptable to him, is not equally demonstrable. This is left to the conscience of every man, upon the best information he is capable of attaining ; and was doubtless so left for the moral benefit of mankind. The different sects feeling a deep interest in approving to the world the superior excellence of their particular religious tenets, manner of service, and worship, are set as watchmen on the moral conduct of each other. This situation always, as men, where they are not involved in the ignorance of bigotry, or led astray by the delusive visions of enthusiasm, judge of religious opinions and modes, and the sincerity of those who profess them, by the good effect on their lives and conversation in society, excites a moral emulation among the different sects, beneficial to them and to mankind. Of this we have full proof in the history of the sixteenth century, which includes the commencement of the great reformation from popery. While the whole christian world was involved in the ignorance and bigotry of that superstition ; when the Pope, as the head of the Church, was held to be infallible and the character of the clergy was held too sacred to be submitted to the judgment of the profane laity ; when the Pope assumed the power of pardoning past sins, however enormous, for the sums at which he had severally rated to them ; of selling dispensations from the most solemn engagements, and indulgences for future crimes, and none dared to hint a censure of these things, the profligacy of the clergy and the universal corruption of manners was such as to render an impartial history of those times almost incredible at this day. The contest that ensued with a powerful hierarchy, excited a spirit of enquiry among the reformers, invigorated their minds, and opened to them the stores of learning which had lain buried for centuries, under the rubbish of a vain philosophy and scholastic jargon. This enabled them to rend the veil of ignorance, under which the world had long been enveloped, and to expose the errors and corruptions of the Church of Rome with an intelligence and force, that threatened the final subversion of the hierarchy. The learners of the reformers could no longer be resisted by ignorance, nor the arguments be opposed by disregarded thunders of the Vatican. The Romish clergy were compelled to become learned in their own defence ; and, to prevent a total defection of their followers, they found it necessary to reform their lives, so strongly contrasted with the sober demeanor and strict moral lives of their opponents. Each party noted with severity the conduct of the other. Among the protestant reformers themselves, differences of opinion, modes of worship, and discipline, to which was added a zeal for gaining proselytes, although they sometimes ran into excess, contributed to the same moral end. These are justly to be considered as the first and principal causes of the great improvements, in moral knowledge, in literature, and science, in the European world during the two last centuries.

In these United States religious liberty is secured, and the rights of conscience enjoyed to their full extent. No state establishment of religion, no religious test is permitted by the constitution. All the different sects enjoy equal prvileges and equal rights natural, civil, and political. The only restriction which operates equally on all is that no one in the exercise of his liberty, shall infringe the liberty of others, do any thing to disturb their rights, or to the injury of society. All causes of jealousy, civil and political, being removed, moral emulation operates without envy, and the different sects live in peace and charity with each other. In elections by the people, and in appointments to office, no enquiry is made what are the religious tenets, but what is the fitness, what the talents and integrity of the candidate.

To violate the rights of others, to disturb the peace and good order of society under pretence of conscience, or of religious duty are acts equally criminal as though perpetrated under any pretence whatever.—They are equally prohibited by the laws of nature; they are prohibited by the Supreme Being, the Author of religion, and the object of all religious worship, and justly punishable by the laws of society. To punish the abuse, instead of being a restraint upon liberty, is in fact, its greatest surety.

The right of propagating a religious opinion stands on the same ground.—The propagation of an opinion which does not result in any acts injurious to society, cannot with justice, be subjected to restraint by human laws. But this right may be abused and made the instrument of the most flagitious crimes, destructive of the order, peace, happiness, and of the very being of civil society. Such were the opinions formerly held by the Roman Catholic Church. It was sedulously inculcated as an essential article of their religious creed, that no faith was to be kept with heretics, dissenters from the doctrines of that Church—that it was meritorious in the sight of Heaven to assassinate heretical princes and rulers, and to subvert by any means, every government which rejected its dogmas, and declined its authority. This was not intended to be a mere speculative doctrine and to rest in theory.—It was reduced to practice by the ministers and agents of that Church, to the terror of one half of the christian world. Such was the violation of the safe conduct given by the emperor of Germany to Jerome of Prague, who, with his associates was sentenced to the flames.

Such the assassination of Henry IV. of France, by the fanatic Monk Ravaillac, for granting toleration to his protestant subjects. Such the gun powder plot in England in the reign of James I.— a plot for blowing up at once, the king and the whole English parliament. From the same source proceeded the numerous plots and rebellions devised principally by the Roman Catholics in England, down to the middle of the last century, by which, the government and liberties of the nation were exposed to perpetual danger, and sometimes brought to the brink of ruin. So intimately had they connected these pernicious opinions with the most important articles of their religious creed, such their faith in the priest of their order, so submissive were they found to the mandates of the sovereign Pontiff, that no penalties could provide an effectual restraint upon men, who were persuaded they merited the favor of Heaven by the commission of the most horrid crimes.

It became therefore necessary, as far as possible, to prevent the propagation of a religion so inseparably blended with such pernicious opinions. For this end, persons professing the Romish religion, were forbidden to keep or teach any school under pain of perpetual imprisonment. They were forbidden to hear or to say mass, that is, to attend worship according to the Romish ritual.—No person might send another abroad to be educated in the Roman Catholic religion, or contribute to his expenses, while abroad for that purpose, under numerous and severe penalties. Popish priests and bishops were forbidden to celebrate mass, or to exercise any of their functions in England, except in the house of a foreign ambassador, under penalty of perpetual imprisonment. To the same end were imposed many disabilities, and other severe penalties, but generally not of a sanguinary character. Without entering into the question, whether laws less severe might not have been equally effectual, I believe every unprejudiced person will see and acknowledge that the restraints imposed by these laws, were no more inconsistent with true religious liberty, than the laws of society for the prevention of theft, robbery, and murder, are inconsistent with civil liberty. It is due here to observe that if the Pope and the Romish Church have not formally disavowed those pernicious opinions, they have of late years been generally discarded by the professors of that religion,—that the Roman Catholics of Great Britain have universally renounced them as gross heresies, in consequence of which those severe laws have been repealed and they have been restored to all their rights, civil, political, and religious, as fully as the other sects dissenting from the established national Church had been by the repeal of the test and other laws.

We come now to the second division of our subject, the liberty of political opinion, which is defined to be " the right and liberty of every citizen to discuss and propagate his opinion on every subject relating to the government, institutions, and laws, the measures pursued by its ministers, and functionaries, and to act agreeable to that opinion, with this only condition, that in so acting he violate not the rights of others, or injure the community, of which he is a member." It is unnecessary here to add any thing on the right of private opinion. The right of discussing and propagating political opinions requires further examination, as it comprehends the liberty of speech and of the press—subjects of great importance in a free government. By the liberty of the speech and of the press, is to be understood what is substantially expressed in the foregoing definition, the right of every citizen freely to express, either in conversation, or by means of the press, his opinions in relation to the constitution of the government, its administration, and laws, the conduct, abilities, and integrity of the officers and functionaries, and the tendency, whether good or bad, of the measures pursued,—to an arbitrary government nothing can be more hostile than liberty of speech and of the press. Where that liberty prevails in any considerable degree, nothing is more efficient in the diffusion of knowledge among the people. They of course become enlightened, and by a free interchange of sentiments and opinions, learn what rights they are entitled to claim as intelligent and social beings, and feel more keenly the arbitrary exactions and oppressive acts of the government. They soon discover that the whole physical strength of the community is in their hands and that nothing is wanting but a union of sentiments and action, and a prudent and steady direction of

that strength so set them free by crushing their oppressors.*
Very different is the case under free institutions where the
rulers are elected by the free suffrages of the people, and hold
their power in trust, under constant accountability to their
constituents for the manner in which they exercise the trust.
The government have no support, no energy, but what
depends on the sentiment of the people ; and the more they
are enlightened, to understand their rights and the true end of
civil institutions, the firmer and more rational will be their
support of the government, if administered on just principles,
and the more forcibly will the rulers feel their accountability.
To this nothing can more contribute, than well conducted
Journals and periodicals, and it becomes the interest of the
government, which is no other than the interest of the whole
community, to provide for a safe, speedy, and cheap distribution
of them through every part of the State. Under these
considerations, it is the duty, as it is the interest of the
government, to cherish and to guard with every proper caution
the true liberty of the press.—But the same rule holds here as
in other cases. No one is allowed to exercise this right so
as to injure the right of another. It becomes necessary
therefore to distinguish between the just liberty, and the

---

*The following incident will shew the influence of a free press in
disseminating liberal principles, and among what classes it principally
operates.

In the charter granted by Louis XVIII, to the French nation in 1814,
which was called the constitution of the government, was an article for
securing in some degree the liberty of the press,—subject, however, to many
restrictions. In consequence many liberal Journals were circulated through
the kingdom, but not without many vexations practised by the court on the
editors. Some five or six years now past, an article was published in one of
the ultra loyal Journals, in which the editor complains bitterly of the want of
support through the loss of subscribers—and that whenever a loyal subscriber
died, the son sent him an obituary for publication and the next day subscribed
for a liberal Journal. It will be recollected that the revolution of July 1830
was brought about by the indignation excited throughout France by the
arrêt of Charles X., for suppressing the liberal Journals and seizing the
presses; which terminated in a few days in the deposition of Charles, the
banishment of himself and family from France, and the election of the duke
of Orleans to the throne.

licentiousness of the press. The right of character is a personal right highly regarded by the laws of every civilized country. If one person by slander injure the character of another, by words spoken, which is simply denominated defamation, or by writing, or printing, which is denominated a libel, an action is given to the party injured, against the slanderer, to recover damages according to the nature and extent of the injury. The publication of a libel from the extent to which it may readily be circulated, the permanent nature of the injury, and its tendency to disturb the peace of society, has been made a criminal offence and liable to penalties more or less severe. In civil prosecutions for this injury, the person bringing the action, is considered to have put his character in issue. If the defendant can prove the matter charged as defamatory or libellous to be true, it is deemed a good defence ; the plaintiff is found not to possess a character to which the law attaches the right of protection. A distinction has been made in most countries, and certainly is in England, between a civil and criminal prosecution for a libel.—In the former the truth is allowed to be a good defence, in the latter, not ; and on an indictment for some species of libel,* it has been considered a sound maxim of law, that the greater the truth, the greater the offence.

In these United States, generally, I believe I may say universally, the law is different. The truth is admitted to be a good defence as well in a criminal as a civil prosecution for a libel. This is perfectly consonant to the nature of our institutions and in accordance with the general interest. It is, in a political point of view, the interest of all to obtain a full knowledge of the true character of those who may be candidates for the offices of trust and confidence in the state, the appointments to which depend mediately or immediately on the suffrages of the people. This principle also serves to establish a well marked and a prominent line of distinction between the liberty and the licentiousness of the press ;—the distinction between truth and falsehood.—It does not, however, extend to every case of licentiousness ; for the facts published

---

* Scandalum Magnatum.—Defamation of the great men of the realm.

may be true, and yet the matter may be expressed in language so grossly indecent as to be an offence against good morals and justly punishable as such ; but this is a matter entirely distinct from the civil injury. It is merely an offence against society, and cannot be justified by alleging the truth of the facts.

If these principles are correct, of which it appears to me impossible to doubt, a palpable line of distinction so far as civil and political rights are concerned, has been drawn, between liberty and licentiousness in the case under consideration, so that the licentiousness may be restraind and punished, not only without danger, but with additional security to the liberty of speech and of the press.

BOOK V.

OF THE FORMATION OF GOVERNMENT—THE DISTRIBUTION AND LIMITATION OF THE CIVIL AND POLITICAL POWER.

CHAPTER I.

Of the Civil Compact.

By the social and civil compact is usually understood the agreement of a people to form themselves into a civil government, providing the mode and the means of making and adopting rules of civil conduct and of carrying them into effect.

Baron Puffendorf, who was very observant of all the forms and distinctions of the ancient schools, tells us, every civil compact, in its nature, consits of two covenants and one decree : that whenever any number of people, in a state of independence, are about to form themselves into a civil state—" here it will be necessary for all, each with the other, to join, in one lasting society ; and in particular, to concert the measures for their safety and welfare, by the public vote. Next it is necessary that a decree should be made, specifying what form of government shall be settled among them.—After this decree is past, to settle the form of government, there will then be occasion for a new covenant, when the person or persons, on whom the sovereignty is conferred, shall be appointed, by which the rulers on the one hand engage themselves to take care of the common peace and security, and the subjects on the other to yield them due obedience." *

---

* B. 7. Sec. 7—8.

Hobbes, although he admits the civil compact to be necessary in establishing a government, yet excludes Puffendorf's second covenant. He says, " the obligation to obey the supreme civil power, doth not arise immediately from that covenant, by which particular persons give up all their right to the state; but only mediately from hence, that without obedience, the right of sovereignty would have been vain, and insignificant, and of course no commonwealth could have been formed,"* that is, the sovereignty is not conferred by any act of the people.

Of the former author we may observe, that his two covenants and one decree savors more of the subtle schoolman than of the civil jurist ; and of the latter, that his civil compact is made a stepping stone by which the tyrant mounts the throne, and which is afterward to serve only for his foot-stool. It is sufficient for us to say, there are but two kinds of simple civil compacts. The one is between the people themselves, by which the whole government is settled,—as in the establishment of a pure democracy and the improved form derived from that, a government by representation ; and this we shall denominate a mutual compact. The other is a compact between the people on the one hand, and the ruling power on the other, whether that power be constituted of one or more persons,—and this we shall call a reciprocal compact. But a government formed on this compact, unless there be intervened an effectual provision to secure a faithful performance of the stipulations, as well on the part of the people, as of the rulers, will soon degenerate into anarchy on the one hand, or into despotism, a government of force, on the other ;—In either of which events all civil compact is annihilated. Such has, in all ages, been the fate of every government, the establishment of which has been attempted on this sole foundation.

From these two simple forms of civil compact has been derived a third kind, of a complex nature, partly mutual and partly reciprocal, in which a certain portion of the power has been retained and exercised by the people, another portion vested in a monarch, and a third portion in a body of nobles,

---

* De Cive. Ch. 5. Sec. 7—13.

thus forming three co-ordinate branches of the government, and providing, in a good degree, security against anarchy on the one side, and against the exercise of arbitrary power on the other.

It is doubtless true, that in the earliest stages of society no civil compact was ever formed by the deliberate act and express consent of any people. In such a state of things, every civil constitution has been the child of custom;—It seems not to have preceded some rules of civil conduct but to have been introduced with such rules, or for the sake of them.

The social compact, if it be proper to give that name to the mode, in which the social state is attained, has not its origin, although it may have its consummation, in the invention or deliberate act of man, but is imposed by nature, in the manner explained in a former chapter. In subsequent periods, however, there is often a deliberate act of choosing between two or more societies, already existing, or a preconcert of individuals to form a new and independent association. But whatever be the origin of the social state; it is impossible to conceive of any rights or duties, civil or moral, independent of that state, in a total seclusion of all social relations.

Mr. Paley, in his Elements of Political Knowledge, lays it down, that all governments were at first either patriarchal or military; that of a father of a family, or a military commander over his soldiers. This cannot be correct,—it cannot be conceived that in the primordial state of man, military government should have immediately succeeded the patriarchal.—Whether we admit the patriarchal among the forms of civil government or not, certainly, in the simple state of one only family existing, it was all that was necessary. But the first patriarchal government could continue no longer than the life of the first patriarch, or common progenitor. If any of the children of the first patriarch separated themselves from the family and settled into different regions, they might continue the patriarchal government each in his own family, but on the death of each patriarch, his descendants, who continued in the same society, were left without a common governor, and a complete and entire separation of all the families, as they came on the stage, cannot be imagined. In this way, however, we may suppose, and ancient tradition justifies the supposition, that numerous races and tribes were formed each on the death of its common progenitor, left in a state of independence, as far as relates to civil institutions, united by the social habits and affections only, which they had acquired while under the government of their common parent. It cannot, with any degree of probability, be supposed, that in this infant state of the human race, a state of conquest was effected, before or coeval with the transition from the patriarchal state of independent families, to that of nations and tribes, without which we cannot suppose the introduction of a military government.

This we may, then, consider as the primitive state, not of man, but of society, beyond the precincts of families ; of nations or rather of tribes,—that independent state of society with which political writers have commenced their speculations, and which must, at one time or another, have been the situation of every original people on the face of the earth. Authentic history does not, perhaps, reach back to this state of any nation, but the traditions of all concur in pointing us to its former existence.—In this situation, on the demise of the patriarch in any tribe, there is already an association, which consists of families, rather than individuals, each father acting for those of his immediate family ;—The people have become capable of sustaining the moral and social relations, few and simple indeed, pertaining to that state and of appreciating their results, so far as that state furnishes sufficient knowledge. Now if we do not suppose the civil state already commenced in such society, it is impossible, the people should long continue, without passing into that state. And a general conception of social rights and duties, with a general acknowledgment of them, among a people, is the first commencement of civil institutions. These rights and duties from common feelings, common experience and observation, are in a course of time, more and more developed, more comprehended, and more respected by the common sentiment, until at last they become fully consecrated by custom. It is natural to suppose, that the form of government adopted by a people, in the state just described, would be similar to the patriarchal government, which they had experienced, and of which alone they could be able to form a conception, and would be commenced, perhaps, by a tacit submission to an elder brother, who, from his age and experience, had acquired an influence over their minds during the life of their common parent. In the same mode there might be a succession of chiefs, for several generations ; but in process of time, the people, become more numerous and farther removed from the common stock, would naturally fall into some mode of election. Under such a government no restrictions, were probably, at first, imposed on the chief, whose power, or more properly influence was that of advice, rather than compulsion. This I apprehend to be the first simple form of civil government among an infant people. The next step is generally towards a democracy. The chief, seeing the strength of the community wholly in the people, seeks to strengthen himself by their approbation. In such a situation, the people compact in settlement, and being not very numerous and easily assembled, their resolutions thenceforward, become the rule or law of the state, whether they relate to the mode of convening the assemblies, to the election, powers, and duties of their chiefs, or the rights and duties of the citizens. But for want of records, they are remembered only as ancient usages, and considered binding as customs, not distinguished from those introduced by tacit consent,—the first mode of legislation with every infant people. All customs, that have generally obtained in any nation, whether they relate to the constitution, the formal mode of government, or to the civil conduct of the citizens, and whether they originate in formal resolutions of the people or in usages tacitly permitted until they have grown up into customs, derive their binding force from general assent ; and that to which the people have generally assented, whether that assent be expressly and formally given, andproved by records, or tacitly, and proved by general and uninterrupted usage, is equally a mutual agreement of the people, and is equally relied upon as such. A government so formed, whatever degree of improvement it may have attained, is a government founded in compact, and in that compact is founded the duty of civil obedience.

A confirmation of this theory of the origin of civil institutions, is found in the early governments of ancient Greece. In the first accounts of authentic history they are represented as pure democracy or partaking of that form, although their petty governments were frequently seized by tyrants, who were again sooner or later expelled. In the commonwealth of Athens, the democratic form appears to be of very high antiquity. The constitution and laws of this government, which before consisted of ancient usages, were revised first by Draco, and afterwards by Solon, and expressly confirmed by the people. These laws, as well the municipal laws as the laws of the constitution, for they made no distinction between them, were, by their political writers and statesmen, denominated compacts of the state. The government of Sparta, although it exhibited the singular phenomenon of two kings or chief magistrates, hereditary in two ancient families, was nevertheless a popular government. In this government, besides a senate there were five magistrates chosen by the people, who were called ephori, or supervisors, who in fact during their office exercised the principal authority, and had the power of calling the kings themselves to account for infractions of the laws, and of punishing them even with death; a power they sometimes exercised. All the original governments of Greece, settled in different parts of that country, in Asia Minor, in Italy, and Sicily, were generally formed after the model of one or the other of those two governments, but more generally after that of Athens, as being the most popular; and they continued those forms, although sometimes under foreign dominion, until they were swallowed up in the Roman empire. As a further confirmation, we find, that at the commencement of the Roman commonwealth, after the expulsion of the Tarquins, the states of ancient Italy were almost universally under popular forms of government. The people were, however, in these states, divided into two classes, the Plebeians, or common people, and the Patricians, or noble families, who in some states exercised the principal, in others the whole powers of government, under the form of an aristocracy.

Similar institutions prevailed among all of the nations of ancient Germany, down to the time of the emperor Vespasian. We are informed by Tacitus the historian of those times that in all the German nations, there were classes of nobles, whose rank was hereditary in their families. The chiefs and all subordinate magistrates, although taken from the noble families only, were elected by the people ; but these chiefs had very little power. They had not the power of punishing offences, that power was committed solely to the priests. All public concerns of smaller moment were decided in the council of the nobles ; but all matters of general importance, in the great council of the nation, consisting both of the nobles and the people. As there was among all these nations a general ignorance of letters, their civil institutions were to be found only in their several customs originating in usages confirmed by the tacit consent of the people. Were it necessary, modern examples might be adduced among the aboriginal tribes of the new world, and of some who have made far less advances in civil institutions, than most of the ancient German tribes. But enough have been adduced to satisfy this part of the subject. I will however after making a few observations on Mr. Paley's second kind of primitive government,—the military, and its derivatives in absolute government, produce, very briefly, an example of the rise, progress, and consummation of an institution in the third kind of civil compact, mentioned above—that of a mixed nature.

A military government has never been considered as a civil institution. In its origin it differs very little, except in its objects, from that government which we have supposed to succeed to the patriarchal, a voluntary but, generally, a temporary, submission to a military chief. It is no more, than that, entitled to be called a primitive government. When, in a course of time, war became an art and profession ; strict discipline and prompt obedience became indispensable. To effect this, an unlimited authority in the chief became equally indispensable. When wars were made for conquest, the conquered people were governed with the same unlimited authority. From this source have sprung all, or nearly all, the absolute governments that have appeared in the world. This government is properly denominated a government of force ; for such, in fact, is every absolute government. Mr. Locke has asserted that an absolute monarchy is inconsistent with civil society, and so is no form of civil government ;* and his reason for this opinion briefly is, that in case of an injury done by the prince to the subject, there is no known authority to which the subject can appeal for redress. This is certainly correct, and it applies to every shape of absolute government. The people or subject, and the monarch, are, in relation to each other in a state of nature. A compact between them is not in the nature of a civil compact ; but of a treaty between independent nations.—If upon this compact, a controversy arise between the parties, it is not to be decided by a reference to any civil rule or law, but by the law of nature and nations,—an appeal to the law of force. Such were, or such finally became, nearly all the governments established in every conquered country by the northern nation who subdued the Roman empire, when again the tide of conquest rolled back on the conquering nations, and expunged nearly every vestige of the civil compact from the code, and from the memory of almost every people in Europe.

The English, however, descended from the Saxons, an ancient German tribe, had retained and improved many of their ancient customs, and enjoyed a good degree of civil liberty under their monarchical government. In this situation it was their fate to be subjected by William the Norman, who, as a conqueror, assumed and exercised an unlimited sovereign power,—but having introduced the feudal system, parcelled out many of the confiscated lands of the English in feudal baronies to his Norman followers, and subjected most of the estates of the English nobles, who were spared to the same tenure, he thereby raised an order, who soon became a sacred estate in the kingdom. Under the successors of William, these noble feudatories claimed certain rights and privileges, which the king refused to allow. Exasperated by this refusal, the nobles or barons, as they were then generally called, among whom were many of the English nobility, who cherished a fondness for the liberties enjoyed under the former Saxon government, rose with their followers in arms, and compelled the king, who from his

---

*Locke on Government p. 116.

unpopularity was unable to meet them with an equal force, to allow the rights and privileges claimed, and to confirm them by a charter executed with great formality in the grand council of the nation, and ratified by the most solemn oaths. This charter not only confirmed the rights and privileges of the barons, but confirmed some very important privileges to the people. It was called the great charter, and has always been considered as the foundation of English liberty. But king John, who granted it, considered the concessions it contained, as so many restrictions of the inherent, inalienable, and indefeasible rights of the monarch, and therefore not binding, however solemnly ratified. Consequently he paid no regard to those concessions further than he was compelled by circumstances. The same charter was, in substance, several times renewed by succeeding monarchs, and by them repeatedly violated on the same plea,—the inalienable and indefeasible rights of the crown.

In those early times there were but two estates of the realm. The monarch was deemed the first estate, as lord paramount, who always sought to abridge the power of the barons, which interfered with what were then deemed the inherent prerogatives of the crown. The barons composed the second estate, who as zealously strove to support and extend the power and privileges of their order, by limiting or abridging the royal prerogative. Thence arose frequent feuds and civil wars, in which sometimes the barons, but more frequently the king, prevailed ; while the people, who had been oppressed by both, began now to be courted by one side and the other, to engage their support in these contests ; but they generally inclined to the king, who was most able to favor and protect them.* The barons had the privilege of not being taxed without the consent of their order, and taxes or subsidies, as they were then called, were granted to the king by the barons assembled in parliament, which then consisted of two branches, the king and the house of lords or barons.

Although the king, whether as a continuance or revival of

---

* Note, Distinction between the people and vassals.

the ancient Saxon polity in favor of the commons, had granted
to certain towns, cities, and districts the privilege of sending
representatives to parliament ; yet they sat and voted
promiscuously with the barons, and, being much a minority had
very little influence.   The lords having been permitted,
gradually to alienate their vast landed property, much of it fell
into the possesion of the wealthy commons.   As the people
under the favor of the monarch, rose in wealth and importance,
it was deemed proper that they should have the same privilege
as the nobles, of being taxed by their own consent only.   For
this purpose, the right of representation was considerably
extended, and ·the representatives of the people ·met by
thmselves, forming what has since been called the house of
commons, and no longer mingled with the barons in their
deliberations.   But further than granting subsidies they had no
direct voice in legislation.   They had the privilege of preferring
petitions for the redress of some grievance, or for the passage
of some law for the benefit of their constituents, which were
sometimes granted, and sometimes denied, by the king or the
barons in parliament, according to the nature of the subject,
and the order of proceedings in those times.   Thus the people,
by their representatives in the house of commons, became a
constituent, but subordinate order in the government.   By
degrees, the commons, favored by circumstances, rose in power
and importance, until they have long since, become a co-
ordinate, and in some instances a paramount branch of the
legislature, and a third estate of the kingdom.

   Thus constituted, the legislature have the power both of
civil and political legislation ; the power of altering, amending,
and explaining every part of the constitution.   This power has
been often exercised and fully confirmed.   But to the validity
of every act and law, civil and political, the separate assent of
the three estates is necessary ; as well of the people by their
representatives in the house of commons, as of the king and
the house of lords.   By this authority, the mutual assent of the
three estates, and however it commenced, and which for a long
time was known only in their customs, that government has
been brought to its present form.   Many of the ancient
customs have been abrogated, changed, or modified ;—some

have been suffered to remain entire, and many new articles
have been added, to adapt it to modern times and modern
improvements. All these acts by which that constitution, has
been altered, amended, and confirmed by competent authority,
in their very nature, constitute the civil compact of that state,—
a compact of the mixed kind, mutual as between the people
themselves, and reciprocal as between the people and the
other branches of the government, the king and the house of
lords.

If, however, the opinion of Mr. Paley be correct, all our
speculations upon this subject are vain and elusory. He wholly
rejects the notion of a civil compact in the establishment of
government.—He denies that any such compact was ever
made, or if made, an adherence to it could be practicable in any
form of government; and that it can afford no ground of
obligation to civil obedience. This is a matter of great
importance to the people of these states, as they have ever
believed their civil institutions to be founded on the civil
compact, and that in this compact is found the obligation, the
measure, and limits of civil obedience ; and as the Treatise on
Moral Philosophy, and the Elements of Political Knowledge, in
which this opinion is maintained, is considered a classical work
of high authority, and is put into the hands of our youth in
most or all of our colleges and universities, I shall examine
that opinion with all the attention and candor which it merits,
as coming from such an author.

In the second part of his work, which he entitles, " Elements
of Political Knowledge," he undertakes to refute the opinion
of those writers, who have laid the foundation of all legitimate
government in the civil compact. To this refutation he has
devoted the third chapter in which he undertakes to explain
the duty of civil obedience upon a different principle. He tells
us, that " In order to prove civil obedience to be a moral duty,
and an obligation upon conscience, it has been usual with many
political writers, at the head of whom we find the venerable
name of Locke, to state a compact between the citizens and
the state, as the ground, and cause of the relation between
them ; which compact, binding the parties for the same general
reason, that private contracts do, resolves the duty of submission

to civil government, into the universal obligation of fidelity in the performance of promises. This compact is two fold,— first, an express compact, by the primitive founders of the state; who are supposed to have convened for the express purpose of settling the terms of their political union and a future constitution of government. The whole body is supposed in the first place to be bound by the resolutions of the majority;—in the next place to have fixed certain fundamental regulations, and then to have constituted, either in one person or an assembly, (the rule of succession, or appointment being at the same time determined,) a standing legislature, to whom under these established restrictions, the government of the state was thenceforward committed, and whose laws the several members of the convention were, by their first undertaking, personally engaged to obey. This transaction is sometimes called the social compact, and these supposed original regulations compose what are meant by the constitution, the fundamental laws of the constitution; and form on the one side, the inherent, indefeasible prerogatives of the crown, and on the other, the inalienable, imprescriptible birthright of the subject,—secondly, a tacit or implied compact by all succeeding members of the state, who by accepting its protection, consent to be bound by its laws, in like manner, as whosoever enters into a private society is understood without more explicit stipulation to promise a conformity with the rules and obedience to the government of that society, as the known conditions upon which he is admitted to a participation of its privileges." "This account" he says "labors under the following objections,—that it is false in fact, and leading to dangerous conclusions. No social compact such as here described, was ever made and entered into in reality. No such original convention of the people was ever actually holden, or in any country could be holden, antecedent to the existence of civil government in that country. It is to suppose it possible to call savages out of caves and deserts, to vote and deliberate on topics which the experience, and studies, and refinements of civilized life alone suggest."

It will be observed that the compact here stated is what I have called the reciprocal compact between the people on one side, and the person or persons appointed to exercise the powers of government on the other, and who are supposed to have a property in the government, and rights distinct from the people.. This form, unless the mutual compact be intervened, as an effectual guaranty between the parties, degenerates in the instant of its formation into absolute monarchy, which annihilates all civil compacts. Were this all, however the author may have mistaken the true ground of his objection, I would not throw away a word on the subject, but he proceeds either in terms or by direct inference, to deny the possible existence of any social or civil compact, and to condemn the principle as impracticable in its operation, and dangerous in its consequences to any government.

For my part, I never understood those writers to whom he refers, to suppose that an express compact was ever formed by the primitive founders of any government in the first ages of the world, or by any infant people. They considered that a compact formed by the tacit consent, and confirmed by the usages of a people, had as real an existence and was as obligatory on the parties, as though it had been committed to writing, and unanimously confirmed by a convention of the people assembled for that express purpose. Those writers were also sufficiently acquainted with history to know, what the author himself well knew, that governments had been remodelled and reformed, new articles added, old articles retrenched, altered, and amended by the people themselves, or by their authorised agents, and to these solemn acts so confirmed, they gave the name of state compacts, what they purported to be, and in fact were.

The author proceeds,—" Some imitations of a social compact may have taken place at a revolution.—The present age has been witness to a transaction that bears the nearest resemblance to that idea of any, of which history has preserved the account. I refer to the establishment of the United States of North America.—We saw the people assembled to elect deputies, for the avowed purpose of framing a constitution for a new empire; we saw these deputies of the people deliberating and resolving upon a form of government, erecting a permanent legislature, distributing the functions of sovereignty, establishing and promulgating a code of fundamental ordinances, which were to be considered by succeeding generations, not merely as laws and acts of the state, but as the very terms and conditions of the confederation ; as binding not only upon the subjects and magistrates of the state, but as limitations of power, which were to control and regulate the future legislature. Yet here much was pre-supposed.—In settling the constitution much was presumed to be already settled. The constituents who were permitted to vote in the elections of members of congress as well as the mode of electing the representatives were taken from the old forms of government."

It is indeed, an article of that constitution, settled and agreed, that " the house of representatives shall consist of members, chosen every second year by the people of the several states, and the electors in each state shall have the qualifications requisite for electors of the most numerous branch of the state legislature. According to our author, then, if the parties making a contract, borrow the form or expressions of any known instrument, or by special reference adopt an article from such instrument, with whatever solemnity they may execute the act, it cannot have the force, although it may have the nearest resemblance to a contract ;—one is astonished at such an argument from such a source.

He-tells us further, that in forming the constitution, "that was wanting from which every social union should set off, and which alone makes the act of the society the act of the individual, the unconstrained consent of all to be bound by the decision of the majority ; and yet, without this previous consent, the revolt and the regulations which followed were compulsory upon dissentients."

The inference intended to be drawn is, that because at the commencement of the revolution, the votes of the majority were made compulsory on a dissenting minority. The United States, notwithstanding the subsequent acknowledgment of their independence by the mother country, and by the world, never have, and never can make a valid civil compact. This by itself needs no answer.—But the principle, from which the author sets off merits a discussion. And let it be observed, that no question is here made of the right of the majority to resist the measures of the British government, or of their right to final independence. All this is, in the argument, taken for granted.

First then, suppose a number of men, in what is called a state of nature, collected together, and a large majority of them agreeing to unite in a civil society,—a few dissent, and retain each his independent state. What will be the situation of such dissenting individuals in relation to that society? Certainly the society and the dissenting individuals are to each other in a state of nature, a state of independence, the same as independent nations,—each party is the judge in its own cause, and the avenger of its own wrongs. Suppose any dissentient to remain in the midst of the society and to commit an act of violence on the person or property of one of the members. Considered as independent, he has committed an act of hostility against the society, which is bound to protect its members; the society have, therefore, against the aggressor a right of war, the same as though the aggression had been made by an independent nation; but instead of treating him as a public enemy, they adopt a milder course,—give him the chance of a trial as though he were a member of the community, and sentence him according to their own laws to make reparation. No one will say, this is a usurpation, but a mitigation of the right; and such is indeed the law practised among all civilized nations.

Again, suppose a society formed, and about to decide on a measure, but no rule has been adopted or suggested, what number or proportion of voices should constitute a binding vote, whether a majority; or whether a unanimity should be required; what would be the decision of natural justice, of the law of nature, in the case? This at once involves the question, what is expedient? what will best promote the general interest of the community? As a general rule, the major interest of the community must be supposed to be contained in that of a majority of its members. Now if a greater proportion, as two thirds, or three fourths, or even unanimity, be required, it will often be in the power of a small minority, representing a minor and sometimes, insignificant interest, down to a single voter, to prevent the adoption of measures necessary to promote and secure the general interest;

and to hold the society in a state of inaction frequently no less ruinous than a course of the most pernicious action. It is, therefore, a general rule, agreeable to the law of nature, founded in general utility, that a majority of votes shall be binding on the whole community. I say, as a general rule, for there may be cases in which the necessity or expediency of a greater unanimity outweighs the inconvenience of a different rule.

But there is still a further view of this subject. An association was formed in the colonies, by an overwhelming majority of the inhabitants, to oppose the measures of the British government. Of the right of this association there is now no question. The British government sent an armed force to put down that resistance, which they considered a rebellion, and which produced a civil war between that government and the associated colonies, who assumed and maintained a state of independence. What was then the situation of the dissentients in relation to the colonies, now states, engaged in war? The dissentients did not claim the situation of independent individuals.—They claimed to continue subjects of Great Britain, to owe allegiance to that government, and thus identified themselves with the enemy actually at war. They considered themselves, by their allegiance, bound in conscience to aid that government by all means in their power, to crush the rebellion, as they deemed the war on the part of the colonies. Their situation was, therefore, very peculiar; if suffered to depart, they might add to the force,—if suffered to depart with their property, they would add to the means—of the enemy.—If suffered to remain they might serve as spies and join the hostile forces, in incursions into their country. Under these circumstances, some were suffered to depart; others fled to the enemy, and their estates were confiscated; some, who were considered too dangerous to be permitted their liberty, were imprisoned;—some few, for unequivocal acts of hostility, while remaining in the country, suffered death as traitors:— some were confined to certain limits under strict surveillance;— others, on assurance given, or from the confidence which their neighbors reposed in them, that they would do nothing to the injury of the country, were suffered to remain at large. Most of those who were suffered to remain in the country till the peace, cordially united themselves to the new government, proved valuable citizens and in not a few instances,—eminent statesmen. In this line of conduct the states were justified by the laws of necessity, the laws of war, the laws of nature, and the usages of all civilized nations.

To the argument that has been commonly urged in support of the civil compact, that " as the first members were bound, by express stipulation, to obey the government which they had erected, so the succeeding inhabitants of the same country are understood to promise allegiance to the constitution and government, they find established, by accepting its protection, claiming its privileges, and acquiescing in its laws ; more especially by the purchase and inheritance of lands, to the possession of which allegiance is annexed as the very service and condition of the tenure," he says,—" Smooth as this train of argument proceeds, little will it endure examination. The native subjects of modern states are not conscious of any stipulations with the sovereigns, of ever exercising an election whether they will be bound or not by the acts of the legislature, of any alternative being proposed to their choice, of a promise ever required or given ; nor do they apprehend that the authority of the laws, depends at all upon their recognition or consent. In all stipulations, whether they be express or implied, public or private, formal or constructive, the parties stipulating must both possess the liberty of assent and refusal, and also be conscious of this liberty, which cannot with truth be affirmed of the subjects of civil government, as government now is or ever was actually administered. This is a defect which no argument can excuse or supply ; all presumptions of consent, without this consciousness or in oppression to it, are vain or erroneous. Still less is it possible to reconcile with any idea of stipulation, the practice in which all European nations agree of founding allegiance on the circumstances of nativity, that is, of claiming and treating as subjects all those who are born within the limits of their dominions, although removed to another country in their youth or infancy."

I am not concerned to prove, that there exists any election under a government of force, a despotic government, where the subject is allowed to have no will, all is absorbed in the will of the prince, whose maxim, as well expressed by the Roman satirist, is "Hoc volo; sic jubeo; sit pro ratione voluntas." Nor can I allow that the practice of the modern governments of Europe, or any opinion derived from that practice, does in reality affect the question,—such opinion is the mere echo of the divine, hereditary, and indefeasible right of sovereigns, connected with the ancient state of vassalage;—it is the legitimate offspring of that government, and of that state, and has in many instances survived its parents. It was unknown to the ancient commonwealths of Greece,—it was unknown to the Roman republic;—nor do we find any vestige of it among the ancient Gauls or Germans. All that is necessary to prove is, that in every state, in which the constitution, however established, is sufficient in its provisions to secure the enjoyment of civil liberty, of civil rights, the acession of the citizens as they succeed in civil life, is a voluntary act to lay them under both a civil and moral obligation to obey all the laws and regulations of the government, made agreeable to that constitution. I know, it has often been asserted that no generation can, by any law or compact, bind the succeeding generation. It is true, that the succeeding generation cannot be bound by any act of their predecessors, by the direct force of that act. Each individual is bound by his own voluntary act as he succeeds on the political stage. In civil life men do not succeed by generations—one generation passing off the stage, to make room for another. Nor do individuals become members, in any proper sense, by succession, but by accession;—they accede to the compact, and this I will show, is a voluntary act binding them to obedience.

The accession is of citizens born in the state, and under the protection of its laws. The progress of children in the acquisition of knowledge, is not made at first, by the exertion of intellect, but by imitation. They imitate the actions of those whom they most love, their parents and tutors. They imitate, or what to them is the same thing, learn their opinions; these they adopt without examination, of which they are incapable in early youth; and often retain them through life without attempting to examine, whether they are well founded or not.

It is hardly possible to conceive, that the opinions they imbibe under such circumstances and under such a government, should not be highly in favor of the country of their birth and education, and of its institutions. The youth come forward with an ardent desire of becoming members of the state, of enjoying the rights and privileges it secures, of fulfilling the duties it requires, and of meriting its honors; and besides, they have been taught that they have a right to all this; that they derive that right from their birth and parentage, and that the country requires these things of them. And so is the truth; for one great end of the institution which the framers had constantly in view, was to secure its rights and privileges to their children, and children's children, if possible, through all generations; and these rights and privileges, civil and political, are capable of communication and transmission no less than other rights, and hereditaments corporeal and incorporeal. The children come forward conscious of their rights and their duties;—they are conscious of a desire to be admitted to the exercise of those rights, and the performance of those duties; nor does the idea of compulsion enter their minds; so far from it, that to be deprived of what they esteem so great a privilege, would be felt as a grievous act of oppression.

Under such circumstances, are they not conscious that their accession, or if that term displease, their adhesion to the compact, the constitution of the state is a free and voluntary act? It is—if any can be such, where predilections are formed, a voluntary, a moral act, sufficient to bind the party. The author himself, would admit it to be a binding act, in any government founded on compact, and actually existing on that foundation. Such, clearly is the government of these United States, and of all the republican governments, lately established throughout almost the whole of that vast region extending from the confines of the United States to the southern extremity of the American continent, notwithstanding the author, from a predilection for what he deems a new principle, but which in fact is little other than the divine right of sovereigns, in a new and more fashionable dress, has been induced to deny the validity and even possible existence of such compact.

So far, I have followed the author on his own statement;

but his statement is not full and correct. It is true that the European governments generally, if not universally, agree, in founding allegiance on the circumstance of nativity; yet, there is not a nation I believe, who do not in practice permit, and some have encouraged the emigration of their subjects.; nor are there any who do not, as a general practice, permit emigrants from other states to reside among them, where they, on certain conditions, may obtain the rights of native subjects, at least, so far as relates to the protection of life, liberty, and property, and where the claim of native allegiance cannot reach them; so that in general any one has his election, whether he will continue in obedience to his native government, or emigrate elsewhere. For, as it has been observed, he cannot, by the laws of nature, continue within the jurisdiction of an established government without being amenable to its laws. Thus stated I think the author would not have ventured the same conclusion.

To the position that the taking and holding of land amounts to an acknowledgment of the sovereign, and a virtual promise of allegiance to his laws, he replies, " It is necessary to the validity of this argument, to prove that the inhabitants, who first composed and constituted the state, collectively posessed a right to the country; a right to parcel it out to whom they pleased, and to annex to the donation what conditions they saw fit." Could these objections be removed, and the possessor's title firmly established, the author seems ready to acknowledge the force of the argument; and fortunately he has done this for us. In treating of the right of property in land he says,— " The real foundation of our right is in the law of the land," and concludes, " Hence it appears, that my right to an estate does not at all depend on the manner or the justice of the original acquisition, nor upon the justice of each subsequent change of possession. It is not, for instance, the less, nor ought it to be impeached, because the estate was taken possession of by a family of aboriginal Britons, who happened to be stronger than their neighbors; nor because the British possessor was turned out by a Roman, and the Roman by a Saxon invader; nor because it was seized without color of right by the Norman adventurer, from whom, after many interruptions of fraud and violence, it has at last devolved on me." It is probable the author, when he wrote this, had not matured his theory of submission to civil government ; but certainly, on a revision, he ought for his own credit, to have expunged one passage or the other.

The author next proceeds to state several conclusions, which, in his opinion, follow from the theory of the civil compact, unfavorable to the improvement and to the peace of human society. The first conclusion is, in substance, that on supposition of the constitution having been settled by a compact, formed by the people, there will be fundamental points with which the legislature cannot interfere, and which they have no power to alter. " This serves to embarrass the legislature, and affords dangerous pretences for disputing the authority of the laws ;— it was this kind of reasoning,—so far as any kind of reasoning was made use of in the question—that produced in this (the English) nation, the doubts which so much agitated the minds of men, in the reign of the second Charles whether an act of parliament could alter or limit the succession of the crown." This cannot with propriety be applied to the British government, where the legislature, of which the people by their representatives form a constituent and co-ordinate branch, have at all times, as now, acknowledged the right and power to amend, alter, and expound the constitution in all its parts ; and surely, the author could not but know that the doubt which so much agitated the minds of men in the reign of the second Charles was not entertained by those who supported the principles of the civil compact, but by those, who were no less opposed to those principles than the author himself, and who maintained that the monarch derived his power from God alone, by a right hereditable and indefeasible, beyond the reach of human laws.

Secondly. That " if by virtue of that"—the civil compact,— " the subject owes obedience to civil government, it will follow that he ought to abide by the form of government which he finds established, be it ever so absurd or inconvenient. It is not permitted to any man to retract from his engagements, merely because he finds the performance disadvantageous, or because he has an opportunity of entering into a better. This law of contracts is universal. Resistance to the encroachments of the supreme magistrate may be justified upon this principle ; recourse to arms, for the purpose of bringing about an amendment of the constitution, never can. Nor can it be ever necessary, justifiable, or desirable, under such a government as that of England at present ; that of the United States, or any other government formed upon natural principles, where the people have either the sole right, or an equal right and voice in proposing and adopting all such alterations and amendments of their civil constitution, as shall be found most for the public good. As to what follows,—that "no government contains a provision for its own dissolution," and that "few governments will consent to an extinction or an abridgment of their own power ; it does not therefore appear how a despotic government can ever be altered or mitigated," the reply is, that a despotic government is a government of force and not of compact ; it is, therefore, wholly out of the question.

The third conclusion is, that "Every violation on the part of the governor, releases the subject from his allegiance, and dissolves the government." This is true of an absolute government, where if we suppose any compact to exist, it is in the nature of a treaty between independent nations, where each party is a judge in its own case, and the appeal is to the law of force ; but in a state which has a constitution containing effectual provisions for enforcing a compliance with the compact, a breach of any stipulation on the part of the ruler, neither releases the people from their allegiance, or dissolves the government.

It is a universal law of contracts that forfeitures be considered as odious,—that they be never admitted unless they are inserted in the agreement, or are necessary to effectuate the clear intention of the parties. The law of all contracts, that is, the rule of construction and the effect to be given, is to be collected from the nature of the subject, the situation and apparent intent of the parties, with a constant view to general utility, or to use the language of our author, general expediency. Rules are formed for classes of cases connected by analogy ; and the rule of any class applies to a particular case so far only, as the case comes within the analogy of that class. Civil compacts in the formation of governments, differing in many respects from all private contracts, form a different and distinct class, and so far demand different rules of construction ; this is founded in the highest practical utility. In the government of the United States, no delinquency, no violation of stipulations can, from any analogy, be construed to affect the compact, the constitution, however it may affect the delinquent functionary.

Agreeable to this principle, was the decision in the English parliament, and in the Scotch parliament in the reign of the second James. The English parliament held, as has been holden by all the most eminent political writers of that nation, except Mr. Paley, that their government was founded in the principle of the civil compact, and accordingly expressed their decision in the following words. " Whereas James II. having endeavored to subvert the constitution of this kingdom, by breaking the original compact between the king and the people, and by the advice of Jesuits and other wicked persons, having violated the fundamental laws, and having withdrawn himself from the kingdom has abdicated the government, and the throne has thereby become vacant."

The English parliament did not declare in words, that James had forfeited the crown, but substituted the expression, that he had abdicated government, in compliance with the tories, who then composed a majority of the house of lords, who could not admit that a king, vested with a divine right, could forfeit that right to mortals ; but would finally agree that he might abdicate the right, for which were to be found several royal precedents.

The parliament of Scotland made nearly the same declaration, excepting that they omitted the violation of a compact, and concluded with these remarkable words, " whereby he hath forefaulted the crown, and the throne has become vacant,"—and thereupon both parliaments proceeded to settle the crown on the prince and princess of Orange. Thus the author stands confuted in all his arguments against the civil, or, as he often calls it, the social compact, as well on the fairest principles of reason, as upon facts and precedents of unquestionable authority.

He proceeds, however, to substitute in its place, which he now considers vacant, his new principle of civil obedience, which he thus introduces : " Wherefore, rejecting the intervention of

a compact as unfounded in its principle, and dangerous in its
application, we assign as the only ground of the subject's
obligation,—the will of God, as collected from experience."
Then follows his argument. "The steps by which the argument proceeds are few and direct. It is the will of God that the
happiness of human life be promoted. This is the first step and
the foundation, not only of this, but of every moral conclusion.
Civil society conduces to this end. This is the second proposition. Civil societies cannot be upholden unless in each, the
interest of the whole society be binding on every part and
member of it. This is the third step, and conducts us to the
conclusion, namely, that so long as the interest of the whole
society requires it, that is, so long as the established government
cannot be resisted or changed without public inconvenience, it
is the will of God—which will, universally determines our
duty, that the established government be obeyed and no
longer."

In reading this passage with all possible attention, I am
compelled to say with Shakspeare

> I see before me neither here, nor there,
> Nor what ensues ; but have a fog in ken,
> That I cannot see through—

It is a universal rule of human action, that men are to obey the
will of God ; and with this accords the author's first proposition.
His following propositions and the conclusion are of a very
general nature, although less so than the first proposition, and
are consequent to each other, but not immediately, and finally
conduct us to no tangible rule of acting or judging. A universal
rule is not, by itself tangible, its use is to serve as a test of
general rules, and of general rules to serve as a test of specific
rules, which alone come in immediate contact with the conduct
and action of human life. It is the same with propositions.
A series of propositions, commencing with a universal, and
descending to one or more that are general, and thence drawing
the conclusion, omitting the the specific proposition applicable
to the specific class of actions to which it is intended to conclude,
is of little or no practical utility. An action is relatively good
or bad, right or wrong. The quality of the action depends on

the relation which the agent sustains to the subject. The rule
of conduct with a view to immediate action must be applicable
to that specific class of actions, to which the act required
pertains, and which cannot without modification be applied to
any other class. By attending to this in forming a system of
morals, the specific rules, the most numerous class, are approved
and adopted by the preceding general rules diminishing in
number, and these again, by the universal rule, thus preserving
the harmony of the system, and constantly directing the whole
to the one great and important end.

A neglect of this, and perhaps a fondness for considering action
in the abstract only, has thrown a degree of obscurity over
the author's whole Treatise on Morals, and in his second part,
the Elements of Political Knowledge, has led to some gross
errors. Thus in the passage before us, the propositions, and
the conclusion are floating above, and the medium of immediate
communication with human conduct, wholly omitted. He
seems not to have in his view of the subject, considered that
civil institutions are the device of man influenced, sometimes,
by high passions, appetites, propensities, and necessities, and
sometimes by reason and experience ; that those institutions
are founded in different principles, establishing different rules
and different limits of the authority and obedience ; in some
more, in others less precise ; that they employ different means
and different modes for promoting the general interest. •But for
any thing in the propositions contained in his argument, we
might suppose every civil institution to be a spontaneous
production of nature,—that from this spontaneously flows the
interest of the whole, and of the parts, composing that whole ;
and thence through the same spontaneity springs the duty of
passive obedience and non-resistance. His conclusion, however,
denies this last consequence, and he admits that resistance to
government may become lawful, and even a duty. But he
seems not to suppose, at least, he no where suggests, that the
principles of a government may vary or diminish the justifiable
causes of resistance, or afford any other rule of decision in
the case, than the vague opinion of public expedience, floating
in the mind of each individual.

Now, although different governments may contain no

subordinate principles, which when considered in themselves, are not embraced in the general principle, which aims at human happiness through civil institutions, yet some may contain more, and some less of those subordinate principles, and may in their construction, so harmonize and identify the interest of the whole with the interests of the several parts and render the union so evident and palpable, as greatly to diminish, or wholly supersede all causes that might lead to a justifiable resistance. In a government constituted and administered agreeable to such principles, the liberty of resistance will rarely be admitted, or the duty exist. And in a despotic government, especially an ancient despotism, the liberty of resistance can rarely serve to any other purpose than indiscriminate and atrocious vengeance. If the people, by some more outrageous act of oppression, are roused to resistance, they generally avenge themselves by a massacre of the tyrant and his instruments; but having forgotten or never known any other form of government, they elevate some other person to the same dignity, whom they at once suppose vested with the same unlimited power, the same, to them, sacred rights. They trust to the character of the new sovereign, and never think it either necessary or possible, to provide any security against the same tyrannical acts. In these cases, public expedience is very rarely the object, and still more rarely is a melioration, the issue of such resistance. The principles which we have here advocated, are not the mere visions of philosophy, to be realized only in the closet. They have been realized and cherished by nations whose civil institutions, while they have excited the jealousy of some and the envy of others, have commanded the admiration of all.

I will conclude with two examples by way of illustration, and shall hope to be pardoned, if, for the sake of a more full illustration, I should indulge in some repetitions. The first I shall adduce, is a government of the mixed kind, founded partly on the mutual, and partly on the reciprocal compact. Such is the government of Great Britain or the English constitution. Of the three co-ordinate branches that compose the legislature or great council of the nation, the people by their representatives in the house of commons constitute one equal, and in some nstances, paramount branch ; for they claim the sole right of proposing taxes, and an equal voice in all appropriations. As far as it relates to this branch, the government is founded on the mutual compact—the mutual assent of the people. Between the popular branch and the two others, the house of lords who hold their seats by hereditary rights and enjoy certain privileges independent of the people, and the king whose power is also hereditary and who constitutes one branch of the legislature, with the power of a negative, is the sole executive of the nation, and vested with certain prerogatives, of which one is to be personally accountable to no one for his acts, the compact is reciprocal, as being between different parties. Still it is a fixed principle of the constitution, that both the king and the peers hold their powers in trust for the nation, and that these powers may be modified, limited, or changed by the full consent of the three estates in parliament. Not only the people, but the king and the peers are bound by all constitutional acts of the legislature ; and as the legislature so composed, have also the power of political legislation, the power of altering and amending by their acts, the constitution itself, or the civil compact of the state, although they may pass an improvident act, they cannot pass an unconstitutional law ; because the people, by their representatives, and the king and the lords for themselves give their assent to every alteration and amendment of the constitution, whether contained expressly in an act intended for that purpose, or incidentally in any other act of legislation. In this, which is a practical view of the subject, no resistance can be justly made to any act of the legislature. It is indeed possible, but in the present improved state of knowledge, of the government, and of public opinion, there is little probability, that the king, the peers, or both combined, by an assumption of unconstitutional powers, should render resistance a necessary or justifiable act. And in that case the resistance would not be to the government, but to a functionary or functionaries, who might be removed and replaced with a better or in a better manner ; for if taken as a forfeiture, it extends to the functionary only, and no more effects a dissolution of government than the removal of a minister. The second part or parts have still a sufficient power to apply the proper remedy. Of this, that government has furnished a precedent of the highest authority in those acts which excluded the second James, and elevated the prince and princess of Orange to the throne of the kingdom.

The second example is found in the government of the United States. This government is founded on the mutual compact, an agreement among the people themselves, to form a constitution, which they should by their own engagement be bound to support, and to observe and obey all laws and regulations to be made pursuant to the powers instituted in that constitution. It is a representative government, and all the functionaries are elected, and appointed mediately or immediately by the people, and periodically accountable to them through that medium. The constitution contains limitations of the powers entrusted to the several organs sufficiently specific to afford a fair ground of decision whether these powers shall, in any instance, have been exceeded or abused ; and a tribunal sufficiently independent, and yet sufficiently accountable to decide on the constitutionality of every act, which shall be called in question in any cause before them. If the act be adjudged unconstitutional, it is void. If it be a legislative act, the legislators are accountable to the people through the medium of elections. If it be an executive act, in addition to the avoidance of the act, and the accountability of the officer in the same manner, he is farther liable to removal by impeachment and disqualification for office, to a reparation in damages, and as the case may be, to prosecution and punishment at law for the offence. There is also ample provision in the constitution for such alterations and amendments as shall from time to time be found necessary and expedient, to be made by the people, the original source of power, and the only parties to the compact, in the mode prescribed either by their representatives in their state conventions called for that purpose, or by their representatives in the state legislatures, to whom proposals of amendment, which must be specific, are to be referred. Here all by their own free consent, through which the author's universal principle of obligation is brought down, and placed in immediate communication with human action, are solemnly bound to support the constitution, and support and obey every constitutional act of the government.

It seems therefore impossible to conceive, that with the people, and the people includes every class and grade in the community, under this constitution there ever can arise a justifiable cause for resisting the government.

The precedent and example of our own government would alone have been a sufficient refutation of the author's opinion of the nullity of any civil compact in the establishment of civil institutions, of its impracticability and the dangerous consequences of admitting its principles as a ground of civil union and civil obedience. But I wished also to adduce the example of the British government for several reasons; among others to show how a man of the first reputation for talents and integrity, may be blinded by a favorite theory of which he considers himself to be the author, or has undertaken to be the champion. In no other way, can we account how such a man, fully acquainted with the political writings of those authors who are still the pride of his nation, with the general opinion of his countrymen, with the theory, practice, public acts, and declarations of his government, should have rejected the true and acknowledged principles of that government, and substituted, in their stead, an abstractprin ciple, to the mass of mankind neither visible, nor tangible, and which is rarely, if ever, the immediate motive to action ; thus cutting asunder the strongest ligament of society, the only legitimate bond of union, in the mutual and voluntary assent of its members ; and leaving, without any obligation, voluntarily contracted, every member under the guidance of this principle, so evanescent in practice, and without the intervention of a common judge, to determine the expediency and measure of obedience, and the expediency, time, and measure of resistance, a situation only to be found in a despotic government.

It is true the author wrote at a time when wild and extravagant opinions of civil liberty, or rather political liberty, and the social compact, were beginning to be broached in Europe, which afterwards drove the people of the continent to madness, and made many proselytes in his own country. Probably, the disgust, which he conceived, from the accidental abuse of a good principle, led him, as is too often the case, to declare war against the principle itself, and prevented him from seeing and acknowledging that from this exploded principle, his government were enabled to put down all opposition, and to stand erect amidst that political tempest which prostrated some of the most powerful governments of the old world, and shook others from their base. He did not indeed, live to witness the event, but from the energy of this same principle, his nation rose superior to every danger, maintained their honor and independence against a world in arms, finally triumphed gloriously in the contest, and were hailed the liberators of Europe.

I was also desirous of exhibiting the source, whence we have derived the principles of our government, the popular branch of the English constitution; principles which that nation had found the means of inserting into the foundation of their ancient edifice, and, removing some of the decaying, unsightly, and cumbrous parts, have, on this foundation, in connexion with what remained of the old, raised a magnificent structure, uniting in a good degree, the symmetry, convenience, and beauty of modern architecture, with the venerable grandeur of the ancient, while we upon the same principles, on a foundation more broad, uniform, and solid, have raised an edifice, which if not equally venerable for its antiquity, equally gorgeous and magnificent, yet as we pride ourselves, uniting more symmetry, convenience, and beauty, and less exposed to the shock of political tempests. On the whole, it belongs to both nations, and surely not least to the people of these states to indulge a noble pride, that these principles are making advances in the old world, and in the new, have broken the chains of despotism riveted for ages, have diffused, and are diffusing the blessings of freedom and free institutions throughout one quarter of the globe, the whole continent of America; and to cherish the generous hope that they are destined one day to meliorate the condition of the whole human race.

CHAPTER II.

Of Sovereignty.

By sovereignty is commonly understood supremacy, supreme power, unlimited and uncontrolled. We find, however, that it is used with considerable latitude, in its various applications. When applied to states and nations, in relation to each other, it means nothing more than independence. A sovereign state, in a political sense, is a state or nation in the free and uncontrolled possession of self government; the right of making war and of entering into treaties of amity, alliance, and commerce with other nations, as it shall judge most to promote its own interest. In this application of the term there is no idea of supremacy, but simply that of national independence. such is the meaning of the term when applied to nations as it respects their external relations. It has no reference to their natural powers, or physical force. These may be unequal in the extreme, and yet each remain equally sovereign, equally independent. But when applied to the internal government of a state, it is made to signify a power somewhere vested, competent to regulate, control, and direct the will of the whole and of every subordinate member of the community. To this end, it is supposed to be absolute, unlimited, and incapable of being put under any control.

Various have been the opinions concerning this internal right of sovereignty, and its attributes, and where it can, or ought to be vested. It was long maintained almost universally, throughout the old world, that sovereignty was conferred on kings, and independent princes, by the immediate act of God;

or as it was sometimes expressed,—God transcribes in kings
the right of governing, which he held by virtue of creation.
It was holden, that the sovereignty does not vest in the
monarch by the election of the people, by succession, conquest,
or any kind of occupation of the government, and that election,
succession, conquest, or occupation, cannot be admitted as
secondary causes. They are to be considered as occasions
only, on which God by his immediate act confers the sovereignty
on the prince ; that on a vacancy of the throne, it returned to
the original source, to be again conferred on the immediate
successor. If the succession was broken or contested, it waited
the event to be again conferred on the successful candidate.
But it finally came to be considered the orthodox opinion, that
the sovereignty once conferred on the reigning prince was
thenceforth hereditary, and the right indefeasible, and thus,
on the death of the reigning prince, it passed by a sort of
metempsychosis, and vested eo instante in his lawful heir.
Still it was held that republican governments whether in form
democratic or aristocratic, were incapable of this divine gift,
and were not entitled to the appellation of sovereignty, or
majesty.

Grotius and Puffendorf were the first writers of any note on
the continent of Europe, who called in question this source of the
divine right of sovereignty, and derived it from the civil compact.
Puffendorf speaking of the civil compact, which he here calls
a covenant, says,—" so likewise the same covenant affords a
full and easy title, by which the aforesaid sovereignty appears
established, not by violence, but in a lawful manner, by the
voluntary consent and subjection of the respective members.
This then is the nearest and immediate cause, from which
sovereignty, as a moral quality, doth result."* Yet, such is the
force of association and early habits, he still adheres to
the divine right. At the close of the same section he says,—
" Yet, to secure to the supreme command an especial efficacy
and sacred respect, there is need of another additional principle, besides the submission of the subjects ; and therefore

---

* Puffendorf, B. 7. Sec. 2.

he who affirms sovereignty to result immediately from compact, doth not in the least detract from the sacred character of civil government, or maintain that princes bear rule by human right, and not by divine." Such divine right he undertakes to prove in the next section. The substance of his argument is, that the establishment of civil government is necessary for the peace and safety of men; that the laws of nature dictate such establishments;—that in pursuance of these laws, which could not otherwise among great multitudes be carried into effect, civil governments have been formed, that God who imposed the laws of nature on the human race, thereby commanded the establishment of civil societies, so far as they serve as instruments and means of improving and enforcing those laws. Grotius, who wrote before Puffendorf, had said,—"that men, not influenced by the express command of God, but of their own accord, having experienced the weakness of separate families against the assaults of violence, united in civil societies, the effect of which was civil power, styled on this account by St. Peter the ordinance of man."* Puffendorf, remarking on this passage, says,—" Grotius' opinion is not so profane but that it may be borne with, if assisted by a dexterous interpretation; but that other opinion of Grotius, that the civil authority is therefore termed divine, because God approved of what man wholesomely instituted, we can by no means admit as though God approved of civil government, as it were, ex post facto, or after it had been actually settled.†" Grotius was a citizen of the United Provinces of the Netherlands, enjoying a republican government, and was ready to consider all governments in their formation as human institutions;—still he maintained the opinion, that the divine right of sovereignty and the sacred character of government were necessary to give it efficiency. Puffendorf thought Grotius' opinions of a subsequent divine approbation only erroneous and profane. They differed from each other, and both from former advocates of divine right, in the mode of derivation only. Both Grotius and Puffendorf, according to the metaphysics of the schools, considered sovereignty as an

---

* S. 1. Ch. 4. Sec. 7. n. 3.   † Puff. Ibid.

entity, not a physical, but a moral entity, capable of supporting attributes, and of subsisting in any government; in a republic as well as a monarchy. But whatever the form of government, sovereignty was to be a unity. They allowed that in a republic, it might be committed to several organs according to the form of the government, which did not make a division of the powers; it still continued one and indivisible.* Such was the force allowed to abstract terms, and abstract notions formed in the mind by aggregation, that while the doctrine of abstract entities, the doctrine of the Realists continued, it was at least difficult, if attempted, to consider the notion of sovereignty as a complex idea, capable of being analyzed into separate and distinct powers,—as the legislative power, the power of making laws, the judiciary, that of interpreting and applying the laws, and the executive, or power of executing the laws. It was not sufficiently considered that these powers had been confounded, by having been engrossed by a single organ, and that although they are all equally necessary and contribute equally to the ends of government, yet they are in their nature distinct, and require different modes and different talents in the administration. We may add with propriety, that, although the doctrine of the divine right of sovereigns has long since been rejected, and its absurdities so exposed that none, even of the princes of modern Europe would venture to rest their authority on that ground; and although the doctrine of abstract entities and their unities has been exploded and become obsolete, yet many of its terms remain in use, and without being properly defined, lead not unfrequently to erroneous conclusions.

The most eminent English writers, who have been perhaps inadvertently influenced by the notion of the unity of the sovereignty or supreme power, have, in that nation, vested it in their legislature or parliament, concerning which, judge Blackstone says, that "Legislature is the greatest act of superiority that can be exercised by one being over another; wherefore it is requisite to the very essence of law, that it be made by the supreme power,—sovereignty and legislature are

---

* Vide Puff. 490. B. 7. Ch. 4. Sec. 1.

indeed convertible terms ; one cannot subsist without the other.* And further, having given an account of the parliament, he says,—The power and jurisdiction of parliament, says sir Edward Coke, are so transcendent and absolute that it cannot be confined, either for causes or persons within any bounds. It hath sovereign and uncontrollable authority, in making, confirming, restraining, abrogating, repealing, reviving, and expounding of laws concerning matters of all possible denominations, ecclesiastical or temporal, civil, military, maritime, or criminal,—this being the place where that absolute despotic power, which must in all governments reside somewhere, is entrusted by the constitution of these kingdoms. All mischiefs and grievances, operations and remedies, that transcend the ordinary course of the laws, are within the reach of this extraordinary tribunal. It can alter or new model the succession to the crown ; it can alter the established religion of the land ; it can change and create afresh even the constitution of the kingdom,—and of parliaments themselves. It can, in short, do every thing which is not naturally impossible, and therefore some have not scrupled to call its powers by a figure rather too bold, the omnipotence of parliament."† Other writers have followed in the same opinion, Mr. Paley has embodied it into a universal principle, which he lays down in language the most decisive. " As a series of appeals must be finite, there necessarily exists, in every government, a power from which the constitution has provided no appeal, and which power for that reason may be termed absolute, uncontrollable, arbitrary, despotic,—and is alike in all countries"—the person or assembly in whom this power resides, is called the sovereign, or supreme power of the state ; and since to the same power universally pertains the office of establishing public laws, it is called also the legislature of the state."—(Moral Phi. 2 part.—185.)

Judge Blackstone and Mr. Paley, seem, in penning these passages, to have been influenced by the notion of a unity of the sovereign power, to which the expression " supreme

---

* 1 Comm. 46. †1 Comm. 60.

power," the general explanation of the term sovereignty, may have contributed ; for it would be absurd to say there are two or more supreme powers in the state. They must of necessity be equal, or some must be subordinate, one only can be supreme—that is, above all others. Mr. Christian's note on the passage from Blackstone is applicable to both. He observes, "The omnipotence of parliament, signifies nothing more than the supreme power of the state, or a power of action uncontrolled by any superior.—In this sense the king in the exercise of his prerogatives, and the house of lords in the interpretation of the laws, are omnipotent, that is, free from the control of any superior provided by the constitution.*

Thus the parliament has the sole power in the kingdom of making and repealing laws ; the house of lords, the sole ultimate power of interpreting them, and the king of sending ambassadors, of entering into treaties with foreign nations, and of making war and peace. There is provided by the constitution, no direct power of control over either, when acting within the constitutional limits assigned to each ; but in the all absorbing sense of these writers, as they have expressed themselves, neither the parliament, the house of peers, nor the king, are possessed of sovereign power,—nor is it any where to be found, but in a state of absolute despotism, in which all the powers of government are concentrated in a sole organ, either a single person or an aristocratic body. And here it merits all the epithets so fondly lavished upon it, of absolute, uncontrollable, arbitrary, despotic.

In every state, where any degree of liberty is enjoyed by the subjects, and their rights in any way respected, the powers of government are, in some good degree, separately delegated to distinct organs, and the functionaries are held accountable in some way for the due exercise of the powers with which they are entrusted. The powers of each must be competent to the purposes for which they are delegated ; but no one possesses the sovereign power in that absolute and unlimited sense. It is in an aggregate, an abstract view, only, of all the powers of

* 1 Comm. 161.

government that the sovereignty of such state is found,—such in fact is the constitution of the English government. All the functionaries in every department, are by the constitution placed in a state of accountability, even those over whom no direct control is provided,—and whether the accountability be of a civil, or a moral nature, if indeed by the provisions of the conttitution it is equally a constitutional control. Let us for a moment, examine their constitution with that view.

In the legislature, the members of the house of commons are accountable to the people through the medium of periodical elections. On the good opinion the people entertain of their public conduct, they are dependant for a continuance of their functions. As the house of commons constitutes a co-ordinate branch of the legislature, any control on that branch, operates an equal control on the whole legislative power, since no law can pass without their consent, and although the king is vested with the sole power of sending ambassadors, entering into treaties, and of making war and peace, yet he can neither support his ambassadors, maintain a war, nor carry into effect a treaty in which are any money stipulations on the part of the nation, without the concurrence of the legislature in raising and appropriating money for those purposes. This check is the more effectual, as every law for raising revenue must originate in the house of commons, who will not in that case admit even a proposal of amendment from the other house ; so that in this respect the house of commons hold the purse-strings of the nation. The king's power therefore, in these, as in most instances of his prerogatives, without the aid of parliament, is but a nrveless power ; and although the king is not personally accountable for the abuse of any of his constitutional powers, yet he cannot act without the advice of his ministers, who are required to sign their names to the advice they give ; and if they advise measures that are unconstitutional, illegal, or pernicious to the public interest ; the advisers are liable to severe penalties on impeachment.

There is another check, arising from the nature of the constitution, and which is found in the public opinion of an enlightened community. This, although a moral control, acts on every department of the government, with a force, not unfrequently irresistible. It has obliged the legislature to repeal obnoxious, and to pass popular laws ; it has compelled the king to abandon his favorite measures, to dismiss his favorite ministers, and sometimes to employ others to whom he entertained a strong personal dislike. All the causes decided by the house of lords in their judicial capacity, in which they are assisted by all the judges of the superior courts, are publicly discussed by the most able counsel, and in the presence of the first jurists who lead the opinion of the nation on such subjects ; and the lords, ambitious of the honors of their station, well know that the respect which they claim for their rank, depends on the public opinion of their talents and integrity. If these checks are in some instances of the moral kind only, yet are they induced by the constitution of the government and the nature of its provisions. Nor is it any objection to the view, we have taken of the subject, that secret intrigues and corruption may sometimes render these checks ineffectual. We may then safely pronounce that this enormous, this omnipotent power of united sovereignty is not to be found in any single organ of that government, whether legislative, judicial, or executive.

The government of the United States, as has been often observed, is wholly representative. By the constitution, the different powers are entrusted to different organs, and different functionaries, and are in each defined and limited with sufficient precision. Besides that the functionaries are accountable to the people at their periodical elections, the constitutionality of all legislative and executive acts may be called in question, and decided by a competent judiciary. All executive officers, even the president and judges, are liable to impeachment and removal, for malconduct in office. Neither have the people, the original source of all power, retained to themselves the sovereignty, absolute and unlimited. It is retained under certain modifications and restrictions, agreeable to the constitution which they have submitted to observe. In this constitution there is no where lodged that united sovereignty, that supreme power, absolute, uncontrollable, arbitrary, and despotic, which it is declared, must, in all governments, reside somewhere, and is alike in all countries. If such be the necessary definition, our constitution has no provision of internal sovereignty ; and yet experience has evinced that the powers of this government, so limited and controlled, are fully competent to the great end of all civil institutions, the permanent happiness of the people, and the prosperity of the state.

CHAPTER III.

Of the political power—its depository and limitations in different governments.

This subject has been incidentally anticipated in some degree in the preceeding chapters ; but its importance as the primary and fundamental power in the state, in which originate all the civil powers, and by which alone those powers can be limited, controlled, and directed to their great end,—the security and happiness of the people, renders a further discussion necessary, in which I shall endeavor to be concise, and to avoid repetition, except where it may be necessary to a more full illustration.

The political power is distinguished from the civil powers in the same manner as political rights are distinguished from the civil rights ; and is exercised in forming, altering, or amending the civil compact or constitution of the state,—in which respect it is the power of political legislation ; and in guarding the exercise of the civil powers, and holding the functionaries accountable in such way and manner as is provided in the constitution,—in which respect it is the guardian power of the state. But this power of political legislation has rarely among the nations of the world, been actually and deliberately employed in political systems, or constitutions of government. Few governments, ancient, or modern, have been constituted by an express compact made by the people, a constitution deliberately formed. The powers of government have, in most instances, been on emergencies blindly conferred on one, or a few individuals ; have been assumed by fraud or violence ; or through a succession of ages, been suffered to accumulate in one or more families and to become sacred in their hands. Thus the powers of government came to be considered as the right and privilege of the ruler, distinct from, and paramount to the rights of the people. Men have conducted as though whatever of good was enjoyed by the people was to be derived from the condescension of the rulers, a mere concession of clemency. Doctrines like these have in all ages, by the ambitious few, been but too successfully inculcated on the minds of the people. From this source has been derived the doctrine of the present perfection of government, the infallibility of rulers, and the divine right of kings ; and hence a total annihilation of all the political rights and power of the people.

On the other hand, the people, from a sense of the horrid oppressions which universally accompany such absurd conceptions of power, have at times plunged into the extremes of anarchy and popular violence. They have been driven to a feeling, rather than a rational investigation of their rights. They have been unable to distinguish between a personal right in the ruler, and a mere trust of power ; still less have they been able to establish any laws of accountability, which might operate to prevent the abuse, without a constant resort to violent measures. Thus embarrassed, they have frequently balanced between the horrors of tyranny and the violence of faction.

Neither the Greeks nor the Romans had any correct or definite notions of political and civil liberty and the natural rights of man ; of those relations from which result the sacred laws of his nature. From the ignorance of their lawgivers on these points, which was indeed the ignorance of the age, there were always radical defects in their constitutions of government. In all their systems they made little or no distinction between

the political and civil laws ; between the laws of the constitution
by which the state is organized, and its efficient powers directed
and limited, and the laws of property and personal rights ; and
yet without a careful attention to this distinction, personal rights
can never be permanently secured. The laws of the constitution, the political laws, are to those entrusted with the powers
of government, what the laws made by the government, are
to a court of judicature. Those courts are bound by the laws,
but have no power to make or alter them. In like manner the
government, that is, those organized bodies who are entrusted
with its powers, are bound by the constitution as the supreme
law, but should have no power to alter or add to any of its
provisions.

Hence it is evident, that in an absolute or despotic government, there can be no political laws, laws of the constitution,
binding on those who exercise the powers of government.
The prince, arrogating to himself all powers, political and
civil, can be bound by none of his laws as they relate to his
own conduct. All such laws and regulations, although in the
form of royal ordinances, and promulgated with all possible
solemnity, are nothing more than present resolutions subject
to the caprice and momentary fluctuations of the tyrant's will.
In such governments, however, there will always be found some
custom or ancient usage, from whatever source derived, that
is by the people held more sacred than the authority or person
of the-prince ;—and which, he cannot with impunity, and dares
not violate.

Such is said to be a customary law among the Turks, derived
from some passage in the Koran, that the sultan shall levy no
new tax on his subjects. The sultan knows that an attempt
to enforce such a measure would excite the unrestrained
indignation of every class of his enslaved people, and that his
head or at least that of his favorite minister must be the forfeiture. In a more polished state of society, the absolute monarch,
not only feels himself limited by some custom, some mode of
thinking, which time, or perhaps religious opinion has rendered
sacred among the people, but he is, in a degree, restrained by
that respect, which he finds it necessary to pay to the manners of the age, and of his own country, and to the general

sentiments of his own subjects. Still he can be subjected to no positive laws or regulations in the exercise of authority. Under such a government there can be no political laws, or political rights. Different is the case of all governments founded in legitimate civil compact. They are capable of positive regulations, of constitutional laws limiting with a good degree of precision the powers of government in their exercise, and directing them to the great end of political and civil institutions, the secure enjoyment by the people, of their rights natural, civil, and political, and the promotion of the general interest and happiness of the community.

Of the three forms of government founded in the civil compact, a democracy is the most liable to fluctuation in its political and civil institutions; because in that government, the citizens, who are in possession of unrestrained political liberty, constitute their legislative assemblies, each citizen having an equal voice in passing all laws whether of a civil or political nature, as well as in appointing those who administer the laws; and although every law, while remaining in force, is binding on the whole community as well as on each individual; yet from the nature of the government, they are at all times liable to be altered, changed, and repealed at the will of a majority, subject to all the fluctuations of popular passions, and prejudice.—And further, as all laws are enacted and are under the control of the same body, there can be no distinction of constitutional and unconstitutional law;—the last law passed on every subject is always constitutional, must be so considered by every one in the civil administration. Although it has been often asserted by the advocates for this form of government, that no people will oppress themselves, yet the majority often adopt measures very oppressive to their opponents, the minority, and in the violence of party spirit, not unfrequently with that view—a situation to which all are in turn exposed. The people have also at times, under some powerful excitement, or sinister influence, been induced to adopt those measues that led to the inevitable ruin of their liberties. So true is it that the extreme of liberty verges on the extreme of tyranny,—a situation into which it finally, and often suddenly degenerates.

In a mixed government, of which we have already given a

sketch, political rights are more limited. Yet here the people enjoy an important portion of those rights, derived from the natural right of self government, which they exercise in the periodical election of a co-ordinate branch of the legislature, through which they, as before shown, hold a check over the two other branches consisting of the king and the nobility. Although the exercise of this right may here, on comparison, appear very much restricted, yet it is all that can be exercised by the people with safety to this form of government. Let the right of suffrage be properly secured and guarded, and the representation be apportioned through the whole, as nearly equal as local circumstances will admit, so as to give all the voters a fair and equal chance of exercising their right, at periods not too remote from each other, and it will prove a check no less salutary than efficient.

In this form of government as well as in a democracy, the legislative body necessarily possesses the ordinary as well as the extraordinary—as well the civil as political—powers of legislation. They have the same power to make, repeal, alter, and change any law relating to the constitution, as one relating merely to the civil state; nor can one be made more binding on the legislature than the other. None of their laws can be adjudged to be unconstitutional, however inexpedient they may be, or however they may disturb the symmetry of that constitution.

On a first view of this government, consisting of three branches claiming distinct powers and those often conflicting, few improvements of the constitution were to be expected, particularly in favor of the rights of the people, an extension of which must be a diminution of those claimed by one or both of the higher orders, as they are called, the monarch or the nobles ; and yet on an attentive consideration of the English constitution, the only government from which any example can at present be adduced, we find that great improvements have from time to time been made, and that by acts of their parliament so constructed. The march of improvement has indeed been slow, often encountering violent opposition, and sometimes its footsteps drenched in the best blood of the nation.

The first act passed upon this subject and which has justly been considered the foundation of English liberty was the act of Magna Charta, or the grand charter, passed in the reign of King John. For notwithstanding its form as a charter or grant, and the force put upon the king, it was an act of parliament, agreeable to the parliamentary mode of proceeding at that time, especially in passing all acts which might in any way affect the royal prerogatives. Since that time five centuries have elapsed,—during the three first, improvements made in the constitution accompanying the progress of manners and knowledge, were few, moderate, and far between ; but they were such as prepared the way, and prepared the nation for those that have followed. During the two last centuries, improvements of the constitution have been very numerous and important. I will barely mention some of the principal acts, relating to that subject, passed during the latter period. The act abolishing the court of starchamber and the high commission court, and the act called the petition of rights, passed during the reign of Charles the first. The act abolishing the feudal tenures and their appendages and the habeas corpus act which is considered the palladium, as Magna Charta was the foundation, of English liberty, passed in the reign of Charles the second.—Under William and Mary at the revolution, the bill of rights, the act of settlement, and the acts fixing the duration of parliament, and an act of the 13 William III. changing the tenure of the office of the judges, before, during the pleasure of the king, to be in future held during good behavior, thereby rendering them independent of the crown :—this act was passed on the recommendation of the king from the throne, as was the act of the 1 George III. for continuing the commissions of the judges, notwithstanding the demise of the crown. We might mention the acts uniting Scotland and Ireland with England as political acts, not as improvements of the constitution.

Those who are conversant in the history of the English laws, will find in addition to the acts here mentioned, many others, more or less relating to the same subject, all of which taken together, clearly prove that this form of government has in it a capacity of improvement, which, if with a tardy, yet with a sure pace will follow the improvements of the age. The people under it enjoy less political liberty, than under a.

demoeracy; but they may enjoy as great a portion of civil liberty, and if we can rely on history and observation, it possesses more stability, and promises a longer duration.

Under the representative form of government, the people may enjoy a greater degree of political power and liberty than under a mixed government, and less than in a democracy; and a greater security of their civil liberties, than can be had under any other form. To this end the political rights and powers of the people, and the civil powers of the government must be so distinguished, modified, and regulated as to be exercised separately by those to whom they are severally reserved or delegated. These regulations provided in the constitution, may be so guarded as to prevent any sudden and unnecessary alterations and changes in those fundamental laws through popular excitement so incident to a democracy, and that confusion of powers which is incident both to a democracy and a mixed monarchy. At the same time the obstacles to wholesome and necessary amendments, arising from an opposition of powers and interest, will be wholly removed. The people may voluntarily assemble to express their opinion of the government or the administration, by memorial, petition, or remonstrance; but such assembly will always be partial and without authority, and can make no amendments, no alteration in the constitution or laws.

That the people may constitutionally exercise their powers of political legislation, it must be provided that they shall, by their representatives elected for that purpose, meet in convention, on the call of the ordinary legislature; or the legislature may be authorized to make proposals of amendments of the constitution to the people to be ratified or rejected in their primary assemblies. Nor can the legislature, composed of members from every part of the state, fail of knowing and being influenced by the sentiments of the people on the expediency of such a measure. Some states have authorized the ordinary legislature, to make any amendment of the constitution by their own act; But requiring a greater degree of unanimity than in common cases, and that before its final adoption it shall be passed by two successive sessions that a new election of representatives may intervene, who it is supposed, will have learned, and will be actuated by the sentiments of the people on the proposed amendment. But this must be considered, in a measure, a departure from the principles of the government; as it confounds the several powers of legislation, and in a degree, the obligation of the political and civil laws, which as they are distinct in their nature ought to be kept in a distinct view. It seems highly expedient that every amendment to be laid before the people for their consideration, should be passed with the same caution, and the same delay, that it may be maturely considered before its final adoption. Indeed none but simple propositions ought to be submitted in this way. The people in their primary assemblies are incapable of discussing intricate questions. All amendments, alterations, and changes of the constitution that require a deliberate discussion in order to a proper adjustment ought to be referred to a convention of the people, by their representatives chosen for that special purpose, where they may meet a full and fair discussion, and be adopted or rejected on mature deliberation.

Not less important is it to provide for the free and secure exercise of the right of suffrage by the people, in the periodical elections of the legislators and principal functionaries of the government, which includes the right of calling to account, through that medium, any functionary and organ of that government, that may for the purpose of a better selection be entrusted with the appointments to office, for the propriety of such appointments. Thus the people are constituted the guardians of their own rights as they are the source of all power. All those who administer the government, will be taught by this means that they are only trustees for the people, exercising a delegated power, and accountable to them and to such tribunals as are established by the constitution, for the manner in which they discharge their trust. No one is placed beyond the reach of accountability. Under this form of government is secured and realized that political liberty which has in all ages been the idol of mankind, the dread of tyrants, and which the people themselves have so often abused to their own ruin.

It is true, this form of government is a novelty in the political world, it cannot, it does not, appeal to history for proof of its excellence ; but to present facts. Half a century is hardly elapsed since the experiment was first made in these United States ; during which, its success has been beyond the most sanguine expectations of its friends, and has disappointed the forebodings of its enemies. The sentiment of attachment to its institutions, and the high sense of independence it is calculated to infuse and cherish among the people, are the strength and confidence of the government. An attack upon the government is felt by all, as it in fact is an attack upon themselves, and it is suppressed or repelled with that promptitude and energy which such sentiments and feelings naturally inspire. It has also solved the great problem of *imperium in imperio.* It has been found capable of uniting independent states under one general government, for all national purposes, to any extent, and with increasing security and energy. From the experience we have had, and that on some of the most trying occasions, we have good reason to say, it promises stability and durability, if any thing human can be durable.

CHAPTER IV.

Of the Division and Limitation of the Civil Powers.

From the manner in which, agreeable to the constitution, the civil powers are to be exercised, and the objects of their exertion, there naturally arises a division into a legislative, an executive, and a judiciary department. The exercise of the legislative power, by a representation of the people, is an improvement of modern times. In all the republics of ancient Greece, in Italy, and in Rome itself, where the people had a share in legislation, every freeman was a member of the legislature, and gave his suffrage personally in the assembly of the people. This brought together a body too unwieldy, even in the smallest states; in states of greater extent, where the citizens were almost innumerable, as in the Roman commonwealth, they formed a heterogeneous assemblage of sentiments, passions, and interests, that bade defiance to all hope of compromise by means of rational discussion.

Those who are little capable of reasoning, are nevertheless, capable of strong feelings. Accordingly we find in the public speeches of their most celebrated orators, comparatively little attention to close investigation; all the powers of their eloquence are directed to the passions and sentiments of their audience;—the whole vigor of the soul is collected to this point. The instruction contained in their orations serves principally to mark the state of knowledge,—the manners and sentiments of the times. The glow of imagination, which they discover, the propriety and irresistible force of sentiment and expression, which wrap the whole soul in attention, have justly rendered them the admiration of succeeding ages. All this well accounts for the fluctuation of measures in ancient popular governments. They have, with great propriety, been compared to the fluctuations of the boisterous elements. A republican government upon this model must always be found rash and vacillating in its counsels, and exposed to violent revolutions.

It has been the opinion of the best writers, that a democracy can be adequate to the government of a small territory only; and that, in this institution, population must be stinted, or the number of citizens, who shall have the right of suffrage, limited. The first is a very discouraging consideration. The latter constitutes a more or less numerous aristocracy. Montesquieu clearly agrees in the general opinion. He appears to have had no conception of that improvement upon a democracy, in which the people exercise all the powers of government by representation. In his time no instance of this form had existed in any independent state, and which yet wants an appropriate name. The same author, speaking of the representative branch of the English government, observes,—" The great advantage of representatives is their being capable of discussing affairs; for this the people at large are very unfit; which is one of the inconveniencies of a democracy."* Representatives, elected from various parts of the community, agreeably to a just apportionment, are not only capable of discussing the affairs of the nation, be it ever so extensive or numerous, but they bring to that discussion more knowledge of the general and particular manners, interests, and sentiments of the people whose interest and happiness is alone concerned in their deliberations, and dispositions more congenial to those manners, interests, and sentiments, than can be found in any other body of men.

The legislative department ought, by the constitution, to be again divided into two co-ordinate branches, one of which, less numerous, we denominate the senate, the other the house of representatives. Both are to be in fact equally representatives of the people; the latter more numerous, to be elected from

* Sp. L. B. 1. 184.

smaller districts intended to represent the local and more partial interests of the community ; the former, fewer in number, to be elected from larger districts and intended to represent the more general interests. This division of the legislature into two co-ordinate branches is a very important and necessary provision of the constitution. Public discussion and mature deliberation in the enacting of laws is indispensably necessary. To this end the senate and house of representatives must have equal powers ; and no law be suffered to pass without the concurrence of both. Should one body, through the prevalence of some secret influence or particular prejudice, pass too hastily upon measures, the other may calmly arrest the decision, and prevent the danger arising from too transient or too partial a view of the subject.

There is another advantage accruing from this division of the legislature, in some degree independent of the above consideration. That man or body of men, who have formed any plan, are in some measure incapable of discovering the errors and mistakes that may have intervened. Their ideas when arranged, flow almost unavoidably in the same channel. Those errors and mistakes will be much more readily discovered by others. This is apprehended to be an important consideration in the legislative institution.

The general qualifications, which may be required for members of the legislature, we shall defer until we come to treat of the qualifications of electors, and shall mention but one here, which relates to the senators. It is a good idea that the senate should be considered as a national council, and it may be thought a necessary provision in the constitution, that certain executive measures should receive the approbation of that body. This suggests a distinction of age, to add to the respectability of the body, and give maturity to their deliberations. Public measures, before they are adopted, ought to be considered in every light in which they may affect the passions, the morals, sentiments, and interests of the people, both general and particular. While they provide for present accommodation, they ought not to lose sight of future improvements,—to secure a more deliberate discussion and a more calm investigation, not only ought the warmth and inexperience of youth to be excluded from the senate, but it is a reason why the members should be fewer in number than those of the other branch,—and thus while the house of representatives, actuated by all the passions and sentiments of the community, in turn give a vigor and national spirit to the measures of government, any precipitation, into which they may be hurried, will be prevented by the calm composure of the senate.

The number of representatives seems not to be capable of any precise limitation. The extremes are very discernible, but they are very distant. Too numerous a representation verges on the inconveniences of an assembly of the people. It encumbers discussion, and gives ascendancy to particular passions, which, in a numerous assembly, often with a sympathetic effect pervade the whole body, and irresistibly influence the decisions of the moment. On the other hand, if the representative body are too few in number, their measures are liable to be dictated by limited views and private interests. Possibly we can go no farther than to say, that it ought to be so numerous, as probably to comprehend all the sentiments and interests that have a national influence. The better to effect this comprehension, and to equalize the representation, the state ought to be divided into as many districts as there shall be representatives to be elected, and the districts should, as near as circumstances will permit, be apportioned by the number of inhabitants. This will in general, secure the most equal representation, and the electors will act more understandingly, and with a personal knowledge of the candidates. Where a number of representatives are assigned to a larger district, and especially, as in that case, a plurality of the votes, not a majority, generally determines the choice, every engine of intrigue is commonly put in motion, and the representatives are chosen by some prevailing interest of the district, in exclusion of every other ; and thus it may happen that the interests of the state are but partially represented. There may, however, be found reasons for adopting this mode of electing representatives, that will out-weigh the inconveniences, but they ought to be very powerful.

The senators, who though not in name, yet in fact are no less representatives of the people than the members of the other branch, ought also to be elected by districts, apportioned in the same manner by the number of inhabitants. And let it be indispensable, that the senators, as well as the representatives, shall be fixed inhabitants of the district for which they are respectively chosen. As the senate is to be considered in some respects as a national council, and may by the executive, be called to meet at times when the legislature is not in session, it is proper that they always continue an organized body, retaining a portion of that experience which is acquired by the long service of its members. With this view it is a good provision, that the members shall be distributed equally into three or four classes and numbered accordingly ; the time of service for each class to expire successively at the periods for the election of representatives, and their places to be supplied by new elections in their respective districts.

It is the province as it is the duty of the legislature to frame such laws and adopt such measures as will in a due proportion direct the actions of all the citizens to the promotion of the public interest, will unite the forces of the whole and direct them to the attainment of those important objects of public utility, or public necessity, to which the united forces of all are alone adequate. To the legislature it belongs to enact such laws for the regulation of individual conduct as will, as far as possible, prevent clashing interests and secure right and justice to the citizens in their private intercourse. Under the same head comes a provision for the ascertainment and reparation of injuries, both public and private, and for securing a general observation of the laws by adequate sanctions, by penalties to be inflicted for every violation. It is also the business and duty of the legislature, to devise ways and means of supplying funds for the support of government, for the protection and defence of the state, and the promotion of the common interest and welfare ; to determine the amount of contributions necessary to be raised for those ends, to apportion them on the citizens with a due regard to their means of contributing, and to order the collection in a manner the least burdensome ; and further to make by law a specific appropriation of the national funds for all the objects required, without which no expenditures can be allowed, no monies drawn from the public treasury.

There is still another duty of the legislature, which ought

to be enjoined by the constitution, which indeed is not the first in order, but among the first in importance under this form of government, and that is to make an effectual provision for the diffusion of common and useful learning through every class of the community, by an establishment of common schools every where in convenient districts, that they may be accessible to all, with funds or means suitable to the importance of the object; and to establish seminaries suitably endowed for instruction in the higher walks of literature and science.

The power of making war, or of placing the nation in a state of hostility with other nations has in most governments, and particularly in those of the monarchical form, been considered as pertaining to the executive power, the prerogative of the monarch; but in a government depending on the will of the people, it is a concern too general and too important to be intrusted to the caprice, or even the wisdom of one man, in whatever station he may be placed. If the power be not precisely of a legislative character, it may, nevertheless, be best exercised by the legislative body, as representing the interests and sentiments of the nation. To that body therefore ought to be intrusted the sole power of placing the nation in a state of war. The making of peace belonging to the treaty-making power, should be left to the proper organ.

From a view of their duties it will be seen that the powers entrusted to the legislature ought to be very ample, or—if any one so pleases—sovereign within their proper sphere, which however can mean nothing more than that they be fully competent to the objects of their institution. Powers so ample will, indeed, be liable to abuse, either through inattention or from design. It is, however, a great security, that the members of the legislature are subject to their own laws, and amenable for a violation equally with all others; but this is not sufficient.—It is necessary that the constitution contain a declaration of those rights, which the legislature shall have no power to infringe; and although it is often necessary to make special provisions by law, and to grant relief in particular cases, by which justice may be done to any party without injury to the rights of others; yet, in whatever may affect the common rights, the legislature ought by express provision, to be confined to the passage of general and prospective laws, and prohibited the enactment of personal penalties, *ex post facto* laws, and the granting of privileges to individuals or associated bodies. Such partial laws are the commencement of an attack on equal rights, and a violation of natural principles. This provision, however, ought not to extend to prevent the establishment of subordinate political institutions for local purposes, nor for the purpose of transacting certain business, or of prosecuting certain enterprises, to which the powers of individuals, are from the nature of the subjects incompetent.

By the establishment of companies for such purposes, new powers are created, but the right of no individual is infringed. Nor should the provision extend to a prohibition of laws for the encouragement of useful knowledge. Authors of books by which useful knowledge is disseminated, and of those inventions, by which the labors of life are facilitated, are equally with other citizens entitled to the fruits of their industry, and the application of their powers ; but such is the nature of their productions, that without a legislative provision in their favor, they must remain wholly at the mercy of others. The power of each house of the legislature, to organize itself, to judge of the qualifications and election of its own members, to appoint its own officers, to make all rules necessary to an orderly proceeding, to repress disturbances, and punish contempts seems to be necessarily incident to their institution. There are other powers and duties, which may be entrusted to them, either to both houses jointly, or to one separately ; less in their legislative character than that of general representation of the people, or as bodies already organized to whom such powers and duties may with convenience and safety be committed.

It is requisite that there should be an enquiry into the conduct of public officers ; that prosecutions should be commenced against the guilty, for the purpose of removal, and that there should somewhere exist a constitutional court for their trial. The enquiry, prosecution, and trial, from the importance to the community, the character and situation of the parties, ought to be more public and solemn than those which are appointed for common offenders.—And to this we may add, that the prosecution is for a political delinquency, not for a civil crime the cognizance of which belongs to the civil judicature, and the end is the removal or disqualification of an unworthy public servant, not a vindictive punishment of the offender. For these, among other reasons, the house of representatives has been thought the most proper board to institute the enquiry and to bring forward the accusations of the public, and the senate to constitute the most proper tribunal for the trial of such accusation. Objections may be suggested to this depository of the power of impeachment; but probably no better provision can be made. The introduction of an independent tribunal for the trial of impeachments might have greater inconveniences, without securing the command of more wisdom, integrity, and weight of character in the judges.

It may be a very proper provision, that in the exercise of some powers entrusted to the executive, the advice and consent of the senate should be made necessary to the validity of his acts. An instance of this is found in appointments to office. By subjecting nominations to office by the president to the approbation of the senate, a more judicious selection will generally be made, and the appointment of unworthy persons prevented. The members of that body coming from the different parts of the state may know of objections to the person nominated, which had not come to the knowledge of the executive. So in the case of a treaty, the advice and consent of the senate may well be made necessary to its final ratification. For although the power of making a treaty as a national compact is, with propriety entrusted to the executive; yet, as when ratified, it becomes a law binding on the citizens as well as a compact binding on the state, the senate in this case may be said not to depart altogether from their character as legislators. It may also be sometimes proper for the legislature as general representatives of the people, to advise and recommend to the attention of the executive, the pursuit of some national measure that may be deemed highly necessary or expedient. Their previous advice will give weight to the measure, and a facility to the execution. Such advice, however, should be general and in those matters that are considered discretionary with the executive, and never extend to those particular instances of conduct which may become the ground of impeachment.

Finally, it should be a sacred stipulation in the constitution that all debates in the legislature should be open, except when some measure submitted to their consideration by the executive may require secrecy; and that effectual means be adopted for their publication in course, and to facilitate an early and general circulation among the people. This will prove an efficient and salutary check on the members, by enabling their constituents to form a just estimate of the characters of those to whom they entrust the powers of legislation.

The executive is the ultimately efficient power in the government. For the sake of despatch and unity of action, and of representing the individuality and sovereignty of the state in transactions with other nations, this power ought to be vested in a single person, who with us has been denominated the governor or president. We shall generally adopt the term president. Some have thought that the election of the executive chief may with the greatest safety be entrusted to the legislature. Others have held that this right should be retained by the people. There are certainly very strong objections to committing its exercise to the legislature. It gives an idea of a dependence of the executive on that body, and intercepts his accountability to the people, whose power he ought to represent in his department. All elections by the representative body are subject to intrigues and coalitions which are very injurious in their influence on public measures, and on morals. This evil is increased in proportion to the importance of the election.

An upright and faithful discharge of the duties of the executive office is the most honorable of any in the state,—an abuse, the most dangerous and in no office are the temptations more powerful. It ought therefore to be guarded with every rational check; at the same time, it must not be so encumbered as to clog its necessary activity. The good or bad conduct of the executive, is in most instances of internal administration, immediately felt by the people. To avoid any hurtful coalition between this high officer and the legislative body, and to subject him to the control of public sentiment, his appointment should be by periodical elections by the people. In more complicated governments, such as that of the United States, this mode of electing the president may be extremely inconvenient or even impracticable. When this shall appear to be the case, some other provision must be made; but care should be taken to exclude all legislative interference in the election, unless as may sometimes happen, no choice shall have been made in the mode prescribed, and to make it depend as much as possible on the sentiments of the people.

It will be the duty of the president as head of the executive department, to execute the laws, to carry into effect many provisions of the constitution and the measures directed by the legislature within the limits of their powers, and the decisions of the judiciary in the manner prescribed by the laws and constitution, and to represent the state in public transactions. In the president also will with propriety be vested the chief command of the military, a peculiar department, which by the constitution must be placed in subordination to the civil power. Besides the duties of the executive, just mentioned, there are other duties to be performed very necessary to an orderly and economical arrangement of measures. It will at all times be the duty of the president, the head of this department, to inform the legislature of the situation of public affairs, of the event of measures that have been adopted, and to recommend to their consideration those measures, which demand their more immediate attention.

The business of the executive is too extensive and various to be performed by one man. Many of its duties must be performed by subordinate officers and ministers. According to the ordinary routine of official business, it will be the duty of the subordinate ministers of the executive department, under the direction of the president, as often as shall be required by the legislature, to make proper reports of the matters committed to their management and to accompany them with all the necessary information, which may assist that body to pursue and adopt a regular system in the internal economy of the state and enable it to conduct with propriety and good faith as well towards the citizens, as in the intercourse with foreign nations.

Although there ought to be maintained an amicable intercourse between the legislature and the executive for the purpose of mutual information, and a mutual co-operation of the several departments of the government, in the exercise of their several powers, yet as will appear in the sequel, no one of the departments should be permitted to exercise any of the essential powers, committed to either of the others. The president therefore, as head of the executive department, ought not to have a negative, or any direct controling power in legislation. He may, however, within certain limits, well be allowed a deliberative voice—conversant in the execution of the laws and all the measures of government; his department will be the centre of information on those subjects. It will be his duty at all times to communicate such information to the legislature, so far as will be necessary to assist them in their deliberations. He will more readily than others perceive the difficulties that may arise in the execution of a law from any discrepancy with the provisions of the constitution or the general system of public measures. Every act of the legislature, therefore, ought, before it become a law, to be submitted to the president for his approval. If he approve it, he will affix his signature with his approval simply, whereupon it will become a law. If he do not approve, he should be required to return it with his objections fairly stated in writing to be re-considered by the legislature. If the legislature, on re-consideration, still pass the act, it must become a law, notwithstanding the objection of the president. If this be made a provision of the constitution, as I think it ought, it furnishes an additional reason against the election of the president by the legislature.

Although the members of the legislature cannot, from the nature of their functions, be made accountable for their acts to any other tribunal but that of public sentiment expressed by the people in their elections, yet happily for mankind it has been found, that the executive power is capable of limitations sufficiently precise, by known and established laws. Its ministers therefore, from the president down through every grade, may be subjected to trial before a proper tribunal, to removal and to further punishment for their unconstitutional acts. Impunity should on no account, be annexed to office or dignity. So far is it from consisting with the good of the community, that it is directly opposed to the common interest and safety.

By the constitution it is to be made the province of the judiciary to decide on the laws by interpreting and applying them to particular cases according to their analogy; and by their decisions to pronounce upon whom, and in what way and manner the executive power shall be exercised, either for the satisfaction and reparation of injuries, or the punishment of offenders. To the judges, the ministers of this power, it will belong to interpret all acts of the legislature agreeable to the true spirit of the constitution as founded in natural principles, and the rules therein explicitly given, and to make a just and impartial application in all cases of disputed right ; and as under this form of government the constitution is the supreme law limiting the powers of the several departments, it will be within their power, as it is their duty, to decide in questions coming before them, on all acts both of the legislature and the executive, and in all cases in which the acts of either are opposed to that supreme law or are clearly not warranted by it, to pronounce them unconstitutional and void. By this provision, the rights and interests of all the members of the legislative and executive departments will be kept in union with the rights and interests of the citizens ; all will be equally protected against an unconstitutional law ; all will be equally exposed by an unjust law, or amenable for an arbitrary execution.

The situation of the judges, the ministers of the judiciary department, is very different from the situation of other functionaries of the government. The integrity of their conduct has a powerful influence. It is indispensably necessary to an impartial administration of justice and the security of public and private rights. Their decisions, though sometimes extending to the acts of the other departments, are mostly of local and private rights ; but the precedents established by their decisions, become general rules for the interpretation of the laws which follow the principles of the government. In a republican government, the laws should be interpreted with a spirit of equity, impartiality, and moderation. In the mode of performing the duties of the legislature and the judiciary, there is a very material distinction. In making laws, a regard must be had to the circumstances, the manners and sentiments of the people, as well as to the principles of the constitution. The laws are to be the best the people will bear. In judging, whether between individual citizens, or between private persons and public officers or functionaries, a strict regard is to be had to the very right and justice of the case, agreeable to the laws of the land and the principles of the constitution.

The judges ought not to stand in awe of the frowns of power, or be influenced by the temporary smiles of popular favor. That kind of accountability, therefore, which is supported by popular elections, and which is proper for a member of the legislature, is not proper for a judge. From the interest which men of great property and influence might expect in future decisions, the people might be misled in their judgment of characters. The same observations will hold of a legislative appointment of the judges, in addition to what was before observed of election by the legislature generally, that they excite an idea of dependence on that body, and give rise to intrigues and coalitions, hurtful to public measures. In popular appointments, no one holds himself accountable for the character of the person appointed. In the legislature responsibility is, in a great measure, lost among numbers.

The appointment, or at least the public nomination of the judges ought to be entrusted to the president or head of the executive department. His conduct is constantly, and singly exposed to the public view. He will be holden responsible to the people for the character and talents of those whom he appoints to office, and will sufficiently feel that responsibility. To secure the judges in that degree of independence, that shall place them above a temptation to a bias, they ought to hold their offices during good behavior, and their compensation should be fixed beyond the power of the legislature to alter, at least, to diminish, during their continuance in office. For corruption and mal-conduct in office, although not for mere error of opinion, they ought to be liable to removal by impeachment, as in the case of other officers of the government.

There may, however, be some things in the conduct of a judge, which affect his character and destroy that respectability and public confidence so necessary to produce a ready acquiescence in the decisions of the judiciary, and a prompt obedience to the laws ;—they may nevertheless be of such a natui e, that they cannot be made the subject of impeachment, which will reach nothing but official conduct. To remedy this evil, which has sometimes been found a matter of great consequence in government, and to impress on the minds of the judges the necessity of purity and integrity of character,—a provision may be made for the removal of any one from office on an address to the executive by both branches of the legislature. To prevent the effect of intrigue, and any popular excitement of the moment, it ought to be attended with great deliberation. To this end let it be necessary, that at least two thirds of the members of each house concur in the address. These provisions, it is believed, while they leave the judges sufficiently independent, will also hold them sufficiently accountable.

We have mentioned the compensation of the judges only ; but it is no less necessary than just for a provision to be made, that every officer, every person employed in the service of the government in every department, should be paid a reasonable compensation for his services ;—a stated compensation apportioned to the labor and expense, the respectability and responsible nature of the employment. It would be in vain to expect, and unreasonable to insist on a strict account of services required to be rendered not only without compensation, but often with great hazard and loss.

From what has been said of the powers committed to the three departments and the duties of the functionaries, it is evident that a separation is not intended to produce an opposition, but a mutual co-operation of those powers, without which, there can be neither harmony nor energy in the government. The reason will also obviously appear why they should be committed to different departments in the state, and not be entrusted to one man or body of men. Different knowledge and different abilities are necessary for the making, judging, and executing of laws. They require the exercise of different powers, faculties, and talents. No man, perhaps, ever had a sufficient extent of abilities or versatility of genius to attend to them all at the same time, or in a quick succession. Such a union must frequently occasion a confusion of principles and violation of rights. To commit their exercise to one man

or body of men, constitutes a monarchy or an aristocracy for
the time being. By giving them the power of avoiding all
constitutional enquiry, it places them above a sense of accountability for their conduct. They have it in their power—either
in the enacting, the interpretation or the execution of laws,—
to screen themselves and every member of their body from
account or punishment. The situation itself, suggests to them
views and interests different from those of the people, and
leaves no common judge between them. It places them in
respect to the people in that state of independence which is
so often called the state of nature. In such case, the people,
hopeless under oppression, sink into a state of abject slavery,
or roused to a sense of their wrongs, assume their natural rights
in such situation, and take exemplary vengeance on their
oppressors.

In a government so constituted, the frequency of elections
can serve only to aggravate the evil. The rulers, with all the
powers of government in their hands, will find every instrument of factious violence devoted to their service. They will
always have a hope of continuing themselves in the administration. Should there happen a change of men, a change of
measures, if attempted, would be of short continuance. The
same situation, and the same motives, would sooner or later
produce the same fatal effects. It may be further observed,
that a separation and precise limitation of the powers of government simplifies the duties of its ministers,—their acts are
thereby rendered distinct, enquiry facilitated, and abuses readily traced to their criminal sources, the particular agents. In
addition to this it gives a degree of energy to public sentiment.
Public approbation or censure, when directed to a number of
men, some of whom it is known have acted well or ill, but the
particular agents are concealed, lose much of their force.
The guilty hide their blushes in the crowd. Guilt, or rather
the sense of guilt, is diminished in proportion to the number of
associates. The better to secure the accountability of individuals in the great departments of government, not only ought
the powers of the several departments to be distinctly limited,
but the several members should be declared incapable of holding a place in more than one of the departments at the same

time. The members of one department may in general be
eligible to a place in another; but the acceptance of the latter
ought to vacate the former. A separation into distinct bodies
will be of little avail, if those bodies may be composed principally of the same individuals. The division of powers, will,
in such case, be only matter of form; they will remain substantially united. It may, however, be unnecessary to extend
these distinctions to the lower grade of magistrates. It may
be for them sufficient, that any office partaking of a judiciary
nature, shall be incompatible with one that is in its nature
executive.

CHAPTER V.

Of a Check arising from a Balance of Power, Rotation in Office, and from
Accountability.

Most modern writers upon government, who have entertained
any just notions of liberty, have contended for a distribution of
the powers of government into three departments or branches,
which are to constitute the legislature of the state. They
would have one body of men representing the commonalty, a
smaller body representing the more wealthy and honorable portion of the community, and an executive chief, whether king,
president, or governor, representing the sovereignty of the
state. These are to constitute three co-ordinate branches of
the legislature, and for the purpose of maintaining an exact balance of the several interests in the state, are to have a mutual
negative in passing all laws. The balance is to be supported
22*a*

between these co-ordinate branches, and the liberties and happiness of the people secured by a mutual opposition of rights,
interests and power.

These principles have been adopted from the form of the
English government, where hereditary ranks and powers are
coeval with the existence of the nation. But we are treating
of a government formed by a people, where hereditary ranks
and powers are happily unknown. For a people so situated,
the first article of whose political creed is, that all men are
born equal, and are by nature entitled to equal rights, to admit the necessity of such balance of opposing rights, powers,
and interests, is to abandon their principles, and to confess that
the laws of nature have indulged to certain classes of men
different rights and privileges with distinct interests, and that
the maintenance of those rights and privileges distinct and inviolable, is indispensably necessary to secure the liberty and
happiness of the whole. This position is, on our principles,
wholly inadmissible. There are inequalities among men ; some
have more bodily strength than others, some more strength
of mind. Hence proceeds an inequality in power and in riches. The strong are able to trample on the weak, the cunning
to circumvent the simple. But will it be maintained at this
day, that they have a natural right to do this ? The right of
acquisition is equal and common to all. The law of natural
justice has laid it under this restriction only,—"so use your
own right that you injure not the right of others." My right
of property, depending originally on my right of acquisition,
is not injured, because another, by the application of greater
industry and economy, has brought more of the goods of fortune within his right. If the law give a monopoly of riches,
of power, and honors, and secure them to him against my claims
of justice and of merit, it is an unjust violation of my rights.
These are the darling principles of monarchy and aristocracy.
Men are capable of being actuated by these principles. They
are also capable of many vices. The one contributes no more
to perfection in government than the other in moral conduct,—
one vice may be made to counteract another, and so one evil
principle in government may be employed to divert the pernicious tendency of another evil principle. But surely, where

they do not exist, it is better to prevent their very germination than to maintain a constant struggle against their evil tendency.

In Great Britain, the balance of power maintained in the three branches of that government preserves that portion of liberty which is found among the people, a valuable portion indeed, compared with what is to be found in any other nation of the old world. That government, as we have seen, consist of a monarchy, an aristocracy and a popular branch with co-ordinate powers. Two of these branches claim distinct and hereditary rights. These rights, as far as they extend, place the claim only beyond the reach of one branch of the laws of nature, the law of accountability to man. If these orders have been established in a state, and are to be supported, power must be opposed to power, authority to authority, as a means of self-defence in each. The prerogatives of the crown, and the privileges of the nobility are in diminution of the rights of the people. They are hereditary, and law and custom deem them inherent in the very blood,—their honors, their privileges, and their crimes are held to be above the judgment of the people.

The powers and rights of the monarch are exercised on the same subject,—the people. The restraint of one, as between themselves, is an enlargement of the other. Both are, in their origin, unfounded in natural principles. It is, in some measure a matter of indifference to the people, which has the exercise. These claims of right and power are placed in opposition, and mutual jealousy, sometimes breaking forth into open enmity, is the natural consequence. Every union of their interests, every compromise of their power is a conspiracy against the rights of the people, who have, at times, been justly provoked to assert their injured rights against both. As the claims of the monarch and the nobles are hostile to the rights of the people, so the people are naturally hostile to both. Thus there is constituted in the government, a perpetual war of each against the other, or at best, an armed truce, attended with constant negotiations, and shifting combinations, as if to prevent mutual destruction ; each party in its turn uniting with its enemy against a more powerful enemy.

The history of the English nation, from the time of William the Conqueror, furnishes an incontestable proof of this truth. It is little more than a history of the usurpation of the king and the nobles on the rights of the people ; struggles between the king and the nobles for the greatest share in the usurpation and the opposition of the people to both. What a scene of treachery, faction, and all the horrors of civil war, the legitimate offspring of such principles in their progress is constantly exhibited to our view. At this day great advancement in knowledge has happily introduced into their constitution a better adjustment of opposing claims ; and from the cultivation of the social virtues, those contests have lost their ferocity. What was formerly attempted by open violence is now often effected by the silent, though not less fatal means of corruption. It is the pestilence that walketh in darkness, succeeding to the destruction that wasteth at noon day.

By the constitution of that government, the democratic branch, the representatives of the commons, are become the only depository, and from interest, the only safe guardians of the people's rights. But with these, arising from the nature of the government and the frailties incident to human nature, temptations to betray their trust, and to desert to the opposite ranks, too often prevail. False notions of greatness, hope of office or of rising to the higher orders, and the desire of wealth, the necessary scaffolding of ambition, open wide the door to corruption. Hence, means are not unfrequently found to silence the boldest champion for liberty, and lay prostrate the stubborn virtues of the patriot. And why should a people, where such established orders do not exist, go so much out of their way to erect or cherish powers and interests hostile to each other, which cannot consist with common liberty, and are dangerous to virtue itself.

We, however, reject these principles, only for ourselves, and for those in a similar situation, among whom no such artificial distinctions exist. We readily admit, that with a people, where ranks and orders, a hereditary monarchy and a hereditary nobility, have so long existed, as to become interwoven with the constitution of the state, and of the human mind itself, the British constitution in its present improved state with its checks and balances, by intervening a third and popular branch, is for them the best form ; and indeed,—if we may trust to the experience of some of the first and most enlightened nations of the old world,—the only form of government which can permanently secure to such a people, any considerable portion of happiness, any portion of civil and political rights and liberty.

I am well aware that the necessity of a balance, constituted by an opposition of powers, in every government whatever, has been advocated by an authority which will always be respected. It has been insisted that the distinction of the one, the few, and the many, exists naturally among mankind, that is, the principles of monarchy, aristocracy, and democracy, and that in our representative form of government, for the accommodation of these classes, the adjustment of their several interests, and to guard against an undue preponderance of either, that might prove injurious, a division has been made of the governing powers into three co-ordinate branches ; a single executive chief representing the monarch, a senate representing the aristocratic branch, and the representatives of the people, being the democratic branch. But if we are not wholly deceived in the principles we have been endeavoring to establish, this opinion, although once and perhaps still entertained by some of our first and best men, is nevertheless erroneous. The opinion was, probably, derived from a habit of adducing the reasons of our institutions from British authorities, whence we have derived many of our forms, without sufficiently reflecting on the different nature of the governments, and that the same forms may be adopted in different institutions upon different principles and for very different reasons.

The distinctions insisted on, as forming a natural aristocracy among men, are birth, (or being descended of a respectable family,) wealth, and talents. These are certainly the occasion of individual distinctions ; but they are incidental and fluctuating. The laws of nature have given them no permanency— experience has proved, that neither birth nor riches, if not unduly favored by political institutions, give any permanent or dangerous pre-eminence, or create any real interest not in accordance with that of the whole. The pre-eminence of talents is but transient, unless accompanied with real merit, a character which always harmonizes with the public good.

Although checks, to be created by an opposition of powers and interests, are not in our institutions admissible on any rational grounds, yet there are other reasons well founded for distibuting the powers of government into three distinct departments, and for a further division of the legislature into two branches, a senate and house of representatives, which have been explained in the preceding chapter. If the view there taken of the subject be correct, the legislature forms one entire department of the government, and its division into two branches, and the power of a negative between them, is not designed to provide a power of control for the purpose of mutual defence, but solely to produce amicable discussion, a more thorough examination of public measures, and a general accommodation of the laws, to the manners, sentiments, and interests of the people. It is claimed by the citizens for their sakes only, not for the sake of the rulers. It is made necessary that each body should be satisfied of the goodness of a measure, before it can be adopted; if either be dissatisfied it is to be no farther pursued at that time. Such is the natural consequence between two bodies having equal powers; whenever they disagree, they must have a mutual negative. If one can carry a measure against the other, their powers are no longer equal. Their deliberations will not be mutual, nor will they long be amicable. The superior body will bear a difference of opinion with impatience. Hoc volo—"It is my pleasure" will always be found the most ready the most decisive answer.

As to the third branch, supposed in this theory to be one of the co-ordinate powers constituting the balance,—the executive or president, he has none of the peculiar powers or prerogatives of the monarch. It is generally made his duty to inform and advise the legislature; but he has no power to arrest their proceedings by interposing an absolute negative. Here, even in point of form, the similitude is much less than in the situation of the senate and house of representatives; and instead of a co-ordinate, he possesses no efficient power in legislation. Thus, these two departments, the legislature and executive, are in the exercise of their powers, maintained separate and distinct.

A frequent rotation in all the offices of government, has, by some statesmen of no inconsiderable authority, been esteemed one of the most effectual provisions against the abuse of power. The advocates for this institution urge, that a rotation in office, has the tendency to prevent the danger which constantly arises from an inveterate habit in the exercise of power by one man, family, or set of men on the one hand, and the habit which the people, on the other, are too prone to acquire, of directing their obedience to particular men or families, rather than to the laws and ordinances of their country. That these habits become inveterate, in any way, are not sufficiently checked by the frequency of elections, and always counteract the true principles of a representative government. The experiment, although often tried in ancient as well as more modern republics, has never succeeded in preventing the abuse of power; but has served rather to increase the violence of faction, and the rapacity of rulers, and render government but the more insupportable. The reason of these effects is, I think, obvious. Where a rotation in office is established, there will frequently be found in those who succeed, the want of a thorough knowledge of the business of their trust, a want of address, a degree of which is unavoidable to persons in new employments. But this is of less importance. An interest in the approbation of the people, and a strong sense of accountability in all official conduct is the greatest, or rather the only effectual security against abuses by those who exercise the powers of government. An institution, agreeable to which, the greatest wisdom, the most distinguished patriotism, the highest integrity in a ruler, cannot entitle him to the proper reward of his virtue, an expression of the approbation of his fellow citizens in his re-election to office, diminishes the most flattering interest which he ought to feel in their favor, and in some degree relaxes his sense of accountability to the tribunal of public sentiment.

His interest is seen directed into another channel. He no longer looks for a public reward, but hopes rather that his crimes may escape detection, or that his rapacity, and acts of oppression will furnish the means of baffling future enquiry, and to this end every intrigue will be employed and all the satellites of faction put in motion. An enquiry, if instituted, will soon be found to be pursued with less zeal by a set of men who, while they served to the same offices, served to the same views and the same interest. In a representative government, every thing ought to be avoided, that tends to deprive the people of the right of employing at their option, except in cases of present incompatibility in office, men of known abilities, and experienced integrity, or which tends to diminish in the rulers a deep sense of accountability, a perpetual interest in the approbation of the people.

In the difficult passage from error to truth, the state that succeeds the almost total ignorance of the savage, and which precedes a more general knowledge of the relations of nature and of man in society, a state in which the public voice of the moral sense is lost amid the violence of passions and appetites, may require, at least, it may endure a government founded in violence, and sometimes supported, but more frequently, overthrown, or brought to the brink of ruin by an opposition of powers. The history of Athens, of Rome, and many of the modern states have exhibited mankind mostly in this character. A few men have arisen in almost every nation, great beyond the age, the instruments of providence for the improvement of the world. To these, modern times, after ages of the darkest ignorance, are indebted for the first dawnings of science. As benefactors of mankind, their names will be held in perpetual remembrance ; but the history of their times informs us that they were able to communicate little of their knowledge to the body of the people, to moderate their passions, or to influence, in any considerable degree, the general sentiments.

The governments of those times, were as ill balanced as the passions of the people. Men in such a state are keenly sensible of the present, but almost regardless of the future. They are little capable of adjusting combinations, or of discovering any but the most obvious relations and tendencies. From the history and character of those times, we have reason to conclude that the violence of government, and the violence of the people, who often destroyed one set of tyrants to make room for another and were often guilty of greater abuses than those which they attempted to reform, did not proceed from the want of a balance of power in their civil institutions or any other provision, which in that state of society, human wisdom could have devised, but from the violence of the passions and appetites,—from the weakness of the moral sense, and consequently, of the sense of accountability, which rendered it difficult, we may say, impossible, to provide any sufficient barrier against the tyranny of rulers or the licentiousness of the people. Certainly, arguments drawn from such a state of society and manners, either for or against a check, constituted by a balance of powers or a rotation of office, ought with caution to be applied to the present state, in many respects so widely different.

At this day, great improvement in science, in manners, and in morals has taken place. The art of printing has facilitated the diffusion of knowledge, and rendered it more easily attainable. Useful science is no longer confined to the recluse. Much useful science and useful knowledge is accessible to the people generally. Improvements have begotten improvements, the knowledge of many things which was the fruit of long and laborious application, and for the attainment of which, a long life scarcely sufficed, is now imbibed almost with the milk in infancy. Many an ancient sage in the warmth of his philanthropy would have exulted, could he have foreseen that in many nations of Europe and in many states in America, a world then unknown, plain husbandmen would be found to possess more practical morality, more knowledge applicable in human life, more useful science than all the schools of antiquity could boast.

In the present state of imperfection the abuse of power will never be wholly prevented. But in a situation, in which the idea of inherent power, exclusive rights, and separate interests, shall, in the mode of delegation and the conduct required of rulers, be no longer suggested to their minds,—temptations to abuse, will, in a great measure be removed, and the enjoyment of equal rights will be finally secured to all, by establishing, as a radical and sacred principle in all their institutions, a strict accountability of the functionaries in every department of government,—a principle, which can be established with full effect, in no nation, where knowledge has not, in some good degree, been diffused among the great mass of the people, and their minds freed from the shackles and prejudices of artificial distinctions, which have so long held a great part of the world in thraldom. The application and effect of the principle of accountability has, in treating of the various parts of the constitution, been so often mentioned, and so far explained, that nothing more is necessary here, than to exhibit the whole in a brief and summary view.

1st. The powers of the several departments are so limited and defined as to afford a sufficient ground of decision, whether the legislature or any functionary in the executive department have exceeded or improperly exercised their respective powers. 2nd. The judges are empowered to decide in all questions coming before them upon executive and legislative acts, and if found to be unconstitutional, to pronounce them void. 3d. Although the members of the legislature, consistently with the nature of their functions, and the freedom of debate and opinion, cannot be elsewhere impeached for any of their acts in that body ; yet, as their debates are open, and the opinion of individuals publicly known, the conduct of each is brought under scrutiny at the periodical elections, and this scrutiny will extend not only to the constitutionality, but to the expediency of their public acts ; for, from the nature of the legislative power, they may pass constitutional acts, which are nevertheless inexpedient and unnecessarily burdensome. All those members, whose conduct and opinions meet the disapprobation of their constituents, will be no longer trusted. Their places will be supplied by others, in whom the people can confide for correcting the errors of their predecessors. 4th. The president and all those whose appointment to office is retained by the people, are subject to the same scrutiny and the same judgment of the people at their elections. Executive officers of every grade are also, for their arbitrary and unconstitutional acts, subject to impeachment, to removal, and disqualification for future employment, and are further liable, according to the nature and effects of their arbitrary acts, to a criminal prosecution and punishment, and a reparation in damages to the party injured. 5th. Finally, the judges, although not accountable for mere error of opinion, are, for corruption, mal-practice, and misbehavior in office, liable to removal by impeachment in the same manner as executive officers ; and are further accountable, to the people through their representatives for their character and conduct, being liable to be by them removed from office in the manner prescribed in the constitution. These provisions of the constitution, if we may trust not to theory merely, but to the experience of more than half a century in these United States, are more effectual in preventing the abuse of power in government, in securing the rights and liberties and promoting the interest and happiness of a people, than any thing before known in political institutions.

CHAPTER VI.

Of Election and Appointment to Office.

It has been already observed, that elections ought to be periodical. To prevent, in the members of the legislature, and the executive, every idea of an independent power, of a property in their appointments, they must be elected for a limited time ; a period must be fixed by the constitution when their exercise of power shall cease, and leave them that pre-eminence only, which they may derive from the approbation of the people. The time must be sufficiently long to complete the ordinary routine of business.

In smaller states, a year will be the most convenient period for the house of representatives. In large states, the time necessary for the elections, the nature of the ordinary business, and the magnitude of the subjects which demand their attention, may require a longer period for that body. Reasons may also be found, as has been suggested, for fixing a different period for the members of the senate from that of the representatives, and a different period may be deemed proper for the president and other officers who may receive their appointments by popular elections. But in every instance, some period ought to be fixed, beyond the power of the legislature to alter. Such, provision will, on every occasion, re-call their attention to the interests of the people, and keep their accountability constantly in view. It will be necessary, however, to entrust to the legislature, the power and duty of passing laws to preserve order, to prevent and punish corruption, and to carry into full effect this provision of the constitution, as well as to order elections at other times than the stated periods, when it may be necessary for filling vacancies that may be occasioned by death, resignation, or removal. One important point to be considered is, the qualifications which ought to be required of electors and of candidates for office.

The questions of a general and of a limited right of suffrage and eligibility, have been not a little agitated in these states. Before the revolution, the colonies who had their provincial legislatures, universally followed the example of the mother country in making property a necessary qualification both of the right of suffrage and eligibility. The amount of property was different in the different colonies ; but generally, a freehold property was required ; in some, personal property to a larger amount in value was substituted for freehold. When, upon the revolution, the colonies became independent states, they generally, in forming their constitutions, adopted the same qualifications. On a revision of these constitutions, in several instances the qualifications have been diminished or abolished, and a nearer approach has been made to a general right of suffrage. The right of suffrage, or of the people to elect the great functionaries of the government, is the principal of those political rights, in the free exercise and enjoyment of which, alone, is found any sufficient guaranty for the permanent enjoyment of civil liberty. Whatever reasons there may be in Great Britain, arising from their mixed form of government, or the general state of property, for limiting the right of suffrage, I am persuaded they do not exist with us, or certainly not to the same extent.

In a representative government, where every thing ought to tend, in a good degree, to a general equality, property seems not alone, or even principally, to be a just criterion of the right of suffrage. The natural, civil, and political rights of man, in society, are the subjects of legislative discussion, and provision, and their security,—the great end of all the apparatus of government in every department. The right of property is one of these rights and gives rise to a very extensive influence in society. It is, however, a right which, if it meets a too partial indulgence, if suffered to engross all political rights, will unavoidably suggest to the proprietor the idea, as it furnishes the means of infringing the rights of others with impunity. The interests of industry, of science, and the mechanic arts, have an equal claim on society. The protection and encouragement of these, tends to a more equal distribution of the goods of fortune, and to correct the unequal influence of wealth.

In a state, where, from the prevalence of corrupt principles, or from any other source, all property with its concomitant power, is accumulated in the hands of a few; where the great mass of the people are reduced to dependence, servility, and meanness, from which they can never hope to rise, but on the ruin of their oppressors, a general right of suffrage would be dangerous to the few, and at least for a time, to the people themselves, and might render impracticable the best institutions of which they are in such situation capable. But in the government of these United States, where the law equally regards the rights of the rich and the poor; where few are to be found wholly destitute of property, and fewer still without a well grounded hope of obtaining it; where industry and economy rarely fail to produce a competence, and often lead to wealth; no ill consequences are to be feared from a general right of suffrage.

By general, however, is not to be understood a universal and indiscriminate right; but so far general as to include all who are by law called upon to pay to the support of government, or for the performance of public duties or services. Still, in every well regulated government, necessity and propriety will require exclusions. All females, from the delicate and dependent nature of their sex, and to preserve that purity and simplicity of character, on which the domestic as well as public happiness of mankind so much depends, have, generally, if not universally, been excluded from any share in political transactions. It will also be necessary and proper to exclude from the right of suffrage all those, who, from want of age, are supposed to be wanting in discretion—all who, from any legal disability are not *sui juris*—at their own disposal. Those whom the law deems incapable of governing themselves, can claim no voice in governing the state—and certainly the interests of virtue require, that those should be wholly excluded, who, by their crimes, have manifested a disposition totally corrupt, and by their conduct declared to the world, that they are no longer to be trusted. Indeed all who are, from situation in life, under the control of others so that they cannot be capable of acting their own opinion, ought to be excluded from the right of suffrage. But it is difficult to distinguish in this case. The control is an influence.

If, from the nature of their situation, any class of citizens are placed under a sinister influence, not ordinarily to be resisted by persons in that situation, the class ought to be excluded the right. All act under some kind of influence, who act from motives; but all influence is not inconsistent with the freedom of action. Some are capable of resisting an undue influence arising from almost any situation; others not, and far the greater number in any particular situation are found incapable of resisting, and if the good of the community so require, the whole class ought to be excluded. If it be said, that the right of suffrage is founded in the natural right of self-government, and is therefore not to be violated, the answer is, that if a society be founded in natural principles, the great end is the general utility, the greatest good of that society; and for attaining that end, there is not a right, natural, civil, or political, abstractly considered as belonging to individuals, which is not subject to limitation. No one can justly insist on the exercise of that as a right, which evidently tends to the general injury of the community. But we must be careful not to mistake a partial for a general interest, the interest of a particular class or classes, for the interest of the whole.

I am unable to persuade myself, that any distinction ought, in general, to be made between the right of suffrage and eligibility. I say, in general; for a man may have placed himself in a situation, in which he owes a duty to society, incompatible with certain civil functions, and which the public good requires should not be suspended. A distinction of age also, which to abilities adds experience and maturity of judgment, may well be admitted. It is an honorary distinction, in which there is nothing invidious, and is yielded by mankind, in a certain degree, with general approbation. A distinction of other qualifications is mostly invidious. It tends to introduce a distinction of classes, and to excite a degree of haughtiness in the candidates. The electors, in such a case, feel themselves degraded, and that their class, notwithstanding their right of suffrage, is unrepresented.

If a character for abilities and integrity is to be considered the only qualifications for office, they will be more assiduously cultivated. These are all-important to the people, and of these, in relation to the principal functionaries of the legislative and executive departments, the people are competent judges. The choice of a worthy character reflects honor upon themselves, which they enjoy with the more satisfaction, as they are sensible of no restraint in the choice. From these considerations, I conclude, that the right of suffrage and of eligibility ought to be the same, or, distinguished by no qualifications but that of age, just mentioned. If in any state, different qualifications are found to be necessary, the necessity must have arisen from the different nature of the government and the condition of the people.

It has been the opinion of some, that all the officers and functionaries of the government may, with the greatest safety, and therefore on principle, ought to be elected by the people. This appears to have been the opinion of Mr. Jefferson. In a letter written by him in the year 1816, to a friend, on the subject of a revision of the constitution of Virginia, he says,—"The true foundation of a republican government is the equal right of

every citizen in his person and property, and their management. Try by this, as a tally, every provision of the constitution, and see if it hangs directly on the will of the people ;
reduce the legislature to a sufficient number for free but orderly
discussion ; let every man who fights or pays, exercise his
just and equal right in their election—submit them to approbation or rejection at short intervals ; let the executive be
chosen in the same way, and for the same term, by those whose
agent he is to be, and leave no screen of a council behind which
to skulk from responsibility. It has been thought that the
people are not competent electors of judges learned in the law,
but I do not know that this is true ; and if doubtful, we should
follow principle in this, as in other cases. In one state of the
union, at least, it has long been tried, and with the most satisfactory success. The judges of Connecticut have been chosen
by the people every six months, for nearly two centuries, and
I believe there has hardly ever been an instance of a change,
so powerful is the curb of incessant responsibility."

The judges of the superior courts in Virginia are chosen by
the legislature, and removeable by their own body only, for
misconduct in office. If prejudice should prevail against the
mode of electing judges by the people, he would then give the
appointment to the executive alone. Upon this subject he
says,—" Nomination to office is an executive function. To
give to the legislature as we do, is a violation of the principle
of the separation of the powers. It swerves the members from
correctness, by temptations to intrigue for office themselves, and
to a corrupt barter of votes, and destroys responsibility, by dividing it among a multitude. By leaving nomination in its
proper place among executive functions, the principle of the
separation of powers is preserved, and responsibility weighs
with its heaviest force on a single hand. After the members
of the legislature and chief of the executive, the writer mentions by way of example, the election of the judges only by
the people ; but the view clearly is to extend the same principle to the election of all the civil officers of the state of every
grade ; and in pursuance of this view, he afterwards proposes
that all county officers should be elected by the people of the
several counties.

The principle he would pursue is "the equal right of every citizen in his person and property and their management." This is no other than the right of self-government, which has been shewn to be the foundation of all political rights. It is certain that in all political establishments, we ought to follow principles; but we must always remember, that they are principles of social nature, of social man—that one principle is not to be pursued to the exclusion of others. They are all to be limited and mutually modified and adjusted, as the best interests of the community shall require.

In all political institutions, the right of self-government is ed, in some more, in others less. In a democracy, where it is carried the farthest, the minority are governed by the majority; and in a representative government, the majority of the electors choose the representatives to the legislature against the will of the minority; and a majority of these representatives make laws to govern the whole state. If the people, by the constitution empower the President to make appointments to office, it is no more a departure from the principle of self-government, than it is to empower their representatives to make laws for them. There is indeed this difference,—the representatives who make the laws, are directly accountable to the people, and so is the President making appointments; the officers, however, whom he appoints, are not so accountable, but to such tribunal as the constitution provides. So far as relates to this principle, then, the questions are, whether a better selection for certain offices is to be expected from an executive appointment, or from popular elections? and whether a sufficient provision is made to hold the officers accountable? If these questions be answered in the affirmative, then the public good, which ought to be an overruling principle in all political institutions, decides in favor of an executive appointment. As to the precedent cited of the judges in the state of Connecticut, being elected by the people semi-annually, Mr. Jefferson must have been egregiously misinformed. The people of that state elected their representatives semi-annually. They also elected annually the treasurer and secretary of the state, the governor, lieutenant governor, and assistants or councillors, that with the governor who presided and the lieutenant governor, formed their senate or upper house of legislature. All other officers of the state generally, except town officers so called, captains and subalterns of the militia, who were elected by the people and sheriffs of counties, were, before the late revision of their constitution, appointed by the concurrent acts of the two houses of legislature, and except generals and field officers of the malitia, annually. Sheriffs were appointed by the governor and council, and removeable by them at their pleasure. The precedent, therefore, wholly fails.

I readily agree that for the principle, where there is a probability that an equally good selection will be made for any office by the people, they ought to retain the election, although it might with equal safety be entrusted to some organ of the government. There will be many instances of this kind, besides those whose election has been mentioned in which the election will be better and with more propriety made by the people. Such will be the case with all the officers of a very numerous class of subordinate political institutions of which we shall briefly treat in the next chapter. We shall, therefore, consider here, of the appointment of those officers only who belong to the general government of the state.

I fully agree that the general power of appointment to office ought not, as observed in a former chapter, to be entrusted to the legislature on account of the irresponsible nature of their situation, in that respect, and the tendency which it has to a corrupting influence. Some will think that the nomination or appointment to office is not in its nature strictly, either a legislative or an executive function; but it will be agreed that it better accords with the duties of the executive, than those of the legislature and will be more safely deposited with the head of that department on account of his prominent and single responsibility to the people. There are powers required for the performance of some duties which do not seem strictly to belong to either of the great departments of government, which yet do not require a distinct and separate department. These may be committed to some organ already established, with whose duties it will best comport, and where it will attach the greatest degree of responsibility, and, of consequence, the powers will probably be exercised with a single view to the public good—at any rate committing the power of appointment to the President does not violate a separation of the powers properly belonging to the several departments.

The principal officers, for whose appointment a provision is to be made will belong either to the judiciary or the executive department. Of the propriety and expediency of the judges being appointed by the executive we have already treated.

It will generally be found necessary for the more easy management, and for the sake of simplifying, to distribute the business of the executive into several subordinate departments,—as the department of state, of the finances or treasury, and others as they may be found expedient; but for these it must be left to the discretion of the legislature to provide. The head of these departments ought to be confidential ministers of the President, and under his inspection. Subordinate to these in each department there will necessarily be employed many officers, in whom great trust and confidence must be reposed; but how can the President have a full confidence in those, who are imposed upon him by others, or be in any degree responsible for their character, either for abilities or integrity? It is therefore proper, the President should have the nomination of these ministers and officers; and also, the power of removing them at his discretion as occasion may require. Indeed without this power of removal by the President, in cases of delinquency, great loss and injury would frequently be sustained by the public before a proper remedy could be applied.

But as there ought to be every rational check upon the exercise of power, that may, without too much embarrassment, guard it against abuse. The President's nomination, as has been before observed, may with propriety be referred to the senate for their advice and approbation, without which the appointment cannot be made. This provision should, however, be with an exception of temporary appointments to supply vacancies on certain occasions, and of some other to be provided for by law. Although this advice is not of a legislative nature, it is apprehended not to interfere with any of the appropriate duties of that department, and to have no tendency to a corrupt influence on the members of the senate—and besides the general accountability of the President to the people, it will be an additional inducement to him to nominate to that body none but those, whose known integrity and talents qualify them for the office.

The President may, with the best intentions, be sometimes deceived in his information, for which he must not unfrequently rely upon others. In such case, the senators coming from all the different parts of the state, some of them may know of objections to the person nominated and prevent an improper appointment. It will also be a proper provision of the constitution, that the legislature should have the power to vest certain appointments in the heads of departments, in the courts of law and on some occasions in the President alone.

On a full consideration of this subject and the provisions of the constitution, that may bear upon it, we may fairly come to the conclusion that the President, who must feel a deep interest in the character of those to be appointed, and who must be supposed to know the nature of the duties to be required of each, and the abilities necessary to a proper performance of those duties, will be capable of making a better selection of suitable characters for the several offices, than can be made by the people at their elections ; especially, as it is certain, a great majority of the electors must, in a great variety of instances, act under a total ignorance both of the duties to be performed and of the characters and abilities of the persons elected,—and that such officers will, in their responsibility to the President, under whose inspection they mostly act, feel a more immediate and powerful restraint upon their conduct than can be induced through popular elections. And when we consider that for misconduct in office, they are liable to removal by impeachment, to disqualification for future appointments, and are further subject to punishment at law according to the nature of their offence, and to a reparation in damages, the provision for securing their accountability is as ample as human institutions will admit. We cannot, therefore, hesitate to say,—that under the restrictions proposed, the general appointing power will be the most safely and beneficially entrusted to the executive.

We cannot forbear again to observe, that the mode of appointment to office here advocated, is not a departure from the principle of self-government considered as pertaining to a social being, the great end of which is the promotion of social no less than individual happiness. The maxim, however technical, will here strictly apply,—" Whatever a man does by another he does by himself." Where the principal is able to hold his agents sufficiently responsible for their fidelity and skill, his affairs may not unfrequently be better managed by them than by himself. This, with proper precaution will be found no less true of a people in their political situation, than of an individual in a private station.

CHAPTER VII.

Of Subordinate Political Institutions.

In every state of any considerable extent, there will always be found many local concerns and interests, which, though not at variance with the general interest, of which indeed they form constituent parts, cannot be managed with propriety and to the general advantage by one central administration. For this reason among others, states have been divided into districts, severally organized with administrations adapted to the management of their local concerns, in due subordination to each other, and all to the general administration of the state. Such generally subsist in this country in the several states of the union, deriving their origin from similar institutions in England, the country of our own ancestors. In adapting them to general circumstances, they have received many alterrtions and improvements, on which it is unnecessary to dwell.

The first grand division is generally in these states, into counties, which are again subdivided into towns, so denominated, especially in the Northern states. This division, also, comprehends cities, which are in fact only more populous towns, and the local interests of which become more intricate and important in proportion to their population and wealth, requiring a different organization and more extensive powers. One principal end in view in a division into counties, is the more convenient administration of justice. For this purpose the county is organized with a court, denominated the County Court, with a jurisdiction in causes civil and criminal, more or less extensive, under the supervision of the Supreme Court of the state. It is also generally provided that the trial in all causes pending before any superior court shall be had in their proper counties. By this institution, instead of a forced attendance of the parties at an extreme distance, as might frequently happen, and at an enormous expense, which can be sustained only by the most wealthy class, justice in civil causes is brought within the reach of all ; and in criminal prosecutions it gives the prosecutor the advantage generally of having his witnesses to prove the charge, and the accused to prove his innocence, as we may say, on the spot. The powers of police, and the management of the local interests of the county, has been more frequently vested in the judges of the County Court, sometimes assisted by the sessions. In some states, the power has been vested in a board of supervisors, so called, the members of which are annually elected by the people of the several towns in the county. Their powers and duties are determined and regulated by a general law. They sometimes exercise a legislative power, as in the imposing of taxes on the inhabitants to defray the expenses incident to the county. They have also the direction and regulation of public or county roads. They sometimes act more in a judicial capacity, as in determining the proportion which each shall contribute, and in what manner, where the law has imposed a common duty or burden on two or more towns. Such county institutions best accord with the nature of our free governments.

The next subordinate division is that of towns. Towns in these states have been so called from an analogy which they bear to towns corporate in England, of a lower grade than cities and of a different organization. In this country, especially in the Northern states, the towns are, for the most part, incorporated by a general law. In each state, therefore, the organization is uniform, and the powers and privileges the same. The organization of these corporations, their powers, and the exercise of those powers ought to bear an analogy to the general government of the state as far as their subordinate situation and the end of their institution will permit ; and to attain that end they must be vested with a certain portion of legislative and executive powers. The form of their government, for such it is, on however small a scale, ought, like that of the state, to be republican ; not of the representative kind, but a pure and simple democracy, in which the power of making local laws and regulations, and the appointment to corporate offices will reside in the people, the inhabitants of the town.

It is proper that there should be appointed by law, a meeting to be held annually in each town for the election of town officers, and for the transaction of such other business as shall be found necessary, and within the limits of their powers. They will also be authorized to call meetings at other times on necessary occasions. Among the officers to be annually appointed, will be a town-clerk, and one—or rather a select board—whose duty it shall be to take care of the prudential affairs, and to carry into effect all the legal acts of the town. As to other town officers, how many there will be, and what the nature of their several offices, will depend on the powers vested in the corporation, and the duties enjoined. Some few of these I will mention.

To carry into full effect such local regulations as the towns are empowered to make, and especially in what relates to the maintenance of peace and good order, civil magistrates will be found necessary. Such magistrates will be furnished through the justices of the peace appointed in every town by the proper appointing power of the state.—But there must be appointed by each town a constable, to be empowered by law to arrest disturbers of the peace, and to serve within his limits all process both civil and criminal, issued by a justice of the peace and also one or more officers in each to present and prosecute before some justice, all breaches of the peace and other offences committed within the town for which they are appointed. Such officer has sometimes been denominated a grand-juror. On the towns will properly be enjoined the duty of laying out, making and repairing roads, and of building and repairing bridges, within their respective limits, to perform which there must be an appointment of proper officers. It will also be made the duty of each town to provide for their own poor, agreeable to the provision of the general laws of

the state. To enable the towns to fulfil these duties, it is
necessary that each should have the power of laying and
collecting taxes under proper restrictions, and to appoint an
officer who shall have the powers necessary to make the
collection. It may, and indeed ought to be made the duty of
the towns severally, to appoint annually suitable persons
assessors, for the purpose of taking, in the manner prescribed
by law, a valuation of the taxable property in each, agreeable
to which all state and other taxes authorized by law, shall be
apportioned for collection. In this mode a valuation more just,
equal, and satisfactory, will be obtained, than in any other
which could probably be devised.

The towns may also be entrusted with the appointment of
the collector of state taxes within their several districts, for
whose abilities and the faithful performance of his duties, the
town appointing, should be made responsible to the state
treasury. In no other mode can the public taxes be collected
with equal facility, security, and economy.

It will be further, as I conceive, a very important and
necessary provision, that for the election of representatives,
and all state and public officers to be elected by the suffrages
of the people, the votes should be taken at public meetings to
be appointed by law in the several towns, in each of which,
none should be permitted to vote but the qualified inhabitants
of the same town. Such provision will effectually prevent
that violent excitement, those tumults, and even riots which
are found too often to prevail among the multitude at the poll
from a large district, and besides, it affords an opportunity to a
greater number of citizens to exercise the invaluable right of
suffrage.

There is another division of the several towns, which,
though the lowest in grade, is not the least in its usefulness
and importance, a division of each into school districts. Each
town should have the power of making such divisions as
occasion may require, in the manner best calculated to accom-
modate the inhabitants and the attendance of the scholars at
that early age, when they are to be taught the first rudiments
of common learning. These districts ought to be instituted
with corporate powers, which will be few and simple, adapted

to the end and design of their institution, the establishment and maintenance of common schools. The inhabitants of these districts, severally, must be empowered to appoint proper officers, to tax themselves in such manner as shall be provided by law, for the purpose of building a school house, and maintaining a school, or to raise money by subscription, or in any other mode upon which they shall agree ; to collect such tax and to carry their agreements into effect. They ought also to be enabled to hold funds to a reasonable amount, and entitled to receive each a due proportion of any general fund belonging to the town for the use of schools, or which may be appointed by the state, on such conditions as the law shall prescribe. It is unnecessary here to dwell on the usefulness of such institution to the rising generation, and to the community in general.

Cities, which I have placed in the same division, are to be considered as towns consistering of a more numerous and dense population, where we find, pressed as it were, into contact with each other, people of every condition in life, from the extreme of wealth, to the extreme of poverty, and of character, from the highest degree of integrity and moral worth, to the lowest degree of profligacy, vice, and crime. They will therefore demand a different organization, and powers more extensive and efficient. Cities in this country have generally, in the form and manner of their government, had a more arbitrary cast than what belongs to our free institutions :—the examples have been taken from governments of different principles and a different construction.

The situation and circumstances of cities, above hinted, will require an organization different from that of the common towns, and a more energetic government, and which may have a nearer analogy to the state government. In this case the powers of local legislation cannot be properly exercised by the people in their public meetings, which would bring together a heterogenous and ungovernable multitude, setting at defiance all discussion, all deliberation and every semblance of order. It therefore appears most proper that resort should be had to the system of representation. The power of making all the necessary local laws and regulations may, under proper guards, be vested in a city legislature to consist like the state legislature, of a senate and body of representatives, to be annually elected by the freemen in the several wards, in such numbers and in such manner as shall be provided by the laws of the state by which the corporation is to be constituted. There must also be an executive officer usually called the mayor, to be elected annually by the freemen of the city, and clothed with sufficient powers.

The power of appointing to office may be vested generally in the legislature or in one of its branches, and perhaps in some instances more properly in the mayor. Many officers will be necessary, but to point them out with their several duties would be tedious and uninteresting. I shall content myself with mentioning a few of them generally. There must be city magistrates for various purposes ; an efficient police, with its officers always vigilant, always on the alert ; and a police court to be almost constantly in session. Other courts will be necessary, but one will be indispensably so, in a large and populous city—a city court of common law, for the trial and decision of all such causes, civil and criminal, as shall be submitted to their jurisdiction. The court ought to be of great respectability, and the judges to be appointed, not by the city powers, but by the appointing power of the state, to hold their offices during good behavior, with fixed and adequate salaries, and subordinate to the Supreme Court of the state.

It has not been my design to enter into minute details on the subject, but to exhibit a brief view of these institutions, their organization, and the powers with which they ought to be entrusted. Enough has been said to evince their general utility, and even necessity ; and that they may be better adapted to the management of the several local interests and concerns, frequently varying with situation and circumstances, than can be effected by any provisions of law under the general administration ; and that they may be so ordered and directed as to render important services, and give efficient aid to the general government of the state, of which they are always to be considered constituent, though subordinate parts.

But there is another view, perhaps not less important, to be taken of these institutions. In the several districts of their establishment, which, taken together, are supposed to cover the whole surface of the state, and to embrace all the inhabitants, the exercise of political power is brought down to the people, themselves. Here are held the primary assemblies of the people, severally empowered to manage the affairs of their little communities. These assemblies are, in fact, the primary schools, in which the people practically learn what may, in a political sense, be called the science of self-government. Here the future statesman learns to exercise his powers of deliberation and discussion—and here the people acquire the habit of submitting private to public opinion, to acquiesce in the decisions of the majority, so necessary to the well being of a free government, without which all turns to faction, rushes into anarchy and finally into despotism, the last desperate remedy for more intolerable evils.

CHAPTER VIII.

The Institution of Juries.

In the institution of juries, I comprehend both the grand and petit jury as known in the laws of England and in the United States.

The trial by jury is certainly of considerable antiquity in the English laws, from which we in this country have derived the institution. It has been often asserted that it made a part of the Saxon jurisprudence before the Norman conquest. On this subject, Mr. Crabb, in his History of the English law, observes,— " Whether the trial by jury existed among the Saxons, has, like many other matters connected with those remote periods, been a subject of controversy. From all the records that have been preserved from those times, it is clear that there was no such thing as a jury of twelve men sworn to give their verdict on the evidence offered to them." He further tells us,—" In criminal matters it is clear from a law of Ethelred, that a grand jury existed among the Saxons ; for the law directs, that twelve Thanes, with the sheriff at their head, shall go, and on their oath enquire into all offences, not charging any one falsely nor wilfully, nor suffering any offender to escape. From the condition of the parties and the office required of them, namely, *accusare*, that is to make presentment of offenders, it is beyond all question that they had only to determine what offenders should be put upon their trial and what not."*

---

* History of English Law, p. 35.

It appears probable that the trial by jury was introduced after the Norman conquest, and was extended and improved by slow degrees. In the reign of Henry I. about the beginning of the twelfth century, the trial by jury was recognised in criminal suits ; but in civil suits it seems not to have approached very near to its present form until about the middle of the thirteenth century in the reign of Henry III.* In this reign we find that the office of the grand jury and their oath was nearly the same as at the present day. The jury system has since received many and great improvements, till it has been brought to its present state of perfection, in which it is justly considered the great palladium of liberty, and worthy of a special provison in the constitution of every free government.†

In a mixed government like that of Great Britain, the intervention of juries, both in the prosecution of crimes, and in the decision of private rights, is a principal security to the subject against any dangerous power and influence of the monarchical and aristocratic branches. It is equally necessary in a republic, but for reasons somewhat different. In a republic the powers of government are supported, not by force, but by the sentiments of the people. It is necessary, therefore, to cultivate a sentiment of attachment to the government.—The powers of government are visible in the exercise only.—The mode in which they are exercised, either invigorates or weakens the sentiment.—The exercise of power is not in general agreeable to those who are the subjects of it.—The administration of justice without a view to the consequences, is austere and forbidding, rather than amiable and attractive. ‡ As more men are capable of feeling than reasoning, the first view is generally of something unamiable. The ministers of justice,

---

* History of English Law, p. 164. † Those who are desirous of further information on this subject will do well to consult this work here quoted, and Reeves' History of the Common Law.

‡ Justice when considered as a private virtue, that is, the rendition to every one of his honest due, is directly amiable ; when considered in the distribution of punishments it is not so ; the mind is reconciled to it from a view of the consequences merely, unless when the passion of revenge excites a desire of retaliation.

20

are the objects of these feelings ;—the ideas of una miable severity daily impressed on the minds of the people are not easily corrected by reasoning on the consequences.*

Justice is administered for the redress of some evil, either public or private. The evil is past, and sometimes uncertain, or at least, of difficult investigation. The evil which is inflicted by the ministers of the law, is present and certain. The people cannot, consistent with an impartial administration of the law, have a direct control over them. These considerations have, more or less, a tendency to diminish that sentiment of attachment, which is so necessary in a republic. The institution of juries, in which is to be comprehended both the grand jury, who are to pass on the accusation and find it supported before the person accused can be put on trial, and the petit jury, who pass on the final trial, furnishes an adequate remedy.

In the administration of criminal law, the institution of a grand jury has a very leading influence in a free government.† To guard the innocent against the infamy and oppression of a public accusation, and without favor to bring forward the guilty to trial for their crimes, constitutes the principal duty of the grand jury. Taken from the body of the people, and having, in the prosecution of offences, no interest but the peace and welfare of the community, as far as they are secured by the prevention of crimes, they are placed as a shield between the accused and the interested passions, or malicious attempts of private prosecutors ; and their intervention between the people and the officers of the law, who, from the nature of their employment, may, sometimes, be suspected of interested views,

---

* Hangmen and public executioners, are universally detested. The first impressions which their actions make on the mind,—impressions of inhumanity and cruelty,—are never effaced by reasoning on the justice of their actions or necessity to the community.

† I do not recollect any institution among the ancients similar to that of a grand jury ; nor do I recollect to have met with any in any of the modern governments, that of the English excepted. It was as we have seen established among them before the Norman conquest. Crabb, ubi supra. Blackstone, Comm. 4. 302.

or at least, of a want of feeling, gives a facility to the execution
of criminal law, and reconciles to the sentiments of the people,
the necessary punishment of offenders. The punishment of
the guilty, if, from an oppressive partiality in the prosecution, or
an undue rigor in the execution, it meets not the acquiescence
of the people, can have no salutary effect in society.

It may be made a question, how far the person injured ought
to be admitted to prosecute for the end of punishing. I apprehend this will depend much on the state of manners, and the
principles of the government. In a government supported in
a great measure by force, and in a state of manners in which
the mind is highly inflamed by every, the least private injury,
and the passion of revenge is satisfied with nothing short of
personal retaliation, it may be in a degree necessary to permit
the person injured to prosecute his revenge at law, to prevent
the fatal consequences of private malice. To restrain the spirit
of personal revenge, and subject it to general laws, is a great
point in the progress of society. Still, as prosecutions, for the
end of punishment by the party injured, have a direct tendency
to perpetuate a resentment of injuries, and to make the law
instrumental in the exercise of personal enmity, the practice,
by no means, agrees with a general refinement of manners* or
the humane principles of a popular government. The person
injured ought to rest satisfied with a full security in the right
of reparation. The right of punishment ought to be exercised
solely for the prevention of crimes, and to be permitted to those
only, who are selected by law for that purpose, and who are
supposed to be capable of candor and moderation in their proceedings. The practice of admitting common informers, who
are to receive a share of the penalty as a reward for prosecuting, is still less to be justified. The practice can never be
necessary in any state of manners, nor is it justified by the plea

---

* By refinement of manners is not meant the ettiquette of politeness merely,
which may consist with many traits of barbarous manners. It consists with
the modern point of honor, the practice of duelling to revenge personal af-
fronts, and insults often imaginary. We ought rather to place a refinement
of manners in the sentiments of humanity, and a general spirit of accommodation.

of preventing a greater evil, by the admission of a less. It often serves the purposes of private malice, always fosters in the prosecutors a spirit of plunder, a disposition to prey on others, and serves to excite and disseminate jealousies and private animosities among the citizens. It is calculated for those governments only, in which the rulers foresee the punishment of their own crimes in the unanimity of the people. Can we, then, hesitate to pronounce that in the United States of America, the institution of criminal prosecutions in the name and under the direction of private persons, is opposed to the present state of manners, and the principles of their government? and that the intervention of a grand jury ought to be secured in every constitution, as the sacred right of the people, at least, in all prosecutions for capital, and all other high crimes and misdemeanors?

The observations made on the institution of grand juries, who, by their intervention between the ministers of the law, and the people, and their deliberate and solemn approbation of prosecutions, remove the odium of severity and serve to reconcile the execution of criminal law to the sentiments of the people, apply with more force to petit juries, in proportion as the condemnation is of more consequence than the accusation. This is not all. The institution is the best which has been devised, and probably, that can be devised by human wisdom, for obtaining substantial justice in trials, both criminal and civil. The particular province of the jury, is to weigh evidence and to decide upon facts. It is true, that in all questions to be decided by a jury, justice results from a combination of law and facts ; and it is also true, that in a complicated state of society the law may become intricate and its application not a little difficult. This can happen in questions of a civil nature only. No crimes are to be made out by a construction of dubious facts, or a doubtful application of law. It is the province of the judges to explain and apply the law, and to decide upon it when submitted to them by the jury on a statement of facts. To such statement the jury are fully competent.

Will it be thought strange to assert, that professional and systematic knowledge is less competent to judge of the proof of facts, than plain sense conversant only with the common business of life, and the common characters of men? And yet, to the mortification of the great and the learned, experience has established this to be generally true. It is not therefore without reason, that men acquiesce more readily in the verdict of a jury, than in the opinion of the judges, on matters of fact. There is also another consideration of considerable weight. The judges are often viewed as a distinct class, placed above the common interests and common feelings of the citizens. Hence arises the idea, however ill founded, of a distinct interest and a general bias, upon certain occasions. Juries are, or ought to be, taken from the substantial class of citizens; and effectual provision should be made to guard against every inlet to corruption, and the admission of those to set on the trial who may be subject to prejudices or interested views, in their decisions.* With these precautions, the justice of their decisions will be attributed to the excellence of the administration, and if they should prove unjust, it will be attributed to human frailty; it will be viewed as a temporary inconvenience, for which the laws are not answerable, where unjust decisions made by the judges are considered as dictated by standing, official prejudices, by interest or secret corruption, which, however dangerous, are not easily removed. From this brief view of the subject it appears, that this institution, in which is included both the grand and petit juries, is intimately connected with the principles of a free government. It sufficiently obviates any danger, which might be supposed to arise from the independence of the judges, and secures the administration of justice, in the spirit of impartiality and moderation, the true spirit of a free government.

---

* There is a provision for selecting jurors in some of these states, well worthy of imitation. The law directs that at the annual town meetings, the principal town officers and the civil authority of the town shall select and nominate a suitable number of persons properly qualified to serve as grand and petit jurors, for the year ensuing. When approved by the meeting the names of the persons so selected, are to be deposited in separate boxes in the custody of the town clerk. When a venire is issued for jurymen, the court directs from what towns they shall be taken, and the number from each; and thereupon the summoning officers attend on the town clerk, who is directed to draw by lot from the several boxes, in the presence of the officer, the number required, and the officer is directed to summon the persons whose names are so drawn, and no others. The jurors thus selected, are always respectable, and in very few instances do the parties in court find cause of challenge.

BOOK VI.

OF LAWS.

CHAPTER I.

General idea of Law—Of the Law of Nature.

The principal object in this book, will be to take a brief view of the principles, and the obligation of the law of nature, of the law of nations, and the municipal law.

Judge Blackstone tells us, that "law in its most comprehensive sense, signifies a rule of action, and is applied indiscriminately to all action, whether animate or inanimate, rational or irrational. Thus we say, the laws of motion, of gravitation, of optics, or mechanics, as well as the laws of nature and nations."* When we speak of the laws of nature, with respect to the universe, so far as it comes under our knowledge, we mean those apparent rules, agreeable to which, all its motions and operations, in all its parts, are produced and directed in an unceasing series, regular, orderly, and uniform. The author afterwards observes, that "laws in their more confined sense, denote the rules, not of action in general, but of human action or conduct." Upon which, Mr. Christian very justly remarks, that "this perhaps is the only sense, in which the word law, can be strictly used; for in all cases where it is not applied to human conduct, it may be considered as a metaphor;

---

*1 Comm. p. 38.

and in every instance a more appropriate term may be found. When it is used to express the operations of the Deity, or Creator, it comprehends ideas very different from those, which are included in its signification, when it is applied to man, or his other creatures. The volitions of the Almighty are his laws. He had only to will, " Let there be light, and there was light." When we apply the word law, to motion, matter, or the works of nature or of art, we shall find in every case, that with equal, or greater propriety, we might have used the words, quality, property, or peculiarity."

Yet from a degree of analogy apprehended, it is, unless limited by the nature of the subject, or the manner of expression, generally understood in its most comprehensive sense. In speaking of the laws of nature generally, we include as well the laws which are supposed to govern action, attending matter animate, or inanimate, and which are sometimes called physical laws, as those laws which govern the actions and conduct of man, as a moral intelligence, and which are the subject of our present enquiry. Between the former and the latter there is, however, a very important distinction. Whether we suppose with some, that the Creator, in the formation of the universe, impressed on matter certain principles, from which it cannot depart, without ceasing to exist ; or with others, that according to a predetermined plan, the movements of the whole system, and every operation in all its parts, even the most minute, are effected by an immediate and constant exertion of the Divine agency, or effective will of the Deity ; yet, here the law, as it respects the subjects, is a law, not of obligation, but necessity. The subjects are mere passive means or instruments, without will, intention, or power of resistance. No moral consequences are attached to the action. But the latter, the law of intelligent beings, the law of human conduct, is a law of obligation, not of necessity, as in the case of mere physical laws. Man has, indeed, a body, wonderfully organized, and endued with animal life. As an animal being, he is subject to physical laws ; but he is furnished with intelligence, with a faculty by which he attains the perception of moral relations and their result in duty, in a view to human actions. In considering certain relations, in which he finds himself, he is conscious of an obligation, or perhaps, we shall be as distinctly understood, if we say, he perceives a duty resulting from those relations, to perform a certain action, or to pursue a certain course of actions. This, which is properly called moral perception, is found to be common to the whole human race; although more or less clear, more or less comprehensive in different men, according to their different susceptibilities and means of improvement. Hence is derived the general notion of a moral, which, by way of eminence, is called the natural law, or the law of nature. All who are capable of discerning the law, are capable of discerning the obligation.

Some authors have, with great propriety, taken a two-fold view of the law of nature, as a moral law. They have first considered it as a law universally binding on the consciences of all men, in all cases, and without exception to be obeyed, agreeable to the end and intention of the whole law, as manifested by the Creator, the Omniscient law-giver, and judge of all human actions. Taken in this view, as universally binding the conscience, it is called the internal law. Again, they have considered it in relation to man in society, and under civil institutions; and here they find certain rules admitted, that seem to be exceptions to the general rule. These relate to those duties which are denominated duties of imperfect obligation, and are principally comprehended in the duties of benevolence. In cases of this kind, the law of nature permits each individual to judge for himself; it does not permit to others, whether individuals, societies, or communities, the right ultimately to judge of the duty, or to compel a performance. In this view, they have called it the external law of nature. I shall treat of these in the same order,—and first, of the internal law, as that which is universally binding on every conscience.

It has, I believe, been generally holden, and with the utmost propriety, that this law has its origin in the relation necessarily subsisting between the Creator and his created intelligences, the human race, and in those moral relations, which man is made to sustain, and is capable of sustaining, with a constant regard to the great end and design apparent in his moral constitution, his true interest and happiness.

It has been much disputed, what constitutes moral obligation, or why a man is, in any instance, obliged by the law of nature, to perform a certain action ; although I apprehend the difference is more apparent than real, and has arisen from the different abstract, as well as practical views, which different writers have taken of the subject. Some have asserted that moral obligation arises from the fitness of things—a moral fitness. Do they mean by this an abstract, antecedent fitness, which, in some mysterious way, imposes an obligation on moral beings, and in a conformity to which only all virtue consists ? Or do they mean that moral obligation arises from the moral relations, in which alone can moral obligation be found either theoretically or practically ? Others tell us, that the will of God is the sole foundation of moral obligation, and have so expressed themselves, as to be often understood to mean an irrespective will. It is unquestionably true, that the whole system of natural law, of which we are treating, was established by the Creator, agreeable to his will, and that it has its binding force on the creature man agreeable to that will ; but the question practically is, upon what is moral obligation founded, or, from what does it arise in that system.

And here I think we need not hesitate to repeat, that it arises from the moral relations existing, and in all cases embracing the relation between the creature and the Creator, and the design and end of that system—the interest and happiness of the subject. The divine will, as a moral law, cannot for an instant be supposed without a reference to those relations, for which provision is made, and to the end and design so apparent in the whole constitution. In a practical enquiry, in any case, after the obligation, resort is had to the existing moral relations. A duty is perceived to result from those relations, and because the duty is so perceived, it is concluded to be the will of God, that the duty should be performed. In this case—for I speak not here of positive revelation—it is not the known will that indicates the duty, but the duty perceived indicates the will which completes the obligation.

Accordingly, those appear to me to be the most correct who have holden, that to constitute the efficient of moral obligation, there is necessarily associated in the result the notion of a Supreme power or Being, rightfully ordaining the law and requiring

obedience; that without this association there might arise a
question of utility, the end of all moral action, but there could be
no conception of duty or moral obligation; that in the case of
natural law that Supreme power is perceived to be the great
Creator of the universe, who made man and established him in
a situation to sustain those relations, individual and social, from
which both his private and public duties result, and which point
out to him the laws of his nature ; that this is also accompanied
with a sense of gratitude to the beneficent Author of existence,
which becomes a leading and powerful inducement to obedience.   This mode of accounting for the efficient of moral obligation supports the dignity of the law, and with energy brings
it home to the mind.   There is, indeed, no very material difference between this opinion and that which makes the will
of God, as above explained, the foundation of moral obligation.
The difference appears to arise, principally, from the manner
of expressing an abstract notion.   To say that the will of God
is a law to man, necessarily implies the supremacy and authority
of the law-giver.   Another ground of difference may be found
in a fondness for definition.   The notion of moral obligation
may be explained, but is too complicated to admit a concise
scientific definition ; yet writers have frequently attempted so
to define it ; and each seizing that idea embraced in the term
which appeared to him most prominent, placed it in his definition to the neglect or exclusion of something equally or more
important.   I believe every definition, which has been attempted upon this subject, leaves something to be sought.   Some
seem to have excluded every thing but the will of the law-
giver ; and those who have laid the foundation in an antecedent
fitness of things appear, at least as far as they can be apprehended, to place that will in subordination to their principle.   Some
have laid the whole stress on the moral relations ; while others
have found the obligation in utility only.   There can in this case
be no obligation on the subject, man, without a law,—no law
without a law-giver, who is God.   No obligation can attach
independent of the moral relations ; nor can it exist without a
regard to utility, the end and design of the law ; for what obligation can attach on a moral being to perform and act to no
end, for no manner of use ?   We may here repeat, that the

utility of any class of actions, that is, their general tendency to promote human happiness is a sure, I may say, the only sure test, that the rule requiring them is a genuine law of nature. We may also here observe a material difference between the law of nature as a moral law, and the municipal law. The latter, formed to direct the actions of the subject to a certain object, requires simply obedience, and judges of that obedience by the external act, and no further regards the intention; the former, the law of nature, requires with obedience a regard to the end of that law, and judges of the obedience by the internal act, the intention. The latter is satisfied with prudence in obeying,—the former unites prudence with benevolence.

Vattel, in his introductory discourse, has laid it down as a general law of society, the law of social nature, "that each should do for others what their necessities require, and they are capable of doing without neglecting what they owe to themselves".* This seems intended by the author as a most general or universal rule; and yet if intended to apply to the internal law, I think we may lay down a rule still more general. That it is a law of social nature, that each should so direct his conduct in all his actions, that they shall tend to the general utility, the general interest and happiness of man. The exception expressed in the former rule is certainly just, but it is clearly implied in the latter; for, were every man to neglect the duties which he owes to himself, or wholly to sacrifice his own interest and happiness, in his endeavors to promote the interest and happiness of others, it would, instead of augmenting, tend to diminish if not destroy the general happiness; especially as no one is equally capable as in his own case, of judging what will contribute to the happiness of another. And yet there are cases in which the law of social nature requires a sacrifice to be made. Self preservation is at least one of the first duties. It nevertheless, sometimes, becomes the duty of one man to expose his own life, to a certain degree, to save the life of another in imminent danger. There are other instances, in which it may be the duty of one man to make no

---

* Law of Nations, Preliminaries. § 10.

inconsiderable sacrifices to relieve the necessities of others. Such instances will readily occur, and must be left to every man's conscience.

It may be said, that general utility, the general happiness of the whole human race is an object too vast for the limited faculties of man; that if it be considered as a general rule, and that all our actions are to be directed to its attainment, the rule is of too general a nature to be applied to immediate action in any case. It is true that a general, is never the immediate rule of action, nor is general utility the primary, if I may use the distinction, but the ultimate end to be kept in view. Such is the constitution of our nature, that the primary end in view is the immediate utility of the agent himself; and thence extending to his family and connexions of kindred and society, until it embraces the community of which he is a member, and thence the whole human race. The interests of all these he identifies with his own, or participates in them according to their estimated importance in securing and perpetuating his own happiness. Now in any community the happiness of the whole consists in the happiness of all its parts. It has its commencement with individuals; it depends on the exertion and actions of individuals, and the general direction of those actions. To give a proper direction and tendency of all to the same end, some general rule or rules are necessary to be observed.

The first rule for the attainment of this end, is that rule of the civil law,—"so use your own right, that you injure not the rights of others." This is not only a rule of the civil law, but is a general rule of the law of nature, subordinate to the more general rule, which requires that all the actions of individuals be so directed as to promote the good of the whole. Each individual is supposed best to understand what will contribute to his own interest and happiness, and the individuals of any society, what will most contribute to the interest and prosperity of their society, and they will pursue their own interest with more alacrity as well as knowledge. All have an equal right to the pursuit, and to make use of the proper means; but if no limits are set to the manner of pursuit, some may usurp or monopolize the means to the deprivation of others. They may, temporarily, increase their own enjoyments, but are constantly exposed to the same deprivation by. a more powerful usurper.

The law of nature furnishes a remedy for this state of things, in the application and observance of the general rule above mentioned,—"so use your own right, that you injure not the rights of others". A general observance of this rule affords to every one the liberty of pursuing, by all just means, his own interest, in the way he judges most suitable to his situation, and in that peace and security which constitutes no inconsiderable portion of individual happiness. It is, however, a mere rule of forbearance, and embraces only that prudence, which is required by the municipal law. But to fulfil the plan of nature something further is necessary, and that is benevolence, which augments and gives a peculiar zest to social and individual happiness. To unite benevolence with prudence, which is the consummation of the law of nature, that all the actions of man be directed in their tendency to general utility, or in other words, to promote the happiness of his species, becomes indispensable ; and, as the happiness of the whole, consists in the happiness of all its parts, this rule is emphatically expressed in that command,—" Thou shalt love thy neighbor as thyself." It was said that the rule of forbearance, above mentioned, is a subordinate part of this more general rule ; and it may be added that it is preparatory to it, as the forbearance of injuries, in the order of things, precedes acts of benevolence.

It was, indeed, before observed that general rules, although very important in forming a system of ethics, do not come in immediate contact with human action. To explain this more clearly, it is a rule that every man be holden to perform his agreements with others; it is also a rule that he shall make reparation for injuries. These may be called specific rules of immediate application ; and although they tend to the same end,—the general utility ; yet a man, in fulfilling his agreement, or making a reparation for injuries, may have no regard to the general utility, nor respect for the common good ; but may yield to compulsion, or act solely from a regard to his own private interest, under present circumstances. But although general rules are not the immediate rules of action, yet they are intended to have an important and extensive influence on human conduct. This we will endeavor to illustrate in the present instance, and to show how, by the operation of this general rule upon the mind, the whole course of action, and conduct of the agent, is influenced and directed to the promotion of the general happiness. By a frequent contemplation of the rule, and the excellence of the end to which it directs, a benevolent disposition is acquired; the mind becomes habitually disposed to do good to all, which is, to promote general happiness. This benevolent disposition fixed in the mind of any one is a constant desire to do good to every human being within the sphere of his action and the reach of his power; the only way of accomplishing the great end permitted to his limited capacity.

Although in the common concerns of life, the interest of the agent and his connexions, more or less remote, is the primary and immediate motive to action, yet this benevolent disposition, become habitual, is a constant bias upon his mind, inclining it to beneficence, gives the ultimate direction to his every action, and stamps his whole conduct with the character of benevolence. What renders this principle dear to the benevolent man is, that with a consciousness of acting agreeable to the laws of his nature, he derives from his benevolent acts, a more exalted happiness than he is capable of communicating, and which strongly attaches him to the objects of his beneficence, the occasions of that happiness. It needs hardly to be suggested, that in proportion as this disposition to benevolence is embraced generally by the members of any community, will the happiness of that community be extended; and in proportion as it is embraced by mankind in general, will the happiness of the whole human race be promoted.

Although the municipal law must be satisfied with the prudence of the subjects in obeying, because it cannot scrutinize the conscience or the disposition of the heart; yet it is only where this benevolence of disposition prevails generally in a state, that not only the ordinary laws, but all just and necessary requisitions are cheerfully obeyed, with a sense of duty, and a zeal in its service, that gives facility to its enterprises, success to its measures, and insures the general prosperity, as far as any thing can be insured under human institutions. Under the influence of this principle, this benevolence of disposition, united with honor, and without which, honor is but a dazzling meteor, oft blazing to destroy, the true patriot has at all times dedicated his services, and on great occasions, even his life to his country, with a self devotion that has embalmed his name in the memory of all generations. Thus it is sufficiently explained how the general rule, superinduced upon the specific and immediate rules of conduct, by affecting the disposition of the agent, qualifies his actions, and unites private with the general interest. In the same manner the universal rule, that we are bound in all things to obey the will of God superinduced upon both the general and the specific rules, brings home to the mind and enforces the obligation in all cases. Such are the principles and obligation of the law of nature, considered as the internal law, which comprehends all the duties of man, and for the performance of which he is holden accountable to the Omniscient Lawgiver and Judge.

The external law considers those duties, only as man is accountable to his fellow men for their performance. In this view, duties are distinguished into two classes,—perfect duties, or duties of perfect obligation, and imperfect duties. To every duty there is a corresponding right, that is, if one person owes a duty to another, that other has a corresponding right to demand the performance. In all cases of perfect duties, he, to whom the duty is owing, has a perfect right, a right to constrain him who owes the duty, to perform it. This class comprehends all the duties and rights of justice, which are the great objects of all civil institutions and laws. If one owes to another an imperfect duty, that other may ask as a favor, but has no right to compel the performance. This class comprehends all the duties of benevolence. The rules of the external law exempt this class of duties from the jurisdiction of all civil laws and human tribunals. No man is holden accountable in the sense of being amenable to any of his fellow men or to society, for their neglect or performance. This distinction is founded in the highest reason and utility. It was before observed to be a general rule of natural law, " that each should do for others what their necessities require, and they are capable of doing, without neglecting what he owes to himself,"

which includes his natural and necessary connexions in society.
As far as relates to his fellow men, each is by the law of nature constituted on this subject the sole judge ; he is amenable
only to God and his own conscience. It is a case, in which
from the very nature of the thing, others are incompetent to
judge. The law of nature has therefore denied to man the
right of enforcing these duties by constraint. Were it otherwise, natural liberty would no where be found among men.
Indeed it would change the nature of the duties, and reduce
acts of benevolence, from the rank which they now hold
among the highest virtues, to the grade of necessary actions.
This we constantly see exemplified in those laws, by which
the community make provision for the necessitous and the relief of the unfortunate. The individuals who are called to
contribute to the relief, act under the constraint of law, and
however cheerfully they may contribute, it is a necessary act
of obedience to the law. The benevolent act is the act of the
community, which being composed of moral beings, sustains
the character of a moral person, and is a subject of moral
obligation.

When it is said that man is not accountable to his fellow
men for the performance or neglect of these duties, it is meant
only he is not amenable to them or to any human tribunal ; yet
from the deep interest which every one feels in his own character, from the irrepressible desire of the approbation and
dread of the censure of his fellow men, which nature has
implanted in the breast of every human being, there still remains a strong sense of accountability ; but it is a moral, not a
legal accountability. From this view of the subject it will be
readily perceived that the rules of the external, do not in any
way operate as an exception to the obligation of the internal
law, or in any way to diminish its force. The laws of nature and
the obligations which they impose, are as immutable as the
Supreme Being by whom they are ordained. When we say
the laws of nature are immutable, it must be understood of the
laws themselves ; not of their application. The subject to
which any rule of the law of nature is to be applied may be
changed, in which case the same laws of nature direct, a
correspondent change in the application of the rule. Of this,

we have innumerable instances under human institutions and their various changes. Human institutions, as we have formerly seen, are indicated and rendered necessary by the laws of nature, but the model of these institutions is ever left to the will and the wisdom of man. · All political and civil rights and duties, have their foundation in the law of nature ; but they are permitted by the same law to be modified and varied, to the nature and end of those institutions. Thus the subjects to which the rules of that law are to be applied, are varied, and this renders it necessary, that there should be a correspondent variation in the application of the rules. Civil institutions left to the discretion of man, may be as different as the manners, habits, and opinions of the different people, by whom, or for whom they are formed, and yet all be within the limits, and receive the approbation of the laws of nature, the great end and design of which is, through individuals, societies, and nations, to promote under human institutions, the happiness of the human race. It will be sufficient, here, to mention one instance, which was noticed on a former occasion,—of a total variation in the manner of applying the rules of natural law, rendered necessary by a variation of the subject in the progress of human institutions. In a simple state of society, short of that imaginary independence, which has been called a state of nature, before the improvement of civil institutions, every man is, by the law of nature, as it operates in such society, in most cases, a judge in his own cause, and the avenger of his own injuries. If another violate the laws of nature to his injury, he for himself applies the rule, judges of the injury, the measure of satisfaction due, and is empowered to carry that judgment into execution. In an improved state of society, and a more ample provision of civil institutions and laws, this manner of applying the rule is no longer tolerated. Every man, in cases of injury, is required to submit to the decision of others,—to the civil tribunal, whose duty it is made to judge of the injury, apply the rule, and determine what measure of satisfaction is due ; and that judgment must be executed by an appointed civil officer. The same thing is to be observed of all the rights of justice ; of all claims of right, natural, civil, and political. They are to be submitted to the appointed tribunals, and the rules applied in a manner agreeable to the modification of those rights by the civil institution and laws.

I will here conclude this brief sketch of the law of nature, its principles and obligation, by repeating that it is the ordination of God in the constitution of human nature.—It is his will manifested to men in his works.—"It is a law," as it has been forcibly observed, "binding over all the globe, and at all times. No human laws are of any validity, if contrary to this; and such of them as are valid, derive all their force, all their authority from this original." *

---

* 1. Bl. Comm. 41.

CHAPTER II.

Of the Law of Nations.

Dispersed over the earth, it is impossible that mankind should have continued united in one society. Local, and other circumstances have occasioned a division into states and nations, independent of each other, without that common interest and united councils necessary to the individuality of the whole as one people. When thus separated and formed into states, each assuming a national character, they sustain various relations towards each other according to their various situations, contiguity, reciprocal wants, and mutual or opposing interests. Between independent states, various circumstances of necessity or convenience, induce an intercourse more or less frequent and intimate ; but such intercourse could not subsist at all, or certainly with any degree of security, without certain rules, which each should be bound to observe toward the other.

Nations are, in regard to each other, in a situation similar to that of individuals, in the state of nature supposed to have existed previous to any social compact. Each nation becomes such by the social or civil compact of its individuals, which, whether ever formally made, or only implied from a customary association long continued, is always held to be binding on every person belonging to the same community. As nations are constituted of beings social by the laws of their nature, nations necessarily assume, in respect to each other, a social character. Hence, they are capable of sustaining social and moral relations, from which result reciprocal moral duties, and through which they are mutually holden amenable to the laws of nature ; but in a manner different from individuals in a state of society, and

more especially, under a regular administration of civil government and laws. It has been observed, that the law of nature
differs in its application, as the subjects differ to which it is
applied. Nations are considered as wholly independent,—
each of the other,—each as sovereign. They neither have,
nor acknowledge any common judge or superior. But such
is not the situation of individuals in any known state of society,
be it ever so rude, and that whether the society has been formed by express compact, or by tacit consent, by custom witnessed
by long usage. In the rudest state of society, there are some
rules, by the whole held to be compulsory on individuals, and
although these rules may be few, and the means of compulsion
weak, so that it verges towards a state of individual independence, yet it is very distant from that state of independence,
which is alone acknowledged among nations and in which their
sovereignty consists. Hence, arises a principal source of difference, between the relations of the individuals of a community,
and those of independent nations. A community or state of
which a nation consists, is composed of individuals associated by
compact, for their mutual benefit, their relations between the individuals, from which result, their rights and duties are often
dictated, and always modified by human institutions, intended to
promote the common interest, and each member has for this end
submitted to the direction and control of the whole. The relations between independent nations are not originally dictated
or modified by compact. Their origin and modifications are a
consequence of the social nature of men, of whom nations are
composed, and of the situation in which they are placed in
respect to each other. From these relations, thus viewed,
result the reciprocal rights and duties of independent nations,
and the duties are made obligatory upon them, as are the duties
of individuals, by the laws of nature applied agreeable to the
difference of the situations and circumstances, that is, agreeable
to the difference of the subjects.

The law of nations has usually, and with a sufficient degree of
propriety, been reduced under three heads. First. The necessary, or as it is often denominated, the internal law of nations.
Secondly. The conventional. And thirdly. The customary law of nations. The necessary or internal law of nations,

is analogous to the internal law of nature, of which we treated in the preceding chapter, on which Vattel observes, " It is necessary because nations are absolutely obliged to observe it. This law contains the precepts prescribed by the law of nature to states, to whom that law is not less obligatory than to individuals ; because states are composed of men, their resolutions are taken by men, and the law of nature is obligatory to all men, under whatever relation they act." *

The law of nature, thus applied to nations, has the same great end in view,—the general interest and happiness of man, and embraces the same general law of society, " that each should do for others, what their necessities require and he is capable of doing, without neglecting the duties which he owes to himself." This general law, properly applied in the manner before suggested, is no less binding on nations than individuals. In the application of the law of nature to nations, there exists a similar distinction between perfect and imperfect rights and duties. The difference principally consists in the manner, in which the law of nature gives effect to those rights, and in which these duties are required to be performed. This difference extends to both classes of rights and duties, as well to the duties of benevolence, as to the rights and duties of justice ; but is most obvious in respect to the latter. Between independent nations, no authoritative tribunal, can, as in the case of individuals in civil society, be intervened, to decide their conflicting claims, and give redress to the party injuried, without a prostration of national independence, which the law of nations necessarily holds to be sacred and inviolable on all occasions. Each nation is therefore constituted the sole judge of its rights, of their violation by others, and of the manner, means, and measure of redress. In case of a dispute arising between two nations, other nations may interpose their good offices to effect a reconciliation, but are not permitted an authoritative interposition to impose constraint on either party. Hence it follows as a necessary consequence that in a case of war between two nations, all other nations, as they are not permitted to judge of the

* Law of Nations, Preliminaries, § 7.

right of either, are bound in their conduct towards the belligerents to consider both as having a just cause. If, however, a belligerent, contrary to the law of nations, should use his own rights against his enemy in such a manner as to injure the perfect rights of another nation, that nation is at liberty to see redress in such way as it shall deem proper. It may be, and often is, a justifiable cause of war. For it is no less a rule of the law of nations than of the law of nature, that every one should so use his own right that he injure not the rights of others. The rule is however applied with some difference, arising from the independence of nations and the necessity of their situation, in consequence of which, some restrictions are laid on the usual intercourse between neutrals and belligerents, of which the neutral, as it tends to the common advantage, has no right to complain. With these, and some other modifications of the law of nature in its application, according to the difference of the subjects, and which in this brief sketch it is not necessary further to specify, it is called the voluntary law of nations; because, by its rules are to be decided what duties each may require of others, what duties each is obliged to perform, and to which, therefore, all ought voluntarily to submit. In this view it is also called the external law of nations; and though, like the external law of nature, it does not extend to all that is required by the internal law, yet it does not dispense with the internal obligation, which remains to its full extent binding on the conscience.

A nation, as well as an individual, may lawfully renounce, in favor of others, or compromise its own rights. Any two nations may, therefore, by treaty, vary the voluntary law in relation to their conduct towards each other, and so far establish a new law to themselves. This law is called the conventional, sometimes the arbitrary, law of nations, and is fully obligatory to the contracting parties, provided it in no wise violates the perfect rights of others, or the duties which each owes to itself.

Under the same restrictions, a custom that has obtained in practice between nations, becomes in virture of a tacit consent, mutually binding on those, and only those who have adopted it ; but that obligation may, in general, be discharged by a public declaration of either of the parties to the custom that they will no longer observe it. Such customs constitute what is denominated the customary law of nations. This, as well as the former, is, in strictness conventional; the one being established by the express, the other by a tacit agreement of the parties; and both derive all their validity from the natural law as applied to nations. No custom, however long, however universally it may have obtained, if not founded on the principles of natural law, if it will not endure the sure test of the law, in its tendency to promote the general interest of mankind, can justly be considered as belonging to the general law of nations; and yet such customs have prevailed generally, I may say universally, and still prevail to a great extent among the nations of the earth, and from their general prevalence have been considered as the dictates of nature, and received as her genuine laws. Of these customs it will be sufficient to mention those which governed the rights of war, anciently received as the universal law of nations. This law subjected in full right to the conqueror, the life, liberty, and property of the conquered. To grant to a captive enemy, or a conquered people, their lives in exchange for perpetual servitude, or for the payment of a perpetual tribute, was considered as an act of clemency, a humane relaxation of the right of the conqueror,—proof of the high antiquity of this custom, and its general prevalence we find in Homer, the most ancient profane writer whose works are extant. We meet with allusions to the right of the conqueror, and instances of the rigid exercise of that right, in almost every page; nor does the author once hint a suspicion of its being wrong, or a deviation from the principles of natural justice. A plenary proof of its still higher antiquity we have in the writings of Moses. In that history we find the same law of war prevailing in the very infancy of nations. In the code given by him to the nation of Israel, for reasons of religion, to guard against the introduction of idolatry, a relaxation of the strict right of the conqueror as then held, was prohibited to a certain extent.

Of the nations that dwelt in the land of their inheritance, they were commanded to destroy every thing that breathed.*

---

* Deut. xx. 16. and vii. 2.

If they went out to war against a remote nation, they were directed first to offer terms of peace. If the nation submitted, it was to be made tributary. If the offers of peace were rejected, they were commanded by an ordinance of their law to smite every male with the edge of the sword,—but to take the women and children as captives,—that is for slaves.* By another ordinance, they were commanded, in addition to the males, which was construed to extend to the adult males only, to kill every woman who had known a man. We may learn how inveterate this custom had then become, when we find it was not deemed fit, or perhaps safe, to attempt its abolition in that nation, even by divine authority. Such is still the right of the conqueror as acknowledged by the received law of nations, throughout the dominions of Africa, and the greater part of Asia. The same law is admitted and carried into execution by the aboriginal nations and tribes of the American continent, with augmented barbarity. But among the nations of modern Europe and their descendants in other parts of the world, improvement in knowledge, refinement in manners and morals, and a more humane religion better understood, have nearly banished reproaches of this nature from their international code ; we cannot say, entirely, while the Turk is suffered to remain an exception, and the inhuman trafic in slaves is yet tolerated by some nations of civilized Europe.

It was observed in a former chapter † that a custom in any nation has its origin in the common feelings and sentiments of the people, and if we find the same custom prevailing universally among all nations, it is a proof that the same feelings and sentiments are universal, and may be admitted as a proof that such custom is a law of nature on the subjects which it embraces. But it is further observed, that circumstances very general may produce a perversion of feelings and sentiments, equally general. To such a perversion of feelings and sentiments, the custom under consideration, unquestionably owes its origin.

It may not be uninteresting briefly to examine the circum-

---

* Deut. xx. 10.   † B. iv. c. 3.

stances which gave rise to so general a perversion. These circumstances will readily be perceived in the view taken in a former book, of the first rude state of society. It may be proper, however, to consider that state with a more particular view to this subject. Many tribes, and even considerable nations, even at this day, remain in that rude state in which we can scarcely discover any trace of civil institutions, and of civil subordination. Whatever may have been the original situation of mankind, we cannot find that any nation or tribe have been exempt from that rude and barbarous state. It is the state from which all nations have commenced their improvements in the arts of life, all their discoveries and refinements in social and civil institutions. Some nations, owing to peculiar circumstances, have made more rapid advances, and have more early than others attained a high degree of improvement in their institutions ; yet early history, and the traditions of every people, whatever credit may be due to the marvellous accounts they furnish, generally hold up a faithful mirror of ancient manners, and clearly prove there was a time when the whole human race were found in the same barbarous state, when without any regular systems of laws, without any efficient government, every man in cases of personal violence, was left to be the sole judge and avenger of the wrongs he had suffered. In such a state, every thing is left to be decided under the influence of some predominant passion, generally that of revenge, of all the most violent aud enduring, and the least susceptible of moral restraint. Causes of offence are constantly multiplied, and the passion of revenge kept always on the alert. Every one must depend on his own personal strength and resources. If these are insufficient, he must associate with others for mutual defence, or devote himself to some powerful chief, whose decisions become the measure of right to his followers, and his commands their sole law. Amid such scenes of violence, every man resorts to the law of force,—the right of the strongest. Right is confounded with might in the general mind, and becomes identified with power.

Between neighboring nations, which in such state generally consist of petty tribes, the condition was still worse. The licentious aggressions of individuals, or of marauding chiefs, for the purpose of plunder, or of avenging former injuries, which, handed down from father to son, were never forgotten, kept them in a perpetual state of hostility, so that the name of stranger and enemy became identified. So inveterate were their hostilities, that the destruction of an enemy was considered the only security against future danger. Accordingly we find that in the infancy of nations, all their wars were wars of extermination. The weaker party were in the end put to the sword, or forced to abandon their country. The conqueror was considered as having a full right, or rather I may say, it was deemed an indispensable duty which he owed to his tribe to take the life of the vanquished. Thus the conqueror was held, by his superior power, to have acquired a right not only to the life but to every thing that belonged to the vanquished; and when in after times the strict right was mitigated and their lives were yielded to them in exchange for hereditary slavery, or a weaker nation was spared in consideration of a perpetual tribute, humanity had little share in the motive. The utility of the conquerors, the augmentation of their power, and their public and private resources was the great inducement to this seeming lenity. In such state of irreconcilable hostility, it is evident that when one nation meditated the conquest of another, the justice of the measure made no part of the deliberation; the whole was reduced to a question of power. Thus all the circumstances of the times, both of nations and individuals, served to confound right with power and to identify them in the general opinion. If an opinion has been entertained by an individual until it has become habitual, he believes it to be founded on some natural principle. If an opinion has become general, is entertained by all, they with one consent pronounce it to be a law of nature. Thus on a fair and candid review of the whole subject, so far is the generality of the custom from proving it to be a genuine law of nature, it is a convincing proof to what a degree, a general perversity of situation and circumstances may serve to corrupt the sentiments and pervert the understanding of mankind in opposition to their true interest and happiness, the great end of all the genuine laws of nature.

It has been often observed that among independent states,

from the nature of their situation, no common superior can be admitted to dictate the law and enforce its observance. Although it is not the less obligatory in a moral view as a branch, and a very important branch of the law of nature, yet its observance is, in a great measure, voluntary between the parties; but such is not the case with respect to the individuals of a nation. Modern nations have adopted the law of nations in their respective civil codes, so far as that law may be affected by the conduct of individuals. The government of every state have the power and find it no less their interest than their duty to punish every unauthorised infraction of that law by their own citizens and subjects. Every state is within certain limits holden accountable for all aggressions of its subjects, especially of its public agents, against another state or its citizens. But if the government disavow the act, and punish or deliver up the aggressor, if in its power, it ought to satisfy the offended state.

CHAPTER III.

Of Municipal Laws and their Civil Obligation.

Municipal law is the civil law of a particular country. It has been defined by Judge Blackstone to be "a rule of civil conduct prescribed by the supreme power in the state, commanding what is right and prohibiting what is wrong."* This definition, was, I believe, first introduced into the English law by him, and has since been adopted by most of the succeeding writers upon that law. It is not given as a definition peculiar to the English law, but as a definition of universal application to the municipal law of every country. But from a conviction of its unsoundness, I feel it necessary to question its propriety.

The first branch of the definition is undoubtedly correct, "that municipal law is a rule of civil conduct prescribed," that is, its injunction must be made known to the citizens, or subjects before it can operate as a rule. That a rule should, by retrospect be applied to transactions which were passed before it existed, or was made known, is an absurdity, a violation of all the principles of natural justice, too palpable to require a comment. But that it is a rule prescribed by the supreme power in the state, in the sense of the author as here expressed, is, according to my apprehension, far from being correct. That we may fully comprehend his sense in this part of the definition, it will be necessary to recollect his depository of this supreme power, and the qualities which he supposes it inherently to possess. To this purpose, let us repeat some passages of the author, which have been before cited in

_____

* 1 Comm. 44.

treating of sovereignty. " Legislature* is the greatest act of superiority that can be exercised by one being over another ; wherefore it is necessary to the very essence of law, that it be made by the supreme power." Sovereignty and legislation are convertible terms, and cannot subsist one without the other."† Speaking of the different forms of government, he says,—however they began, or by what right soever they subsist, there must be in all, a supreme, irresistible, absolute and uncontrolled authority, in which the *jura summi imperii*, or the rights of sovereignty reside ;" ‡ and according to him, the residence of this supreme power is in the legislative organ of the state.

All this is true in terms, in a government absolute, arbitrary, and despotic where all the powers of the state are, whether by consent or by usurpation, concentrated in one man or body of men ; but we have before seen, that in a free government, an absolute, uncontrolled, and unlimited power is not committed to any one of its organs, and that it does not actually subsist in the British legislature, for whom it is so strenuously claimed. Certainly such power does not belong to the legislature of every state. It is not vested in the legislature of the United States, nor in that of any state in the union. Each is limited by the constitution from which it derives its power. The constitution is the supreme law established by the people, the ultimate supreme power in every free country ; a law which the legislature is bound to obey in all its acts. Every act not warranted by the constitution is void, and with us is so decided by the courts of law. So far we may, with propriety, apply the definition to the law of the constitution, the fundamental law, that it is a rule of political conduct prescribed by the supreme power in the state ; but it wholly fails, when applied to the derivative, to the municipal law. The positive laws

---

† The word "legislature," is here used in an unaccustomed sense. That term is in the English language, appropriated to express the name of the organ vested with the power of making laws in a state, but the powers and the acts of that organ are appropriately expressed by the term " legislation ;" thus we say the " power of legislation,"—the power of making laws,—"the act of legislation,"—the act of making laws. † 1 Comm. 46. ‡ 1 Comm. 49.

enacted by the legislature, are prescribed by a competent authority instituted and limited by the supreme political power.

Could the author for a moment have called off his attention from the transcendent power of his legislature, I think he would have clearly perceived the deficiency of his definition; that, upon his own principles, it could embrace the positive laws only expressly enacted by the legislature, and that it excludes the customary or common law and which, in fact, comprehends the greatest portion of the municipal laws of every country. So extensive is this branch of the law that it embraces all the common rights of the citizens, decides the manner of their enjoyment and punishes their infringement. By it is decided the validity and the effects of civil contracts in most instances. It furnishes principles for the decision of new cases as they arise, and rules for ordering and regulating the proceedings of courts. It furnishes also, rules and maxims for the construction of written instruments; rules for the interpretation of statute laws, and even of the constitution itself. Nay, in England, the constitution of the government lays its foundation in the common law. This law was not enacted by the legislature, was not prescribed by the supreme power in the sense of the definition. It came in by custom, and derives its authority as law, from a general and tacit consent of the people, and may justly be defined by itself to be a rule of civil conduct introduced by the tacit consent and agreement of the people ratified, prescribed and consecrated by long usage.

We may then, I think, without hesitation pronounce this part of the author's definition to be, not only deficient and unsatisfactory, but injurious in its consequences, leading to a misconception of the nature of our civil and political institutions. The following definition taken from the Institutes of Justinian, is in this point more correct,—at least it is not liable to the same objection. " That law, which any people have established for themselves, is the appropriate law of their state, and is called the civil law, as being the peculiar law of the civil state.*

---

* Quod quisque populus sibi jus constituit, id ipsius proprium civitatis est, vocaturque jus civile, quasi jus proprium ipsius civitatis. Inst. B. 1. T. 2. § 1.

This definition comprehends as well the customary as the positive laws considering both as equally established by the people ; the former, by a general and tacit consent, the latter by positive enactment either by the people themselves, or by some legislative organ, deriving its authority from them. Even the Roman Emperors, absolute and despotic as they held and exercised their powers, claimed the legislative authority as being derived from the same source,—the people. For in the Institutes, after mention of various kinds of law—the *plebiscita*, or acts of the people, and the decrees of the senate ; we find the following declaration of the constitution of the empire, " the ordinance of the Prince hath also the force of law ; for the people by the *lex regia*, which was passed in relation to the empire, conceded to him their whole power ; therefore whatever the Emperor ordains by rescript, decree, or edict is law."*

With Mr. Christian, in his note on the above definition, I consider the latter branch that " municipal law is a rule—commanding what is right and prohibiting what is wrong,"—to be faulty. It leaves us in doubt whether the author meant to refer right and wrong to the rule itself or to the law of nature. If to the rule, it is, as observed, a useless tautology. If to the law of nature, it will be found to be incorrect ; for there are many things, which the law of nature permits, generally, but which the municapal law may justly prohibit, because the general interest of the state requires such prohibition, and hence the distinction of those things which are *mala in se*,† and those which are *mala prohibita*.‡ There are things that may be at least innocently done while not prohibited, but which cannot be so when prohibited. It may, for instance, be for the public interest that fish should be suffered to increase for food. It may therefore be just and expedient by law to prohibit the taking of them in their places of resort during the season of

---

* Sed quod principi placuit, legis habet vigorem : cum lege regia, quæ de ejus imperio lata est, populus ei et in eum, omne imperium suum et potestatem concedat. Quodcunque ergo imperator per epistolam constituit, vel cognoscens decrevit, vel edicto præcepit, legem esse constat. Inst. B. 1. S. 1. T. 2. § 6.

† Wrong in themselves.   ‡ Wrong as being prohibited.

their breeding. Before the prohibition, the taking is innocent; it *is* permited by the law of nature to all. The public interest, public expediency, renders the prohibition just and proper, and the prohibition renders the act of taking, criminal, a public wrong.

I have chosen this instance out of many, because the law in this case is not like the game laws, adduced by Mr. Christian, of an arbitrary or doubtful character,—if it be deemed necessary to embrace something of every branch of the definition in the commentaries, the following will, according to our principles, be unexceptionable.

Municipal law is a rule of civil conduct prescribed by a competent authority in the state, enjoining what ought to be done and prohibiting what ought not to be done. This definition refers the right and the wrong of the action commanded or prohibited to the laws of social nature, as applicable under existing relations; the situation, circumstances, and general interests of the community.

In treating of the general principles of municipal law, I shall consider the subject under a three-fold division. The first division will comprehend those laws which regulate the general intercourse, provide for the security of rights, and for the administration of justice between the citizens of the state, which may, by way of eminence, be denominated the civil code,—under this head I shall also treat of the civil and the moral obligation of laws. The second will comprehend the laws relating to crimes and punishments, which belong to the criminal code. The third division will include the laws which relate to taxation. In the remainder of the present chapter after treating of the principles of the civil code, which embraces principles common to all, I shall discuss the civil obligation of laws. After having so fully treated of rights, natural, civil and political, in the former part of this work, I may well be permitted to indulge brevtiy on the first part of this article.

The principles of the laws ought to coincide with the principles of the constitution. They are the detail of what the constitution contains, the outlines under general heads, and ought to be made in the same spirit. They ought, in the manner prescribed by that instrument to pursue the same end; the interest and happiness of the citizens as inseparably connected with the prosperity of the state. It is the business and duty of the legislature in forming a system of laws, which are to be general rules to all in their social and civil intercourse, to provide for a full and equal enjoyment of rights, and to guard against their abuse, and to harmonize, as far as the nature of things will permit, public and private interests ; the interest of the state with the private interests of the citizens. It is not supposed, however, that the legislature are to adapt their laws to the interest of each individual. The laws must of necessity be general, and ought to be so framed that all, by a steady observance of the rules, which they establish, may find their several interests in accordance with each other, and consequently in unison with the interest of the public. This, next to a code of good and wholesome laws, is to be effected by a provision for an able and impartial administration of justice between man and man, and between the state and its citizens. I will content myself with these general observations, and proceed to examine the civil obligation of municipal laws.

There is a passage in one of the orations of Demosthenes, in which he has given, not, indeed, a definition, but a just and beautiful description of the laws, and pointed us to the immediate efficient of its civil obligation. " The design and object of the law is to ascertain what is just, honorable, and expedient ; and when that is discovered, it is proclaimed as a general ordinance equal and impartial to all. This is the origin of laws which for various reasons all are under obligation to obey ; but especially, because all law is the invention and gift of heaven. The resolution of wise men, the correction of every offence, and the general compact of the state, to live in conformity with which, is the duty of every citizen."* This is not less

---

*Ὁ'ι δε νομοι το δικαιον καὶ το καλον καὶ το συμφερον βου'λονται, καὶ τατο ζητᾶσι, καὶ ἐπειδαν ευρεθη, κοινον τᾶτο προςαγμα απεδειχθη, πασιν ἴσον καὶ "ομοιον, και τατ' ἐςι ιὁμος, ω παντας προσηκει πειθεσθαι δια πολλα, καὶ μεγισθ'"οτι πας ἐςι νο'μος ευ"ρημα μεν καὶ δωρον θεων, δο'γμα δ''ανθρωπων φρονιμων, ·ἐπανο'ρθωμα δε των ἐκᾶσιων καὶ α'κᾶσιων α'μαρτημωτων, πο'λεως δε συνθηκη κοινη καθ' 'ην πασι προυηκει ζην τοῖς εν τη πο'λει.—Orat. 1. cont. Aristogit.

just, than elegant and forcible. It gives us the true ground of
our obligation, both civil and moral, to obey the law, " because
it is the invention and gift of heaven" that is sanctioned by the
laws of nature. " The resolution of wise men,"—the proper
organ of legislation : " The correction of every error,"—necessary to preserve the peace and happiness of society : " The
compact of the state,"—what all the citizens have solemnly
agreed to observe as the rule of their civil conduct. In this is
exhibited the only true ground on which it is possible to rest
the civil obligation. The wisest of the ancients considered
the law as a solemn compact, to which all the citizens were
parties, and to observe and obey which, all were mutually
pledged to each other, and to the state. Upon this they rested
the binding force of the laws.—Some modern writers upon
general law have wholly rejected this principle of compact.

Baron Puffendorf, whose high reputation appears to have had
great influence on the opinions of the first English jurists, and
to have involved them in some very palpable inconsistencies,
tells us that " Law, though it ought not to want its reasons, yet
these reasons are not the cause why obedience is paid to it,
but the power of the exactor, who, when he has signified his
pleasure, lays an obligation on the subject to act in conformity
to his decree. We obey the laws, principally, not on account
of the matter of them, but on account of the maker's will."*
Here is found the germ of the definition in the Commentaries.
In the next section he adds,—" Neither are they accurate
enough in their expressions, who frequently apply to the laws
the names of common agreements. The points of distinction
between a compact or covenant, and a law, are obvious. For
a compact is a promise, but a law is a command. In a compact
the manner of speaking is, I will do so ; but in a law, the form
runs thus, Do thou so, after an imperative manner." Let us
examine these positions, and see how far they are true, how
far they support the inferences which have been deduced from
them.

We need not question their propriety, when applied to an

*B. 1. Ch. 6. § 1.

absolute, despotic government, provided we may be allowed to substitute terror for will, and compulsion for obligation. But in a free government, the legislature consists of agents appointed by the people, and empowered under certain restrictions, to agree for all, including the agents themselves, on certain rules for their government, which rules so agreed, the people have bound themselves, in their original compact, the constitution, to observe and keep; and have also provided the means of compelling the observance, should any be found to neglect or disobey. Whatever tone or form the rule may assume, it is clearly a compact, but a compact of a peculiar nature, mutual between the individuals of the society and the aggregate. The consideration is no less than the protection, security, and happiness of each and of all. That a man may be as firmly bound by a contract made by his agent, as one made in his own person, is agreeable to the common sentiments of mankind, and is adopted in the laws and practice of every people on the globe, and that an agent may bind himself jointly with his principals, is known and adopted in every partnership concern.

But, says the author last mentioned, " It is a maxim that a man cannot bind himself," and this maxim he tells us, is not confined to single individuals, but extends to whole societies. And further, "for a person to oblige himself under the notion of a law-giver is impossible." That notion of a superior in this case, in the sense of the author, has been before shown to be unfounded. But instead of theoretical notions, let us resort to practical instances. He might not have known or not have recollected, that in England, the members of the legislature, were, as they still are, bound by the laws made by that body as fully as any other subject. The king is indeed not bound unless he is specially named in the act; if named, he is also bound in virtue of his assent.

But is it possible, that the author, writing on general law, should have overlooked not only the laws and customs of private partnerships, but of public incorporated companies, known in every country, and as old as the civil law itself, in which he was deeply versed, the great object of which laws and customs has always been, to enable the society or company by itself or its agents to bind the whole body by their contracts?

There were, and are, beside, numerous corporations of various descriptions which have the power of making certain laws, each binding on its own members. That a man cannot bind himself to himself, in the common acceptation of the term, is indeed true. In whatever form of words a person may to himself express his intention to perform some certain acts, it is but an intention or resolution, from the nature of the thing still holden under consideration, and the performance still remains optional ; but let the intention, being in itself lawful, be expressed by way of promise to another person upon a good and lawful consideration, surely the person so promising binds himself to the performance, and by the same act gives that other a full right to demand the performance. To every obligation or duty on the one part, there is a corresponding right on the other. This right is voluntarily conferred by the obligor, and cannot be arbitrarily assumed by the obligee. This is a first principle of universal law,—the law of nature.

To support the doctrine of an absolute sovereignty, an arbitrary, despotic power in the legislature, whether that legislature consist of a single man or body of men, the principle is reversed. Instead of the right of the obligee originating in the voluntary act of the obligor, it is made to originate in the arbitrary will and pleasure of the obligee. The advocates for this doctrine act consistently, in clothing their legislature with omnipotence, for certainly nothing short of that power could effect such a reversal of the law of nature. Power or force may impose a necessity, but can never impose an obligation, in any intelligible sense of the term. Necessity, arising from compulsion by force, and the duty arising from obligation, civil or moral, can no more coalesce than the veriest opposites in nature. But it is said there is an obvious distinction between the language of a compact and the language of a law. The language of a compact is,—" I will do so ;" but the language of a law is,—" thou shalt do so." This language is, from the nature of the case, very proper. When one of the parties enters into a bond, the language is,—" I acknowledge myself bound to do so ;" or if a simple contract,—" I promise to do so." But when a compact is pronounced by a third person mutually empowered by the parties, it is often expressed in the imperative style of a law,—such is the case of an award.

Two persons having a controversy, submit the decision to a third person, an arbitrator, who having heard the parties, pronounces his award in the usual style of command. "I do award and order that A. B.—one of the parties, pay the other such a sum, and that the other release. Here the language is after an imperative manner, and yet if the party against whom the award has been made, neglect to perform, the other may have an action, as on contract either of debt or assumpsit,—a promise, according to the nature of the submission.

Notwithstanding the imperative language of the award, it is still a contract, or rather consummation of a contract, inchoate in the submission of the parties from which it derives its binding force. Frequently a person by agreement binds himself to obey the commands of his employer, and in virtue of such agreement, and that only, he is bound to obey the commands according to his stipulation, with this proviso,—that the commands be lawful, and such as are usual and customary in the employment.

It may appear trifling and beneath the dignity of the subject to descend to the refutation of agreements drawn from the mere forms of expression ; but let it be recollected that those arguments having been adopted and urged with great gravity by authors of high reputation, in those writings from which are universally taught the rudiments of jurisprudence, and from which the student, the future law-giver and statesman collects his principles as from an infallible source, they assume an importance, to which they would not otherwise be entitled.

Thus on a full and fair investigation of principles, it may safely be pronounced, that, in a free government, the civil obligation to obey the law immediately originates in compact ;*

---

* If it should be decided, that a law itself is not in any strict sense a compact, still the argument and the conclusion, that the obligation to obey the law originates in compact, will remain in full force ; for it will not be denied, that, in all free governments, the constitution by which the legislative power is authorised, is established by compact, to which the people are the parties, and in forming which it is explicitly understood, that all shall be bound by that constitution, and by all the laws made under and in pursuance of its authority. Still farther, the people, through their representatives, give

a compact of a high and sacred nature, entered into on a high and valuable consideration; that hence, both customary and positive laws derive their binding force; that a statute law, whatever may be its form of expression, is a rule of civil conduct, which the people have agreed to observe, an agreement inchoate in the civil compact and consummated by the same people through their representatives. Although the civil obligation to obey the law, immediately originates in compact, yet the law of nature, which has rendered civil government necessary to man, necessary to the attainment in any considerable degree of that happiness which he is destined to seek in society, and which is the great object of all, attaches a peculiar sacredness to that obligation, and to the civil, adds the force of moral obligation, which I shall proceed to consider in the next chapter.

---

their assent to every law that is passed. Whatever force therefore, of obligation can arise from compact, contract, agreement, or assent, for they are in fact the same, that force the law has as an obligation, and no other. Compulsion may be superinduced, but that is a thing distinct from obligation in the sense here intended.

CHAPTER IV.

Moral Obligation of Civil Laws.

In the preceding chapter we treated of the civil obligation of municipal law only and the ground of compact; on which that was established, so closely connects the civil with the moral obligation, it might be thought that little could remain to be said on the subject of this chapter; but as a distinction has been taken that some laws are binding, and that others, although necessary and expedient for the public good, are not binding on the conscience, I shall treat the subject more fully. In doing this it will be necessary to recite at some length, those passages in the Commentaries, in which the author has endeavored to establish that distinction.

After having briefly treated of the law of nature, and the law of revelation, he tells us " upon these two foundations,— the law of nature, and the law of revelation,—depend all human laws; that is to say, no human laws should be suffered to contradict these. There are, it is true, a great number of indifferent points in which the divine law and the natural, leave a man at his liberty; but which are found necessary for the benefit of society to be restrained within certain limits; and herein it is that human laws have their greatest force, and efficacy; for with regard to such points as are not indifferent, human laws are only declaratory of, and act in subordination to the power. To instance in the case of murder,—this is expressly forbidden by the divine, and demonstrably by the natural laws; and from these two prohibitions, arises the true unlawfulness of the crime. Those human laws which annex a punishment to them, do not at all increase the moral guilt, or add any fresh obligations in *foro conscientiæ* to abstain from the perpetration. Nay, if any human laws should allow or enjoin us to commit it, we are bound to transgress that human law, or else we offend both the natural and the divine. But with regard to matters that are in themselves indifferent, and are not commanded by those superior laws, such, for instance, as exporting wool into foreign countries; here the inferior legislature has scope and opportunity to interpose, and to make that unlawful which before was not so."* Again, " Where rewards are proposed as well as punishments threatened, the obligation of the law seems chiefly to consist in the penalty; for rewards, in their nature, can only persuade and allure; nothing is compulsory but punishment."

Here it is evident the author has confounded the obligation to obey the law with the external force provided to compel that obedience. It is true he is speaking of the external obligation of the law, which alone is the direct concern of human laws and human tribunals; and does not here in any case, discharge the internal obligation.† But in the following passage he is very explicit.

" It is true, it hath been holden and very justly by the principal of our ethical writers, that human laws are binding on men's consciences. But if that were the only or most forcible obligation the good only would regard the laws, and the bad would set them at defiance—and true as this principle is, it must still be understood with some restriction. It holds I apprehend as to rights; and that when the law has determined the field to belong to Titius, it is a matter of conscience no longer to withhold or invade it—so also in natural duties, and such offences as are *mala in se*, here we are bound in conscience, because we are bound by superior laws, before these human laws were in being, to perform the one and abstain from the other. But in relation to these laws, which only enjoin positive duties and forbid only such things as are not *mala in se*, but *mala prohibita* merely, without any intermixture of mor-

* 1 Comm. 42, 43.   †1 Comm. 57.

al guilt, annexing a penalty to noncompliance ; here I apprehend conscience is no farther concerned than by decreeing a submission to the penalty, in case of our breach of those laws. For, otherwise, the multitude of penal laws would not only be looked upon as impolitic, but would also be a very wicked thing, if every such law were a snare for the conscience of the subject. But in these cases the alternative is offered to every man, either to do this or submit to the penalty, and his conscience will be clear, whichever side of the alternative he thinks proper to take."

The author might have been induced to this conclusion, partly from a consideration of that unlimited, arbitrary, and despotic power, with which he had thought it necessary to invest his legislature, a power to impose on the subject an equally unlimited civil obligation to obey all laws by them enacted, be they ever so absurd, violent, and oppressive. He could not but be sensible that such laws, whatever prudence might dictate, could never be felt as binding on conscience, and partly from a view of the criminal and penal code as it then stood and perhaps still stands in Great Britain. It was not his principal design to improve the laws of England, but to facilitate the study ; not to write a criticism, or to examine their merits, but to exhibit in a connected system a body of laws already formed. Had his subject led him to consider the extent of moral obligation, and the nature of all human laws, as founded in the principles of society and the only end that can be admitted in a free government, he would probably have found reason for a different opinion. Much deference is due to the author of the Commentaries as a luminous, and with few exceptions, a correct law-writer ; but the doctrine he has here advanced is certainly erroneous and dangerous to be admitted in society.

The question which this doctrine involves respecting the moral obligation of positive and penal law is important and requires a more extensive discussion than the limits prescribed to this portion of the work would permit, had not the greater part of the principles on which a correct decision depends, been as I apprehend already settled, in treating the subjects which have preceded. By the assistance and application of these principles, I shall hope to bring the question to a full and fair decision without transgressing those limits.

An opinion once advocated by many, although not admitted by the author, seems nevertheless to have influenced his reasonings. That a state of individual independence, or very little in advance of that condition is the natural state of man, and that all social improvements, as they are called, beyond that state, are a departure from nature. And that in an advanced state of social and civil improvement it becomes necessary, if not right, for the support of the community and protection of its members to make many laws, which—if not contrary to the original law of nature, yet have not the sanction of that law, and although allowed to be civilly binding, are not morally so,—do not effect the conscience.

But we have before seen there is by nature, implanted in man, a capacity for improvement. A state of nature may be a state of weakness and ignorance ; but a state of knowledge and improvement, is not therefore a departure from a state of nature ; as well might we make the assertion of the infant and the adult. An endeavor after knowledge, an improvement of his powers, individual and social, is indicated to him,—nay is imposed upon him by the very laws of his nature. That rude state so often immagined, if ever it did exist, is a state forced and unnatural. It cannot exist without a violation or dereliction of almost all the laws constituted by God in the formation of man. It must be either a state of brute violence, in which there can be no law but the law of the strongest ; or it must be a state of seclusion, in which the solitary individual has almost no use of any of the laws of his nature, scarcely have any of his powers, his mental faculties, his passion or appetites, either excitement or object ;—he is indeed exempted from some of the evils, and some of the vices found in a state of society ; but he is also excluded from all its endearing charities, —all its enjoyments. In a word, he is not entitled to the rank of man. He is in possession of himself, and entitled to his rank in society only. It is the state to which all his powers and faculties are adapted,—to which the laws of his nature bind him, and which gives him the full privilege of those laws.

Civil government, as we have already shewn, is the natural

and necessary consequence of a state of society, and is legitimately founded in the principles arising out of the social nature of man. The laws of nature have ordained that men, brought together in society, shall seek to promote and secure their own happiness through civil institutions and laws, and thus in their several spheres concur in the end and design of the great original Law-giver, to promote the general utility,—the happiness of the whole human race. Although the laws of nature have ordained civil institutions, they have prescribed no particular forms, but have submitted them to the discretion *of each society. These laws indeed, make it the duty of all to endeavor after perfection, but do not make its attainment, the condition of their concurrence and approbation. It is sufficient for each, that it in some degree secures and promotes the happiness of its members, at least without impeding the happiness of others.

Man is formed with dispositions and principles, that both allure and impel him to the adoption of civil institutions. Governments may originally be formed on different models; and each in a course of improvement may receive many and great alterations. There are, however, principles common to all arising from the general nature and end of all legitimate government. From a variety of circumstances, situation of country, different degrees of improvements in arts, science, and manners, they may have particular principles arising from the particular nature of each; but all governments have one common end in view, and all the members of each have in it a common interest. This consists in the means of securing to all, and mutually adjusting their social and individual rights. To effect this end, laws to regulate the general conduct of the members and direct their actions to the great object of society, the common good, are indispensably necessary. A power must therefore be somewhere intrusted to make such laws and enforce their observance. The mode of constituting this power must always be left to the wisdom of man, and will vary more or less, will be more or less perfect, according to the wisdom, integrity and means employed to effect the end; but the constitution of such a power, is, as we have shewn, not only permitted, but required by the law of nature. Surely then every civil law made in the spirit and agreeable to the intent of such constitution, whether it relate to the security of individual rights and interests, to the security and improvement of social intercourse, internal or external, or to the support and maintenance of the state, is ultimately derived from the law of nature, has the sanction of that law and carries with it the force of moral obligation.

The author, in the passage above cited, appears to understand by natural duties and offences *mala in se*, that is, offences against natural rights, those duties that are required and those offences that are forbidden by the primary rules of the law of nature, which were in force before any human laws were in being, as he expresses it, that is, those primary rules which were discovered by all men in that state of society which is supposed to have existed, previous to the adoption of civil institutions—and he calls those duties positive, and those offences *mala prohibita* which become such merely in consequence of the relations arising in civil society, and which are not comprehended in his first class. Thus, he calls the civil laws relating to the first class " auxiliary" to the laws of nature—those relating to the other class, " positive laws." This is, doubtless, a very proper, civil distinction, very proper in a treatise on civil law ; but is, I think, insufficient to support the moral distinction which he has founded upon it. If pursued through all its consequences, it would reduce the law of nature, considered as a moral law within very narrow limits. Of this, from an exception he has made to his general rule, and which we shall notice presently, it appears the author was in some degree aware. It may be difficult to decide with precision, the dividing line between the two classes ; but we may perhaps make an approximation sufficiently near.

Mr. Christian, who dissents from the doctrine of the author, observes that the principles of moral, that is natural, and positive law are the same, viz. utility, or the general happiness and true interest of mankind. But he farther observes, that the necessity of one set of laws is seen prior to experience ; the other posterior. The first observation is as just as it is important ; for although we may not allow utility to be the sole efficient of moral obligation, it is a *sine qua nan*, that without which it could not exist. It would be vain and useless, imposed for no end. But that the necessity of one set of laws, that is, laws of nature, is seen prior to experience, is not correct. For although nature has furnished man with a susceptibility of moral impressions, and capacity for attaining the exercise of that mental power or faculty which we call reason ; yet reason as a discriminating power, is not innate any more than the ideas on which it is exercised. It is, we know, attained by slow and almost imperceptible degrees. All the subjects on which it is exercised, and all the data from which it makes even the most obvious conclusion are furnished only by observation and experience. So true is it that we can in no instance reason but from what we know.

In any state of society a very little experience and observation is sufficient to discover the injurious effects of some actions, and the benficial tendency of others; and the necessity of rules to enforce the one class and to restrain the other. Their necessity, or in other words their utility, or high degree of expedience, is obvious to almost any degree of reason and experience ; but is not the discovery of intuitive reason.—Kill not, rob not, perform all promises,—are rules equally obvious and equally obligatory in every part of the world ; still their obligation is not a thing of intuition ; it is a deduction from experience and observation, it is derived from a conviction of the justice and utility of the rules.

There are other rules, which appear to be subsequent, the utility of which becomes obvious and their necessity is very early discovered in the same manner by experience. That all those who are united in the same society shall mutually protect each other and defend the whole against foreign aggressions, no one, I believe, will dispute, is a natural law, and obligatory on all as such. There are other rules, which do not relate to the general society in the same manner. Such is the rule, that parents shall support and maintain their offspring during their helpless state, and that rule which makes it the duty of children to maintain their parents when incapable of supporting themselves. These, if any, have always been considered as natural duties and their obligation imposed by the law of nature. If it should be said, that those rules are suggested by parental or filial affections, it may be replied, that the affections themselves, although we may reject the notion of their being instinctive, are natural and that they embrace the rules for their utility.

There are certain principles and relations common to all societies and governments in the earliest and rudest state, and which continue unchanged through every successive degree of improvement. The laws and duties discovered as resulting from these relations, have, with one consent, been pre-eminently denominated laws of nature and natural duties. This pre-eminence they have obtained from their permanence and universality, and these again from the constant and universal experience of their necessity, their universal utility. Such are the laws and duties just enumerated to which others might be added were it necessary to the present purpose. The people of each society in its progress, in the same manner discover by farther experience other rules adapted to their particular circumstances and growing interests. Such rules are at first, from a general representation and conviction of their utility, adopted by a general but tacit consent, and become the custom of the community. Many such rules have been already mentioned and the manner of their adoption explained, particularly those rules by which the right of property have been extended, enlarged and secured according to the exigencies of the present social state—and which it is unnecessary here to repeat.

In the gradual advancement of the society, their situation becomes less simple. Their relations and interests more numerous and complex. Further regulations are generally perceived to be necessary, but the particular rules that ought to be adopted are less obvious to the common mind.—They are comprehended only by the wiser part, consisting of those, who from their age, have had more opportunity for experience and observation. Such rules are by them adopted from a conviction of their expedience and general utility, are received by others on their recommendation and authority, and by a silent acquiescence ingrafted into their customs. Whatever is become habitual to any people, is by them considered as natural. They, therefore, consider their customary laws, as so many laws of nature, and their obligation is referred to the same source.

Accordingly, one who violates an established custom, is con

sidered not merely as the violator of a human law, but as an impious person,—as an offender against religion, a contemner of the divinity, under whatever forms they may have conceived of the divine power. And certainly their opinion of the obligation of their customary laws, as being of the moral kind, and enforced by the law of nature is correct, if we have been correct in our explanation of the source of moral obligation and the extent of the law of nature. • Let it be observed that we are here speaking of those customs of any people which have been adopted from just views of their situation, not such as have sometimes prevailed from a general perversion of sentiments.

We have hitherto been considering men in what is generally called a state of society, not having yet adopted by express compact, any particular form of civil institutions, or proceed by tacit consent to an organization of the civil powers. A little advance in the state we have been describing, renders their situation and interests too complicated for their simple, or as I may say, natural and primitive mode of legislation. New regulations, new laws are found to be necessary; but to adjust the different interests, and by fair and impartial rules to direct the whole to the promotion of the general interest, is now no longer obvious to the common apprehension. The remedy, which in this situation most naturally presents itself, is to call an assembly of the people, to collect and compare the different opinions and experience of all, and on deliberation to agree on such new laws or such modifications of the laws and customs as shall be deemed by the majority to be most expedient,—most conducive to the common interest; or which frequently happens, the people delegate that power to one or more persons in highest repute for wisdom and experience. Whichever mode be adopted, this is the first distinct organization, the first express civil compact, by which all agree to submit to such laws as shall be ordained by a majority of the assembled people, or by the authority of the select legislative organ.

The laws enacted under this new organization will be received with less veneration as coming from human, not from divine authority which has been attributed to the primitive laws and customs of every people. To question their author-ity, or to disobey their injunctions, will not in the same man-ner be considered as impious, as an offence against religion, which they have been accustomed to associate with all inter-nal obligation, which to be efficacious is always a sentiment no less than a dictate of reason,—nay, which with the weak and uninformed often sets reason at defiance.

It is true, as before shewn, the civil compact induces a moral obligation to all laws made agreeable to that compact—that is, such laws as the common interest requires; but until positive laws have, from their obvious utility, or from long habit, ob-tained in the minds of the people the moral character of their ancient customs, the obligation will appear to rest in the com-pact, and not to arise from, or to be immediately united in, the law—a distinction which will readily be perceived. Hence, perhaps, men first learn to make a distinction between the civil and the moral obligation. They find in their own minds a difference in the force of the obligation,—the question, how-ever, is not of the degree of moral obligation to obey any particular law or class of laws, but of the reality of such obli-gation ; for, while we admit different degrees in crimes, we must necessarily admit different degrees in obligation, and this is equally true of both positive and natural law. All laws, therefore, which come within the definition which we have given,—a definition equally applicable to moral and positive law,—" a rule enjoining that which ought to be done, and pro-hibiting that which ought not to be done,"—and it would be absurd to suppose the author, notwithstanding he has adopted an exceptionable mode of expression, did not intend the same, carry with them a moral obligation.

It certainly was not the intention of the author, as it was not his business in this instance, to discuss what obligation, or whether any would attach to arbitrary and tyrannical laws. Taken in this view, the exception which he has admitted to his general position, and to which we have before alluded, at once annihilates his distinction : For, after having laid it down that a certain class of penal laws " do not make the transgres-sion a moral offence or sin ; the only obligation in conscience is to submit to the penalty if levied ;"* he concludes the whole with this sentence,—" but where disobedience to the law involves in it also any degree of public mischief or private injury, it falls within our former distinction and is also an offence against conscience." What law can there be, "enjoining what ought to be done and prohibiting what ought not to be done," the violation of which does not necessarily involve some public mischief, or private injury ?

As to the alternative said to be offered to every one to abstain from the violation or submit to the penalty ; this is wholly to mistake the intention of the law—nor does the delinquent ever act on that intention. It is his great object while he transgresses the law to evade the penalty. Take away all hope of evasion, and the law will never be deliberately violated. According to the author's expression, it concerns the conscience to submit to the penalty in case only of its being levied, that is, if the delinquent be taken and convicted. How fully and clearly a man may discharge his conscience by a compulsory submission to the penalty under the bolts and bars of a prison, bound under the lash of the beadle, or mounted a public spectacle on the pillory, let some nicer casuist decide. One thing, however, is certain, that however he may have discharged his conscience of the offence, he will ever after remain conscious of the infamy he incurred by the manner of that discharge.

On this subject it has been justly observed, " Punishments or penalties are never intended as an equivalent, or compensation for the commission of the offence ; but they are that degree of pain or inconvenience, which are supposed to be sufficient to deter men fiom introducing that greater degree of inconvenience, which would result to the community from the commission of that act which the law prohibits. It is no recompense to a man's country for the consequences of an illegal act, that he should afterwards be whipped, or should stand in the pillory, or lie in jail."

Let us instance in a few of those laws which are generally considered as *juris positivi*. Those enacted for the prevention

---

* 1 Comm. 58.

of frauds in the collection and payment of the public revenue;
—to prevent the introduction of pestilential diseases and the
spreading of conflagrations. What compensation can the personal penalty or punishment of the delinquent be to the state
for a sum of money withdrawn or purloined from the public
treasury, either by smuggling or peculation? What compensation, what atonement can any penalty suffered by the offender,—
who by a violation of the laws on those subjects, has been the
means of letting loose conflagration and pestilence to the destruction of the lives and property, perhaps of thousands of his
fellow men,—be either to the public or to the suffering individuals?

The moral reason which the author gives for permitting in
penal law the alternative, that one may either obey the law or
clear his conscience by submitting to the penalty, is altogether
inadequate.—" That otherwise the multitude of penal laws in
a state would not only be looked upon as impolitic, but a very
wicked thing, if every such law were a snare for the conscience of the subject." Was it ever thought that the multitude of moral rules in any state of society ought to be looked
upon as a very wicked thing, or that they were a snare to men's
consciences, and not rather a safe guide? However complicated the state of society, and however numerous the rules,
their application is left to be discovered as the result of situation, circumstances, and relations; nor is it thought a task too
difficult. In matters that become the subject of positive law
the difficulty is much less; many actions are considered as
good only when enjoined, or as evil when prohibited.

Hence, the duty of the subject arises on the requisition of the
law, and is clearly explained in the law itself. Not that the
positive law creates, if I may use the expression, but induces
the moral obligation, and that in perfect consistence with the
definition given of municipal law. It is presupposed that in the
existing situation, the actions which are to be the subject of the
law, are such as public good—the general interest—requires
should be enjoined or prohibited according to their nature and
tendency. It is here with the public right, the same as in the
case of an individual, who may, by his acquiescence, suffer others
to reap advantage from the use of his rights or property. So

the government may suffer the citizens or subjects, to do, or neglect to do things, which it may have become the public interest either to enjoin, or to prohibit; and from the nature of civil liberty the permission continues until a law be interposed by public authority. In the former case, if the individual interpose his rightful claim, for others to persist in, the use becomes a private wrong; in the latter, if government interpose a law, to persist in opposition to the law, becomes a public wrong, a moral no less that a civil wrong.

The author, seemingly, to prepare the way for his doctrine, has supposed there are many matters in themselves indifferent and which are not commanded or prohibited by those superior laws, the primary laws of nature of which he had been speaking; here, he says, the inferior legislature has scope and opportunity to interpose and to make that action unlawful which before was not so. It may, perhaps be difficult to fix the precise meaning of the word indifferent as here intended. That there are things indifferent, in the sense that they are neither right or wrong, considered independent of the relation under which they exist, and that they take their moral quality from those relations is true; but it is equally true, that independent of those relations they can never be a proper subject of legislation. They become such from their relation to the public interest; and when from that relation, the public good requires the interposition of a law on any matter it is no longer a matter of indifference.

For the legislature to interpose a law on a matter, if any such could be found, totally indifferent, would be an unnecessary and wanton restraint both of the civil and natural liberty of the subject. It is also true that when a necessary end is sought to be effected by a law proposed, several subjects may be presented, and it may appear to the legislature a matter of indifference, or rather, of serious deliberation which shall be preferred; but when the choice is made, that indifference is not transferred to the law to interrupt the moral, any more than the civil obligation. Nor does it affect the reality of the obligation that the choice has been made of a subject less proper than another to attain the end sought.

We may here repeat what has been said, at least in substance,

The laws of nature have ordained that men, brought together in society, shall seek to promote and secure their own happiness through civil institutions and laws, and thus concur in the end and design of the great Lawgiver, to promote the general utility,—the happiness of mankind. But although the laws of nature have ordained civil institutions generally, yet they have not ordained any particular forms, or specific civil rules. These are left to the wisdom and discretion of each society; and though they make it the duty of all to endeavor after perfection, they do not make its attainment a condition of their approbation. It is sufficient to induce their moral obligation in each society, that its civil institutions and laws in some degree tend to promote the happiness of its members at least without impeding the happiness of others, and thus concur in the original design of promoting human happiness.

Thus, in every view which can be taken of the subject, it is clearly proved, that all municipal laws, whether civil or criminal, that is, penal, which the public interest, the general happiness require, and which in their tendency promote that happiness, are, in addition to the obligation of the civil compact, of strict moral obligation, and are inforced by the general moral law, the law of nature. In fact, they are rules of that law discovered by the wisdom of man as applicable to the existing situation of the civil state. To erect crimes upon actions wholly indifferent to the interest of the society, if any such are to be found, to gratify the pride and caprice of one class of citizens by allowing to them what is forbidden to others; to inflict penalties to support a system of monopoly, or the mere purpose of revenue, is to confound every idea of right and wrong in a criminal code. Such laws are to be found in many states. Such, perhaps, are the English laws to which the author has referred, the game laws and some others; but if they discover this character, they do not as we have shewn come within the definition of municipal law, or the purview of his subject—it demands a different discussion. Harrassed with such laws, and unable to find any moral restraint, men learn to make a distinction between what is morally wrong and what is only partially so.

Among a great variety of laws, some arbitrary and some not, their minds are wearied with the difficulties of discriminating. They readily admit the author's doctrine, and refer the violation of the primary class of duties in society to the class of *mala in se*, the others to the class of *mala prohibita*. Probably, however, no two men in any community will be found to agree in the classification. Laws which violate the principles, or neglect the interest of the society for which they are made, will be resisted, or will be obeyed with reluctance.— Obedience will sometimes be considered as a matter of prudence ; never as a matter of conscience. Men would be in a deplorable situation, if the law of morals inforced obedience to every act of legislation. The laws when once enacted would be received with veneration. The facility of execution would supersede the necessity of repeated examination, and frequent recurrence to the principles of the government, and the rights, interests, and sentiments of the people, without which the best intention of the legislature can afford no sufficient security against the danger of tyrannical laws.

CHAPTER V.

THE SAME SUBJECT CONTINUED.

Principles of the Government as they affect the Moral Obligation of Laws.

From the different nature or constitution of governments, their principles and the spirit of their laws will be different. Fear, supported by terror of punishments, or a superstitious veneration for the reigning family, or both, are the principles, that is, the great object of the laws and the sole motive of obedience, in a despotic government.

Monarchy does not lose sight of the principle of fear, but blends with it, chiefly in regard to the order of nobility, the principle of honor, a sentiment merely personal and devoted to all the caprices of opinion. The principle of an aristocracy, as it relates to the people, differs little from that of despotism. Republican, or rather, popular and representative governments have for their principle, that is, the end of their institution and the motive of obedience, a sentimental attachment of the people to the community, its institutions, its laws and government. A mixed government partakes of all these principles, each of which predominates in proportion to the prevalence of one or other of its constituent parts. Where fear is the governing motive of every social action, all happiness in social intercourse, all social improvements are not neglected only, but opposed by the genius of the government. Blended with fear, however, honor—that principle of all the most capricious, sometimes irradiates, but more frequently obscures the social horizon. Neither of them have any principal regard to the happiness of the people, or the interests of morality. The principle of a popular government, a sentimental attachment to the community, its institutions and laws, need not,—neither can it—endure the intervention of the other two principles, as they are usually understood by writers on government :—principles, which regard the whole society as constituted to gratify the passions and appetites of one, or a few individuals. Such a mixture of heterogeneous principles, in a government with pains adjusted, must of necessity have a very considerable effect upon its legislation, upon the interpretation and the execution of its laws. It will have a tendency to dictate acts and rules of civil conduct, which can in no view claim the sanction of the moral sense. The spirit of the laws is directed by the effective principle,—the principle by the constitution, or nature of the government. Perhaps the laws of England are the best that can consist with the mixed principles of that government. If this be true, Judge Blackstone's distinction between those laws that are morally binding, and those that are only politically so, is, so far as it applies to English laws, just and necessary ; but he should not have considered it as he has done,—a common and necessary distinction in every code. . It is, however, a severe, though an undesigned stroke at the principles of that government.

Can there be a more sure, a more safe criterion for deciding the goodness of any government than the tendency of its principles in legislation? That government, that constitution of society, the principles of which dictate those laws and those only, that are adapted to the present state of men and manners, and tend to social improvement, which induce a moral obligation under the sentence of the laws of nature, not of savage solitary nature, but of social nature in its improved and improvable state, is incontrovertibly good ; so far as it deviates it is clearly faulty. Upon a candid examination, upon a fair comparison, it will be found that a representative republic is pre-eminently, if not alone, capable of these principles to their fullest extent. It is true, that in any government, circumstances foreign to its principles, may—and in this state of imperfection frequently will—concur to the adoption of bad laws ; but if the constitution and principles be good, such laws will not have a long continuance.

The governments of the several American states, as well as that of the Union, are of the representative kind. We ought to know their principles, to study well their tendency, and to be able, both in theory and practice, to exclude all foreign principles.

Judge Blackstone was a British subject, high in favor with the government. He was enamored with the principles of their constitution ; he has emblazoned them with all his rhetoric, and not the least some that are the most faulty ; and probably to this, not less than to his great talents, he was indebted for the great reputation he enjoyed in that country. Unhappily his Commentaries contain the only general treatise of law, to which the law students in these States have access. In every section of the criminal code, and in all questions of a civil nature, where the prerogatives of the crown or the privileges of the peers intervene, the principles of the government have given a cast to his reasonings. I wish not to detract from the merit of the author, as a British subject; a writer, who has in a masterly manner delineated the laws and jurisprudence of a great nation, but under a government very different from our own. There are many things in his Commentaries which accord with the principles of our own governments, and which are founded on the universal principles of jurisprudence. These will, however, be found mostly to be derived from the popular part of the British constitution. The student should carefully learn to distinguish those principles, which are peculiar to that government, or governments of a similar constitution ; to distinguish the reasons which are accommodated to those principles, or solely dictated by them. He ought to know that they are not universal ; that in a repesentative republic they are wholly inadmissible. This is not enough ; he ought to be led through a system of laws founded on the principles of our own governments, and a train of reasoning congenial to those principles. Such a system is yet a desideratum.*

---

* Since this was written that desideratum has been most amply and happily supplied by the publication of " *Commentaries on American Law,* By JAMES KENT." In 4 Vols.

CHAPTER V.

Of Penal Laws.

Penal laws and laws relating to taxation, or for the purpose of raising a revenue to government, merit more particular attention, because they more than others immediately affect the lives, liberty, and property of the subjects. In treating of them, I shall consider the right and power of government, and the legitimate end to be attained in each.

Under penal laws I comprehend all those laws which inflict a penalty, whether it be capital, pecuniary, or personal, for the violation or neglect of any duty enjoined, either by the primary laws of nature, or the positive laws of society.

The right to punish individuals for crimes against society is not an arbitrary institution of civil policy. It has its foundation in the moral and social nature of man and is derived to government from that source through the civil compact. We have already seen that man was not formed for individual independence, but for society, for civil union in government. All the liberty of an individual, all his rights which can any way effect the rights and liberty of others are placed in an accommodation, a mutual compromise with the rights and liberties of all and every member of the society. To facilitate this accommodation and to render a compromise practicable, mutual and safe, is the object of civil institutions and laws.

If man be by nature a social being, it is an obvious conclusion that it is his duty to forbear any injury to the society of which he is a member ; and that the violation of this duty is a violation of the laws of his nature. It may, perhaps, be here thought sufficient to say, that rights and duties are reciprocal ; every society must have a right corresponding with the duty of the individual ; if the individual violate his duty to the society, the society have a clear right to take a satisfaction. But as this subject is of great importance in national jurisprudence, I shall endeavor to analyze the right and trace it to its source in the moral nature of man. Deity in the constitution of nature has not done every thing for man ; he has established certain relations, from which result the laws that ought to govern his moral and social actions. He has given him powers and faculties to enable him to discover these relations and the laws that result from them. The mode of giving these laws their full effect is left to his sagacity, to the exercise of his reasoning powers. To enable him more steadily to pursue them he is furnished with a moral perception of right and wrong, and a sense of merit or demerit attending the observance or non-observance—the moral sense and the sense of accountability as before explained, and which are generally comprehended, in the term conscience, which, when rightly informed, extends its authority to every moral, every social, and every civil action. Hence, on the perpetration of a crime, arise in the mind of the perpetrator the feelings of guilt, and the consciousness of a desert of punishment. These sentiments are common to men, both in a review of their own actions and in passing judgment on the actions of others. What might at first seem to be inconsistent with that universal desire of happiness, which belongs to the nature of every individual is, that guilt is sometimes in the mind of the guilty, attended with a strong desire of punishment ; this is, what we generally call remorse. If punishment be inflicted by no other hand, self-punishment is well known to be the gratification provided by nature for the violent affection of remorse. From this view of the subject the right of punishing the guilty is clearly perceived to be derived from the relation of men in society. It was not alone from an extraordinary impression of the Divine anger on the mind of Cain, after the murder of his brother, but from a perception of those relations and the right resulting from them, that he is made to say, " whoso findeth me shall slay me."

The Marquis Beccaria has founded the right of punishing on

the same principles. " Let us (says he) consult the human heart ; and there we shall find the foundation of the sovereign's right to punish ; for no advantage in civil policy can be lasting, which is not founded in the indelible sentiments of the heart of man." In cases of mere private injury, the right is perceived to belong to the party injured. He has a right to demand reparation for the injury, and a caution against the like injury in future. The mode of obtaining both is to be regulated by the present nature of social rights. Where the right cannot be exercised by the party injured without danger to the social rights of others, the laws of social nature dictate a submission to an impartial tribunal ; a provision which can be made and enforced in the union of civil society only. When a person is guilty of a violation of those rights, which more immediately affect the interest and happiness,—the peace and security of the whole, the right of prosecuting the injury is perceived to belong to the community, although the end is not generally the same as in the case of a more private injury, as we shall see presently.

In a state of any considerable degree of social and civil improvements, men endure with reluctance the exercise of the right of punishment by the party injured. This happens, not because men are more unfit for the exercise in this state, but because they have a nicer sense of right and wrong. Their social feelings are extended and refined.—The security and happiness of each individual member becomes the interest, as it effects the happiness, of the whole. They perceive not only the inhumanity to which the practice tends, but the injustice, of which it is in almost every instance productive. They perceive, that the power of punishing can in almost no case be exercised by the party injuried, without a perpetual violation of the rights of others, of the obligations of morality, and the danger of a total annihilation of social happiness. Hence, it becomes the right, interest, and duty of every civil community, to punish by way of caution, all those injuries which disturb, or have a direct tendency to disturb their happiness, or to render it insecure. And it will extend to whatever the common sentiment has connected with the public happiness. It is evident, then, that the right of government, by way of caution, to punish the crimes of its members, is not an arbitrary institution, nor does it originate in necessity only, but in the sentiments of the human heart, the existing relations of men in society, and has the full sanction of the laws of nature.

The organ by which the right of punishing shall be exercised in government is a consideration of propriety, safety, and convenience. A slight attention to the subject will discover it to be a branch of the right of legislation and intimately connected with the duties of that department. Without the right of punishing for the violation of a law, the right of legislation would be perfectly nugatory.

There is a three-fold division of the right of punishment, or of the exercise of that right, corresponding with the general division of the powers of government. First, the decreeing of penalties for the breach of any law. This involves a consideration of the importance of the law to the interests of the state, and the means of preventing crimes, the true end of all punishments, and corresponds with the right of legislation. To that branch, therefore, it can alone be intrusted. Secondly, the application of the law to particular cases for the purpose of determining whether it has been violated and who is the offender. This is clearly the proper business of the judiciary. Thirdly, the execution of the sentence upon the criminal, which falls to the province of the executive. The right of punishment is, in practice, frequently limited only by the will of the legislature, and the decisions of the judiciary; but the laws of nature have not left it arbitrary. Those laws have assigned certain limits, beyond which the right ceases, and the exercise of the power becomes a crime against society. These limits are not, in every sense, permanent and invariable. It is universally true that the right is limited by the end of preventing crimes and securing obedience to the laws. It is also true, that the penalties, which, in one state of society and manners are adequate to that end may, in a different state, be wholly inadequate.

Not only the state of manners, but the principles of the government, affect the severity of punishment. Where the support of the reigning powers, without any regard to the good of the people, is the sole end of every measure of state, fear, which is inculcated by the severity of punishment, is the sole principle of obedience. Such governments set limits neither to crimes, nor to the severity of punishments. No actions are considered to be criminal because they are injurious to the people, or against the laws of nature; but because they are supposed to be dangerous to the reigning power, and a contempt of its authority. In proportion as governments have ascended to natural principles and made the happiness of the people the end of their institutions, crimes and punishments have admitted of more definite limits. It has been proved and acknowledged, that, in a civil view, those actions only are criminal, which are injurious to the community at large, or to individuals, whose rights and happiness the community are bound to protect, and secure; that the prevention of crimes is the sole end of punishments, and that all beyond this is the spirit of revenge and wanton cruelty.

I repeat it, the sole end of punishment is, or ought to be the prevention of crimes. Under crimes, I comprehend, not only the doing of those things which are directly detrimental to the community, but the omission of those things which are necessary to its support and general happiness; for if man be a social being, it clearly follows that he is bound not only to forbear injuries to the society, but to contribute his equal share to its well-being. It is an obligation arising not from necessity merely, but an original, indispensable obligation.

We have seen that the Deity has been pleased, by the strongest and most intimate relation,—the relation of cause and effect,—to connect happiness with the virtuous actions of moral agents,—misery with their vices. These are the rewards and punishments in the government of providence. To this system man, in the original constitution of his nature, is admirably adapted, by means of the moral faculty of which we have before treated, his perception of the moral right and wrong of his actions, his desire of the approbation of others, and a consequent dread of their censure; a consciousness when he has done right that he is deserving of their approbation, when wrong—of censure or punishment. To this constitution of nature, all civil laws and political institutions ought to be adapted. Hence are to be derived the true principles of all penal laws and criminal jurisprudence,—principles which can alone produce and support a coincidence between the civil and moral obligation of those laws. Upon no other principles will punishments be perceived to be just; upon no other principles can they have a salutary effect on the life,—on the manners of men, to promote the ends of civil society.

It is worthy of remark, that in the progress of society, no science has, in general, received so little improvement as the science of criminal jurisprudence.* It is true that the outrageous violence with which capital and other punishments were inflicted, has in some nations been abolished or greatly mitigated, but it may with equal truth, be observed, that among nations, who boast of the highest degree of refinement, the greatest degree of improvement in their civil policy, the number of capital punishments has been increased out of all proportion to the reform in point of cruelty. The British government, which in civil improvements, and the justice and humanity of its civil code, has gone beyond most of the European nations,—has proceeded with a degree of wantonness in the enactment of capital punishments. One hundred and sixty crimes, declared to be worthy of immediate death, hardly completes the murderous catalogue.

The following just and pointed observations not only on the inutility, but the injurious consequences of this multiplicity of capital offences, made some years ago by a British senator in the house of commons, ought to be carefully preserved and deeply fixed in the mind of every legislator.—" Whether hanging ever did, or can answer any good purpose, I doubt; but the cruel exhibition of every execution day, is a proof, that hanging carries no terror with it. And I am confident that every new sanguinary law operates as an encouragement to commit capital offences; for it is not the mode, but the certainty of the punishment that creates terror. What men know they must endure, they fear; what they think they may escape they

---

* The world is more indebted to the Marquis Beccaria for his little " Treatise on Crimes and Punishments" than to all other writers on the subject.

despise. The multiplicity of our hanging laws, has produced these two things ; frequency of executions and frequent pardons. As hope is the first and greatest spring of action, if it was so, that out of twenty convicts one only was to be pardoned, the thief would say, " why may not I be that one ?" But since, as our laws are actually administered, not one in twenty is executed, the thief acts on a chance of twenty to one in his favor ; he acts on a fair and reasonable presumption of indemnity ; and I verily believe, that the confident hope of indemnity is the cause of nineteen in twenty robberies that are committed."

Several causes have concurred to prevent any considerable improvement in the criminal code. Men appear often to entertain an idea of justice as of a physical being or power, something which physically exists,* whereas, it is only the result of certain relations ; civil justice results from the relations of men in civil society ; beyond these, it has no relation nor even mental existence. This notion has done infinite mischief in the world. It has represented justice, as really offended in proportion to the degree of the crime committed, and inexorably demanding satisfaction by a certain determinate punishment to be inflicted on the offender ; like the malevolent deities of some nations who are propitiated by human sacrifices only. By considering a satisfaction to justice as the principal end of punishment, and disregarding its utility to society, the safe and certain criterion of the justice and propriety of any class of civil or social actions, it has served to reconcile people, in other respects of a refined sensibility, to an excess of cruelty in the enacting and the execution of laws.

A punishment annexed to a crime is, by association, viewed in connexion with the crime, and often serves as a measure for the degree of its guilt, which arises only from its relation to society. When from any cause the perpetration of any particular species of crimes has become frequent, the minds of legislators are irritated against the perpetrators and against the crime. Determined to apply an effectual remedy they are

---

* Beccaria on Crimes and Punishments, Ch. 2

too prone, without adverting to the cause of the evil, to enhance the penalty, thus augmenting the uncertainty of the punishment, which was perhaps before the most powerful cause.

It is, however, for the interest of humanity and a wise disposition of providence, that in a state of any considerable degree of refinement, sanguinary laws should always defeat the end of their institution. If the penalty imposed by law exceed the demerit of the crime in the estimation of the people, whose general semtiments are, in this case, the best criterion of what ought to have been done, the law is rarely executed. Humanity, whose dictates are more readily obeyed than the requisitions of such laws, is interested in the escape or acquittal of the criminal. When the severity of the punishment excites the compassion of the people, the effect of the punishment is more than lost. While they pity the criminal, they forget his crime, or diminish its guilt, and conceive an abhorrence of the law. If the criminal be detected and condemned, he is viewed as unfortunate, rather than guilty.

From an attention to the state of crimes in different societies we shall find, that in those governments whose legislators have swelled the list of capital offences and by applying the same ultimate punishment to crimes of very different grades have confounded all degrees of guilt, the same crimes are more frequently committed, than in those governments where the laws have been enacted with more mildness, and different degrees of guilt distinguished by different degrees of punishment. The punishment ought never to exceed, but to rather fall short of the demerit of the crime in the sentiments of the people. Where this is the case, humanity is engaged on the side of the law, and the punishment is rendered as certain as the perpetration of the crime. This adds a mild, but irresistible energy to the execution of the law. It is universally true, that certainty of punishment has a much more powerful effect than severity in the prevention of crimes. Indeed, the resentment and contempt of mankind, which always pursue the perpetrator of a crime, if not converted into compassion by the severity of the law, constitute a punishment of no inconsiderable efficacy.

Such is the right of government to punish, and such the principles which ought to be invariably pursued in the enactment of all penal laws. I add with entire satisfaction, that under no form of government is a certain degree of mildness more requisite, in none more effectual to the prevention of crimes, than under the representative form of popular government. An equitable moderation in punishments, while it exhibits the powers of government in the amicable light of humanity, cherishes and invigorates its only efficient principle, a sentimental attachment to its institutions and laws.

CHAPTER VI.

Of Taxation, or Laws for raising a Public Revenue.

The right of taxation is no more than the right of punishment on arbitrary institutions of civil government. To whatever organ the exercise of the right is committed, it is a trust for the benefit of the community. It is perceived, even by the most simple, that from the relations of men in civil society, there results a duty upon them, not only to forbear to injure the society, but also to contribute to its support and prosperity; that common conception of the individuality of a society, which has been before explained, has no inconsiderable effect in rendering the perception of this duty distinct and in collecting and fixing its object. The duty may be called the duty of contribution on the one hand, from which, on the other, results the right of taxation. The right of taxation is nothing more than the right to enforce the duty of contribution, to which every member of the community is originally bound. The duty, and he right wherever it resides are reciprocal. The duty is the same upon every individual, as to the reality, not as to the quantity of the contribution.

No civil duty, perhaps, can less be intrusted to the voluntary conduct of individuals ;—none more needs a provision of general rules, to secure equal justice, both to individuals and the community. The utility of the community cannot be opposed to that of the individual members in gereral ; nevertheless, the latter, from its being more immediate, so far outweighs the former, that they are often viewed in opposition. The duty would, therefore, never be performed, unless there somewhere resided a right, with authority, as well to enforce it, as to apportion the several quotas. The end of this right and duty is the utility of the community ; not indeed in an absolute sense, but in certain relation, proportion, and agreement with the utility of individuals.

The right of determining the amount, of apportioning the contribution, and enforcing the duty—which is the right of taxation—is originally in the community, considered as an aggregate body. The organ by which it shall be exercised, is, as in the case of punishment, a consideration of propriety, safety, and convenience, and the apportionment must be made by equal and general rules, and the demand enforced by the sanction of law. It is, therefore, with propriety and convenience, committed to the legislative body. If such body be composed of a full and equal representation of the several interests of the citizens, the trust is safely deposited with them. The power and right of taxation can be safely intrusted to no man, or body of men, who are not amenable to the people for the exercise, and who do not equally share the burdens which they impose, without a moral certainty of oppression, the final annihilation of liberty, and all security of private property.

The great question, therefore, about taxation, and representation, is a question about the mode, rather than the right ; a consideration of safety to the rights of the people. It is, indeed a most important consideration ; but it does not reach the original right of taxation, founded on the duty of contribution. The representation of any portion of the people in the national legislature is a proof of an intimate civil connexion which clearly subjects them to the duty of contribution ; but if the people choose to intrust the power of taxation in any other mode, or to any other body, the exercise, if not equally safe, may be equally legitimate. It is not easy, perhaps, to ascertain with precision, what degree of social union among individuals will incur the duty of contribution. It is, however, clear that one community can have no right to tax personally the members of another community, where the citizens of both are not united ultimately by an internal, reciprocal, civil connexion.

States in league, may, as far as the league extends, incur one to another, the duty of contribution; but the duty is demandable against each state collectively, not against the individual citizens. Each state has a demand against the other, and the several states against their citizens individually, to enable them to fulfil their engagements. Between the several states the right to enforce the duty resides equally in every part, till by mutual agreement, a body is formed for its exercise. Till this has taken place, it remains, like that of independent individuals, a voluntary duty, or to be enforced only by the law of nations,—the right of the sword.

So different are the interests, both general and particular, in different states, that no general rules can be prescribed as to the particular mode of taxation, which shall be equally applicable to all; it must ever be considered as a matter of public convenience and private equity. There are, however, certain principles which ought ever to be considered as fundamental, in all laws upon this subject. The lawful interest of no citizen or class of citizens, can, without injustice, and a violation of equal rights, be sacrificed to that of another, or even that of the whole. That mode ought to be adopted which, as far as general rules can extend, will operate agreeable to the rule of mutual compromise,—a rule very general indeed, which is applied in ethics, may, with great propriety, be applied in this case. Requisition shall be made of a man according to that which he hath,—not according to that which he hath not. Taxes, therefore, ought not to be apportioned upon persons, but upon things—upon property possessed or used by individuals.

Smith, in his Wealth of Nations, in treating of taxes, has laid down the four following rules, or maxims as he calls them;–

" I. The subjects of every state ought to contribute toward the support of government, as nearly as possible in proportion to their respective abilities ; that is, in proportion to the revenue which they respectively enjoy under the protection of the state.

" II. The tax which each individual is bound to pay, ought to be certain and not arbitrary. The time of payment, the manner of payment, the quantity to be paid, ought to be clear and plain to the contributor, and to every other person.

" III. Every tax ought to be levied at the time, or in the manner in which it is most likely to be convenient to the contributor.

" IV. Every tax ought to be so contrived, as both to take out and to keep out of the pockets of the people, as little as possible over and above what it brings into the treasury of the state."—To which may be added—

V. Every tax ought to be so contrived, as to cause as little vexation, and to embarrass as little as possible the common business of the citizens.

Taxes have generally been reckoned of two kinds, and denominated direct and indirect taxes. Those of the first class are called direct taxes, because they are assessed upon the person or upon the property in his possession or use, and of which he is supposed to be the proprietor. Of this we shall first treat :— some of our observations will, however, be alike applicable to both kinds of taxes.

First. A direct tax, we have said, is assessed upon the person, or on the property. That which is assessed on the person is called a capitation tax. In the assessment of this tax no regard is had to the means of payment. The same sum is demanded of the poorest as of the wealthiest subject of the same rank; it is in its operation unequal in the extreme, and can never be adopted by a government that would pay any regard to the just and equal distribution of the public burdens.

When direct taxes are assessed upon property, it has been used to apportion them upon a valuation of the property or thing to be taxed. This will be just and equal, provided the valuation be made—not according to the market value, but— according to the income it may produce with ordinary manage-

ment. There are, however, some exceptions which will occur in their proper place.

Protection has, by many, been held to be the consideration,
on the one side, on which is founded the right of taxation on
the other. If it were so, the degree of protection should serve
as a measure for the apportionment of taxes on individuals. But
this is not the case. The mutual protection of its members is
one great end proposed in the civil compact. But the duty of
contribution, and consequently the right of taxation, arises from
the whole relation in which men stand in society. The same
thing is true of every civil right and duty. The general relations are connected and form a certain internal relation among
themselves. If we take away one relation, it deranges the connexion, varies the mutual relations, and of course the result.

In those governments in which the rights of the sovereign
are supposed to be original, and independent of the rights of
the people, it is in perfect consistency with the principles of
the government, to derive the sovereign's right of taxation from
the protection afforded to the subject, although in practice as
it always happens with such absurd principles ; it is destructive
of the consideration itself, and the source of the most grievous
oppression. But where, as in popular governments, those who
exercise the sovereign power are merely constituted organs,
and exercise only the power of the people, associated in civil
government, that consideration between the sovereign and the
people does not exist. The sovereign power,—the whole right
is the power and right of the people thus associated,—not individually, but collectively.

It is true, that the laws of nature, from which result all civil
rights and duties, are always directed to some useful end ; but
the useful end to be attained is the criterion by which to judge
of their authenticity, rather than the consideration of the duty
imposed ; the final, rather than the efficient cause. The right
of the citizen to civil protection does not arise from any such
consideration, and an apportionment of taxes upon that principle,
would be grossly unequal and oppressive. It would make the
poor and the weak the greatest debtors to the state ; for, contributors they could not be. The consideration of abstract relations and abstract rights,—fabrications of the mind only,

which may or may not justly comprehend the rights of nature,
and are, perhaps, never precisely the same in the conceptions
of any two individuals,—can furnish no sufficient data for the
apportionment of taxes. It is necessary to find something more
fixed and certain, and to take real quantities, as well in the data as in the product.

The only plausible theory, and which is capable of being
reduced to practice by the application of real quantities is, that
every contributor, in any community, shall be taxed to its support in proportion to his enjoyments, as a member of that
community. In this, however, no regard is to be had to mental,
but to apparent and sensible enjoyments. Upon this principle,
the possession and the use of property become the data for
apportioning taxes upon the contributors. I have added the
use, which will comprehend the consumption, at least, beyond
what is common and necessary to every class ; because some
will place the enjoyment in the use of consumption, rather than
of profit in the possession. They may choose—while others
hoard for use or profit—to spend their acquisitions in the gratification of their passions or appetites.

It has been held by some, that taxes ought to be assessed by a
fixed and general valuation of property, and such has been the
practice in some states. In favor of this mode it has been
urged that though it may be subject to considerable inequalities,
yet they will not be greater than in the case of particular assessments ; and should it happen that taxes may fall more
equally in the latter mode, yet in the former they would be
more known and certain,—a very important consideration in
the levying of taxes ; that the contributor is thus enabled to
foresee with a good degree of certainty, the amount of his
taxes, and to take it into his calculation, both of economy and
enterprize, which will rarely be disappointed through the intervention of an unexpected demand ; that it is, perhaps, a
consideration of nearly equal weight, that men are generally
less dissatisfied with the inequalities of fortune, than those
which are imposed by the ignorance, prejudice, or caprice of
their fellow citizens.

Plausible as these reasons may appear, there are unanswera-
ble objections to the mode. A general valuation must be an

average valuation ;—for instance, a certain sum for every acre of land, without regard to the quality ; and so of a horse, or other personal property. The real value, or the income that may be derived from different kinds of land, often varies in the extreme. One acre may yield an income of twenty, or even an hundred dollars, while another hardly pays the labor of cultivation. There are, besides, many local and other causes, which are constantly producing a difference in the value of land. The difference in the actual value of personal property, may be as great. We know from observation and experience, that the most valuable property falls to the share of the more wealthy class. It is evident, therefore, where taxes are high, and assessed agreeable to such valuation, the poorer class of contributors must be ruined long before such taxes reach the amount which the whole might be able to pay, on a judicious assessment apportioned as near as may be agreeable to the income that the property may afford, to which it is believed some near approach might be made. To this end, it will be necessary that proper boards of assessors should be appointed to make, under proper regulations, a valuation annually, of the property of each individual liable to direct taxes ; and provision may easily be made that their acts should be public and known to each contributor as far as concerns his interest.

Taxes ought not only to be equal, but, as far as the reasonable exigencies of the state require, and general rules can extend, to be apportioned to the visible means of the contributors, both collectively and individually. This, however, must be understood with some limitation. The apportionment ought not to be according to the means of living, but to the means of payment ; or, what upon an ordinary calculation ought to be the means of payment. This object can be attained only by an extensive knowledge of the different interests, employments, modes, and necessary expense of living, of the different classes of citizens. With such knowledge, and with a particular attention to the subjects of taxation, the legislature may, in a great measure, if not altogether exempt from the burden of taxes, the necessary means of living, to the poorer classes of citizens, who, though they may contribute nothing directly to the support of government, are far from being the least useful class to the state.

The exigencies of the state must limit the aggregate sum to be demanded in taxes. But the demand ought not, for any continuance, to equal the sum of private revenue, much less ought it to be suffered to diminish the capital stock. Were the government, by thus anticipating the revenue of its citizens, to deprive them of the comfortable prospect of a provision for the future, it would take away all incitement to enterprize, and even the spirit of private industry and economy. If, in addition to this, the enormity of the demand should constantly diminish the capital stock, nothing would be presented to the view but the gloomy prospect of inevitable poverty and distress. The same observations will apply to those burdens which, through the unequal mode of assessment, fall most severely on particular classes only.

The mode of apportionment ought not to be directed by the interests of any single classes of citizens, but by the interests of the whole, which consists in a certain ratio of the particular interests. If, in the political consideration of taxes, the interest of the state,—by which nothing more is generally meant than the interest of the majority,—come in competition with the interest of a particular class of citizens in their lawful pursuits, their interests ought not to be wholly sacrificed to that of the state,—much less to that of another class. Every affair of this nature ought to be conducted upon the principles of a compromise of interests. In adjusting the compromise, however, the magnitude of any interests in competition is not to be adopted as the only rule of preference. Such rule would frequently prove a total sacrifice of the minor interest. Where it is demanded of particular persons or particular classes, that they give up their interest for the public service, they are as fully—as in cases that arise between individuals—entitled to a compensation for all that which exceeds their just proportion.

Second. Indirect taxes are such as are assessed upon subjects, not in regard to the revenue they may produce to individuals or their use in possession, but to their use in consumption. Such are duties on the importation and exportation of articles for a sale of consumption, whether the consumption intended be

foreign or domestic. So also an excise on domestic productions, as on beer brewed, or spirits distilled in the country, or
on the sale of such articles as have been imported. In all these
cases, such is the nature of the subjects, that they sooner or
later perish in the use. Under the same head of indirect taxes,
comes duties on sales and transfers on registration, on certificates, and licences; and duties on stamps made necessary for
the authentication of written instruments.

I do not here pretend to enumerate all the subjects of taxation
in this mode; such taxes have been almost infinitely extended by
the ingenuity of financiers. They have been extended, not only
to all the productions of human industry, and the enjoyments of
domestic comfort, but to the common gifts of nature,—to light
and genial heat. Such is the window tax, and hearth tax in
England, and other countries. Taxes of this kind, unless
laid on the absolute necessaries of life, which ought always
to be avoided if possible, are never compulsory on the contributor, the consumer. He is left to his own option whether he
will purchase for his use, the article taxed or not. It is true,
that in general, it is the safest, cheapest, and least onorous mode
of collecting and realizing a tax by government.—It is advanced by the exporter, importer, and producer of the articles taxed,
wherever that mode can be adopted, who recompense themselves by adding the amount of tax, with reasonable profits, to
the price of the article sold; so that the consumer, becomes
the ultimate contributor, by paying his proportion of the tax
in the price of the article he chooses to purchase. It is true,
the ultimate inequality on the contributors may be as great in
the payment of indirect as of direct taxes; but in the latter, the
inequality is compulsory; in the former, voluntary. The contributor may, at his election, pay either more or less than would
be his proportion according to his actual income.

It has another advantage over direct taxation; that when
once in steady operation, the contributor can never be sur-
prised, or his plans of economy or enterprize be deranged by
an unexpected demand on his finances. Uncalled for and unnoticed by itself, it necessarily, and if I may use the word,
spontaneously unites itself in all the data from which he makes
his calculations. Indirect taxes will therefore be preferred in a

good degree to direct, taxes, by every government which has a due regard to the ease and happiness of the people.

In modern times, besides financial purposes, indirect taxes have been employed as a principal engine of a state, for regulating commerce, foreign and domestic, and for directing the industry of the citizens into those particular channels of arts, manufactures, and commerce which are deemed most to conduce to the present interest of the community. A British writer observes—" taxes may be so contrived as to rival bounties in promoting industry, manufactures, and commerce." The policy, expedience, and justice of such application of taxes by which a preference may be given of one branch of industry over another, and to domestic over foreign manufactures, has been called in question. It has been said to be an interference of government, with the affairs and pursuits of individuals, by an attempt to direct the employment of their stock and industry into certain channels ;—that individuals are the best judges in what mode and in what channels they can employ their stock and their industry to the most profit, much better than the community at large, or than any legislative body ;—therefore, not only a true regard to the rights of the citizens, but the true interest of the community requires that every one should be left free to employ his stock and his industry as he shall please;—in a word, to manage his own concerns in his own way. All this may be, and indeed, is very true; and yet it does not effect the question arising on this subject.

The principal question is, whether the community, or rather the legislature may not, from their general information, be more capable of judging whether the employment of part of the stock and industry of the country, in some branches of arts and manufactures, not at present occupied by their citizens, or not sufficiently cultivated to produce a domestic supply, may be, I do not say more profitable to individuals in the present situation, but more advantageous to the community at large, if it can be made profitable to individuals.

The only specious answer to this question has been, that the whole stock or capital of a nation is made up of the capitals of individuals,—that the increase of the national capital depends on the increase of individual capitals ; and this increase of individual capitals must ordinarily arise from the profits made by each in the management of his stock and the application of industry, and that from the nature of the thing each employer of stock must be the best,—and ought to be the only,—judge in what branch of industry, what branch of arts, manufactures, or commerce he can employ his stock most for his advantage,—most to his own profit. A very slight consideration will, however, evince that the answer is, indeed, specious, and nothing more. It does not follow that because an individual capitalist is the best judge in what mode, or in what branch of industry he may employ his capital to his own private advantage, he is, therefore, the best judge of what—in a situation supposed to be practicable—would be most advantageous to the community. A situation may be produced in which capital employed in establishing some needful branch of manufactures now neglected, may yield to the employer a profit equal to that expected in the established branches. Nor does it follow that every employment of capital, profitable to the employer, is equally advantageous to the public; were it so, the greater the profit to the individual, the greater must be the advantage to the public,—and the monopolist would become the great benefactor of his country; and the more enormous his profits, the greater the benefaction.

If we suppose two persons employing equal capitals, and with equal profits,—the one in the importation of foreign manufactures for the consumption of his country, the other in the domestic manufacture of articles needed in the country, and to be there consumed ;—the former, by the manner in which he employs his capital enables a foreign manufacturer to put in motion and reward a certain quantity of foreign industry. The other employs his capital at home—employs and rewards—we will suppose—the same quantity of domestic industry, and increases domestic circulation, by whatever he disburses; while the other is added to foreign capital, and goes into foreign circulation. And if we suppose the articles imported from abroad by the one, and the articles manufactured by the other,—equally necessary for the consumption of the country, there can be no doubt that the capital employed in the domestic manufacture is employed with most advantage and affords more accommodation to the community at large. And this is the more apparent when we find the raw material of the manufacture indigenous, and the means of subsistance abundant. Besides every commercial and manufacturing nation make regulations to favor their own manufactures and productions of every kind; and for that purpose frequently lay heavy duties, not only on the articles of manufacture imported from abroad, but upon every article of subsistence, and materials which are found, or can be produced among themselves, and sometimes amounting to a prohibition. These duties extend to almost every article of remittance, and are paid by that nation who are supplied with their manufactures. This evil can generally be corrected, only by retalliating duties on the part of the nation thus supplied, and which is, in fact, made tributary to the supplying nation. But in discriminating duties, it will be necessary to act with prudence and a great degree of caution,—whether the increase of duties be intended for the regulation of foreign or of internal commerce,—for the encouragement of domestic manufactures,—lest it should effect too suddenly a diminution of profits in any particular branch already established, to the great injury, or perhaps ruin of those who are employed in it.

The limits prescribed in this work will not permit us here to enter into a more particular detail upon this subject which constitutes a very extensive branch of political economy, and has been discussed at large, by writers of the first talents whose works are in the hands, or at the command of all those who may be desirous of further and more particular information.

BOOK VII.

OF THE GOVERNMEMT OF THE UNITED STATES.

CHAPTER I.

Political Situation of the Colonies,—afterwards Independent States—previous to the Establishment of the present Constitution of the United States.

The government of the United States exhibits a new scene, and may truly be said to commence a new era in the political history of the world, when a number of integral republics, each, then sovereign and independent, undertook to establish over the whole, a general government with full powers of legislation for all national purposes, and of executing its laws on the citizens, independent of the local authorities. The experiment was new, and the event has been watched with anxiety by the friends and the enemies of free institutions. A system so complicated,—so different from that of a simple, or single government, of which we have been treating, must have an effect in the application of the laws of nature, from which the general principles are derived to give a different modification to those principles, owing to the different combination, and relative circumstances of the constituent parts, and to have an influence on the organization of the general government, and the adjustment of the powers of all and each, to the relations it is intended they should sustain with each other.

The several American states, while they remained colonies, or provinces of the British empire, had no political connexion, or governmental dependence on each other. They were, though situated in the same vicinity, and professing allegiance to the same sovereign, united only through the government of Great Britain, the common head. There existed a similarity of manners, which might with propriety be denominated national. There were, indeed, provincial differences, but not greater than are to be found within the limits of England. As Americans they had little national sentiment.—It was by different channels centered in Great Britain, or rather in England,—the mother country. Any collected and permanent national sentiment among themselves, was opposed by that connexion. It was the policy of the British government to foment divisions among them to a certain degree, and to cherish their local prejudices. The similarity of their circumstances, however, and the difficulties of making settlements in a wild, uncultivated country, at a great distance from any part of the civilized world, introduced some degree of direct attachment. This attachment was increased and cemented in a considerable degree by the necessity of defence against a common enemy. Bloody wars waged against them by the savages instigated and aided by the French, the ancient enemies of the English, suggested the expediency and necessity of common counsels and united exertions.

Consultations were held by delegates from the several colonies, measures for the common defence were devised, and afterwards executed, in pursuance of their common counsels. This was the germ of that general union of counsels and sentiments, which produced the American revolution. For a time, it acquired its utmost force from the oppressive measures of the British government, which equally effected the liberties of all the colonies,—now the United States of America. The first inhabitants had brought with them all the liberal principles of the British government, and had communicated them nearly free and unmixed to the great body of their descendents. Their love of liberty had been cherished and heightened by an equal enjoyment of rights and property, under equitable laws, mostly formed by themselves ; and they had been stimulated to a thorough investigation of their lights to which the extraordinary claims of power on the part of Great Britain had given rise.

The principles of monarchy and aristocracy, had, however, prevailed, more or less, among some classes, in most of the colonial governments. They were, in form, epitomies of the British government. In each there was a governor, who represented the king, a council representing the house of lords, and an assembly of the people, the commons of America. In most of the colonies, the governor and council were mere creatures of the crown. They were wholly dependent on the king. He appointed them as well as the judges at pleasure. This created an aristocratical influence, hostile, in a degree, to the liberties and interests of the people.

Happily, the plan of establishing a hereditary nobility in America was never adopted. Had such establishment been introduced at an early period, it is not an easy matter to determine, what obstacles it might have interposed in the great struggle for liberty and independence, by securing a deeper and more permanent interest in the aristocratical principles of the British constitution. When the measures which gave rise to the American revolution were adopted by the government of Britian, the great body of the people had not been corrupted by those principles. The sentiments of attachment, which originated in their descent from a common stock, had been cherished by a similarity of circumstances and adventures, and strengthened by their common counsels and united exertions, in a long and bloody war.

These common exertions had confirmed an opinion of their united importance. A more general acquaintance had been introduced, and a reciprocation of counsels and good offices had tended to soften and remove local prejudices. A similarity of situation and similarity of danger, from the same quarter, united their sentiments and interests, and forcibly suggested the plan of again uniting their counsels to obtain redress. This produced the first congress. A number of delegates from the several colonies assembled for mutual counsel, on the common situation, in which they were placed by the measures of the British parliament, from which as the opening source, we may-trace, through all the succeeding political revolutions and changes, the rise and final establishment of our present national government. A second congress was assembled, when on the 19th of April 1775, Great Britain commenced her military operations against what she termed her rebellious colonies.

From that time a congress directed the affairs of the country. The British authorities were every where put down and all were left without even the form of government, except the colonies of Connecticut and Rhode-Island, who alone had retained their charters, and the election of their governors and all the functionaries of their respective governments. These still continued their ancient forms. The other colonies, generally, resorted to the expedient of conventions and committes of safety to supply the place of regular government, until the 4th of July 1776, when the thirteen colonies were, with their consent, declared by congress to be free and independent; on which each colony, now state, formed for itself a constitution, generally after the model of the British government as to form, but, by the provisons of which, on the true principles of republican government, all the functionaries were to be elected, either directly or indirectly by the people, and made accountable to the tribunal of public sentiment for their conduct in office. Thus each assumed the character, and became, in fact, a sovereign and independent state. At the same time it was perceived and acknowledged by all that some bond of union was wanting and that it was necessary congress should be vested with powers adequate to the management of the common concerns of the whole. With this view, and in consequence of instructions from their constituents congress prepared articles of confederation, which on the 15th day of November 1776, were submitted to the several states for their approbation, and being approved constituted what was denominated the Federal Government. An examination of this confederation, its inefficiency, and the causes of that inefficiency will be the subject of the next chapter.

CHAPTER II.

Of the former Consideration of the United States.

Several instances occur both in ancient and modern history of small states confederated with a view to a national union in the pursuit of national measures. The great object,—the means of accomplishing which, had always been a desideratum in federal politics—was to bring the people to have a sense of a common national interest and all the states of the confederacy, effectually, to act in concert in those measures, which relate immediately to the good of the whole. There are two principal modes, in which this has been attempted.

The first mode, because the most ancient, was by a council appointed to legislate on the several states composing the confederacy. Of this kind was the council of the Amphictions at the head of the confederated states of ancient Greece. But as this body were not furnished with executive power or means, they could do nothing more than issue their decrees. Under such a federal institution, as none but states can refuse to obey, a delinquent can be nothing less than a state already provided with arms or counsels for a formidable opposition. To enforce the decrees of the federal council, which ought to have the force of laws, it becomes necessary, in case of a refusal of any part, to draw out the powers of the complying states, and to compel obedience by force of arms. The history of ancient Greece is for many years, infamous for a succession of such wars. Such was the sacred war. The famous Peloponesian war which raged for nearly thirty years, and drew in almost all the states of Greece on one side or the other, must be attributed to the same cause—the want of an efficient power in the national council. Such ever has been, and such ever will be the effect of this kind of federal government if it deserve that name, unless its decrees are suffered to fall into neglect producing in the end a total disolution of the confederacy.

The second mode is by a council empowered to propose measures to the confederated states, subject to the ratifications of the states individually before they acquire the force of laws, or can be carried into effect by the general authority. The United Provinces of the Netherlands furnished at that time, an example of this mode of confederation. The state's general was the grand council of the confederacy. This council, though pompously styled their high mightinesses, had in all matters of national concern, whether of greater or less moment, a power to propose only. The several states had reserved to themselves the right of ratification, and which in each state descended even to the burghs. No law could be constitutionally binding until it had been ratified by each. The veto of a single state, or of a single burgh, might disconcert, and actually has disconcerted the national counsels in measures of pressing necessity. Frequently on great emergencies, such has been the delay before all the states could be brought to agree, that the opportunity of acting was wholly lost. This induced the state's general, aided by the prince of Orange, who, as stadtholder administered the republic, sometimes to act without the authority of the smaller states. Such a disregard of the constitutional principles of the confederacy, produced at times, among that people, not remarkable for a spirit of faction, high domestic violence, and convulsed the government with dangerous insurrections.

The congress of the United States had nominally more power than the council of Amphictions, but they were not authorized to call one state to arm against another for the purpose of enforcing their ordinances. Nor like the government of the United Provinces, had the several states reserved to themselves the right of final ratification ; but in a total absence of all executive power, in congress, the execution of their measures depended on the good pleasure of each state. In my observations on the articles of confederation, I shall be more particular, because the prominent defects of that system, as discovered in its administration, will serve as a key to the construction,—to the true intent of some of the most important provisions of the present constitution of the United States, which has at times, been the occasion of no small degree of jealousy with some.—From a perusal of the several articles of that confederation, it is evident that it was intended to form a national union, and to serve as a national government, so far as the general interests were concerned. It is evident, that it did not contemplate, or certainly that it could not effect a national union of the people of several states. It was, in fact, nothing more than a treaty of perpetual alliance and federal union, between sovereign and independent states, by which in that capacity, they agreed to submit their common concerns and interests to a board of delegates to be appointed by each state, but without the provision of a common judge or of an executive power. The first article merely declares the style of the confederacy to be " The United States of America." The second article is in the following words :—" Each state retains its sovereignty, freedom, and independence, and every jurisdiction and right, which is not by this confederation delegated to the United States in congress assembled." Article third is—" The said states hereby enter into a firm league of friendship with each other for their common defence,— the security of their liberties, and their mutual and general welfare, binding themselves to assist each other against all force offered to, or made upon them, or any of them on account of religion, sovereignty, trade, or any other pretence whatever." These articles fully develope the nature of the confederation. For the more convenient management of the affairs of the United States, delegates were to be annually appointed in such manner as the legislature of each state should direct, to assemble on a certain day in each year— each state to be represented by not less than two, nor more than seven members. In determining questions in congress, as all independent sovereigns are equal in dignity, however unequal in other respects, each state was to have one vote only.

Most of the powers stipulated in this federal league to be

conferred on congress, were in many respects, nearly the same as those afterwards delegated to the general government by the constitution of the United States, and the limitations and prohibitions, nearly the same. Congress were not provided with any power to raise a revenue, with any semblance of an executive power, or judiciary commensurate with their stipulated powers. Congress were, indeed, empowered to appoint courts for the trial of piracies and felonies committed on the high seas and courts for receiving appeals in all cases of capture. And also for the determination of controversies between two or more states, and in controversies between private persons respecting certain grants of land, congress were empowered on application to nominate a certain number of persons, from whom judges were to be selected much in the manner of a struck jury with a power of final decision.

All the acts of congress, as well as the articles of confederation, were subject to the interpretation of the legislatures and judicial tribunals of thirteen sovereign and independent states, and their execution was dependent on the good pleasure of the same sovereign states. Congress had the power of making treaties, but not the power of fulfilling them—that rested with the several states—congress had the power of declaring war ; but had the command of no resources for maintaining a war. They had no power to lay and collect taxes of any kind direct or indirect. Their power went no farther than to ascertain the sum necessary to be raised for the public service, and apportion it according to a rule prescribed, among the several states, with a request that they should raise, and pay over to the general treasury the amount of their respective quotas ;—which each as an independent sovereign might choose or refuse, and often did refuse with impunity. They were empowered to borrow money, and to emit bills of credit of the United States ; but without the command of funds to pay the one or redeem the other. They issued their acts which they denominated ordinances. They never ventured to give them the name of laws ; for what property of a law has an act, which all and every of the parties is at liberty to obey or not at its sovereign will and pleasure ?

It is true, that the pressure of the war, and the patriotic zeal of the citizens in a common cause, in which their all, life, liberty, and property was at stake, supplied, in some good degree, the want of an energetic system of national government. In addition to these, a fortunate concurrence of circumstances in the political world enabled congress to engage in the cause of the country some of the most powerful nations of Europe ; to triumph in the event, and obtain from Great Britain a full acknowledgment of the sovereignty and independence of the United States. But no sooner was war ended, and peace restored to the country, than the evils of this imbecile system of confederation were fully developed to the astonishment of many and the regret of all. An enormous debt had been contracted, and public credit had fallen to the lowest and most humiliating state of depreciation. The pressure of circumstances ceasing with the war, congress found that they possessed none of the efficient powers of government, legislative, executive, or judicial. Their ordinances were disregarded. The states, from inability, or indisposition, neglected or refused to pay their respective quotas of the national expenditures,—the price of their liberty and independence. In some states the treaties made with foreign nations, particularly with Great Rritain, were disregarded or openly violated. The authority of congress was lost in the power of the several states now found to be, in fact, so many independent nations. Former prejudices, which had subsided during the struggle for liberty were rapidly reviving. Each state pursuing its local and separate interests seemed to bid defiance to any national union of the whole. The effect of this situation began to be apparent in the manners of the people, and in the administration of the state governments. They were verging to the state of small, independent tribes, in the same vicinity. This state of things was visibly contracting the views of the people and forming them to a spirit of faction. The state governments found themselves mostly, incapable of pursuing any energetic system of administration, and the whole country was clearly in a state of moral and political retrogradation. The effect on the minds of the people was no less moral than political.

The want of public credit and its concomitant evil, a depreciated and depreciating paper, had nearly rrined their morals, their industry, and their commerce, as well as private credit. Other causes, not necessary here to be enumerated, concurred to enhance the evil. Many began to suppose that the liberty for which they had risked so much blood and treasure, was but the phantom of imagination, the enjoyment of which was never to be realized under any form of government. Some of the wisest and best citizens did not dispair of the republic. They had conceived, that an energetic national government alone could inspire hope of restoring public and private credit, of reviving commerce, of giving any degree of nationality to the union, of securing the faith of public treaties, and in a word, of preventing or repelling the numerous impending evils, which threatened to plunge the country into anarchy and all the miseries of civil war. Congress, fully sensible of the inefficiency of their powers to any national purpose, recommended to the several states to meet in convention by their delegates, to deliberate on a plan of national government which might be equal to the exigencies of the whole. Agreeable to that recommendation a convention of delegates assembled, and proposed the present constitution of the United States, as the result of their deliberations. This constitution is a unique in federal politics— an actual, deliberate, and solemn compact, ratified by the concurrent act of the sovereign people of each state, severally assembled in convention, by their delegates elected for that purpose.

CHAPTER III.

The Constitution of the United States.

The power by which the constitution of the United States was ratified, and from which is derived all the authority of the national government thereby instituted, as well as the great end of its institution, is fully expressed in the declatory clause prefixed to that instrument.

" We the people of the United States, in order to form a more perfect union, establish justice, insure domestic tranquillity, provide for the common defence, promote the general welfare, and secure the blessings of liberty to ourselves and our posterity, do ordain and establish this constitution for the United States of America."

The government of the United States is constituted with legislative, executive, and judicial powers, vested in distinct and separate departments. The legislative power is vested in a congress consisting of two branches, a senate and house of representatives, whose powers in legislation are mutual and co-ordinate. The representatives are chosen by the people of the several states every second year, and are apportioned by the number of people in each state to be ascertained by an actual enumeration taken once in every ten years. The provision upon this subject as expressed in the constitution is—" Representatives and direct taxes shall be apportioned among the several states which may be included within this Union, according to their respective numbers, which shall be determined by adding to the whole number of free persons, including those bound to service for a term of years, and excluding Indians not taxed, three-fifths of all other persons. The actual enumeration shall be made within three years after the first meeting of the congress of the United States, and within every subsequent term of ten years, in such manner as they shall by law direct. The number of representatives shall not exceed one for every thirty thousand, but each state shall have at least one representative; and until such enumeration shall be made, the state of New Hampshire shall be entitled to choose three; Massachusetts, eight; Rhode Island and Providence Plantations, one; Connecticut, five; New York, six; New Jersey, four; Pensylvania, eight; Delaware, one; Maryland, six; Virginia, ten; North Carolina, five; South Carolina, five; and Georgia, three.

The qualifications for the electors of the representatives are not reduced to a uniform rule throughout the Union, but are to be the same in each state as for the electors of the most numerous branch of the state legislature. To be eligible as a representative, three qualifications are necessary, neither of which introduces any odious distinction of classes. To be eligible, a person must have attained the age of twenty-five years, have been seven years a citizen of the United States, and at the time of his election an inhabitant of the state for which he is elected. Property is, in many of the states, a qualification, both of electors and candidates; so far it is a qualification for the electors of the federal representatives; but not for the candidates. Hence it may happen that a person may be elected, who has not a right of suffrage in the election. There is in this, at least, some degree of inconsistency, which it would have been desirable to avoid by extending more uniformly the right of suffrage. It is probable, however, that difficulties on this point would have arisen from an attachment to local usages. When a vacancy shall happen in the representation of a state, the executive authority of the state are to issue writs of election to fill such vacancies. The house of representatives are to choose their speaker and other officers, and to have the sole power of impeachment.

The senate of the United States is composed of two senators from each state chosen by its legislature. The senators are divided into three classes. The seats of one class are vacated every second year, and the vacancy supplied by the legislatures of the states, to which the senators of such class respectively belong. Their election is, therefore, in reality sexeniel, and the senate can never be composed of more than one third new members. There are three qualifications for a senator.—He must have attained the age of thirty years, have been nine years a citizen of the United States, and at the time of his election an inhabitant of the state for which he is chosen. To the senate is given the sole power to try all impeachments. When sitting for that purpose, they are to be on oath or affirmation, and when the President of the United States is tried, the chief justice is to preside, and no person can be convicted without the concurrence of two thirds of the members present. Judgments in cases of impeachment can extend no farther than to removal from office, and disqualification to hold and enjoy any office of honor, trust, or profit under the United States; but the party convicted is, nevertheless, still subject to indictment, trial, judgment, and punishment according to law.

We may with satisfaction observe, that in the qualifications of the senators, there is no feature of aristocracy,—nothing that tends to any permanent distinction of rank. The qualifications both of the senators and representatives, tend only to secure in the national legislature a maturity of experience and abilities, an attachment to the national interests, and the interests of the respective states.

The senate choose their own officers,—except that the Vice-President of the United States, for the time being, is President of the senate—and are the sole judges of the elections, returns, and qualifications of their own members. The times, places, and manner of holding elections for senators and representatives are prescribed by the legislature of each state; but congress have power by law, to make or alter such regulations, except as to the place of electing senators. This exception was made that congress might not have it in their power to remove the state legislatures from place to place at their pleasure. Congress are to assemble at least once in every year, which meeting is to be on the first Monday in December, unless they shall by law appoint a different day. A majority of each house, that is, of the members elected, constitutes a quorum for doing business, but a smaller number may adjourn from day to day, and may be authorized to compel the attendance of absent members in such manner, and under such penalties as each house may provide. Each house has the right to determine the rules of its proceedings, to punish its members for disorderly behavior, and with the concurrence of two thirds, expel a member. Each house is enjoined to keep a journal of its proceedings, and to publish the same from time to time, except such parts as may in their judgment require secrecy. And the yeas and nays of the members are, at the desire of one fifth of those present, to be entered on the journals. Neither house, during the session of congress, is permitted, without the consent of the other, to adjourn for more than three days, nor to any other place than that in which they shall be sitting.

To provide against a servile dependence and to remove temptations to corruption, the senators and representatives are to receive a compensation for their services, to be ascertained by law. They enjoy certain privileges and are subject to certain disabilities. They are, except in cases of treason, felony, and breach of the peace, privileged from arrests during their attendance on the business of their appointment. To prevent an undue influence in any measure or department of the government, senators and representatives are incapable of being appointed to any civil office under the United States, which has been erected or the emoluments of which have been increased during such time, nor can a person holding any office under the United States, be a member of either house during his continuance in office.

No bill can pass into a law, without the concurrence of both houses, and a bill may indifferently originate in either. There is, indeed, one exception, and that, a wise and proper one, relative to raising a revenue. These can originate in the house of representatives only. The revenue is to be raised upon the people, to whom the representatives are directly amenable,—not upon the states collectively. In such case, however, the senate may propose or concur with amendments as on other bills.

In the legislative functions of the government, the President has a deliberative voice, but not a final negative upon any act.

representatives, must, before it becomes a law, be laid before the President. If he approve, he signs it, and then it has all the force of a law. If he disapprove, he returns it with his objections in writing, to that house in which it originated, for reconsideration. If, on such reconsideration by both houses, two thirds of each house still agree to pass the bill, it becomes a law, otherwise not. If the President neglect to return a bill for ten days after it shall have been laid before him, it becomes a law in the same manner as if he had approved and signed it; unless the return within the time be prevented by an adjournment of congress,—in which case it does not become a law. The same proceedings, under the regulations are necessary to the validity of every order, resolution, or vote, to which the concurrence of both houses is required, except in cases of adjournment.

For the purpose of directing and limiting the powers of congress to those objects only, which are of national necessity or utility, and to prevent, in the exercise of their proper functions, any interference between the national and the state governments,—the constitution has pointed out generally, the objects of federal legislation, and has limited and modified as well the powers of the general government as the powers of the several states.

Congress are by the constitution empowered to lay and collect taxes, duties, and excises, for the purpose of paying the debts and providing for the common defence and general welfare of the United States; to regulate commerce with foreign nations among the several states, and with the Indian tribes; to establish a uniform rule of naturalization, and uniform laws on the subject of bankruptcy throughout the United States; to coin money, regulate its value, the value of foreign coins, and fix the standard of weights and measures, and to provide for the punishment of counterfeiting the securities, and current coin of the United States. They are empowered to facilitate and secure an extensive national communication by the establishment of post offices and post roads; to promote the progress of science, and useful arts, by securing for a limited time, to the authors and inventors, an exclusive right to their respective writings and discoveries.

To this body it is referred to define and punish piracies on the high seas, and offences against the laws of nations. They have the power of declaring war, granting letters of marque and reprisal, and of making rules concerning captures on land and water ; to raise and support armies with this restriction, that no money shall be appropriated to that use for a longer term than two years ; to provide and maintain a navy ; to make rules for the government of the land and naval forces; to provide for calling forth the militia to execute the laws of the union ; to suppress insurrections and repel invasions ; to provide for organizing, arming, and training the militia, and for their government while in actual service. The states, however, have the appointment of the officers, and the authority of training the militia according to the discipline prescribed by congress.

Congress are also empowered to exercise exclusive legislation, in all cases over the district of ten miles square—now the district of Columbia—ceded for the seat of government, and to exercise a like authority over all places, purchased by the consent of the legislature of any state, in which the same shall be, for the erection of forts, magazines, arsenals, dock yards, and other needful buildings ; and finally, congress is empowered to make all laws, which shall be necessary and proper for carrying into execution the foregoing powers, and all other powers vested by the constitution in the government of the United States, or in any department or officer of the government.

Such are the powers with which congress are entrusted for the purposes of national government. To render these powers in exercise equal in every part of the Union, to prevent any preference of one state to another, to guard against the dangers of oppression ; of profligacy in the national expenditures; of peculation in its officers, and if possible to avert every tendency to corruption in the principles of the government, certain restrictions and limitations are provided. It is expressly provided that all taxes, duties, imposts, and excises shall be uniform throughout the United States ; that the privilege of the writ of *habeas corpus* shall not be suspended, unless, when in cases of rebellion or invasion, the public safety shall require it ; no bill of attainder, the oppressive engine of state in many governments, or *ex post facto* law, is permitted to be past by the national legislature. No capitation or other direct tax may be laid unless it be in proportion to the census of the inhabitants of the several states. No tax or duty can be laid on any article exported from any state ; nor may any preference be given, in any regulations of commerce or revenue to the ports of one state over those of another, nor vessels bound to or from one state, be obliged to enter, clear, or pay duties in another. No money is permitted to be drawn from the national treasury, but in consequence of appropriations made by law, and an account of the receipt and expenditures of public monies, is directed to be published from time to time, for the information of the people. The national government is prohibited to grant any title of nobility ; and to exclude an undue foreign influence, in measures of government, no person holding any office of profit or trust under the United States, may, without the consent of congress, accept of any present, emolument, office, or title whatever from any king, prince, or foreign state.

It was obvious these powers, so indispensably necessary to any national union, and national sovereignty, could not, while the several states retained that independent sovereignty, which had been vested in each by their respective constitutions, and expressly reserved under the articles of confederation, be exercised by the general government without being perpetually exposed to dangerous collisions, with the state governments. To avoid these otherwise irremediable evils, it was determined that this independent sovereignty ought no longer to be retained, but the powers of the several states should in future, be confined in exercise to those only, which pertain to the internal and municipal sovereignty, within their local limits respectively ; and even that, under certain modifications and restrictions, which were deemed essential to the general interest. To this end it is expressly provided in the constitution, that no state in the Union shall enter into any treaty of alliance or confederation ; grant letters of marque and reprisal ; coin money ; emit bills of credit ; make any thing but gold and silver coin, a tender in payment of debts ; pass any bill of attainder, *ex post facto* law, or law impairing the obligation of contracts, or grant any title of nobility. No state shall, without the consent of congress, lay imposts or duties, on imports or exports, except what shall be absolutely necessary for executing its inspection laws ; and the net produce of all duties and imposts, laid by the several states on imports or exports shall be for the use of the treasury of the United States ; and all such laws shall be subject to the revision and control of congress. No state shall, without the consent of congress, keep troops, or ships of war, in times of peace, or enter into any agreement or compact with another state, or with a foreign power, or engage in war, unless actually invaded, or in such iminent danger as not to admit of delay.

The executive power is by the constitution vested in the President of the United States, who is to hold his office for the term of four years, and together with the Vice-President chosen for the same term, is to be elected in the manner, following:

Each state is to appoint, in such manner as its legislature shall direct, a number of electors, equal to the whole number of senators and representatives, to which such state is entitled. No person is capable of being appointed an elector, who at the time shall be a senator or representative in congress, or hold any office of profit or trust under the United States. Congress has the power to determine the time of choosing the electors and the day on which they shall give their votes, which is to be the same in every state. The electors are to meet in their respective states, and to vote by ballot for President and Vice-President, one of whom, at least, shall not be an inhabitant of the same state as themselves. They are to name in their ballots the person voted for as President, and in distinct ballots the person voted for as Vice-President, and to make distinct lists of all the persons voted for as President and of all persons voted for as Vice-President, and of the number of votes for each, which lists they are directed to sign and certify, and transmit sealed to the seat of the government of the United States, directed to the President of the senate, who, in the presence of the senate and house of representatives, is to open all the certificates, and the votes are there to be counted ; a majority of the votes of all the electors appointed, is necessary to the election of the President, and also of the Vice-President. If no person is found to have such majority for President, the house of representatives are immediately to choose by ballot a President, in which case the votes are to be taken by states, the representatives from each state having one vote, and a quorum must consist of a member or members from two thirds of the states, and a majority of all the states is made necessary to a choice. If the house of representatives, whenever the right of choice shall devolve on them, shall not choose a President before the fourth day of March next following the day on which the President elect is to enter on the duties of his office, then the Vice-President is to act as President as in case of the death or other constitutional disability of the President. Should there be no choice of Vice-President by the electors, it devolves on the senate to choose a Vice-President from the two highest on the list, under the same regulations as are prescribed for the house of representatives in the choice of President.*

The qualifications for the office of President are, that he be a natural born citizen, or a citizen of the United States, at the time when the constitution was adopted ; that he shall have attained the age of thirty-five years, and have been fourteen years a resident within the United States. In case of the removal of the President from office, or of his death, resignation, or disability to discharge the powers and duties of his office, the same devolves on the Vice-President; congress is empowered by law to make provision to supply the place, both of the President and Vice-President, until the disability shall be removed or a President shall be elected. The President is to receive at stated times a compensation for his services, which shall neither be increased nor diminished during the period for which he shall have been elected, nor shall he receive within that period any other emolument from the United States or either of them. Before entering on the execution of his office he must take the following oath :—

" I do solemnly swear (or affirm) that I will faithfully execute the office of president of the United States, and will, to the best of my ability, preserve, protect, and defend the constitution of the United States." It is provided that the

---

* Vide Amendment.

President shall be commander in chief of the army and navy of the United States, and of the militia of the several states when called into the actual service of the United States; that he may require the opinion in writing of the principal officer, in each of the executive departments, upon any subject relating to the duties of their respective departments, and shall have power to grant reprieves and pardons for all offences against the United States, except in cases of impeachment; that he shall have power, by and with the consent of the senate, to make treaties, provided two thirds of the senate present concur; and to nominate by and with the consent of the senate, ambassadors, other public ministers and consuls, judges of the Supreme Court, and all other officers of the United States, whose appointments are not by the constitution otherwise provided for, but the congress may, by law, vest the appointment of such inferior officers as they think proper, in the President alone, in the courts of law, or the heads of departments. The President has also the power to fill up all vacancies that may happen during the recess of the senate by granting commissions, which shall expire at the end of their next session.

It is made his duty to give to congress from time to time, information of the state of the union, and to recommend to their consideration such measures as he shall judge necessary and expedient; he may, on extraordinary occasions, convene both houses or either of them; and in case of a disagreement between them with respect to the time of adjournment, he may adjourn them to such time as he shall think proper. He is to receive ambassadors and other public ministers, and to take care that the laws be faithfully executed, and to commission all officers of the United States. It is also provided that the President, Vice-President, and all civil officers of the United States shall be removed from office on impeachment, and conviction of treason, bribery, or other high crimes and misdemeanors.

The judicial power of the United States is vested in one Supreme Court and such inferior courts as congress shall, from time to time, ordain and appoint. The judges of all the courts hold their offices during good behavior, and are at stated times to receive a compensation for their services, which may not be diminished during their continuance in office. The judicial power is extended to all cases in law and equity, arising under the constitution and laws of the United States, and treaties made, and to be made, under the same authority ; to all cases of admiralty and maritime jurisdiction ; to controversies to which the United States shall be a party, to controversies between two or more states ; between a state and the citizens of another state ; between the citizens of different states ; between citizens of the same state, claiming land under grants of different states ; and between a state and its citizens, and foreign states, citizens, or subjects. Such was the provision in the original constitution ; but this has been so far altered by a subsequent amendment, that no action can be commenced or prosecuted against one of the United States, by citizens of another state, or by citizens or subjects of a foreign state. In all cases affecting ambassadors, other public ministers and consuls, and those in which a state is a party, the Supreme Court has original jurisdiction ; in all the other cases before mentioned, the Supreme Court has an appellate jurisdiction, both as to law and fact, with such exceptions, and under such regulations as congress shall make.

Ample provision is made to secure among the several states a mutual confidence; to establish among the citizens of the whole, a reciprocal enjoyment of rights in their public and private intercourse ; to cultivate and extend a national sentiment in every part of the union, and to prevent those injuries, which might arise from a difference of local laws and customs. It is provided that full faith and credit is to be given in each state to the public acts, records, and judicial proceedings of every other state, and congress may by general laws prescribe the manner in which such acts, records, and proceedings shall be proved, and their effect,—that the citizens of each state are entitled to all the privileges and immunities of citizens in the several states,—that a person charged with treason, felony, or other crime, who shall fly from justice and be found in another state, shall, on demand of the executive authority of the state from which he fled, be delivered up to the state having jurisdiction of the crime ; and that no person holden to service or labor in one state, under its laws, escaping into another state shall, in consequence of any law or regulation in that state, be discharged from such service or labor; but shall be delivered up, on claim of the person to whom such service or labor is due. New states may be admitted by congress into the union, but no new state may be erected or formed by the junction of two or more states or parts of states, without the consent of the states concerned, as well as of congress. Congress is vested with the power to dispose of, and make all necessary rules and regulations respecting the territory, or other property belonging to the United States, and nothing in the constitution shall be so construed as to prejudice the claims of the United States on any particular state.

There are other clauses, which are intended as a declaration of rights, to guard against an undue exercise of power in the administration of the general government, as it may affect the rights of the several states, or of individual citizens. It is declared that all trials for crimes, except in cases of impeachment, shall be by jury, and such trial shall be held in the state where such crime shall have been committed, but when not committed within a state, the trial shall be at such place or places as congress may by law have directed—that treason against the United States shall consist only in levying war against them, or adhering to their enemies, giving them aid and comfort—and no person shall be convicted of treason, unless on the testimony of two witnesses to the same overt act on confession in open court. Congress have the power to declare the punishment of treason, but no attainder of treason shall work a corruption of blood or forfeiture, except during the life of the person attainted. It is declared that congress shall make no law respecting an establishment of religion or prohibiting its free exercise; or abridging the freedom of speech or of the press; or the right of the people peaceably to assemble, and to petition the government for a redress of grievances, or to infringe the right of the people to bear arms.

Provision is made to prevent oppression from the quartering of soldiers on the people, and from unreasonable search or seizure on general warrants; that no person shall be held to answer for a capital or otherwise infamous crime, unless on a presentment or on indictment of a Grand Jury, except in cases arising in the land or naval forces, or in the malitia when in actual service in time of war or public danger, and that no person shall be subject for the same offence to be twice put in jeopardy of life or limbs—nor be compelled in any criminal case to be a witness against himself—nor shall be deprived of life, liberty or property, without due process of law,—nor private property be taken for public use without due compensation ; that in all criminal prosecutions, the accused shall enjoy the right to a speedy and public trial by an impartial jury of the state and district in which the crime shall have been committed, which district shall have been previously ascertained by law, to be informed of the nature and cause of the accusation, to be confronted with witnesses against him, to have compulsory process for obtaining witnesses in his favor, and to have the assistance of counsel for his defence.   It is further provided that in suits at common law, where the matter in demand shall exceed twenty dollars, the right of trial by jury shall be preserved, and that no fact tried by a jury shall be otherwise re-examined in the courts of the United States, than according to the rules of the common law ; that excessive bail shall not be required, nor cruel and unusual punishment be inflicted ;—and it is finally declared, that the enumeration in the constitution of certain rights shall not be construed to deny or disparage other rights retained by the people, and that the powers not delegated to the United States by the constitution, nor prohibited by it to the states, are reserved to the states or to the people respectively.

That the people may avail themselves of those improvements in government, which time and experience may discover and render necessary in the progress of social improvements, and yet sufficiently to hold in check that dangerous spirit of innovation which no government, however well constituted can satisfy, it is further provided that—" Congress, whenever two thirds of both houses shall deem it necessary, shall propose amendments to this constitution, or on the application of the legislators of two thirds of the several states shall call a convention for proposing amendments, which, in either case, shall be valid to all intents and purposes, as part of this constitution, when ratified by the legislatures of three fourths of the several states, or by conventions in three fourths thereof, as the one or the other mode of ratification may be proposed by congress ; provided that no state shall be deprived of its equal suffrage in the senate." There was also a further proviso with respect to the admission of slaves, which is now become immaterial.

All debts contracted, and engagements entered into, before the adoption of the constitution, are declared to be as valid against the United States under this constitution as under the confederation. And, finally, it is declared, that " This constitution, and the laws of the United States which shall be made in pursuance thereof, and all treaties made, or which shall be made under the authority of the United States, shall be the supreme law of the land; and the judges in every state shall be bound thereby; any thing in the laws or constitution of any state to the contrary notwithstanding;" and, that " The senators and representatives before mentioned, (in congress,) and the members of the several state legislatures, and all executive and judicial officers both of the United States, and of the several states, shall be bound by oath or affirmation to support this constitution ; but no religious test shall be required as a qualification to any office or public trust under the United States."

I have thus exhibited a full and correct view of the constitution of the United States, embracing the subsequent amendments, as ratified by a competent authority, by the solemn and concurrent act of the sovereign people of each state, forming an express compact of national union and government equally binding on themselves and their several state governments.

CHAPTER IV.

Of the construction of the Constitution, with observations on some of the principal powers, general and incidental.

It is not my design here to enter into a detailed construction of every article and clause of the constitution. This would require volumes; such a work would be interesting, as well as highly necessary to professional men ; but less interesting, and might even appear tedious, to the general reader, who is in search of general principles, and is satisfied with a few brief and pertinent illustrations.

To attain even a general understanding of the constitution, it will be necessary to establish some general rules of construction. These are to be derived from various sources; from the common law ; in some instances, from the law of nations; from clauses and expressions in the constitution ; from the general end and design of the government established by the constitution. In treating the subject, however, I shall not confine myself to the precise order here indicated. I shall also reserve for a more full discussion in the following chapters, some important questions, which have been raised on the construction of the constitution respecting the nature of the union, the parties to the constitution ; the relation to the general government, in which the several states are placed ; and the relation established between the several departments of that government.

By the common law, is here to be understood the common law of England, so called ; its principles, its rules, and maxims. From that country it was brought by our fathers,—the country of their birth and education. Its language was to them their native language,—not merely the language of their lips, but of their thoughts upon law, government, and all institutions, civil and political. They claimed the common law as their birth-right, and transmitted it to their posterity in this country. Such was the language, and such the habits of thinking, both of those who framed, and of those who ratified the constitution. To the common law we must resort to learn what is meant by a legislative, an executive, and a judicial power in government, by an impeachment, by a court of law, a jury, a Grand Jury, an indictment, and a trial by jury The same observation will be found applicable to almost every clause of the constitution. It may be proper here, once for all, to observe, that the common law as understood by us, is not precisely the common law of England as known and taught in that country, but as corrected by long experience and observation, and adapted to our civil and political institutions.

It is an established rule of the common law, that in the construction of a statute, the words are to be understood in the sense in which they were understood by the law makers; and the same rule is to be applied in the construction of the constitution. If, in course of time, as is often the case with language, the meaning of words or terms is changed, the meaning of the constitution is not therefore changed. In such case it is necessary to seek and learn the meaning intended by the framers. For this we must resort, first, to cotemporary writers, and cotemporary documents on the same, or similar subjects; and secondly, the construction given and acted upon at the same time, or in the times immediately following the institution. If a construction of the constitution has prevailed, has been acted upon, and acquiesced in for a reasonable length of time, it is to be considered as a precedent in the case.* If, in addition, it shall have been approved by a course of judicial decisions, it has then acquired all the sanction, all the force of a rule of the common law,—a common law precedent; and can be thereafter changed by that power only to which is reserved the right of altering and amending the constitution-itself. In

---

* See Mr. Madison's letter on the bank question, No. 2, in the appendix.

many cases the constitution will be found its own best interpreter. The true meaning of any particular part, article, or clause, will frequently be best learned, by considering the scope, end, and design of the whole,—the great end which the framers had in view,—as it must necessarily be supposed to have been their intention, that all the parts, all the provisions should conspire to promote that end. The government of the United States is different from any thing of the kind before known in the world. The great end of its institution was to form a national, instead of a federal union; to unite a number of independent states into one national sovereignty for all purposes merely national; and to unite the citizens of the whole, in a national character; and at the same time to secure to the several. states the full exercise of the municipal sovereignty within their local limits respectively, except in certain cases in which the interests of the whole were considered to be affected. To this end, therefore, there are certain restrictions and limitations on the powers delegated to the general government, and certain prohibitions and restrictions on the exercise of certain powers by the governments of the several states, with a view of drawing a line of distinction between the national sovereignty to be exercised by the general government, and the municipal sovereignty retained by the states. To these limitations, restrictions, and prohibitions, and the end for which they were imposed, a constant regard must be had in the construction of the constitution, as it respects the general, as well as the incidental powers.

The powers delegated by the constitution are for the most part expressed in general terms. It is a general rule of construction, that a grant made in general terms, is a grant of all that which is appurtenant to the thing granted, which is necessary to its enjoyment, or rather, without which the grant could not have the effect manifestly intended. It is the same with respect to powers delegated in general terms. A general power can in no other way be carried into effect, than by an exercise of the incidental powers comprehended in the general term.—Powers delegated in general terms are to be considered as the general and the incidental powers, the species comprehended in each. However obvious this mode of construction may appear, yet, lest some doubt might arise on the subject, the framers of the constitution, after the enumeration of general powers, which it was declared congress should have, added the following clause.. " The power (that is, congress shall have the power) to make all laws necessary and proper for carrying into effect the foregoing powers, and all other powers vested by this constitution in the government of the United States, and in any department or officer thereof." This clause was certainly introduced from abundant caution, and contains nothing more than what, on a sound construction of the constitution, was fully implied. It is very cautiously worded, because it obviously gives to congress a very great discretion in the exercise of the specific, or incidental powers,—in the choice of means to effect a legitimate end :—they must be necessary and proper. The word " necessary," is not here to be understood in the sense of that necessity which is usually denominated absolute, intending something without which the end could not be possibly effected, but is to be understood in its more usual and popular sense,—of that which is expedient and-convenient, of the degree and urgency of which congress are to judge. The word " proper," is intended to qualify the term " necessary ;" the measure proposed must not only be expedient, but proper as it respects the object, and as it respects the nature and end of the government,—the limitations of power on the one hand, and the reservation of rights on the other. Of the same nature is the clause which declares, that the constitution, the laws made in pursuance of it, and treaties made under its authorities shall be the supreme law of the land ; and the article of amendment, declaring, that the powers not delegated by the constitution, nor prohibited by it to the states, are reserved to the states and to the people respectively. The former is implied in the very nature, end, and design of the government, intended to be a government over the whole, of which it must wholly fail, if not vested with that supremacy in the exercise of its power ; and the latter, " that the powers not delegated are so reserved," is clearly implied from the manner in which that government is formed by a delegation of enumerated powers with certain limitations of those powers, and in the prohibitions to the states to exercise certain powers,

or to exercise them in certain cases. These precautions were
necessary and proper ; they were cases of too much importance
to be left solely to construction.

There are other cases in which the implication arises from
the very nature and end of government. It is the duty of
every government to seek the welfare of the nation. Every
duty on government implies the right and the power of fulfilling
it. This duty, although it is no where expressly declared in
the constitution of the United States, is clearly pre-supposed.
In the grant of power to lay and collect taxes, the purposes
for which they are to be laid and collected, is declared to be
" to pay the debts, and to provide for the common defence and
general welfare of the United States." I do not suggest that
the expression in this clause, of the purpose for which the power
of taxation is granted, is an imposition of the duty or the grant
of a substantive power to fulfil it, but that it pre-supposes that
duty and that power as necessarily and unavoidably implied
from the nature and end of the government. Such were evidently the views of those who framed the constitution, and
they therefore provided congress with the means of accomplishing the purpose. Hence is derived the right and power
of congress to make those internal improvements which tend
to promote the general welfare ; such as the clearing of harbors ; the erection of break-waters for the protection of shipping ; the building of light-houses ; the removing of obstruc-
tions in navigable rivers ; and the making of roads and canals
for the promotion of internal intercourse. From the same
source of construction, the duty to promote the general welfare, we would derive the right of congress to promote domestic manufactures by means of discriminating duties, which
may enable the domestic manufacturer to maintain in the
market a competition with the foreign manufacturer of the
same article. This is different from the case of internal improvements mentioned above. In that case, the money raised
by taxes is appropriated to the purpose ; but in this, the end
is sought to be attained by the manner in which the tax—
generally duties of imposts—is assessed. The mode and manner, is, in general, a question of policy and expedience,
which, unless in cases of positive restriction, is left to the

discretion of the legislature, and does not involve the question of constitutionality.

There are, in my view, some other things necessary to render this power of making internal improvements, and encouraging manufactures fully constitutional, or perhaps I may rather say, to justify its exercise.—First, that the benefit to accrue should not be merely local, but general. Secondly, that it should be of sufficient magnitude in a national point of view to justify the expense. And thirdly, that it shall have a relation to, or be capable of being brought to aid some of the general powers expressly granted in the constitution. The two first requisites are of necessity, submitted to the discretion of congress; the last,—that it shall have a relation to, or be capable of being brought to aid some of the general powers, I consider as of a more positive nature. Let us then try the cases of internal improvements and manufactures above mentioned, by this standard. They have all a more or less intimate relation to the war power and the consequent power and duty committed to congress, of protecting the country against invasion and suppressing insurrections. Secure and commodious harbors, and even light-houses are absolutely necessary for the safety of the navy, and to provide for protection and defence of the coasts. Navigable rivers, roads, and canals, in proportion to their goodness, extent, and direction, will serve greatly to expedite the march of troops, and the transport of the munitions of war, and all that is necessary for the support of armies. The encouragement given to domestic manufactures may serve to secure a supply of arms, of clothing, and all the materials of war. They have also a near relation to the power vested in congress, of regulating commerce with other nations, and among the several states, which includes the power of encouragement and protection, so far as the public interest may require. I know that this opinion has been strenuously opposed by men of the first talents; but it has been supported by men of equal talents, and is sustained by the general sense of the community.*

---

* See Mr. Madison's letters, No. 3 and 4, in the appendix.

Power is given to congress to punish certain crimes as expressed in the constitution. This has always been construed not to exclude the power of punishing in other cases. It results from the nature of government, and is contained in the clause last recited, giving to congress the power to make all laws necessary and proper for carrying the constitution into effect, that congress have the power to enact penalties in all cases where it may be necessary for carrying their measures into effect, and to make laws for the punishment of all crimes which may impede the measures, obstruct the authority of the government, or injuriously affect it in any and all its departments; but congress have not, unless in places over which they have exclusive jurisdiction, the power to punish crimes because they are injurious to society merely. This belongs to the municipal sovereignty, and is reserved to the several states. For this, among other reasons, it has been always held that the courts of the United States cannot exercise common law jurisdiction in criminal cases. I shall conclude this chapter with some brief observations on the construction arising out of the article by which the judicial power is granted in the constitution. That power is appointed to be exercised by one Supreme Court and by such inferior courts as congress may ordain and appoint. The courts of the United States are not common law courts in the sense that they derive their authority from the common law, or look to that law for the extent or limits of their jurisdiction. In order that we may, at once, have a full view of the subject, I will here repeat the passage as it stands in the constitution. " The judicial power shall extend to all cases in law and equity, arising under this constitution, the laws of the United States, and treaties made, or which shall be made under their authority ; to all cases affecting ambassadors, other public ministers and consuls ; to all cases of admiralty and maritime jurisdiction ; to all controversies to which the United States shall be a party ; to controversies between two or more states; between a state and the citizens of another state ; between the citizens of different states ; between citizens of the same state, claiming land under grants of different states; and between a state and the citizens thereof, and foreign states, citizens or subjects. In all cases affecting ambassadors, other public ministers and consuls, and those in which a state shall be a party, the Supreme Court shall have, original jurisdiction. In all the other cases before mentioned, the Supreme Court shall have appellate jurisdiction, both as to law and fact, with such exceptions, and under such regulations as congress shall make."

The true construction, and which has always been adopted, is, that the courts of the United States have a limited jurisdiction, and that it cannot be extended to any case not described in the grant, and that, therefore, in every case brought before any of those courts, it must appear on the face of the proceedings, that it comes within the description, or it must be dismissed for want of jurisdiction.

The appellate jurisdiction has by the laws of congress been extended to cases decided in the state courts, and provision made for their removal by writ of error into the Supreme Court of the United States for final decision. The provision is " that a final judgment or decree in the highest court of law or equity in a state, in which a decision in the suit, could be had ; where is drawn in question the validity of a treaty, or statute of, or an authority exercised under the United States, and the decision is against the validity ; or where is drawn in question the validity of a statute or an authority exercised under any state on the ground of their being repugnant to the constitution, treaties, or laws of the United States, and the decision is in favor of their validity, or where is drawn in question any clause of the constitution, or of a treaty or statute of, or commission held under the United States, and the decision is against the title, right, privilege, or exemption especially set up, or claimed by either party under such clause of the constitution, treaty, statute, or commission, may be reversed or affirmed in the Supreme Court by writ of error. But no other error shall be assigned or regarded as ground of reversal in any such case, than such as appears on the face of the record, and immediately respects the before-mentioned questions of validity or construction of the constitution, treaties, statutes, commissions, or authorities in dispute.

It has been very warmly contended by some, that this is a violent construction of the constitution, and an unwarrantable interference with state authority ; that the appellate jurisdiction is, on a fair construction of the constitution, confined to decisions in the inferior courts of the union, and is not extended to decisions in the state courts. But when we examine the constitution, we find no mention of the court, but of the case to which the appellate jurisdiction shall extend ; and when we examine the law, we find that all the cases in which a removal is allowed, are cases to which the judicial power is expressly extended by the constitution,—cases arising under the constitution, laws, and treaties of the United States. It is evident, therefore, that congress have adopted the true construction. Let us see what would be the consequence of a different construction. There are, and will be numerous cases brought before the state courts in which a proper decision will depend on a just construction of the constitution and laws of the United States. If in such cases the decisions of those courts were to be final, there could be no hope of a uniformity of construction. The constitution and laws would be one thing in one state, and something very different in another, and perhaps not the same in any two states. There is every reason to believe that the framers of the constitution, aware of these injurious consequences, intended so to express the appellate jurisdiction as to extend it to the state courts, as well as to the inferior courts of the union, so as to secure a uniformity of decisions in matters of such immediate consequence to the government, and to the nation. It will be observed that jurisdiction is, in many cases given to the courts of the United States, not by reason of the origin of the case, but the character of the parties ; and that this must bring before those courts many which have not arisen under the constitution, laws, or treaties of the United States, many which have arisen solely under the state laws. This, it might be feared, would have a tendency to disturb the course of decisions as it respects those laws, to obviate which, and to preserve a uniformity in the administrations of justice, it has been the established construction of the power and duty of the judges, that they are holden in all cases coming before them, to decide according to the law of the case,—the law under which it arose ; and that the rules of law, of property, and of evidence, whether derived from the laws, or from the adjudications of the judicial tribunals of the state, must furnish the rules and guides in the courts of the union in all cases, where the constitution, treaties, or laws of the United States do not interpose.

CHAPTER V.

Nature of the union established by the confederation, and of the union established by the constitution of the United States.—The different parties to their several establishments and their different powers.

The several different states now composing the United States, as before observed, became on the declaration of independence, each, sovereign and independent. There had subsisted between them, from the commencement of the revolutionary contest with Great Britain, while yet colonies, a union of counsels, and a concert of measures, suggested and supported, only by a sense of common interest in a common cause. Although in all their counsels, and in all their acts, they styled themselves the United States, there had been no express or formal compact of union entered into between the several states, until the ratification of the articles of confederation, about two years after the declaration of independence. The confederation was a league or treaty of alliance between sovereign and independent states, or in other words, nations. and to prevent any misconception of its nature, it was expressly declared by the second article, that " each state retains its sovereignty, freedom, and independence."* Although it is expressly declared to be a firm league of friendship, yet its firmness, or binding force depended on the good faith only, of each of the states,—the sovereign parties, agreeable to the law of nations by which it was governed, and by which it was necessarily to be interpreted ; not by the rules of the civil

*See articles of confederation, No. 1, in the appendix.

state ; for it was not in fact a civil, but a political institution. It presents a case in which each party is for itself the sole interpreter of the stipulations, the sole judge of its obligations ; and in the event of a violation by either, the ultimate remedy is a resort to war, to the law of force, the only final arbiter admitted by the law of nations between sovereign states. It was a union of the states, not of the people of the several states. The people as citizens, owed obedience to their respective state governments only. They were not citizens of the United States, but of their respective states. Upon them the acts of congress had no binding force, as such ; they were a mere dead letter, until animated by state authority. The union was therefore a federal, not a national union ; and we shall presently see that the parties contracting had not the power of forming any other, nor could any other exist while they retained their character of independent sovereigns. The congress organized by the confederation, was indeed called a government, and was denominated the government of the United States, but more familiarly the federal government ; although it wanted the essential requisites of a real government, an executive and judicial power.

On the other hand, it was clearly intended by the framers of the constitution, and was so understood by the parties ratifying that instrument, that the union to be formed should be, not a federal, but a national union, under a national government, vested with all the powers necessary to form a real and efficient government, legislative, executive, and judicial ; with full power in that government to carry the laws into effect by acting immediately upon the people, the individual citizens throughout the United States, and that independent of the state authorities. Agreeable to this intention, the people, by the final ratification of the constitution, were brought into a national union,* and acquired a national character, that of

* When the question of the constitution was depending, those who were in favor of its adoption, assumed the name of federalists, and bestowed on the party opposed, the name of anti-federalists; intending thereby, as is well remembered, to intimate that the opposers of the constitution were opposed to any union of the states; but the fact was not so. That party were in favor of continuing the existing federal system, while the other were for

citizens of the United States, in which only they have since been known, and still are known to all foreign nations.

Such was the union intended by the general convention, who framed the constitution, and fully explains the sense of the expression in their report to congress accompanying the draught of that instrument, ' the consolidation of our union.' "In all our deliberations," say they, " we kept steadily in our view, that which appears to us the greatest interest of every true American, the consolidation of our union, in which is involved our prosperity, felicity, safety, and perhaps our national existence." This consolidation, it was intended, should be effected by uniting the people of all the states in a national character, and national sentiments, under a general government for all purposes deemed truly national, but still preserving to all, the character and rights of citizens of their respective states. The same idea of a national union is conveyed, though differently expressed, in the introductory clause of the constitution. "We, the people of the United States, in order to form a more perfect union, establish justice, secure domestic tranquillity, provide for the common defence, promote the general welfare, and secure the blessings of liberty to ourselves and our posterity, do ordain and establish this constitution for the United States of America." Indeed we have the most convincing proof in the history of the confederation and its failure, and in the history of the formation and establishment of the constitution, that the great end in view, was, instead of a federal, to form a national union, without which all were convinced, by a long and disastrous experiment, no efficient national government could be established. And we may be further convinced, if any thing further can be necessary, from an enquiry, who were the real efficient parties, that finally estab-

---

abolishing it, in favor of the national union proposed by the constitution. The parties ought in propriety to have exchanged names. The term "federal," has been handed down and is familiarly applied to the present constitution and government in this reversed sense ; and it is often not a little amusing to find a writer or speaker, while earnestly contending that the union is national, and not federal, in the same line or the same breath, applying to the government the term federal, as a proper and distinctive appellation.

lished the several compacts, that of the confederation, and that of the constitution of the United States.

Who were the parties to the act of confederation, there has never been raised a doubt. It is conceded by all, that the parties to this compact were the several states acting in their capacity of independent sovereigns. But it has been made an important question who were the original and efficient parties to the national compact, the constitution of the United States. Whether the several states acting in the capacity of independent sovereigns, but each acting through the people of their states respectively ;—whether the people of all the states acting as an aggregate political community ;—or whether the constitution derives all its authority from the people of each state acting separately in their capacity of primitive sovereignty within their own limits, and in concurrence with the people of the several states, acting separately, and in the same primitive capacity. The history of that transaction proves that the people of all the states did not act as one aggregate political community. Nor did the states by themselves, or by the people, act in the character of independent sovereigns in the ratification of that instrument. The people of the several states, by their representatives in the state conventions acted separately for themselves, and their respective communities. They acted, however, in no instance in the character of that sovereignty, which they had intrusted to their respective state governments as organized. They acted in the character of that primitive and ultimate sovereignty, in virtue of which they had formed their state constitutions, and not as servants or agents of their respective governments. In this manner the constitution of the United States was ratified by the people of each state in concurrence with the people of all the states, and thus it became a mutual compact between all, binding upon all, and upon their respective state governments. The people were, in fact, the original and only efficient parties in the character, and the manner described, and the state governments became their authorized agents so far as they were empowered by their several state constitutions and the constitution of the United States. The governments of the several states, by which we are to understand the functionaries of

those governments, were not authorized, they were not competent to ratify the compact, to establish the national government
proposed.* They are in each, but servants of the people,
trustees for administering the powers instituted in the constitution, which is to them the supreme law ; every act not warranted
by that law, or act done in violation of it, is null and void. By
the ratification of the constitution, and the establishment of a
general government over the whole, many important alterations were to be made in the state constitutions ; many of the
powers and rights in which consisted the sovereignty of the
individual states, were to be surrendered. It will be sufficient
to mention but two or three instances. It is declared in the
constitution that no state shall enter into any treaty of alliance
or confederation,—grant letters of marque and reprisal,—nor,
without the consent of congress, enter into any compact with
any other state, or engage in war, unless actually invaded or in
such imminent danger as will not admit of delay. All, therefore,
that the governments of the several states could do, they did.

---

*I find that it has lately been asserted by an authority, from whom I would dis-
sent with reluctance, and certainly, not without great consideration, that the
constitution is not in strictness of language, a compact, but is acknowledged
to be founded on compact, meaning nothing more by compact than voluntary
consent or agreement,–that it is the result of a contract, meaning nothing more
by contract, than assent. Certainly nothing more can be meant, nor can more
forcible words be used than consent, and assent, taken in their technical
sense, which they always are, when applied to the act of contracting. After every consideration which I have been able to bestow on the subject, it appears
to me that the distinction taken, was irrelevant to the point in debate, which
was, whether the several states in the character of independent sovereigns,
or the people of the United States were the actual parties to the constitution.
Now if the constitution be founded on compact, of whatever nature it may
be, it will amount to the same thing, to consider the states as parties to that
compact ; and if the states cannot be parties to the constitution because it is
not a compact, neither can the people, nor can there be any parties at all for
the same reason. I think it also incorrect. The word agreement, as well
as compact, contract, and many other words in the language, are often used
to express the cause, and to express the effect ;—to express an action, and
the subject matter of that action ; although to express the action, we often
use another manner, and say to agree, to contract,—to make an agreement,
a contract or compact, but always call the subject matter simply—an agreement, contract, or compact. If the agreement be reduced to writing, assented

According to the recommendation of the general convention, and of congress, each submitted the constitution to the people from whom they derived their powers respectively, and by whom those powers were limited. According to the first principles of our political institutions, it was necessary and proper that the constitution of the general government should be submitted to the people of the United States for ratification, because the laws of that government were intended to operate generally and to be carried into effect, not on the states as such, but on the people as citizens of the United States. It was also necessary that it should be submitted to the people of each state separately, because to any beneficial effect of the national government, it was necessary that important alterations should be made in the state constitutions, and that as far as it related to that government, they should be reduced to a uniformity. This was proposed to be effected by provisions inserted in the general constitution which being adopted and ratified by the only competent authority, the people of each state by themselves, all the necessary alterations and limitations of power in the several state constitutions would be effected, and the

---

to by the parties, the instrument is properly called the agreement or contract as containing the subject matter agreed or assented to. The subject matter contained in the instrument, is indeed the result of the act of agreeing, and that result is the agreement itself, completed by the act of the parties. The constitution of the state, has for centuries been denominated by all political writers and publicists, (Mr. Paley, as far as I recollect, alone excepted,) a compact and by way of distinction, the civil compact. I have always considered the constitution of the United States as a compact, to which the people of the United States were the only efficient parties. Every constitution of government is a compact sui generis. One thing that distinguishes it from ordinary compacts is, that in and by it is instituted a power to make laws and rules for the conduct of the citizens, and a power to enforce obedience to those laws; — essential powers of government. These powers are instituted by provisions contained in certain articles of the compact, the constitution, which were agreed and ratified with the whole. If we look at the doings of the conventions, we find that they all, in their final act, used words of compact, that they "agree to, and ratify" or "assent to and ratify" the constitution. The word "ratify" is more appropriate to public bodies, and functionaries, concluding and giving final effect to public compacts, as to ratify a treaty ; and from its solemn use, it strikes the mind with more force, and seems to give a higher sanction to the compact, than the common words of agreement.

requisite uniformity produced. But the people of one state can have no right or power to act with the people of another state in framing or making alterations in their constitution. It was therefore necessary that for this purpose, the conventions of the people in each state should act separately, and that at the same time, as it relates to the establishment of a national union and a national government, each, to render the act binding on all, or even on any, should act in concurrence with all. Such was the mode proposed, and is contained in substance, in the seventh and last article of the constitution. " The ratification of nine states shall be sufficient for the establishment of this constitution between the states so ratifying the same. All the thirteen states did finally concur in ratifying the constitution. But, if after the ratification by nine states, the remaining four states, or any of them had ultimately refused to concur, those refusing would have continued sovereign and independent, each with all the rights of an independent nation; and the confederation being dissolved, they would have stood connected among themselves, and with all other independent states by the laws of nature and nations only. If, however, a different mode had been adopted, and the people of the several states, had, as a preliminary step, made the same alterations in their respective constitutions, which were effected by the constitution of the United States, and then sent their delegates to a general convention, with powers for that purpose, and such convention had ratified the constitution as proposed, this act would have been equally binding on the people of the states and their respective governments; the force of the compact would have been the same, and the parties would have been the same as they now are; it is not in the power of human ingenuity to make or to find any available distinction. Indeed every article of the constitution of the United States that any way affects the constitutions of the several states, whether by a prohibition or modification of powers, or an injunction of duties is to all intents and purposes a part of their several state constitutions, as much as though it had been inserted in each by the direct act of the sovereign people. There is, however, this difference, that all the articles and provisions of the state constitutions, not any way affecting the constitution of the general government, may be altered and changed at the sovereign pleasure of the people of each state respectively, but not so as to affect any article of that constitution without the consent of two thirds of all the states in the manner prescribed.

From this brief, but I trust, clear and distinct view of the subject, it must be evident to every unprejudiced mind in the least capable of comprehending the subject, that the several states acting in the capacity of independent sovereigns were not, the real parties to the national compact; but that the people acting in the capacity of their primary sovereignty were the real and efficient parties; that such was the intention apparent in the constitution, is expressed in the report of the general convention to congress, and in the resolution of congress recommending to the state legislatures to submit that instrument for ratification to the people of their respective states, and that the several legislatures by submitting it accordingly, fully complied with that intention, and provided for its full effect. The great point, however, is not so much what precise character the states sustained at that time, as whether the compact was executed by a power in each state, competent to bind the community and all its members, and, in concurrence with the same power in all the states, to bind the whole in a national union, under a national government. This point cannot be successfully controverted, nor that such power resides in the sovereign people only, without sapping the very foundations of all our civil institutions.

CHAPTER VI.

Of the relation established by the Constitution of the United States, between the general government and the several states composing the union.

In the last chapter we discussed the question, whether the several states in their capacities of independent sovereigns which they then sustained, were parties to that compact by which the constitution of the national government was established, and, I trust, have demonstrated that the states were not parties in that or any other character, but that the people in their character of primary sovereignty, were the only acting and efficient, indeed the only competent parties. But there is presented another question more important in its consequences,— what character the several states now sustain, in what relation they are now placed to the national government. It has been strenuously contended by many, of very high character as statesmen and political jurists, not only that the several states in the character of independent sovereigns were the original parties to the constitution, but that they still retain that character with all the rights and powers pertaining to it, and that as between independent sovereigns, no common judge can be authoritatively interposed without impairing, and even annihilating the sovereignty each state retains—the sovereign right to judge for itself of all the acts of the general government, and to interpose its authority to suspend and annul all the acts of that government which it shall judge to be unconstitutional, or a dangerous usurpation of power not granted. This presents, indeed, an interesting question. Still it is of little consequence what character the several states sustained under the confederation, or at the time of establishing the general government, but what character they now sustain in respect to that government, in what relation they have been placed by an authority which all must allow to be competent, the sovereign people of each state. It is material to observe, that in the present constitution, which suceeded the confederation, the article by which each state retained its sovereignty is wholly omitted, and that the omission was made from a full and experimental conviction that such retention of independent sovereignty by the several states was incompatible with any national union of the whole, and with any efficient national government. This is clearly expressed by the general convention in their report to congress. "It is" say they, "obviously impossible in this federal government of these states, to secure all rights of independent sovereignty to each, and yet provide for the interest and safety of all." Indeed, neither the term sovereign and independent,—or the word sovereign is to be found in the constitution. The term seems to have been purposely avoided by the framers of that instrument, and that perhaps, because they considered it not applicable under our institutions, to the powers and to the relative situation of the general and state governments, in that absolute sense in which, as we have seen, it has been used by former political writers and jurists. They might, therefore, deem it safer to enumerate the powers delegated to the general government with those withheld or limited on the one hand, and the powers limited, modified, or prohibited to the state governments on the other, without expressing the result by a term or terms, which might lead to an erroneous or doubtful construction.

Sovereignty, as before observed, when applied to states or nations, in relation to each other, means nothing more than independence. A sovereign state, in a political sense, is a state or nation in the free and uncontrolled possession and exercise of self-government, a right of making war and peace, and entering into treaties of amity, alliance, and commerce, as it shall judge conducive to its own interest. There is, in this sense of the term, no idea of supremacy, but simply of national independence.

The sovereignty of a nation, in another sense, embraces, also the internal or municipal government, and excludes all interference, all control of its citizens or subjects, by a foreign power ; and in governments of a simple form, this sovereignty is denominated the supreme power of the state. The opinion formerly entertained, as has been shewn, that the sovereignty of a state was a sort of indivisible escence, a power absolute, uncontrolled and uncontrollable, has been corrected in modern times. Experience has proved that it is capable of division ; that under a general superintending power, there may be, indeed, in all free institutions there must be a division of the sovereignty, or rather of the powers of which it consists among the several departments, each exercising its allotted portion, in a certain degree of independence, and yet those powers so adjusted in the exercise, that all shall conspire in their subordinate spheres to the same end, and harmoneously effect the entire government of the state. Of this, a complete example is to be found in our institutions, and those of some other nations, in a division of the powers of government into the legislative, executive, and judicial, vested in separate and distinct departments. We have another conspicuous example, in the division and distribution of powers between the national government, and the several states of the union ;—a subject, which it is necessary should be explained and fully understood. This division consists in the sovereignty resulting from the powers delegated to the general government by the constitution of the United States, and the sovereignty resulting from the powers retained by the several states. The United States as a nation, are sovereign and independent. That sovereignty results from the powers delegated by the constitution, and is vested in the general government. In all the relations with foreign powers, and intercourse with independent nations, that sovereignty is absolute and independent, in the sense of the law of nations, which places all sovereign states on the ground of equality ; but in the relations of that government to the people and to the state governments, it is a limited sovereignty ; and though its laws are declared to be supreme, they are supreme only within the limits prescribed by the constitution. On the other hand, the several states, as the result of the powers retained, may with propriety be denominated sovereign, but not independent. Each state possesses a portion of sovereign power, but it is limited and adapted to the superior sovereignty of the national government. The sovereignty of the several states is local, confined in each within its local limits. It is wholly municipal in its character, and embraces those local concerns and interests, which were considered as not having a national character, or not to affect the interest of all as forming a national whole. Thus, while the general government is vested with supreme power in all matters that involve the common interest and welfare of the union in a national view, the state governments within their respective jurisdictions, retain as sovereign, all those powers, which in their due administration most endear the social state to mankind. To them it belongs to protect their respective citizens in the secure enjoyment of all their personal rights ; to regulate the mode of acquiring, and to secure the acquisitions of property, to cherish and protect all the social relations; to provide for an equal administration of justice ; to provide the means of education, and facilitate the diffusion of useful knowledge ; to animadvert upon morals, and to provide for the prevention and punishment of all those crimes, that attack private property, or in any way violate the rights, or disturb the peace of community. Each of the states may be said to be independent in the exercise of the municipal sovereignty, in one sense, that no power external to the state has a right to interfere or to control it, while exercised within the limits prescribed, but not in the sense of sovereign and independent, because the general government has, among other things, the power and right to execute its laws on the citizens of the several states within and throughout the limits of their respective jurisdictions ; and because certain limits are set to that sovereignty, as it relates to the general government, which the state governments are forbidden to exceed, and of which the constitution of the United States has made the former the sole guardians, and the sole judges of the excess. What is conclusive upon this point, if any thing can be conclusive, is that the right of final decision in all cases arising under the constitution and laws of the United States, and treaties made under its authority, in all controversies to which the United States shall be a party, or in which a state shall be a party, is vested in the general government, through the proper department, the judiciary of the United States; nor is there to be found a single instance, in which a state is by the constitution permitted the right to judge finally for itself in any question relating to the powers and acts of that government; a right incident to the sovereignty and independence of any state, and without which, no such independence can exist. As we have seen, the constitution and laws of the United States are declared to be the supreme law of the land, and binding on all the judges in every state, any thing in the constitution or laws of any state to the contrary notwithstanding; and all the functionaries and officers of the several states, legislative, executive, and judicial, are required to be bound by oath to support that constitution, that is, to support the government in all its constitutional acts, in all its departments. Each and every state with the several governments is, therefore, bound by the same solemn obligation,—a state or government without functionaries by whom it is administered is a mere abstract entity, incapable of energy, incapable of action.—It is a self-evident truth, that the obligation of a state or government is identical with that of its functionaries. The several states are, therefore, bound by all the constitutional acts of the general government; but that government is not bound in the same sense by the laws of any state, nor of every state, should all enact the same thing. I am here speaking of the ordinary power of legislation, which belongs to the state governments, not of the extraordinary power of legislation which belongs to the sovereign people, and is employed solely in enacting, altering, and amending the constitution of the government, and has no bearing on the present subject. I say, the general government is not bound by a state law.—That government is, indeed bound to respect the laws of the several states, not transcending the limits of their municipal sovereignty, as established by their respective constitutions and the constitution of the United States.

The United States, that is, the national government, are bound to guaranty to every state in the union, a republican form of government, and to protect each of them against invasion, and on application of the legislature or of the executive as the case may be, against domestic violence. In this is expressed the obligation of the general government as wielding the national force, to protect the several parts of the united whole, in the peaceable enjoyment of their respective rights, privileges, and immunities. It is not the obligation merely, of an equal, of an ally, but of a superior, of the national government, and places that government in the situation and grade, whatever that grade may be, of guardian and protector of the several states. The same superiority is clearly implied in the prohibitions to the several states to exercise certain, powers or to exercise them without the consent of congress. It is true, the consent is a permissive, not a compulsory act, but it is compulsory on the states, not to act without the consent.

I know that all subordination of the states to the general government is denied by some, and among others, by Mr. Jefferson, whose opinions stand high in the scale of authority. He has said, " with respect to our state and federal government, I do not think their relations correctly understood by foreigners. They generally suppose the former subordinate to the latter ; but this is not the case. They are co-ordinate departments of one simple and integral whole ; to the state governments are reserved all legislation and administration in affairs which concerns their own citizens only ; and to the federal government is given whatever concerns foreigners, or the citizens of other states. The one is the foreign, the other the domestic branch of the same government, neither having control over the other, but within its own department. There are one or two exceptions to this partition of power."*

If, however, we include all the cases which belong as well to the municipal as to the national sovereignty, which we certainly ought, and in which either by expressions in the grant, or by prohibitions to the states, the powers are exclusively vested in the general government, the exceptions are considerably more numerous than is here represented, and some of them very important. It is true that the general, and state governments are parts of one integral whole in this sense, that they embrace the whole government of the country, and exercise

---

* Jefferson's Memoirs, vol. iv. 396,

the whole sovereignty, national and municipal; each the portion and within the limits allotted and prescribed by the constitution. It is evident, the writer does not here use the term co-ordinate in the common acceptation, when applied to departments of governments, in which case the appropriate meaning is, that the several departments are vested with co-ordinate powers, which must co-operate to produce an intended effect, that is, that a concurrence of all the departments is necessary to the validity of any act.

No concurrence is here necessary to give validity to the acts of either, when exercising their powers within the limits prescribed by the constitution; he does not, therefore, use it in that sense. The original meaning of the epithet is, an equality of rank or degree, without reference to power. It is evident, however, that he includes an equality of power in each of his departments, so that when they come into collision, on any subject, the power of each is neutralized,—for he proceeds—" But, you will say, if the two departments should claim the same subject of power, where is the common umpire to decide between them? In cases of little importance or urgency, the prudence of both parties will keep them aloof from the questionable ground, but if it can neither be avoided nor compromised; a convention of the states must be called, to ascribe the doubtful power, to which they may think best."

This clearly goes on the assumption, that the powers of the general government and of the state governments as distributed and established by the constitution, are equal, that there is no common judge provided with power and right to decide between them, and that in cases of collision, the only resort is to the people, the original source of all political power. This is altogether incorrect. If there is to be found any intelligible meaning in words and expressions, if there is any force of inference, any reliance on the most obvious construction, it is demonstrably clear, that not only are the powers of the general government, to the extent granted superior, whenever there arises a collision of claims, but that for the decision of such claims, a common judge is established by the constitution in the judicial power delegated to the general government, the jurisdiction of which is expressly extended to all cases in law and equity that shall arise un-

der the constitution and laws of the United States, declared to
be the supreme law, and to all parties that may become inter-
rested in the decision of any question so arising, whether
states including the United States or individuals. Now it is
presumed that no one will venture to deny that the question
whether the power over the subject supposed, is exclusively
granted to the general government, or reserved to the states,
or whether the power is so disposed that both may exercise it
on the same subject, as in most instances of taxation, are
questions or cases arising under the constitution, and to be
decided by a sound construction of that instrument, the supreme law, as applicable to the subject.

As to a compromise, the general government can have no
right to surrender or transfer any power which has been
vested in it on any subject. Nor can the state governments
surrender any power or right reserved to them, but by the
consent of the people from whom the power or right was derived, and in the mode prescribed. Although there is but one
mode provided in the constitution for settling the existing
rights of the parties, by the national judiciary, there is another
mode provided for settling its exercise for the future, by an
amendment of the constitution, which may assign the right to
one party or the other, or wholly prohibit its exercise, as shall
be deemed most conducive to the general good. An authority
for this purpose is found in the fifth article of the constitution,
which provides, among other things, that on the application of
the legislatures of two thirds of the several states, congress
shall call a general convention of the states, not with a power
to decide on the existing rights or claims of the parties, or a
power of final action, but to propose amendments to the constitution, and which can have no validity until afterwards ratified by the legislatures of three fourths of the several states,
or by conventions in three fourths of the states, as congress
shall direct one or the other mode of ratification.

Mr. Jefferson had, undoubtedly, reference to the calling of
such convention ; for we are not to suppose that he contemplated in this instance an innovation of the constitution. On a
fair and candid view, it will be clearly perceived that such
convention could not be empowered to decide the existing

rights or powers of the parties, the general and state governments, or the relations existing between them ; although the amendments which they should propose, might, if duly ratified vary those powers, rights, and relations for the future. We need not, therefore, hesitate to say that the answer which he has given to the objection he had raised for the purpose of illustration, does not serve in the least to illustrate or strengthen his proposition.

Another opinion of Mr. Jefferson, connected with the same subject, is, that " to give the general government the final and conclusive right to judge of its own powers, is to make its discretion, and not the constitution the measure of its powers," and further, " that in all cases of compact between parties having no common judge, each party has an equal right to judge for itself, as well of the operation, as of the mode and measure of redress." The first proposition must be understood to mean, that to give such right of judging finally to any department of the government, is to make its discretion and not the constitution the measure of its powers, and thence to conclude that such right was not granted. This might have been proper to be urged against inserting in the constitution, a provision granting the right. It was in fact powerfully urged, both in the general convention, and in the several state conventions ; but it was over-ruled, and the provision inserted and ratified with the constitution. Nor was there any attempt to restrict it by any amendments proposed by any of the state conventions, nor has it been suggested by any subsequent amendment.

In the second proposition, it is again assumed that by the constitution no common judge is instituted between the parties. Now the only real parties to the compact were the several states, or in truth, the people of the several states in the manner and character already described. But the general government now established becomes a party on the one hand, and the several states constitute the party on the other, and these appear to be the parties here intended. Before making any further observations, I will here, to save a repetition of the same arguments, add the resolutions of the general assembly of the state of Virginia, passed in the years 1798 and

1799, more fully expressing the same opinion; and I do this the more readily, because it appears from Mr. Jefferson's Memoirs, if he did not dictate those resolutions, they were brought forward by his advice and had the authority of his approbation, as it was well understood at the time.

The first resolution concludes in the following words:— "That this assembly doth explicitly and peremptorily declare, that it views the powers of the federal government as resulting from a compact to which the states are parties as limited by the plain sense of the instrument stipulating that compact, as no farther valid than they are authorized by the grants enumerated in that compact, and that in case of a deliberate, palpable, and dangerous exercise of powers not granted by the said compact, the states who are parties to that compact have a right, and are in duty bound to interpose for arresting the progress of the evil and for maintaining within their respective limits, the authorities, rights, and liberties pertaining to them." This resolution was understood at the time as implicitly asserting that the right of finally deciding on the powers granted to the general government, or the constitutionality of its acts, is not vested in the judiciary of the union ; but that the states, as parties to the compact establishing that government, have the final right to judge of its acts, each for itself, whether they are the exercise of powers not granted, and if judged to be such, to interpose and prevent their execution within the limits of their respective jurisdictions.

It has indeed been otherwise explained by very respectable authority ;* but the subsequent resolution of 1799 puts it beyond all manner of doubt. That resolution was past on the report of a committee appointed for the purpose of explaining the former resolution. The committee, speaking of the right of a state to interpose for the preservation of her reserved rights, say,—"It is objected that the judicial authority is to be regarded as the sole expositor of the constitution. To this objection it might be observed,—first, that there may be instances of assumed powers, which, from the forms of the

* See Mr. Madison's letter, No. 5, in the appendix.

constitution, cannot be drawn before the judiciary department. Secondly, that if the judiciary be raised above the sovereign parties to the constitution, the decisions of the other departments not carried by the forms of the constitution, before the judiciary, must be equally conclusive and final with the decisions of that department. But the proper answer to the objection is, that the resolution of the general assembly relates to those great and extraordinary cases, in which all the forms of the constitution may prove inefficient against infractions dangerous to the rights of the parties to it. The resolution supposes, that dangerous powers not delegated, may not only be usurped and executed, but the judiciary department may also exercise and sanction dangerous powers beyond the grant of the constitution, and consequently, that the ultimate right of the parties to judge whether the compact has been dangerously violated, extends to violations by one delegated authority, as well as by another—as well by the judiciary as by executive and legislative."

All this is but a further development and explanation of the principles asserted in the former resolution, and in accordance with the principles advanced by Mr. Jefferson. It is intended as an answer to the objection against the state right claimed by the first resolution, 'that the judicial authority of the United States is to be considered as the sole expositor of the constitution.' As the answer here attempted, is, at first sight, plausible, and as it is a subject of great importance in our political system, I shall examine it at some length, perhaps at the hazard of being thought prolix. "On this objection," say they, "it might be observed,—first, that there may be instances of usurped powers, which, by the forms of the constitution, cannot be drawn within the control of the judicial department." There is in every part of this report, a confusion of ideas, the want, not of a subtle and metaphysical, but of an obvious and practical distinction—a distinction between the unconstitutionality and the inexpedience or impolicy of a law or measure of the government.

In the first case, the unconstitutionality of a law or measure, or as it is called in the report, the usurpation of a power not granted, the constitution itself,—the supreme law—gives the rule of decision ; nor can there be found a single instance of a case, which cannot by the forms of the constitution, be drawn within the control of the judicial department ; not a case, where the party injured may not bring to a legal decision the question, whether the act complained of be the usurpation of a power not granted, or the exercise of a power granted by the constitution. But as to the expedience, or inexpedience, the policy, or impolicy, of an act or measure, in the exercise of a legitimate power, the constitution furnishes no rule, nor can it, in the nature of things, be so formed as to furnish any rule of decision to a court of law. The constitution has, therefore, necessarily; and I will add, wisely left questions of mere policy and expedience, to the discretion of the legislative or executive department, to which the power is committed in trust. But the constitution has not left this power uncontrolled. It is by the provisions of that instrument, placed under the control of public sentiment; which is exercised by the people, and the state legislatures, in the elections of the President, Vice-President, and the members of the national legislature, both of the senate and house of representatives. The frequency of elections, renders this control constant and powerful, and of which those who are the subjects of it, can never be unmindful.

If the distinction taken above, and the consequences drawn from it be correct, of which it appears impossible to entertain a doubt, it proves the assertion that there may be instances of usurped powers, which cannot be drawn within the control of the judicial department to be without all foundation. It also shows that there is no force in Mr. Jefferson's objection that "to give the general government the right to judge of its own powers, is to make its discretion, and not the constitution, the measure of its powers." Had he duly considered and fully comprehended the nature and principles of that government, he must have seen and acknowledged, that without such power vested in the judicial department, it could not, more than any other, even subsist as a government, and that under our free institutions, such investment is no less safe than necessary.

The committee proceed to observe, " secondly, if the decisions of the judiciary be raised above the sovereign parties to the constitution, the decisions of the other departments not carried by the forms of the constitution before the judiciary must be equally authoritative and final with the decisions of that department." The distinction, which was taken above is equally applicable, and equally available here. The decisions of the judiciary are final on the parties in all cases submitted to its jurisdiction, and this includes all cases in which the constitutionality of any act or measure of the other departments may be brought in question. But, as before observed, all questions arising on the policy of their measures, are referred to the tribunal of public sentiment. There can, therefore, be perceived no more force of reason in this observation than in the former.—They are equally unfounded.

The report then proceeds,—" But the proper answer to the objection is, that the resolution of the general assembly refers to those great and extraordinary cases in which all the forms of the constitution may prove ineffectual against infractions dangerous to the essential rights of the parties to it. The resolution supposes dangerous powers not delegated, may not only be usurped by the other departments, but that the judicial departments may exercise and sanction dangerous powers beyond the grant of the constitution, and consequently the ultimate right of the parties to judge, whether the constitution has been dangerously violated, must extend to one delegated authority as well as by another ; as well by the judiciary, as by the executive and legislative."—This is putting an extreme case, which, like extreme cases in general, prove nothing in establishing general rules, but must be left to make a rule for itself.

Still more, it is a case that never can happen under our institutions ; a case that necessarily implies a general corruption of the whole mass, at least a very powerful majority of the people, who have diffused that corruption through every department of the government, who have created, and who support and cherish their oppressors, and have become the willing instruments of their own slavery. But were it possible it should happen, a remedy would not be sought or obtained by any right reserved to the people by the constitution. No constitution of government among men, ever has provided or ever can provide for a lawful resistance to its authority, without insuring a perpetual suspension, or even an annihilation of its necessary energies—a universal anarchy. But it will be asked, can no lawful resistance be in any case, made to the oppressive acts of government? As it relates to human institutions, there cannot, any further than may be done by a resort to the constituted tribunals, among which is included that of public sentiment, and which, under free institutions, has an all-prevaling influence.

But in cases of violent oppression, where all constitutional remedies have been tried, and have become hopeless, a people in that situation, are discharged and freed from all the obligations of the constitution, however solemnly ratified, and are thrown back upon the law of nature,—the law of self-protection;—that law which authorizes, and enjoins as a duty, resistance to oppression, under the guidance of reason and prudence. In such case of oppression happening under our government, should any portion of the people be roused to resistance, that resistance would not be the exercise of any right granted or reserved by the constitution, but a resumption of their natural rights in defiance of the constitution.

Conclusive as this reasoning appears to me, I will, nevertheless, add the opinion of the well known Patrick Henry, on the same subject, whose character as a true and sound patriot, and as a civil and political jurist, will not suffer on a comparison with Mr. Jefferson, or any other man of his day. In an address to the people of Charlotte county, speaking of the first resolution above recited, he remarks that the state had quitted the sphere in which the constitution had placed her, and in daring to pronounce upon the federal laws had gone out of her jurisdiction in a manner not warranted by any authority, and in a manner in the highest degree alarming to every considerate man. He adds that he had seen with regret the purse and the sword, consigned to the federal government, but he had been overruled, and it was now time to submit to the constitutional power. "If I am asked," he says, "what is to be done, when a people feel themselves intolerably oppressed? My answer is ready,—overturn the government!" This, in a few words, goes the whole length of the argument.

Before closing this subject, it will not be improper to consider two objections that have been urged against the powers
here attributed to the national government, with an apparent
conviction of their weight, by the advocates for the continuing
sovereignty, independence, and consequent rights of the states.
First. That to give to the general government, through whatever department, the sole right to judge of its own powers,
is in effect, to reduce the several states from being independent
governments, to the subordinate grade of corporations, existing
at the will and pleasure of that government and dependent
upon it for the powers they may be permitted to exercise.
Second. That to make the general government to any purpose
and within any limits superior to the state governments, is to
make the creature greater than the creator. As to the first
objection, what analogy is to be found between the state
governments as they exist under the constitution of the United
States and a corporation in the sense intended ?

A corporation is the mere creature of the superior government, from which it derives its existence, and on the laws of
which it is dependent for its powers and its continuance. Not
so the state governments. Admitting all the powers vindicated
for the general government, in no sense do they derive their
existence or their powers from that government; nor are they
dependent on its laws for their continuance, or the exercise of
their rightful powers, within the limits of their respective
jurisdictions. The general government and the several state
governments, derive their existence, their powers, and the limitation of those powers, from the same source of all political power,
the sovereign people, and both are dependent on the same
sovereign people alone for their continuance.

The government of each state derives its powers from the
act of the people within its local limits and the general
government from the concurrent act of the people of all the
states, as we have seen, and the people still retain solely to
themselves in the same sovereign capacity the right to alter,
to enlarge, or limit the powers of both, or either, as they shall
think will best promote the public good. One thing that gives
a permanent security to the state governments, and to state
rights, is, that the members of congress are elected, those of

the house of representatives, on a certain ration, by the people of each state from their own citizens, and those of the senate by the state legislature, for short periods, so that they are holden constantly accountable to their constituents, deeply interested with themselves in the maintenance of those rights. There is, therefore, no possible force in the objection.

As to the second objection, it is a general truth, that the creature cannot be made greater than the creator; but in what sense does this apply to government? The people in their associated and sovereign capacity create, or rather institute the government for this very end, that it shall rule over themselves as individuals in society. It has been shown that society is the necessary and the natural state of man, that civil government is necessary to the social state, and is agreeable to the laws of nature, but the institution is left to man in his social state. How these institutions have been formed in the early stages of society, and have become binding by the force of custom, need not be here repeated. We will advance at once to that state of social and civil improvement in which the people have entered into an express civil compact, a written constitution, forming and organizing a government for themselves, instituting, limiting, and directing its necessary powers, to the end intended; providing for the selection and appointment of the functionaries to administer those powers in the several departments, and the manner in which they shall be held accountable for their conduct in the administration.

In thus forming and establishing their government, the people act in their united sovereign capacity in which they are the source of all power, civil and political. They have, also provided that this their sovereign power, shall in future remain dormant until again called into action on the same subject— the constitution, on the occasions only, and in the manner which they shall have prescribed. The government thus instituted is made supreme over the people, who now no longer act as such in their sovereign capacity, but as individuals in society subordinate to that government by their own solemn agreement and consent. There is, therefore, no absurdity in the case, that the people should, one and all, become subject in their individual capacities to the government which they have established in their aggregate capacity.

This reasoning applies as well to the several states under the general government, as to the people under a government of a more simple form; for let each state be considered as a party to the compact establishing the constitution, each was, undeniably, made a party by the sovereign act of the people of the state, the government of which is the creature of that people, and binding as their act only. If then the people as the several states, by themselves, or through the agency of their several governments, by concurrent act have instituted another and general government, that government is the creature of the whole, as the government of each state is the creature of its separate and distinct people ; and each people have the power over the creature they have made, and the right to place it in such relation to the creature made by the whole, as they please, and in such degree of subordination as they may conceive to be most conducive to their interest, and to the common interest of the whole. Indeed, if we reject this reasoning, we must of necessity resort to the exploded doctrine of the divine right of sovereignty. Nothing short of that can establish the authority of any government.

Thus from every view we are able to take of the subject, it conclusively follows that the relation established by the constitution of the United States between the general or national government and the state governments, is a subordination of the latter to the former; but a subordination *quoad hoc* only, within the limits of the powers delegated to that government, and to the end for which they were delegated. Could I find a term in our language less offensive to state pride, than the word subordination, thus qualified, to express the relation in which the constitution has placed the states in respect to the general government, I would readily adopt it ; but I can find no other word that will so correctly express that relation, and I conceive it a matter of the first consequence that we should form a correct opinion upon that subject.

CHAPTER VII.

On the Relations established between the three departments of the General Government.

In the preceding chapter we have treated of the relation established between the general government and the several states; in the present chapter, we shall treat of the relations established between the several departments of the general government, the legislative, executive, and judicial.

The reasons for this division and distribution of powers are so obvious that they hardly need be repeated. To vest all the powers of government,—the power of making, the power of executing, and the power of interpreting and applying the laws,—a power of final decision between the people and the government, in a single man, or body of men, is to constitute an absolute despotism, subject to no restraint but that of brute force. To prevent so enormous an evil, the government has, under our institutions, been divided into three separate and distinct departments; the legislative, the executive, and the judicial, and to each is allotted a portion of the power of government, suited to their several functions. The legislative branch to make all laws; the executive, to give them effect in execution; and the judiciary to interpret and apply the laws, of which the constitution is the supreme law binding on the government, and on each of the departments, by which the validity of every act, legislative and executive is to be decided. From the manner in which these powers are distributed between the several departments and the order in which they are brought to bear on each other, it results that the legislature are bound by the constitution alone in all their acts and measures. The President in whom is vested the executive power, is bound by the constitution, and all constitutional laws of the legislature committed to him for execution. The judges of the Supreme Court, the functionaries of the judicial department in deciding on the acts and measures of the other departments whenever regularly brought in question before them, are bound to decide agreeable to what is, in their best judgment, the true interpretation, the true intent and meaning of the constitutional provisions on the subject.

To that department, the Supreme Court of the United States, the constitution has intrusted the power of final decision. It is expressly provided that the judicial power shall extend to all cases in law and equity arising under the constitution and laws of the United States, and treaties made under their authority. The court, is, therefore, competent to such decision ; and as there is no provision for a revisal of any judgment or sentence of that court, in any case, its decision is necessarily, final and conclusive. From the manner in which the powers are distributed, and the order of their exercise, congress in whom is vested the powers of legislation, must first act, before any matter can be brought before the judiciary for decision. Congress must, therefore, judge for themselves, for the guidance of their own action, what is the meaning of the constitution as it respects the powers they are to exercise. The constitution has made no provision for obtaining a judicial decision, or judicial advice previous to their action. The same is the situation of the executive ; but in neither case is that judgment final and conclusive ; since, by the provisions of the constitution it may be brought in question before the judiciary, the Supreme Court, and that judgment, in effect reversed by a decision that the act is a violation of the constitution, or not warranted by any of the powers therein granted ; and as this decision is made final, it is conclusive of the meaning of the constitution on the points embraced in that decision,—as well on the functionaries of the other departments, as on the states and the people. This is clear to a demonstration, when we reflect that the consequence of such decision against the constitutionality of an act is to arrest its force. It cannot thence be carried into effect.

37

It is an effective declaration of its nullity. Such is the relation established by the constitution between the great departments of the government, as it respects their powers in exercise.

A very different opinion has, however, been maintained upon this subject, by some of the first characters in the country, of whom we may consider Mr. Jefferson as standing at the head. An opinion supported by an authority so respectable, merits a full, careful, and candid investigation. I will recite this opinion as expressed by Mr. Jefferson in two passages found in his correspondence lately published, with his observations, not to say, reasonings on the subject. The first, is in a letter to Mrs. Adams, of September 11th, 1804, while he was President of the United States. " You seem to think it devolved on them, (the judges,) to decide on the validity of the sedition law. But nothing in the constitution has given them a right to decide for the executive, more than to the executive to decide for them. Both magistrates are equally independent in the sphere of action assigned to them. The judges believing the law constitutional, had a right to pass a sentence of fine and imprisonment ; because the power was placed in their hands by the constitution. But the executive, believing the law to be unconstitutional, were bound to remit the execution ; because that power has been confided to them by the constitution. That instrument intended that its co-ordinate branches should be checks on each other. But the opinion which gives the judges their right to decide what laws are constitutional, and what not,—not only for themselves, in their own sphere of action, but for the other departments, would make the judiciary a despotic branch."

The second passage is in a letter to Judge Roane, of the 6th of September 1819. " In denying the right, they (the judges) usurp of exclusively explaining the constitution, I go further than you do, if I understand, rightly, your quotation from the Federalist, of an opinion, that the judiciary is the last resort in relation to the *other departments* of the government, but not in relation to the rights of the parties to the compact, under which the judiciary is derived. If this opinion be sound, then, indeed, is our constitution a complete *felo de se*. For intending to establish three departments co-ordinate and independent that they might check and balance one another it has given, according to this opinion, to one of them alone, the right to prescribe rules for the government of the others, and to that one too that is unelected by them and independent of the nation." " My construction of the constitution is very different from that you quote. It is that each department is truly independent of the others, and has an equal right to decide for itself what is the meaning of the constitution, in the cases submitted to its action; and especially, where it is to act ultimately and without appeal." He then goes on to explain by relating what he did in cases under the sedition law as in the passage above recited from his letter to Mrs. Adams. Before proceeding to discuss the opinion here advanced I will make a few observations.

First, the position here taken by Mr. Jefferson, places the decisions of the executive above the decisions of the other departments—the legislature and the judiciary ; for although he assumes to decide for himself on his own act only ; yet that very act overrules the decisions of both the others, and vindicates independence to the executive alone.

Second, the power of pardoning was not submitted to the executive for such purpose. It was submitted to the President in trust that he might exercise not merely his own clemency, but the clemency of the government, where justified by the circumstances of the case, or by well considered reasons of state. But such is the nature of the subject and of the trust, that it must necessarily be submitted to the discretion of the department by which it is to be exercised. Nor can that discretion be so restrained by any exception or limitations, as always to prevent its perversion to purposes not intended.

Third, a decision of the judiciary, which is the act of that department, is as much an act of the government as a constitutional act of the legislature, or of the executive, and is equally binding on every department as well as all others whom it may concern, and besides, it is in its nature and order an ultimate act. The doctrine advanced, with so much confidence, in the passages above recited, appears to me subversive of the harmony, that ought to subsist in the departments, of all unity of action, and energy in the government. It forbids all expectation of a uniform interpretation, either of the constitution or the laws, all must be in a perpetual state of change with a change of rulers. It removes the principal, indeed, almost the only guard against the unconstitutional, dangerous, and oppressive acts of the legislature and the executive, from which departments alone such oppressive acts can be exercised, and by excluding the enterposition of a judiciary power, be forced upon the people.

We have a written constitution, and that constitution is a rule of action to the citizens. The powers granted by the constitution, are assigned to different departments of the government, the legislative, the executive, and the judicial. To give effect to those powers, the action of the legislative department is first necessary. On that department it devolves by their laws to give energy to those powers, by directing how, in what manner, and upon what subjects the powers shall be exercised to attain the end intended by the constitution. In the exercise of these—their legislative functions—the constitution is their law and their guide. It is the superior law imperiously binding on the government, the states, and the people. Every act of congress is to be judged by this superior law, the constitution; if not supported, if not warranted by the law, it is illegitimate, it is a mere nullity.

To the executive, the President of the United States, besides certain other powers and duties not necessary here to be specified, is committed the authority, as it is made his duty, to take care that the laws be faithfully executed; and in the exercise of this authority, the acts of the President depend for their ultimate jurisdiction on the rule of the same supreme law, the constitution of the United States.

The judicial department has no concern in originating, or forming the laws, or any of the measures committed to the other departments. The duty assigned to that department is to administer justice by deciding in all cases regularly brought before them, according to the laws of the land, of which the constitution is made supreme. The constitution does not undertake expressly to point out the relation subsisting between the departments, or to what extent the act of one shall effect any act of the other; but has left that generally to be determined by inference from a sound construction of the instrument agreeable to the nature of the subject.

Now, says Mr. Jefferson, "my opinion is, that each department is truly independent of the other, and has a right to decide for itself, what is the meaning of the constitution in cases submitted to its action, especially where it is to act ultimately and without appeal." Certainly in all cases submitted without appeal. But the general proposition embraces all cases whatever submitted to the action of the department, whether ultimately and without appeal or not; although the latter are considered as more evidently so to the common understanding. There are two classes of cases presented ; one, of cases submitted to the ultimate decision of the department without appeal ; the other, of cases submitted to the action of the department in which there may be an appeal or ulterior decision. We will first enquire what are the cases, what the actions thus submitted without appeal, and to what extent. These are cases of discretion, and of discretion only. A discretion is permitted to the legislative and to the executive department. But this extends only to the mode, manner, and occasion, to the expediency and policy of a law or measure proposed ; and on this discretion we find certain limitations imposed, as on the power of pardoning committed to the discretion of the President, that it shall not extend to a conviction on impeachment, and the mode of taxation by the legislature, to prevent an inequality of burdens. No discretion is permitted in any case to dispense with any rule of the constitution positive or negative, or with any modification or limititation of powers. I come now to the other class of cases, in which, as I contend, there is allowed an appeal, that there is provided, by the constitution, a power and right of ulterior decision. This is denied by the terms of the general proposition, " that each department is truly independent of the other, and has a right to decide for its If, what is the meaning of the constitution in all cases submitted to its action," although in the concluding sentence it seems to be strongly implied that such appeal is allowed, with certain special exceptions.

By an appeal, in this case, is to be understood the right of one department subsequently to decide, with effect, on the constitutionality of the act of another department, or to decide what is the true meaning of the constitution in the case. It is not to be understood of a formal and technical appeal—the removal of a cause from an inferior to a superior court by writ of error or in any other mode. If any other department has, agreeable to the provision of the constitution, the power and right to decide on the constitutionality of the act whether it be valid—within the meaning of that sacred instrument, the supreme law—to all the departments ; and if in their opinion it be not valid within that meaning, to pronounce it a nullity, unconstitutional and void ; then it is a case in which there is an appeal in the sense intended.

Let us take a strong case. Suppose congress, the legislative department with the approbation of the President, the executive, to pass an act suspending the writ of habeas corpus, in a time of profound peace. A person committed by process and under the government, applies to the Supreme Court for a writ of habeas corpus, on a proper case laid before the court. The suspending act is offered as an objection to the granting of the writ, or to the liberation of the prisoner. Nevertheless, it being known to the court that no case had happened which, agreeable to the constitution could authorze a suspension of the writ, it would be not only the right, but the imperious duty of the court to pronounce judicially this act of the legislature to be unconstitutional and void. Nor is any executive act, in a similar case exempt from judicial cognizance. The court cannot evoke the case from the legislature or the executive. They can decide upon it when, and only when it becomes a material point in a cause properly before them.

On an examination of the constitution, it will be found, that the judicial is the ultimate department, not merely in the arrangement there made, but in point of action from the nature of the powers and duties assigned to it. The judges,—the functionaries of that department, have no concurrent voice, or even advisary, in the acts or measures adopted by the other departments. None of the acts of congress, or measures of the executive, in any way come before the judiciary, until they have received the sanction of the department to which they belong, and have been put in exercise. The acts may thereafter in the course of administration, come before the judiciary,—the court, for decision. In all cases of a prosecution,

civil or criminal, for the infraction of a law, or unlawful opposition, the party prosecuted has a right, as well as any one
who shall have commenced an action for an injury sustained
in the execution of the law, to impeach its constitutional validity, and to claim the decision of the judges on that point. In
making this decision the very nature of the duty forbids that
the judges should be biassed by the previous decision of the
legislature supposed to have been made in passing or determining on the act. They are bound by the rule of the constitution,—the supreme law only. But whether they decide for, or
against its validity, that decision does not affect the constitutionality, or unconstitutionality of the act. It is an authoritative declaration only, for the government of themselves and
others, of a fact already existing. This construction of the
constitution furnishes the only efficient check on those departments of the government which are in a situation to usurp and
exercise dangerous powers ; while it serves to give a uniform
and consistent direction to the acts of the whole, bringing all
to the test of the constitution,—the true standard of political
action, and the value of the test depends wholly on a steady
and uniform interpretation.

In every free government it is an object, the importance
of which can never be too highly appreciated, to make effectual provision for a uniform interpretation of all its laws. As
this object can never be effected, if the interpretation be submitted to different departments independent of each other, and
as is almost inevitably the case, actuated by different views,
interests, and prejudices, the judicial department has been
established by our constitution, and in that department one
Court Supreme over the other, whose decisions are final, fur-
nishing a rule of interpretation in analagous cases binding on
all inferior courts, and a rule of action as well to the government and its functionaries, as to the people. Where, as with
us, there is a written constitution which is the supreme law of
the land, and, emphatically, the supreme law of the government,
and of all its departments, no less in the administration of justice, than in the enacting and execution of laws, the judges who
are under the obligation of an oath to support the constitution,
are bound to administer justice, according to that supreme law,

and by that law, as a rule not to be dispensed with, to interpret all subordinate laws, the acts of the legislature, and in the application of this rule, they must be governed by their own best judgment, whether in testing the validity of the subordinate laws, or directing its interpretation, it is no less necessary that there should be a fixed, steady, and uniform interpretation of the constitution, than of the subordinate laws, and that the binding effect should be no less extensive.

If all admit Mr. Jefferson's opinion to be correct, that each department is so independent of the others that it has a right to decide for itself what is the meaning of the constitution, as respects the extent and limits of its powers, in all cases submitted to its action, there can never, as it respects the powers of government, be established any uniform construction, any steady and uniform interpretation of the constitution; consequently, there will rarely be found a consent of action between the departments, which, although dangerous in cases of conspiracy, is absolutely necessary to any beneficial, practical, and constitutional administration of the government. For from their different construction of their several powers, they will often be found at variance not unfrequently, in irreconcilable opposition, each in duty bound, according to its own construction, to defeat the acts of the other. Of this, Mr. Jefferson has himself, perhaps unwarily, furnished a very notable instance, in the passages above recited from his correspondence.

Adopting Mr. Jefferson's construction, of what avail is a written constitution? Instead of being a rule of action to the government,—the supreme law, it has hardly the force of an admonition. To give to each department the sole right to judge of its own powers, to whatever extent, is to that extent, to use the emphatic language of Mr. Jefferson on another occasion, to make its discretion, and not the constitution, the measure of its powers. It is very obvious from a perusal of the constitution, that, as before observed, every dangerous abuse of power, every oppressive act of the government, must originate with the legislative or the executive department, and must be matured and carried into effect by one or both of those departments; none can originate with the judiciary. The judges may from ignorance or corruption, sanction a dangerous abuse of power, or an oppressive act of the government; but this is not to be presumed; especially, when we consider the manner of their selection and appointment, and the independent situation in which they are placed.

I will finish this chapter by observing that the doctrine which I have here advocated of the power and right of final decision vested by the constitution in the judicial department, has been supported by the first characters in and out of the government, as well as by the great body of the people, who rest upon it as the great safe-guard of their constitutional rights and security against any oppressive acts of the government.

Such opinion of the office and duty of the judges, has been maintained from the commencement of our republican institutions, not in theory merely, but in practice; not only in the general government, but in every state government in the union, all formed on the same republican principles. It is true that a different opinion has been expressed by individuals, and in some instances, by public bodies, during the excess of public excitement, but it has on the subsidence of that excitement, generally been abandoned as untenable, with some few exceptions.

CHAPTER VIII.

Observations on the tendency in government to dissolution, from a corruption of its principles.—Plan of reformation incorporated in the constitution.—Its probable effects in perpetuating its duration.

Montesquieu, speaking of that kind of government, which was established through Europe by the conquerors of the Roman Empire, says—"It was a good government that had in itself a capacity of growing better." This capacity of growing better was not the effect of any direct intention of the founders, nor, if perceived, was its cultivation, generally, an object of pursuit. Accordingly, we have seen this kind of government almost universally, degenerating into a species of despotism, under an absolute monarchy, or an aristocracy equally absolute. If any of those governments have admitted improvements, these improvements never have been deliberately made, in consequence of any plan of reformation adopted in the constitution. They have been constantly introduced by violence, or, in a concurrence of circumstances, little, if at all intended or foreseen.

Notwithstanding the foregoing observation of Montesquieu, he appears to join in the opinion, which has very generally prevailed, that governments, like men, carry in themselves from their very origin, the seeds of dissolution; that man is fatally incapable of forming any which shall endure without degenerating. I am, however, apprehensive, that on enquiry, we may, so far as it relates to government, find reason to doubt the correctness of this opinion. A more general development of the laws of social nature, and the principles resulting from those laws, may discover, that although in the infancy of mankind, from which, perhaps, those nations who have made the greatest advances, have hardly emerged, this may be true, yet man is by nature, capable of improvements, which may render an amelioration in the science of government, as easy and familiar as in any other science. The same fate has attended all sciences of more difficult investigation. Their establishment and improvement have generally, been attempted by reasonings *apriori*, in which imagination is the principal agent. It has fared in the same manner with the various systems of natural philosophy, morality, and theology which have succeeded each other in the world.

Within the last two centuries, experimental reasonings have banished innumerable absurdities, and in many sciences, seem to have laid a foundation of knowledge as fixed and as durable as the course of nature.

It is at length perceived that all nature is subjected to certain laws established by deity in the original constitution of things, and that while some of those laws extend to inert matter only, to physical operations and effects, others extend to social beings, moral agents, to regulate and direct their actions, and that nothing can be durable, that is calculated to thwart those laws, or divert them from their course ; but with this difference in the character of those laws ; the laws of inert matter are, to the material agents irresistible, not so the laws of moral action.—The laws of moral action respect the design of the agent ; the laws of inert matter, have no respect to the design of the material agents ; the former are obligatory and precede the action ; the other necessary and accompany the operation. A knowledge of one class of these laws is denominated physical science ; a knowledge of the other, with their proper application and direction is denominated moral science, and such is political science, or the science of government. That science consists in a knowledge of the laws of moral action, the laws of social nature,—their application and their effect on the actions of men under government and laws, and their direction for attaining the great end of all moral laws, the happiness of social beings. For this, by the same laws, is left to the wisdom of man. The science of government is not merely theoretical, but a practical science. It requires not only a knowledge of the laws of nature, but of the subject on which they are brought to operate ; the nature of man in society, and the nature of the society, which is the subject of the government.

The state of society is rarely stationary for any length of time. Under an absolute government, where the people are slaves, society is generally in a retrograde course until it has reached the lowest point of degradation, in which it may remain stationary as long as the government shall continue.

Under free institutions of government, the state of society will always be progressive—there will be a constant improvement in manners and in knowledge. Such improvements in a community will, from time to time, require corresponding improvements in their civil institutions, to adapt them to the existing state of things; besides, in the best institutions that can be formed by fallible man, imperfections will be admitted, for the correction of which provision ought to be made in the constitution. No such provision was made in the institution of those governments, mentioned by Montesquieu. Each government, however, or rather the rulers who assumed the government, had a power to alter the constitution; but as they were not holden accountable or sufficiently accountable to the people, and therefore not in a situation to be restrained by any efficient fundamental laws, such alterations only could be expected as might serve to augment the power of the rulers, with little or no attention to the rights of the people. Here we find the principal cause of the degeneracy of those governments. In more modern times, from a fortunate concurrence of circumstances, among which, may be reckoned a more free and extended intercourse between nations, even the benumbning influence of a despotic government has not been sufficient to prevent an advance, and in many instances, a rapid advance in knowledge, through the greatest portion of the civilized world. And the effect has been, and it is to be hoped always will be a correspondent amelioration of the government, as in England,—or the total subversion of it as in France; although the horrors which attended that catastrophe are deeply to be lamented.

The political institutions of the United States in which we include the constitution of the general government are, in many respects, essentially different from all preceding institutions. Their great leading principles are—first, that the sole end of all government ought to be, to promote and secure the happiness of the people. And second, that the people are the only legitimate source of political power, that the ultimate sovereignty resides in the people subject to such regulations only as they themselves shall have prescribed. These two leading principles embrace all the laws of social nature, which have any relation to the subject of government, and furnish the means of making amendments to the constitution corresponding with the progress of the citizens in social improvements and political science ; they furnish also the means of establishing fundamental laws binding on every department of the government, legislative, executive, and judicial, as well as the means of giving full effect to those laws by subjecting to the test of the constitution all the act of those departments from which is to be apprehended any danger to the legitimate rights and liberty of the people and holding all the great functionaries of the government accountable for the constitutional discharge of their several trust to the established tribunals, and through the medium of periodical elections, constantly accountable to the tribunal of public sentiment—the people—as we have before seen.

The idea of incorporating in the constitution of the government a plan of reformation, which without encouraging a spirit of innovation, the parent of anarchy and final despotism might enable the people, with deliberation, and more mature experience to correct what should be, at any time, found wrong in the form, principles, or operation of the government, was first, adopted in practice by the states of the union, in forming their several constitutions. It has been found not only practicable in the exercise, but its happy effect in ameliorating their institutions had in several instances been fully evinced. The idea was taken up and pursued in framing the constitution for the government of the United States,—and to carry it into full effect, an article was introduced, which requires no comment for its explanation, or to manifest the wisdom and propriety of its provisions and their accordance with the best principles of the government. I shall therefore, content myself with a simple repetition of the article. " Congress, whenever two thirds of both houses shall deem it necessary, shall propose amendments to the constitution, or on application of two thirds of the several states, shall call a convention for proposing amendments, which in either case shall be valid to all intents and purposes, as parts of the constitution, when ratified by the legislatures of three fourths of the several states, or by conventions in three fourths thereof as the one or the other mode shall be proposed by congress." There remains one restriction in respect to amendments, " that no state shall, without its consent be deprived of its equal suffrage in the senate."

In virtue of the power vested in congress and the powers reserved to the states and the people by this article several important amendments to the constitution have been adopted ; and we have reason to believe, that whatever shall be found deficient in principle will be added ; whatever shall be found dangerous to the rights of the people or the states or impracticable in operation will be retrenched and corrected. The wisdom that formed it, aided and matured by experience, may improve its principles and extend its provisions in accordance with the progress of social improvements, and carry it to a greater degree of perfection than any thing yet known in government.

Let us not then rashly, or from the pride of a prophetic spirit, conclude that this beautiful system, is, with the craggy empires of antiquity, or the ill constructed governments of former times, destined to inevitable, and perhaps speedy dissolution ; or that it must in time, through the degeneracy of the people,—and a corruption of its principles, of necessity, give place to a system of remediless tyranny and oppression. Let us rather, while we entertain a rational hope that it may endure as long as the successive generations of men, attend with the calmness of philosophy to the enjoyment of its blessings and the improvement of its principles. To an ardent wish for its perpetual duration let us add the only means of securing it ; let us endeavor to diffuse extensively the principles of useful knowledge, and to impress, on the minds of the rising generation, the sentiments of liberal virtue and genuine patriotism.

APPENDIX.

Number 1.—*p.* 259.

*Articles of confederation and perpetual union between the states of New Hamp-
shire, Massachusetts Bay, Rhode Island and Providence Plantations, Connecticut, New York, New Jersey, Pennsylvania, Delaware, Maryland, Virginia,
North Carolina, South Carolina, and Georgia.*

ARTICLE I. The style of this confederacy shall be "The United States
of America."

ART. II. Each state retains its sovereignty, freedom, and independence,
and every power, jurisdiction, and right, which is not by this confederation
expressly delegated to the United States in congress assembled.

ART. III. The said states hereby severally enter into a firm league of
friendship with each other, for their common defence, the security of their
liberties, and their mutual and general welfare ; binding themselves to assist
each other, against all force offered to, or attacks made upon them, or any of
them, on account of religion, sovereignty, trade, or any other pretence
whatever.

ART. IV. The better to secure and perpetuate mutual friendship and
intercourse among the people of the different states in this union, the free
inhabitants of each of these states, paupers, vagabonds, and fugitives from
justice excepted, shall be entitled to all privileges and immunities of free
citizens in the several states ; and the people of each state shall have free
ingress and egress to and from any other state, and shall enjoy therein all
the privileges of trade and commerce, subject to the same duties, impositions,
and restrictions as the inhabitants thereof respectively, provided that such
restrictions shall not extend so far as to prevent the removal of property
imported into any state, to any other state of which the owner is an inhabitant ; provided also that no imposition, duties, or restriction shall be laid
by any state, on the property of the United States, or either of them.

If any person guilty of, or charged with treason, felony, or other high
misdemeanor in any state, shall flee from justice, and be found in any of the

United States, he shall, upon demand of the government or executive power of the state from which he fled, be delivered up and removed to the state having jurisdiction of his offence.

Full faith and credit shall be given in each of these states to the records, acts, and judicial proceedings of the courts and magistrates of every other state.

ART. V.   For the more convenient management of the general interests of the United States, delegates shall be annually appointed, in such manner as the legislature of each state shall direct, to meet in congress on the first Monday in November, in every year; with a power reserved to each state, to recall its delegates, or any of them, at any time within the year, and to send others in their stead, for the remainder of the year.

No state shall be represented in congress by less than two, nor more than seven members ; and no person shall be capable of being a delegate for more than three years in any term of six years ; nor shall any person, being a delegate, be capable of holding any office under the United States, for which he, or another for his benefit, receives any salary, fees, or emolument of any kind.

Each state shall maintain its own delegates in a meeting of the states, and while they act as members of the committee of the states.

In determining questions in the United States, in congress assembled, each state shall have one vote.

Freedom of speech and debate in congress shall not be impeached or questioned in any court, or place out of congress, and the members of congress shall be protected in their persons from arrests and imprisonments, during the time of their going to, and from, and attendance on congress, except for treason, felony, or breach of the peace.

ART. VI.   No state, without the consent of the United States in congress assembled, shall send any embassy to, or receive any embassy from, or enter into any conference, agreement, alliance, or treaty with any king, prince, or state ; nor shall any person holding any office of profit or trust under the United States, or any of them, accept of any present, emolument, office, or title of any kind whatever from any king, prince, or foreign state ; nor shall the United States in congress assembled, or any of them grant any title of nobility.

No two or more states shall enter into any treaty, confederation, or alliance whatever between them, whithout the consent of the United States in con- gress assembled, specifying accurately the purposes for which the same is to be entered into, and how long it shall continue.

No state shall lay any imposts or duties, which may interfere with any stip- ulations in treaties, entered into by the United States in congress assembled, with any king, prince, or state, in pursuance of any treaties already proposed by congress, to the courts of France and Spain.

No vessels of war shall be kept up in time of peace by any state, except such number only, as shall be deemed necessary by the United States in congress assembled, for the defence of such state, or its trade ; nor shall any body of forces be kept up by any state, in time of peace, except such number only, as in the judgment of the United States, in congress assembled, shall be deemed requisite to garrison the forts necessary for .the defence of such state; but every state shall always keep up a well-regulated and disciplined militia, sufficiently armed and accoutred, and shall provide and constantly have ready for use, in public stores, a due number of field-pieces and tents, and a proper quantity of arms, ammunition, and camp-equipage.

No state shall engage in any war without the consent of the United States in congress assembled, unless such state be actually invaded by enemies, or shall have received certain advice of a resolution being formed by some nation of Indians to invade such state, and the danger is so iminent as not to admit of a delay, till the United States in congress assembled, can be consulted: nor shall any state grant commissions to any ships or vessels of war, nor letters of marque or reprisal, except it be after a declaration of war by the United States in congress assembled, and then only against the kingdom or state and .the subjects thereof, against which war has been so declared, and under such regulations as shall be established by the United States in congress assembled; unless such state be infested by pirates, in which case vessels of war may be fitted out for that occasion, and kept so long as the danger shall continue, or until the United States in congress assembled shall determine otherwise.

ART. VII. When land forces are raised by any state for the common defence, all officers of or under the rank of colonel shall be appointed by the legislature of each state respectively, by whom such forces shall be raised, or in such manner as such state shall direct; and all vacancies shall be filled up by the state which first made the appointment.

ART. VIII. All charges of war, and all other expenses that shall be incurred for the common defence or general welfare, and allowed by the United States in congress assembled, shall b defrayed out of a common treasury, which shall be supplied by the several states, in proportion to the value of all land within each state, granted to or surveyed for any person, as such land and the buildings and improvements thereon shall be estimated, according to such mode as the United States in congress assembled shall from time to time direct and appoint.

The taxes for paying that proportion shall be laid and levied by the authority and direction of the legislatures of the several states, within the time agreed upon by the United States in congress assembled.

ART. IX. The United States in congress assembled shall have the sole and exclusive right and power of determining on peace and war, except in the cases mentioned in the sixth article—of sending and receiving ambassadors—entering into treaties and alliances, provided that no treaty of commerce shall be made, whereby the legislative power of the respective states shall be restrained from imposing such imposts and duties on foreigners, as their own people are subjected to, or from prohibiting the exportation or importation of any species of goods or commodities whatsoever—of establishing rules for deciding, in all cases, what captures on land or water shall be legal, and in what manner prizes taken by land or naval forces in the service of the United States shall be divided or appropriated—of granting letters of marque and reprisal in times of peace—appointing courts for the trial of piracies and felonies committed on the high seas—and establishing courts for receiving and determining finally appeals in all cases of captures, provided that no member of congress shall be appointed a judge of any of the said courts.

The United States in congress assembled shall also be the last resort on appeal in all disputes and differences now subsisting, or that hereafter may arise between two or more states, concerning boundary, jurisdiction, or any other cause whatever; which authority shall always be exercised in the manner following. Whenever the legislative or executive authority, or lawful agent of any state in controversy with another, shall present a petition to congress stating the matter in question, and praying for a hearing, notice thereof shall be given by order of congress to the legislative or executive authority of the other state in controversy, and a day assigned for the appearance of the parties by their lawful agents, who shall then be directed to appoint, by joint consent, commissioners or judges to constitute a court for hearing and determining the matter in question: but if they cannot agree congress shall name three persons out of each of the United States, and from the list of such persons each party shall alternately strike out one, the petitioners beginning, until the number shall be reduced to thirteen; and from that number not less than seven nor more than nine names, as congress shall direct, shall in the presence of congress be drawn out by lot, and the persons whose names shall be so drawn, or any five of them, shall be commissioners or judges to hear and finally determine the controversy, so always as a major part of the judges who shall hear the cause shall agree in the determination: and if either party shall neglect to attend at the day appointed, without showing reasons which congress shall judge sufficient, or being present shall refuse to strike, the congress shall proceed to nominate three persons out of each state, and the secretary of congress shall strike in behalf of such party absent or refusing; and the judgment and sentence of the court to be appointed, in the manner before prescribed, shall be final and conclusive; and if any of the parties shall refuse to submit to the authority of such court, or to appear or defend their claim or cause, the court shall nevertheless proceed to pronounce sentence, or judgment, which shall in like manner be final and decisive; the judgment or sentence and other proceedings being in either case transmitted to congress, and lodged among the acts of congress, for the security of the parties concerned: provided that every commissioner before he sits in judgment, shall take an oath, to be administered by one of the judges of the Supreme or superior Court of the state, where the cause shall be tried, "*well and truly to hear and determine the matter in question, according to the best of his judgment, without favor, affection, or hope of reward:*" provided also that no state shall be deprived of territory for the benefit of the United States.

All controversies concerning the private right of soil, claimed under different grants of two or more states, whose jurisdictions, as they may respect such lands, and the states which passed such grants, are adjusted, the said grants or either of them being at the same time claimed to have originated antecedent to such settlement of jurisdiction, shall, on the petition of either party to the congress of the United States, be finally determined as near as may be in the same manner as is before prescribed for deciding disputes respecting territorial jurisdiction between different states.

The United States in congress assembled shall also have the sole and exclusive right and power of regulating the alloy and value of coin struck by their own authority, or by that of the respective states—fixing the standard of weights and measures throughout the United States—regulating the trade and managing all affairs with the Indians, not members of any of the states, provided that the legislative right of any state within its own limits be not infringed or violated—establishing and regulating post-offices from one state to another, throughout all the United States, and exacting such postage on the papers passing through the same as may be requisite to defray the expenses of the said office—appointing all officers of the land forces, in the service of the United States, excepting regimental officers—appointing all the officers of the naval forces, and commissioning all officers whatever in the service of the United States—making rules for the government and regulation of the said land and naval forces, and directing their operations.

The United States in congress assembled shall have authority to appoint a committee to sit in the recess of congress, to be denominated " a committee of the states," and to consist of one delegate from each state ; and to appoint such other committees and civil officers as may be necessary for managing the general affairs of the United States under their direction—to appoint one of their number to preside, provided that no person be allowed to serve in the office of president more than one year in any term of three years; to ascertain the necessary sums of money to be raised for the service of the United States, and to appropriate and apply the same for defraying the public expenses—to borrow money, or emit bills on the credit of the United States, transmitting every half year to the respective states an account of the sums of money so borrowed or emitted—to build and equip a navy—to agree upon the number of land forces, and to make requisitions from each state for its quota, in proportion to the number of white inhabitants in such state ; which requisitions shall be binding, and thereupon the legislature of each state shall appoint the regimental officers, raise the men, and clothe, arm, and equip them in a soldier-like manner, at the expense of the United States ; and the officers and men so clothed, armed, and equipped, shall march to the place appointed, and within the time agreed on by the United States in congress assembled : but if the United States in congress assembled shall, on consideration of circumstances, judge proper that any state should not raise men, or should raise a smaller number than its quota, and that any other state should raise a greater number of men than the quota thereof, such extra number shall be raised, officered, clothed, armed, and equipped in the same manner as the quota of such state, unless the legislature of such state shall judge that such extra number cannot be safely spared out of the same, in which case they shall raise, officer, clothe, arm, and equip as many of such extra number as they judge can be safely spared.

And the officers and men so clothed, armed, and equipped, shall march to the place appointed, and within the time agreed on by the United States in congress assembled.

The United States in congress assembled shall never engage in a war, nor grant letters of marque and reprisal in time of peace, nor enter into any treaties or alliances, nor coin money, nor regulate the value thereof, nor ascertain the sums and expenses necessary for the defence and welfare of the United States or any of them, nor emit bills, nor borrow money on the credit of the United States, nor appropriate money, nor agree upon the number of vessels of war, to be built or purchased, or the number of land or sea forces to be raised, nor appoint a commander-in-chief of the army or navy, unless nine states assent to the same : nor shall a question on any other point, except for adjourning from day to day, be determined, unless by the votes of a majority of the United States in congress assembled.

The congress of the United States shall have power to adjourn to any time within the year, and to any place within the United States, so that no period of adjournment be for a longer duration than the space of six months ; and shall publish the journal of their proceedings monthly, except such parts thereof relating to treaties, alliances, or military operations, as in their judgment require secrecy ; and the yeas and nays of the delegates of each state on any question shall be entered on the journal, when it is desired by any delegate ; and the delegates of a state, or any of them, at his or their request, shall be furnished with a transcript of the said journal, except such parts as are above excepted, to lay before the legislatures of the several states.

Art. X. The committee of the states, or any nine of them, shall be authorized to execute, in the recess of congress, such of the powers of congress as the United States in congress assembled, by the consent of nine states, shall from time to time think expedient to vest them with ; provided that no power be delegated to the said committee, for the exercise of which, by the articles of confederation, the voice of nine states in the congress of the United States assembled is requisite.

Art. XI. Canada acceding to this confederation, and joining in the measures of the United States, shall be admitted into, and entitled to all the advantages of this union : but no other colony shall be admitted into the same, unless such admission be agreed to by nine states.

Art. XII. All bills of credit emitted, moneys borrowed, and debts contracted by, or under the authority of congress, before the assembling of the United States, in pursuance of the present confederation, shall be deemed and considered as a charge against the United States, for payment and satisfaction whereof, the said United States, and the public faith are hereby solemnly pledged.

Art. XII. Every state shall abide by the determinations of the United States in congress assembled, on all questions which by this confederation are submitted to them. And the articles of this confederation shall be inviolably observed by every state, and the union shall be perpetual ; nor shall any alteration at any time hereafter be made in any of them, unless such alteration be agreed to by a congress of the United States, and be afterwards confirmed by the legislatures of every state.

And whereas it hath pleased the great Governor of the world to incline the hearts of the legislatures we respectively represent in congress, to approve of, and to authorize us to ratify the said articles of confederation and perpetual union: KNOW YE, that we, the undersigned delegates, by virtue of the power and authority to us given for that purpose, do by these presents, in the name and behalf of our respective constituents, fully and entirely ratify and confirm each and every of the said articles of confederation and perpetual union, and all and singular the matters and things therein contained: and we do further solemny plight and engage the faith of our respective constituents, that they shall abide by the determinations of the United States in congress assembled, on all questions, which by the said confederation are submitted to them; and that the articles thereof shall be inviolably observed by the states we respectively represent, and that the union shall be perpetual.

In witness whereof, we have hereunto set our hands in congress. Done at Philadelphia in the state of Pennsylvania the ninth day of July in the year of our Lord one thousand seven hundred and seventy-eight, and in the third year of the independence of America.

Number 2.—p. 254.

Mr. Madison to Mr. Ingersoll.

Montpelier, June 25, 1831.

DEAR SIR:—I have received your friendly letter of the 18th instant. The few lines which answered your former one, of the 21st of January last, were written in haste and in bad health: but they expressed, though without the attention in some respects due to the occasion, a dissent from the views of the President, as to a Bank of the United States, and a substitute for it; to which I cannot but adhere. The objections to the latter have appeared to me to preponderate greatly over the advantages expected from it, and the constitutionality of the former I still regard as sustained by the considerations to which I yielded in giving my assent to the existing bank.

The charge of inconsistency between my objection to the constitutionality of such a bank in 1791, and my assent in 1817, turns on the question, how far legislative precedents, expounding the constitution, ought to guide succeeding legislatures, and to overrule individual opinions.

Some obscurity has been thrown over the question, by confounding it with the respect due from one legislature to laws passed by preceding legislatures. But the two cases are essentially different. A constitution being derived from a superior authority, is to be expounded and obeyed, not controlled or varied, by the subordinate authority of a legislature. A law, on the other hand, resting on no higher authority than that possessed by every successive legislature, its expediency as well as its meaning is within the scope of the latter.

The case in question has its analogy in the obligation arising from judicial exposions of the law on succeeding judges; the constitution being a law to the legislator, as a law is a rule of decision to a judge.

And why are judicial precedents, when formed on due discussion and consideration, and deliberately sanctioned by reviews and repetitions, regarded as of binding influence, or rather of authoritative force, in settling the meaning of a law? It must be answered, 1st. Because it is a reasonable and established axiom, that the good of society requires, that the rules of conduct of its members should be certain and known, which would not be the case if any judge, disregarding the decisions of his predecessors, should vary the rule of law according to his inividual interpretation of it. Misera est servitus ubi jus est aut vagum aut incognitum. 2d. Because an exposition of the law, publicly made, and repeatedly confirmed by the constituted authority, carries with it by fair inference the sanction of those who, having made the law through their legislative organ, appear, under such circumstances, to have determined its meaning through their judiciary organ.

Can it be of less consequence that the meaning of a constitution should be fixed and known, than that the meaning of a law should be so? Can, indeed, a law be fixed in its meaning and operation, unless the constitution be so? On the contrary, if a particular legislature, differing in the construction of the constitution from a series of preceding constructions, proceed to act on that difference, they not only introduce uncertainty and instability in the constitution, but in the laws themselves; inasmuch as all laws preceding the new construction and inconsistent with it are not only annulled for the future, but virtually pronounced nullities from the beginning.

But it is said that the legislator, having sworn to support the constitution, must support it in his own construction of it, however different from that put on it by his predecessors, or whatever be the consequences of the construction. And is not the judge under the same oath to support the law? yet has it ever been supposed that he was required, or at liberty to disregard all precedents, however solemnly repeated and regularly observed; and, by giving effect to his own abstract and individual opinions, to disturb the established course of practice in the business of the community? Has the wisest and most conscientious judges ever scrupled to acquiesce in decisions in which he has been overruled by the mature opinions of the majority of his colleagues, and subsequently to conform himself thereto, as to authoritative expositions of the law? And is it not reasonable that the same view of the official oath should be taken by a legislator, acting under the constitution, which is his guide as is taken by a judge, acting under the law, which is his?

There is in fact, and in common understanding, a necessity of regarding a course of practice, as above characterized, in the light of a legal rule of interpreting a law: and there is a like necessity of considering it a constitutional rule of interpreting a constitution.

That there may be extraordinary and peculiar circumstances controlling the rule in both cases, may be admitted: but with such exceptions, the rule will force itself upon the practical judgment of the most ardent theorist. He will find it impossible to adhere to, and act officially upon, his solitary opinions as to the meaning of the law or constitution, in opposition to a construction reduced to practice, during a reasonable period of time : more especially where no prospect existed of a change of construction by the public or its agents. And if a reasonable period of time, marked with the usual sanctions, would not bar the individual prerogative, there could be no limitation to its exercise, although the danger of error must increase with the increasing oblivion of explanatory circumstances, and with the continual changes of the import of words and phrases.

Let it then be left to the decision of every intelligent and candid judge, which, on the whole, is most to be relied on for the true and safe construction of a constitution—that which has the uniform sanction of successive legislative bodies through a period of years, and under the varied ascendency of parties; or that which depends upon the opinions of every new legislature, heated as it may be by the spirit of party, eager in the pursuit of some favorite object, or led astray by the eloquence and address of popular statesmen, themselves, perhaps, under the influence of the same misleading causes.

It was in conformity with the view here taken, of the respect due to deliberate and reiterated precedents, that the Bank of the United States, though on the original question held to be unconstitutional, received the executive signature in the year 1817. The act originally establishing a bank had undergone ample discussions in its passage through the several branches of the government. It had been carried into execution throughout a period of twenty years with annual legislative recognitions; in one instance indeed, with a positive ramification of it into a new state; and with the entire acquiescence of all the local authorities, as well as of the nation at large; to all of which may be added, a decreasing prospect of any change in the public opinion adverse to the constitutionality of such an institution. A veto from the executive under these circumstances, with an admission of the expediency and almost necessity of the measure, would have been a defiance of all the obligations derived from a course of precedents amounting to the requisite evidence of the national judgment and intention.

It has been contended that the authority of precedents was in that case invalidated by the consideration that they proved only a respect for the stipulated duration of the bank, with a toleration of it until the law should expire, and by the casting vote given in the senate by the Vice-President in the year 1811, against a bill for establishing a national bank, the vote being expressly given on the ground of unconstitutionality. But if the law itself was unconstitutional, the stipulation was void, and could not be constitutionally fulfilled or tolerated. And as to the negative of the senate by the casting vote of the presiding officer, it is a fact well understood at the time, that it resulted not from an equality of opinions in that assembly on the power of congress to establish a bank, but from a junction of those who admitted the power, but disapproved the plan, with those who denied the power. On a simple question of constitutionality, there was a decided majority in favor of it.   JAMES MADISON.

Mr. Ingersoll.

Number 3.— p. 258.

Mr. Madison to Mr. Cabell.

Montpelier, Sept. 18, 1828.

DEAR SIR:—Your late letter reminds me of our conversation on the constitutionality of the power in congress to impose a tariff for the encouragement of manufactures; and of my promise to sketch the grounds of the confident opinion I had expressed, that it was among the powers vested in that body. I had not forgotten my promise, and had even begun the task of fulfilling it; but frequent interruption from other causes, being followed by billious indisposition, I have not been able sooner to comply with your request. The subjoined view of the subject might have been advantageously expanded, but I leave that improvement to your own reflections and researches.

The constitution vests in congress, expressly, "the power to lay and collect taxes, duties, imposts, and excises;" and "the power to regulate trade."

That the former power, if not particularly expressed, would have been included in the latter as one of the objects of a general power to regulate trade, is not necessarily impugned by its being so expressed. Examples of this sort cannot sometimes be easily avoided, and are to be seen elsewhere in the constitution. Thus the power "to define and punish offences against the law of nations," includes the power, afterwards particularly expressed, "to make rules concerning captures, &c. from offending neutrals." So also a power "to coin money" would doubtless include that of "regulating its value," had not the latter power been expressly inserted. The term taxes, if standing *alone*, would certainly have included duties, imposts, and excises. In another clause it is said, "no tax or duties shall be laid on exports, &c." Here the two terms are used as synonymous. And in another clause, where it is said, "no state shall lay any imposts or duties, &c," the terms imposts and duties are synonymous. Pleonasms, tautologies, and the promiscuous use of terms and phrases, differing in their shads of meaning, (always to be expounded with reference to the context, and under the control of the general character and manifest scope of the instrument in which they are found), are to be ascribed, sometimes to the purpose of greater caution—sometimes to the imperfections of language, and sometimes to the imperfection of man himself. In this view of the subject, it was quite natural, however certainly the general power to regulate trade might include a power to impose duties on it, not to omit it in a clause enumerating the several modes of revenue authorized by the constitution. In a few cases could the "ex majori cautela" occur with more claim to respect.

Nor can it be inferred, that a power to regulate trade does not involve a power to tax it, from a distinction made in the original controversy with Great Britain, between a power to regulate trade with the colonies, and a power to tax them. A power to regulate trade between different parts of the empire, was confessedly *necessary*; and was admitted to lie, as far as that was the case, in the British parliament; the taxing part being at the same time denied to the parliament, and asserted to be necessarily inherent in the colonial legislatures, as sufficient, and the only safe depositories of the power. So difficult was it, nevertheless, to maintain the distinction in practice, that the ingredient of revenue was occasionally overlooked or disregarded in the British regulations, as in the duty on sugar and molasses imported into the colonies. And it was fortunate that the attempt at an internal and direct tax, in the case of the stamp act, produced a radical examination of the subject before a regulation of trade with a view to revenue had grown into an established authority. One thing at least is certain, that the main and admitted object of the parliamentary *regulations* of trade with the colonies, was the encouragement of *manufactures* in Great Britain.

But the present question is unconnected with the former relation between Great Britain and her colonies, which were of a peculiar, a complicated, and, in several respects, of an undefined character. It is a simple question under the constitution of the United States, whether " the power to regulate trade with foreign nations" as a distinct and substantive item in the enumerated powers, embraces the object of encouraging by duties, restrictions and prohibitions, the manufactures and products of the country? And the affirmative must be inferred from the following considerations:

1. The meaning of the phrase " to regulate trade," must be sought in the general use of it ; in other words, in the objects to which the power was generally understood to be applicable, when the phrase was inserted in the constitution.

2. The power has been understood and used by all commercial and manufacturing nations, as embracing the objects of encouraging manufactures. It is believed that not a single exception can be named.

3. This has been particularly the case with Great Britain, whose commercial vocabulary is the parent of ours. A primary object of her commercial regulations is well known to have been the protection and encouragement of her manufactures.

4. Such was understood to be a proper use of the power by the states most prepared for manufacturing industry, whilst retaining the power over their foreign trade.

5. Such a use of the power, by congress, accords with the intention and expectation of the states, in transferring the power over trade from themselves to the government of the United States. This was emphatically the case in the eastern, the more manufacturing members of the confederacy. Hear the language in the convention of Massachusetts.

By M. Dawes, an advocate for the constitution, it was observed, " our manufactures are another great subject which has received no encouragement by national duties of foreign manufactures, and they never can by any authority in the old confederation." Again, " if we wish to *encourage our own manufactures*, to preserve our own commerce, to raise the value of our own lands, we must give congress the power in question."

By Mr. Widgery, an opponent: " all we hear is, that the merchant and farmer will flourish, and that the mechanic and tradesman are to make their fortunes directly, if the constitution goes down."

The convention of Massachusetts was the only one in New England whose debates have been preserved. But it cannot be doubted that the sentiment there expressed was common to the other states in that quarter, more especially to Connecticut and Rhode Island, the most thickly peopled of all the states, and having of course their thoughts most turned to the subject of manufactures. A like inference may be confidently applied to New Jersey, whose debates in convention have not been preserved. In the populous and manufacturing state of Pennsylvania, a partial account only of the debates having been published, nothing certain is known of what had passed in her convention on this point. But ample evidence may be found elsewhere, that regulations of trade, for the encouragement of manufactures, were considered as within the power to be granted to the new congress, as well as within the scope of the national policy. Of the states south of Pennsylvania, the only two in whose conventions the debates have been preserved are Virginia and North Carolina, and from these no adverse inferences can be drawn. Nor is there the slightest indication that either of the two states farthest south, whose debates in convention, if preserved, have not been made public, viewed the encouragement of manufactures, as not within the general power over trade to be transferred to the government of the United States.

6. If congress have not the power, it is annihilated for the nation ; a policy without example in any other nation, and not within the reason of the solitary one in our own. The example alluded to, is the prohibition of a tax on exports, which resulting from the apparent impossibility of raising, in that mode, a revenue from the states proportioned to the ability to pay it—the ability of some being derived, in a great measure, not from their exports, but from their fisheries, from their freights and from commerce at large, in some of its branches altogether external to the United States ; the profits from all which, being invisible and intangible, would escape a tax on exports. A tax on imports, on the other hand, being a tax on consumption, which is in proportion to the ability of the consumer whencesoever derived, was free from that inequality.

7. If revenue be the sole object of a legitimate impost, and the encouragement of domestic articles be not within the power of regulating trade, it would follow that no monopolizing or unequal regulations of foreign nations could be counteracted ; that neither the staple articles of subsistence, nor the essential implements for the public safety, could, under any circumstances, be insured or fostered at home, by regulations of commerce, the usual and most convenient mode of providing for both, and that the American navigation, though the source of naval defence, of a cheapening competition in carrying our valuable and bulky articles to market, and of an independent carriage of them during foreign wars, when a foreign navigation might be withdrawn, must be at once abandoned, or speedily destroyed ; it being evident that a tonnage duty in foreign ports against our vessels, and an exemption from such a duty in our ports, in favor of foreign vessels, must have the inevitable effect of banishing ours from the ocean.

To assume a power to protect our navigation, and the cultivation and fabrication of all articles requisite for the public safety, as incident to the war power, would be a more latitudinary construction of the text of the constitution, than to consider it embraced by the specified power to regulate trade; a power which has been exercised by all nations for those purposes, and which effects those purposes with less of interference with the authority and conveniency of the states, than might result from internal and direct modes of encouraging the articles, any of which modes would be authorized, as far as deemed " necessary and proper," by considering the power as an incidental power.

8. That the encouragement of manufactures was an object of the power to regulate trade, is proved by the use made of the power for that object, in the first session of the first congress under the constitution; when among the members present were so many who had been members of the federal convention which framed the constitution, and of the state conventions which ratified it; each of these classes consisting also of members who had opposed and who had espoused the constitution, in its actual form. It does not appear from the printed proceedings of congress on that occasion, that the power was denied by any of them. And it may be remarked, that members of Virginia, in particular, as well of the anti-federal as the federal party, the names then distinguishing those who had opposed and those who had approved the constitution, did not hesitate to propose duties and to snggest even prohibitions in favor of several articles of her production. By one a duty was proposed on mineral coal, in favor of Virginia coal pits; by another a duty on hemp was proposed, to encourage the growth of that article; and by a third, a prohibition even of foreign beef was suggested, as a measure of sound policy.   [See Lloyd's debates.]

` A further evidence in support of the constitutional power to protect and foster manufactures by regulations of trade, an evidence that ought, of itself, to settle the question, is the uniform and practical sanction given to the power, by the general government, for nearly forty years; with a concurrence or acquiescence of every state government, throughout the same period; and, it may be added, through all the vicissitudes of party which marked the period. No novel construction, however ingeniously devised, or however respectable and patriotic its patrons, can withstand the weight of such authorities, or the unbroken current of so prolonged and universal a practice. And well it is that this cannot be done, without the intervention of the same authority which made the constitution. If it could be so done, there would be an end to that stability in government and in laws, which is essential to good government and good laws, a stability, the want of which is the imputation which has at all times been levelled against republicanism, with most effect, by its most dexterous adversaries. The imputation ought never therefore, to be countenanced by innovating constructions without any plea of a precipitancy or a paucity of the constructive precedents they oppose, without any appeal to material facts newly brought to light; and without any claim to a better knowledge of the original evils and inconveniences, for which remedies were needed, the very best keys to the true object and meaning of all laws and constitutions.

And may it not be fairly left to the unbiased judgment of all men of experience and of intelligence, to decide, which is most to be relied on for a sound and safe test of the meaning of a constitution, a uniform interpretation by all the successive authorities under it, commencing with its birth, and continued for a long period, through the varied state of political contests ; or the opinion of every new legislature, heated as it may be by the strife of parties—or warped, as often happens, by the eager pursuit of some favorite object—or carried away, possibly, by the powerful eloquence or captivating address of a few popular statesmen, themselves, perhaps, influenced by the same misleading causes ? If the latter test is to prevail, every new legislative opinion might make a new constitution, as the foot of every new chancellor would make a new standard of measure.

It is seen with no little surprise, that an attempt has been made, in a highly respectable quarter, and at length reduced to a resolution, formally proposed in congress, to substitute for the power of congress to regulate trade so as to encourage manufactures, a power in the several states to do so, with the consent of that body ; and this expedient is derived from a clause in the tenth section of article first of the constitution, which says : " no state shall without the consent of congress, lay any imposts or duties on imports or exports, except what may be absolutely necessary for executing its inspection laws ; and the net produce of all duties, and imposts laid by any state on imports and exports, shall be for the use of the treasury of the United States ; and all such laws shall be subject to the revision and control of the congress."

To say nothing on the clear indications in the journal of the convention of 1787 that the clause was intended merely to provide for expenses incurred by particular states, in their inspection laws, and in such improvements as they might choose to make in their harbors and rivers, with the sanction of congress—objects to which the reserved power has been applied in several instances, at the request of Virginia and Georgia—how could it ever be imagined that any state would wish to tax its own trade for the encouragement of manufactures, if possessed of the authority, or could, in fact do so, if wishing it ?

A tax on imports would be a tax on its own consumption ; and the net proceeds going, according to the clause, not into its own treasury, but into the treasury of the United States, the state would tax itself separately for the equal gain of all other states ; and as far as the manufactures, so encouraged, might succeed in ultimately increasing the stock in market, and lowering the price by competition, this advantage, also, procured at the sole expense of the state, would be common to all the others.

But the very suggestion of such an expedient to any state, would have an air of mockery, when its *experienced* impracticability is taken into view. No one, who recollects or recurs to the period when the power over commerce was in the individual states, and separate attempts were made to tax, or otherwise regulate it, need be told that the attempts were not only abortive, but by demonstrating the necessity of general uniform regulations, gave the original impulse to the constitutional reform, which provided for such regulations.

To refer a state, therefore, to the exercise of a power, as reserved to her by the constitution, the impossibility of exercising which was an inducement to adopt the constitution, is of all remedial devices, the last that ought to be brought forward. And what renders it the more extraordinary, is, that, as the tax on commerce, as far as it could be separately collected, instead of belonging to the treasury of the state, as previous to the constitution, would be a tribute to the United States, the state would be in a worse condition, after the adoption of the constitution, than before, in reference to an important interest, the improvement of which was a particular object in adopting the constitution.

Were congress to make the proposed declaration of consent to state tariffs in favor of state manufactures, and the permitted attempts did not defeat themselves, what would be the situation of states deriving their foreign supplies through the ports of other states? It is evident that they might be compelled to pay, in their consumption of particular articles imported, a tax for the common treasury, not common to all the states, without having any manufacture or product of their own, to partake of the contemplated benefit.

Of the impracticability of separate regulations of trade, and the resulting necessity of general regulations, no state was more sensible than Virginia. She was accordingly among the most earnest for granting to congress a power adequate to the object. On more occasions than one, in the proceedings of her legislative councils, it was recited " that the relative situation of the states had been found, on *trial*, to require *uniformity* in their commercial regulations as the *only* effectual policy for obtaining in the ports of foreign nations a stipulation of privileges reciprocal to those enjoyed by the subjects of such nations in the ports of the United States; for preventing animosities which cannot fail to arise among the several states from the interference of partial and separate regulations; and for deriving from commerce such aids to the public revenue as it ought to contribute, &c."

During the delays and discouragements experienced in the attempts to invest congress with the necessary powers, the state of Virginia made various trials of what could be done by her individual laws. She ventured on duties and imposts as a source of revenue : resolutions were passed at one time to encourage and protect her own navigation and ship building; and in consequence of complaints and petitions from Norfolk, Alexandria and other places, against the monopolizing navigation laws of Great Britain, particularly in the trade *between the United States and the British West Indies*, she deliberated, with a purpose controlled only by the inefficiency of separate measures, on the experiment of forcing a reciprocity by prohibitory regulations of her own. [See Journal of house of delegates in 1785.]

The effect of her separate attempts to raise revenue by duties on imports, soon appeared in representations from her merchants, that the commerce of the state was banished by them into other channels, especially of Maryland, where imports were less burdened than in Virginia. [See do. for 1786.]

Such a tendency of separate regulations was indeed too manifest to escape anticipation. Among the projects prompted by the want of federal authority over commerce was that of a concert first proposed on the part of Maryland for a uniformity of regulations between the two states, and commissioners were appointed for that purpose. It was perceived, however, that the concurrence of Pennsylvania was as necessary to Maryland as of Maryland to Virginia, and the concurrence of Pennsylvania was accordingly invited. But Pennsylvania could no more concur without New York than Maryland without Pennsylvania, nor New York without the concurrence of Boston, &c.

These projects were suprerseded for the moment by that of the convention at Anapolis in 1786, and forever by the convention at Philadelphia, in 1787, and the constitution which was the fruit of it.

There is a passage in Mr. Neeker's work on the finances of France which affords a signal illustration of the difficulty of collecting, in contiguous communities, indirect taxes, when not the same in all, by the violent means resorted to against smuggling from one to another of them. Previous to the late revolutionary war in that country, the taxes were of very different rates in the different provinces; particularly the tax on salt, which was high in the interior provinces and low in the maritime; and the tax on tobacco, which was very high in general, whilst in some of the provinces the use of the article was altogether free. The consequence was, that the standing army of patrols against smuggling had swoln to the number of twenty-three thousand; the annual arrest of men, women, and children, engaged in smuggling, to five thousand five hundred and fifty; and the number annually arrested on account of salt and tobacco alone, to seventeen or eighteen hundred, more than three hundred of whom were consigned to the terrible punishment of the gallies.

May it not be regarded as among the providential blessings to these states, that their geographical relations, multiplied as they will be by artificial channels of intercourse, give such additional force to the many obligations to cherish that union which alone secures their peace, their safety, and their prosperity! Apart from the more obvious and awful consequences of their entire separation into independent sovereignties, it is worthy of special consideration, that, divided from each other as they must be by narrow waters and territorial lines merely, the facility of surreptitious introductions of contraband articles, would defeat every attempt at revenue in the easy and indirect modes of impost and excise; so that whilst their expenditures would be necessarily and vastly increased by their new situation, they would, in providing for them, be limited to direct taxes on land or other property, to arbitrary assessments on invisible funds, and to the odious tax on persons.

You will observe, that I have confined myself, in what has been said, to the constitutionality and expediency of the power in congress to encourage domestic products by regulations of commerce. In the exercise of the power, they are responsible to their constituents, whose right and duty it is in that as in all other cases, to bring their measures to the test of justice and of the general good. With great esteem and cordial regard,

Jos. C. Cabell, Esq.   JAMES MADISON.

Number 4.—p. 258.

Mr. Madison to Mr. Cabell.

Montpelier, Oct. 30, 1828.

DEAR SIR:—In my letter of Sept. 18, I stated briefly the grounds on which I rested my opinion, that a power to impose duties and restrictions on imports, with a view to encourage domestic productions, was constitutionally lodged in congress. In the observations then made was involved the opinion, also, that the power was properly there lodged. As this last opinion necessarily implies that there are cases in which the power may be usefully exercised by congress,- the only body within our political system capable of exercising it with effect, you may think it incumbent on me to point out cases of that description.

I will premise that I concur in the opinion, that, as a *general* rule, individuals ought to be deemed the best judges of the best application of their industry and resources.

I am ready to admit, also, that there is no country in which the application may, with more safety, be left to the intelligence and enterprise of individuals, than in the United States.

Finally, I shall not deny, that in all doubtful cases, it becomes every government to lean rather to a confidence in the judgment of individuals, than to interpositions controlling the free exercise of it.

With all these concessions, I think it can be satisfactorily shown, that there are exceptions to the general rule, now expressed by the phrase, " let us alone," forming cases which call for interpositions of the competent authority, and which are not inconsistent with the generality of the rule.

1. The theory of " let us alone" supposes that all nations concur in a perfect freedom of commercial intercourse. Were this the case, they would, in a commercial view, be but one nation, as much as the several districts composing a particular nation ; and the theory would be as applicable to the former as to the latter. But this golden age of free trade has not yet arrived ; nor is there a single nation that has set the example. No nation can, indeed, safely do so, until a reciprocity, at least, be ensured to it. Take for proof, the familiar case of the navigation employed on a foreign commerce. If a nation, adhering to the rule of never interposing a countervailing protection of its vessels, admits foreign vessels into its ports free of duty, whilst its own vessels are subject to a duty, in foreign ports, the ruinous effect is so obvious, that the warmest advocate for the theory in question must shrink from a *universal* application of it.

A nation leaving its foreign trade, in all cases, to regulate itself, might soon find it regulated by other nations into a subserviency to a foreign interest. In the interval between the peace of 1783 and the establishment of the present constitution of the United States, the want of a ganeral authority to regulate trade, is known to have had this consequence. And have not the pretensions and policy lately exhibited by Great Britain, given warning of a like result, from a renunciation of all countervailing regulations on the part of the United States? Were she permitted, by conferring on certain portions of her domain the name of colonies, to open from these a trade for herself, to foreign countries, and to exclude, at the same time, a reciprocal trade to such colonies, by foreign countries, the use to be made of the monopoly need not be traced. Its character will be placed in a just relief, by supposing that one of the colonial islands, instead of its present distance, happened to be in the vicinity of Great Britain; or that one of the islands in that vicinity should receive the name and be regarded in the light of a colony, with the peculiar privileges claimed for colonies. Is it not manifest, that, in this case, the favored island might be made the sole medium of the commercial intercourse with foreign nations, and the parent country thence enjoy every essential advantage, as to the terms of it, which would flow from an *unreciprocal* trade from her other ports, with other nations?

Fortunately, the British claims, however speciously colored or adroitly managed, were repelled at the commencement of our commercial career as an independent people, and at successive epochs under the existing constitution both in legislative discussions and in diplomatic negotiations. The claims were repelled on the solid ground that the colonial trade, as a *rightful* monopoly, was limited to the intercourse between the parent country and its colonies, and between one colony and another; the whole being, strictly, in the nature of a coasting trade from one to another port of the same nation; a trade with which no other nation has a right to interfere. It follows, of necessity, that the parent country, whenever it opens a colonial port for a direct trade to a foreign country, departs, itself, from the principle of colonial monopoly, and entitles the foreign country to the same reciprocity in every respect, as in its intercourse with any other ports of the nation.

This is common sense and common right. It is still more, if more could be required. It is in conformity with the established usage of all nations, other than Great Britain, which have colonies. Some of those nations are known to adhere to the monopoly of their colonial trade, with all the rigor and constancy which circumstances permit. But it is also known, that, whenever, and from whatever cause, it has been found necessary or expedient to open their colonial ports to a foreign trade, the rule of reciprocity in favor of the foreign party was not refused, nor, as is believed, a right to refuse it pretended.

It cannot be said that the reciprocity was dictated by a deficiency of the commercial marine. France, at least, could not be, in every instance, governed by that consideration—and Holland still less: to say nothing of the navigating states of Sweden and Denmark, which have rarely, if ever, enforced a colonial monopoly. The remark is, indeed, obvious, that the shipping liberated from the usual conveyance of supplies from the parent country to the colonies might be employed in the new channels opened for them, in supplies from abroad.

Reciprocity, or an equivalent for it, is the only rule of intercourse among independent communities; and no nation ought to admit a doctrine, or adopt an invariable policy, which would preclude the counteracting measures necessary to enforce the rule.

2. The theory supposes, moreover, a perpetual peace; a supposition, it is

to be feared, not less chimerical than a universal freedom of commerce.

The effect of war among the commercial and manufacturing nations of the world, in raising the wages of labor, and the cost of its products; with a like effect on the charges of freight and insurance, need neither proof nor explanation. In order to determine, therefore, a question of economy, between depending on foreign supplies, and encouraging domestic substitutes, it is necessary to compare the probable periods of war with the probable periods of peace; and the cost of the domestic encouragement in times of peace, with the cost added to foreign articles in times of war.

During the last century, the periods of war and peace have been nearly equal. The effect of a state of war in raising the price of imported articles, cannot be estimated with exactness. It is certain, however, that the increased price of particular articles may make it cheaper to manufacture them at home.

Taking, for the sake of illustration, an equality in the two periods, and the cost of an imported yard of cloth in time of war to be nine and a half dollars, and in time of peace, to be seven dollars, whilst the same could at all times be manufactured at home for eight dollars, it is evident that a tariff of one dollar and a quarter on the imported yard would protect the home manufacture in time of peace, and avoid a tax of one dollar and a half imposed by a state of war.

It cannot be said that the manufactories which could not support themselves against foreign competition in periods of peace, would spring up of themselves at the recurrence of war prices. It must be obvious to every one, that, apart from the difficulty of great and sudden changes of employment, no prudent capitalist would engage in expensive establishments of any sort, at the commencement of a war of uncertain duration with a certainty of having them crushed by the return of peace.

The strictest economy therefore suggests, as exceptions to the general rule, an estimate, in every given case, of war and peace periods and prices, with inferences therefrom, of the amount of a tariff which might be afforded during peace, in order to avoid the tax resulting from war. And it will occur at once, that the inferences will be strengthened by adding, to the supposition of wars wholly foreign, that of wars in which our own country might be a party.

3. It is an opinion in which all must agree, that no nation ought to be unnecessarily dependent on others for the munitions of public defence, or for the materials essential to a naval force, where the nation has a maritime frontier or a foreign commerce to protect. To this class of exceptions to the theory, may be added the instruments of agriculture, and of the mechanic arts which supply the other primary wants of the community. The time has been, when many of these were derived from a foreign source, and some of them might relapse into that dependence, were the encouragement of the fabrication of them at home withdrawn. But, as all foreign sources must be liable to interruptions too inconvenient to be hazarded, a provident policy would favor an internal and independent source, as a reasonable exception to the general rule of consulting cheapness alone.

4. There are cases where a nation may be so far advanced in the preré-quisites for a particular branch of manufactures, that this, if once brought into existence, would support itself; and yet, unless aided in its nascent and infant state, by public encouragement and a confidence in public protection, might remain, if not altogether, for a long time unattempted, or attempted without success. Is not our cotton manafacture a fair example? However favored by an advantageous command of the raw material, and a machinery which dispenses in so extraordinary a proportion with manual labor, it is quite probable, that without the impulse given by a war, cutting off foreign supplies, and the patronage of an early tariff, it might not even yet have established itself: and pretty certain, that it would be far short of the prosperous condition which enables it to face, in foreign markets, the fabrics of a nation that defies all other competitors. The number must be small, that would now pronounce this manufacturing boon not to have been cheaply purchased by the tariff which nursed it into its present maturity.

5. Should it happen, as has been suspected, to be an object, though not of a foreign government itself, of its great manufacturing capitalists, to strangle in the cradle the infant manufactures of an extensive customer, or an anticipated rival, it would surely, in such a case, be incumbent on the suffering party, so far to make an exception to the "Let us alone" policy, as to parry the evil by opposite regulations of its foreign commerce.

6. It is a common objection to the public encouragement of particular branches of industry, that it calls off laborers from other branches found to be more profitable; and the objection is in general a weighty one. But it loses that character in proportion to the effect of the encouragement in attracting skilful laborers from abroad. Something of this sort has already taken place among ourselves, and much more of it is in prospect; and, as far as it has taken or may take place, it forms an exception to the general policy in question.

The history of manufactures in Great Britain, the greatest manufacturing nation in the world, informs us that the woollen branch, till of late her greatest branch, owed both its original and subsequent growth to persecuted exiles from the Netherlands; and that her silk manufactures, now a flourishing and favorite branch, were not less indebted to emigrants flying from persecuting edicts of France.—[Anderson's History of Commerce.]

It appears, indeed, from the general history of manufacturing industry, that the prompt and successful introduction of it into new situations, has been the result of emigrations from countries in which manufactures had gradually grown up to a prosperous state, as into Italy on the fall of the Greek empire; from Italy into Spain and Flanders, on the loss of liberty in Florence and other cities; and from Flanders and France, into England, as above noticed.—[Franklin's Canada pamphlet.]

In the selection of cases here made, as exceptions to the "Let us alone" theory, none have been included which were deemed controvertible. And if I have viewed them, or a part of them only, in their true light, they show, what was to be shown, that the power granted to congress to encourage domestic products by regulations of foreign trade, was properly granted, inasmuch as the power is, in effect confined to that body, and may, when exercised with a sound legislative discretion, provide the better for the safety and prosperity of the nation. With great esteem and regard,

JOSEPH C. CABELL, Esq.   JAMES MADISON.

Number 5.— p. 280.

It will be readily understood, that Mr. Madison is the authority alluded to.- At the time of writing that chapter I had seen only an extract of his letter to Mr. Livingstone, on the subject. While the work was in the press I found the following letter published in an appendix to Niles' Register, of May last, (1833.) This letter contains his construction of the Virginia resolution of 1798 at large, and I thought it no more than just that he should be allowed to speak for himself. This subject, however, occupies but a minor portion of the letter; the greater part is occupied with a luminous exposition and powerful vindication of the constitutional doctrines which I have endeavored to support, and a refutation of the nullifying doctrines, which have been advanced in opposition. I have therefore, here republished the whole letter, wish and though it is long, no one can possibly regret its length.

Mr. Madison to Mr. E. Everett.

Montpelier, August, 1830.

DEAR SIR:—I have duly received your letter, in which you refer to the "nullifying doctrine," advocated as a constitutional right, by some of our distinguished fellow citizens; and to the proceedings of the Virginia legislature in '98 and '99, as appealed to in behalf of that doctrine; and you express a for my ideas on those subjects.

I am aware of the delicacy of the task in some respects, and the difficulty in every respect, of doing full justice to it. But, having, in more than one instance, complied with a like request from other friendly quarters, I do not decline a sketch of the views which I have been led to take of the doctrine in question, as well as some others connected with them; and of the grounds from which it appears, that the proceedings of Virginia have been misconceived by those who have appealed to them. In order to understand the true character of the constitution of the United States, the error, not uncommon must be avoided, of viewing it through the medium, either of a consolidated government, or of a confederated government, whilst it is neither the one nor the other; but a mixture of both. And having, in no model, the similitudes and analogies applicable to other systems of government, it must, more than any other, be its own interpreter according to its text and *the facts of the case.*

From these it will be seen that the characteristic peculiarities of the constitution are, 1, the mode of its formation; 2, the division of the supreme powers of government between the states in their united capacity, and the states in their individual capacities.

1. It was formed, not by the governments of the component states, as the federal government for which it was substituted was formed. Nor was it

formed by a majority of the people of the United States, as a single community in the manner of a consolidated government.

It was formed by the states, that is, by the people in each of the states, acting in their highest sovereign capacity ; and formed consequently by the same authority which formed the state constitutions.

Being thus derived from the same source as the constitutions of the states, it has, within each state, the same authority as the constitution of the state ; and is as much a constitution, in the strict sense of the term, within its prescribed sphere, as the constitutions of the states are, within their respective spheres; but with this obvious and essential difference, that being a compact among the states in their highest sovereign capacity, and constituting the people thereof one people for certain purposes, it cannot be altered or annulled at the will of the states individually, as the constitution of a state may be at its individual will.

2. And that it divides the supreme powers of government, between the government of the United States, and the government of the individual states, is stamped on the face of the instrument ; the powers of war and of taxation, of commerce and of treaties, and other enumerated powers vested in the government of the United States, being of as high and sovereign a character, as any of the powers reserved to the state governments.

Nor is the government of the United States, created by the constitution, less a government in the strict sense of the term, within the sphere of its powers, than the governments created by the constitutions of the states are, within their several spheres. It is like them organized into legislative, executive, and judiciary departments. It operates, like them, directly on persons and things. And, like them, it has at command a physical force for executing the powers committed to it. The concurrent operation in certain cases, is one of the features marking the peculiarity of the system.

Between these different constitutional governments, the one operating in all the states, the others operating seperately in each, with the aggregate powers of government divided between them, it could not escape attention, that controversies would arise concerning the boundaries of jurisdiction ; and that some provision ought to be made for such occurrences. A political system that does not provide for a peaceable and authoritative termination of occurring controversies, would not be more than the shadow of a government; the object and end of a real government being, the substitution of law and order, for uncertainty, confusion, and violence.

That, to have left a final decision, in such cases, to each of the states, then thirteen, and already twenty-four, could not fail to make the constitution and laws of the United States different in different States, was obvious ; and not less obvious, that this diversity of independent decisions must altogether distract the government of the union, and speedily put an end to the union itself. An uniform authority of the laws, is in itself a vital principle. Some of the most important laws could not be partially executed. They must be executed in all the states, or they could be duly executed in none. An impost, or an excise, for example, if not in force in some states, would be defeated in others. It is well known that this was among the lessons of experience, which had a primary influence in bringing about the existing constitution. A loss of its general authority would moreover revive the exasperating questions between the states holding ports for foreign commerce, and the adjoining states without them; to which are now added all the inland states, necessarily carrying on their foreign commerce through other states.

To have made the decisions under the authority of the individual states, co-ordinate, in all cases, with decisions under the authority of the United States, would unavoidably produce collisions incompatible with the peace o society, and with the regular and efficient administration, which is of the essence of free governments. Scenes could not be avoided, in which a ministerial officer of the United States, and the correspondent officer of an individual state, would have rencontres in executing conflicting decrees; the result of which would depend on the comparative force of the local posses attending them; and that, a casualty depending on the political opinions and party feelings in different states.

To have referred every clashing decision, under the two authorities, for a final decision, to the states as parties to the constitution, would be attended with delays, with inconveniences, and with expenses, amounting to a prohibition of the expedient; not to mention its tendency to impair the salutary veneration for a system requiring such frequent interpositions, nor the delicate questions which might present themselves as to the form of stating the appeal, and as to the quorum for deciding it.

To have trusted to negotiation for adjusting disputes between the government of the United States and the state governments, as between independent and separate sovereignties, would have lost sight altogether of a constitution and government for the union; and opened a direct road from a failure of that resort, to the *ultima ratio* between nations wholly independent of, and alien to each other. If the idea had its origin in the process of adjustment between separate branches of the same government, the analogy entirely fails. In the case of disputes between independent parts of the same government, neither part being able to consummate its will, nor the government to proceed without a concurrence of the parts, necessity brings about an accommodation. In disputes between a state government, and the government of the United States, the case is practically, as well as theoretically, different; each party possessing all the departments of an organized government legislative, executive, and judiciary; and having each a physical force to support its pretensions. Although the issue of negotiation might sometimes avoid this extremity, how often would it happen among so many states, that an unaccomodating spirit in some would render that resource unavailing? A contrary suppositon would not accord with a knowledge of human nature, or the evidence of our own political history.

The constitution, not relying on any of the preceding modifications, for its safe and successful operation, has expressly declared, on the one hand—1, 'that the constitution, and the laws made in pursuance thereof, and all treaties made under the authority of the United States, shall be the supreme law of the land; 2, that the judges of every state shall be bound thereby, any thing in the constitution and laws of any state to the contrary notwithstanding; 3, that the judicial power of the United States shall extend to all cases in law and equity arising under the constitution, the laws of the United States, and treaties made under their authority, &c.'

On the other hand, as a security of the rights and powers of the states; in their individual capacities, against an undue preponderance of the powers granted to the government over them in their united capacity, the constitution has relied on—1, the responsibility of the senators and representatives in the legislature of the United States to the legislatures and people of the states; 2, the responsibility of the President to the people of the United States; and 3, the liability of the executive and judicial functionaries of the United States, to impeachment by the representatives of the people of the states, in one branch of the legislature of the United States, and trial by the representatives of the states, in the other branch: the state functionaries, legislative, executive, and judicial, being, at the same time, in their appointment and responsibility, altogether independent of the agency or authority of the United States.

How far this structure of the government of the United States is adequate and safe for its objects, time alone can absolutely determine. Experience seems to have shown, that whatever may grow out of future stages of our national career, there is, as yet, a sufficient control in the popular will, over the executive and legislative departments of the government. When the alien and sedition laws were passed in contravention to the opinions and feelings of the community, the first elections that ensued put an end to them. And whatever may have been the character of other acts, in the judgment of many of us, it is but true, that they have generally accorded with the views of a majority of the states and of the people. At the present day it seems well understood, that the laws which have created most dissatisfaction, have had a like sanction without doors; and that whether continued, varied, or repealed, a like proof will be given of the sympathy and responsibility of the representative body to the constituent body. Indeed, the great complaint now is, against the results of this sympathy and responsibility in the legislative policy of the nation.

With respect to the judicial power of the United States, and the authority of the Supreme court in relation to the boundary of jurisdiction between the federal and the state governments, I may be permitted to refer to the thirty-ninth number of the "Federalist,"* for the light in which the subject was regarded by its writer, at the period when the constitution was depending; and it is believed, that the same was the prevailing view then taken of it,

---

*No. 39. It is true that in controversies relating to the boundary between the two jurisdictions, the tribunal which is ultimately to decide, is to be established under the general government. But this does not change the principle of the case. The decision is to be impartially made, according to the rules of the constitution; and all the usual and most effectual precautions are taken to secure this impartiality. Some such tribunal is clearly essential to prevent an appeal to the sword, and a dissolution of the compact; and that it ought to be established under the general, rather than under the local governments; or, to speak more properly, that it could be safely established under the first alone, is a position not likely to be combated.

that the same view has continued to prevail, and that it does so at this time, notwithstanding the eminent exceptions to it.

But it is perfectly consistent with the concession of this power to the Supreme Court, in cases falling within the course of its functions, to maintain that the power has not always been rightly exercised. To say nothing of the period, happily a short one, when judges in thear seats did not abstain from intemperate and party harangues, equally at variance with their dignity, there have been occasional decisions from the bench, which have incurred serious and extensive disapprobation. Still it would seem, that, with but few exceptions, the course of the judiciary has been hitherto sustained by the predominant sense of the nation.

Those who have denied or doubted the supremacy of the judicial power of the United States, and denounce at the same time nullifying power in a state, seem not to have sufficiently adverted to the utter inefficiency of a supremacy in a law of the land, without a supremacy in the exposition and execution of the law; nor to the destruction of all equipoise between the federal government and the state governments, if whilst the functionaries of the federal government are directly or indirectly elected by and responsible to the states, and the functionaries of the states are in their appointment and responsibility wholly independent of the United States, no constitutional control of any sort belonged to the United States, over the states. Under such an organization, it is evident that it would be in the power of the states, individually, to pass unorthorized laws, and to carry them into complete effect, any thing in the constitution and laws of the United States to the contrary notwithstanding. This would be a nullifying power in its plenary character; and whether it had its final effect, through the legislative, executive, or judiciary organ of the state, would be equally fatal to the constituted relation between the two governments.

Should the provisions of the constitution as here reviewed, be found not to secure the government and rights of the states against usurpation and abuses on the part of the United States, the final resort within the purview of the constitution lies in an amendment of the constitution, according to a process applicable by the states.

And in the event of a failure of every constitutional resort, and an accumulation of the usurpations and abuses, rendering passive obedience and non-resistance a greater evil than resistance and revolution, there can remain but one resort, the last of all—an appeal from the cancelled obligations of the compact, to original rights and the law of self-preservation. This is the *ultima ratio* under all governments, whether consolidated, confederated, or a compound of both; and it cannot be doubted that a single member of the union, in the extremity supposed, but in that only, would have a right as an extra and ultra-constitutional right, to make the appeal.

This brings us to the expedient lately advanced, which claims for a single state a right to appeal against an exercise of power by the government of the United States decided by the state to be unconstitutional to the parties to the constitutional compact; the decision of the state to have the effect of nullifying the act of the government of the United States, unless the decision of the state be reversed by three-fourth of the parties.

The distinguished names and high authorities which appear to have asserted and given a practical scope to this doctrine, entitle it to a respect which it might be difficult otherwise to feel for it.

If the doctrine were to be understood as requiring the three-fourths of the states to sustain, instead of that proportion to reverse the decision of the appealing state, the decision to be without effect during the appeal, it would be sufficient to remark that this extra-constitutional course might well give way to that marked out by the constitution, which authorizes two-thirds of the states to institute and three-fourths to effectuate an amendment of the constitution, establishing a permanent rule of the highest authority, in place of an irregular precedent of construction only.

But it is understood that the nullifying doctrine imports that the decision of the state is to be presumed valid, and that it overrules the laws of the United States, unless overruled by three-fourths of the states.

Can more be necessary to demonstrate the inadmissibility of such a doctrine, than that it puts it in the power of the smallest fraction over one-fourth, of the United States, that is, of seven states out of twenty-four, to give the law and even the constitution to seventeen states, each of the seventeen having as parties to the constitution, an equal right with each of the seven, to expound it, and to insist on the exposition? That the seven might, in particular instances be right, and the seventeen wrong, is more than possible. But to establish a positive and permanent rule giving such a power, to such a minority, over such a majority, would overturn the first principle of free government, and in practice necessarily overturn the government itself.

It is to be recollected that the constitution was proposed to the people of the states as *a whole*, and unanimously adopted by the states as *a whole*, it being a part of the c ntution that not less than three-fourths of the states should be competent to make any alteration in what had been unanimously agreed to. So great is the caution on this point, that in two cases where peculiar interests were at stake, a proportion even of three-fourths is distrusted, and unanimity required to make an alteration.

When the constitution was adopted as a whole, it is certain that there were many parts, which, if separately proposed, would have been promptly rejected. It is far from impossible, that every part of a constitution might be rejected by a majority, and yet taken together as a whole, be unanimously accepted. Free constitutio s will rarely if ever be formed, without reciprocal concessions; without artic s conditioned on and balancing each other. Is there a constitution of a s ngle state out of the twenty-four that would bear the experiment of having its component parts submitted to the people and separately decided on?

What the fate of the nstitution of the United States would be if a small proportion of the states . unge parts of it particularly valued by a large majority, can have but one   er.

The difficulty is not removed by limiting the doctrine to cases of construction. How many cases of that sort, involving cardinal provisions of the con stitution have occurred? How many now exist? How many may hereaf ter spring up ? How many might be ingeniously created, if entitled to the privilege of a decision in the mode proposed ?

Is it certain that the principle of that mode would not reach further than is contemplated ? If a single state can of right require three-fourths of its co-states to overrule its exposition of the constitution, because that proportion is authorised to amend it, would the plea be less plausible that, as the constitution was unanimously established, it ought to be unanimously expounded ?

The reply to all such suggestions seems to be unavoidable and irresistible ; that the constitution is a compact, that its text is to be expounded according to the provisions for expounding it—making a part of the compact ; and that none of the parties can rightfully renounce the expounding provision more than any other part. When such a right accrues, as may accrue, it must grow out of abuses of the compact releasing the sufferers from their fealty to it.

In favor of the nullifying claim for the states, individually, it appears, as you observe, that the proceedings of the legislature of Virginia, in '98 and '99, against the alien and sedition acts, are much dwelt upon.

It may often happen, as experience proves, that erroneous constructions, not anticipated, may not be sufficiently guarded against, in the language used ; and it is due to the distinguished individuals, who have misconceived the intention of those proceedings, to suppose that the meaning of the legislature, though well comprehended at the time, may not now be obvious to those unacquainted with the contemporary indications and impressions.

But it is believed that by keeping in view the distinction between the governments of the states, and the states in the sense in which they are parties to the constitution ; between the rights of the parties, in their concurrent and in their individual capacities ; between the several modes and objects of interposition against the abuses of power, and especially between interpositions within the purview of the constitution, and interpositions appealing from the constitution to the rights of nature paramount to all constitutions ; with an intention, always of explanatory use, to the views and arguments which were combatted, the resolutions of Virginia, as vindicated in the report on them, will be found entitled to an exposition, showing a consistency in their parts, and an inconcistency of the whole with the doctrine under consideration.

That the legislature could not have intended to sanction such a doctrine, is to be inferred from the debates in the house of delegates, and from the address of the two houses to their constituents, on the subject of the resolutions. The tenor of the debates, which were ably conducted, and are understood to have been revised for the press by most, if not all, of the speakers, discloses no reference whatever to a constitutional right in an individual state to arrest by force the operation of a law of the United States. Concert among the states for redress against the alien and sedition laws, as acts of usurped power, was a leading sentiment, and the attainment of a concert, the immediate object of the course adopted by the legislature, which was that of inviting the other states to concur in declaring the acts to be unconstitutional, and to *co-operate*, by the necessary and proper measures, in maintaining unimpaired the authorities, rights, and liberties reserved to the states respectively, and to the people.'* That by the necessary and proper measures to be *concurrently* and *co-operatively* taken, were meant measures known to the constitution, particularly the ordinary control of the people and legislatures of the states, over the government of the United States, cannot be doubted ; and the interposition of this control, as the event showed, was equal to the occasion.

It is worthy of remark, and explanatory of the intentions of the legislature, that the words 'not law, but utterly null, void, and of no force or effect,' which had followed, in one of the resolutions, the word 'unconstitutional,' were struck out by common consent. Though the words were in fact synonymous with 'unconstitutional,' yet to guard against a misunderstanding of this phrase as more than declaratory of opinion, the word 'unconstitutional' alone was retained, as not liable to that danger.

The published address of the legislature to the people, their constituents, affords another conclusive evidence of its views. The address warns them against the encroaching spirit of the general government, argues the unconstitutionality of the alien and sedition acts, points to other instances in which the constitutional limits had been overleaped; dwells upon the dangerous mode of deriving power by implication ; and in general presses the necessity of watching over the consolidating tendency of federal policy. But nothing is said that can be understood to look to means of maintaining the rights of the states, beyond the regular ones, within the forms of the constitution.

If any further lights on the subject could be needed, a very strong one is reflected in the answers to the resolutions, by the states which protested against them. The main objection of these, beyond a few general complaints of the inflammatory tendency of the resolutions, was directed against the assumed authority of the state legislature to declare a law of the United States unconstitutional, which they pronounced an unwarrantable interference with the exclusive jurisdiction of the Supreme Court of the United States. Had the resolutions been regarded as avowing and maintaining a right, in an individual state, to arrest by force the execution of a law of the United States, it must be presumed that it would have been a conspicuous object of their denunciation.†   JAMES MADISON.

Mr. E. Everett.

---

* See the concluding resolution of 1798.

† Every one, it is believed, will give full faith and credit to Mr. Madison's sincerity in the opinion, he has expressed ; nor will that faith be weakened by the strong desire he must feel to vindicate the acts of his native state. Still it appears to me, that if such was the meaning intended by those who drew the resolution, they were very unfortunate in their manner of expression. The resolution, as it appears to me, when considered by itself as well as taken in connexion with what may be called the preamble, admits but one construction, that is,—that the right of the state to judge of the acts of congress, and to interpose its authority, is claimed as a constitutional right,—a right reserved to the state by the constitution, and not what may be called a right of revolution, the natural right of a people to resist the intolerable oppressions of the government. Such, after all that has been said, was the construction given to the resolution of the time by all the states that replied to it ; and such was the construction of Patrick Henry, as demonstrably appears from the passage cited from his address. Aware, however, as I am of the extraordinary excitement under which that resolution was passed, and the effect intended to be produced by it, I do not hesitate to believe, that little, if any thought was at the time bestowed on the nature and origin of the right claimed, or of the ultimate consequences, to which it might lead.

www.ingramcontent.com/pod-product-compliance
Lightning Source LLC
Chambersburg PA
CBHW020602270326
41927CB00005B/138